Slavery and Emancipation

BLACKWELL READERS IN AMERICAN SOCIAL AND CULTURAL HISTORY

Series Editor: Jacqueline Jones, Brandeis University

The *Blackwell Readers in American Social and Cultural History* series introduces students to well-defined topics in American history from a socio-cultural perspective. Using primary and secondary sources, the volumes present the most important works available on a particular topic in a succinct and accessible format designed to fit easily into courses offered in American history or American studies.

1 *POPULAR CULTURE IN AMERICAN HISTORY*
edited by Jim Cullen

2 *AMERICAN INDIANS*
edited by Nancy Shoemaker

3 *THE CIVIL RIGHTS MOVEMENT*
edited by Jack E. Davis

4 *THE OLD SOUTH*
edited by Mark M. Smith

5 *AMERICAN RADICALISM*
edited by Daniel Pope

6 *AMERICAN SEXUAL HISTORIES*
edited by Elizabeth Reis

7 *AMERICAN TECHNOLOGY*
edited by Carroll Pursell

8 *AMERICAN RELIGIOUS HISTORY*
edited by Amanda Porterfield

9 *COLONIAL AMERICAN HISTORY*
edited by Kirsten Fischer and Eric Hinderaker

10 *MOVIES AND AMERICAN SOCIETY*
edited by Steven J. Ross

11 *SLAVERY AND EMANCIPATION*
edited by Rick Halpern and Enrico Dal Lago

Slavery and Emancipation

Edited by

Rick Halpern and Enrico Dal Lago

350 Main Street, Malden, MA 02148–5018, USA

108 Cowley Road, Oxford OX4 1JF, UK

550 Swanston Street, Carlton South, Melbourne, Victoria 3053, Australia

Kurfürstendamm 57, 10707 Berlin, Germany

First published 2002 by Blackwell Publishers Ltd

Library of Congress Cataloging-in-Publication Data

Slavery and emancipation / edited by Rick Halpern and Enrico Dal Lago.
p. cm.—(Blackwell readers in American social and cultural history)
Includes bibliographical references and index.
ISBN 0–631–21734–7 (alk. paper)—ISBN 0–631–21735–5 (pbk. :alk. paper)
1. Slavery—United States—History. 2. Slavery—United States—History—Sources. 3. Plantation life—Southern States—History. 4. Plantation life—Southern States—History—Sources. 5. Slaves—Emancipation—United States. 6. Slaves—Emancipation—United States—History—Sources. I. Halpern, Rick. II. Dal Lago, Enrico, 1966– III. Series.

E441 .S6185 2002
306.3′62′0973—dc21

2002066418

ISBN 0–631–21734–7 (hardback); ISBN 0–631–21735–5 (paperback)

A catalogue record for this title is available from the British Library.

Set in 10 on 12pt Plantin
by Kolam Information Services Pvt Ltd, Pondicherry, India
Printed and bound in the United Kingdom
by MPG Books Ltd, Bodmin, Cornwall

For further information on
Blackwell Publishing, visit our website:
http://www.blackwellpublishing.com

Contents

Series Editor's Preface

The purpose of the Blackwell Readers in American Social and Cultural History is to introduce students to cutting-edge historical scholarship that draws upon a variety of disciplines, and to encourage students to "do" history themselves by examining some of the primary texts upon which that scholarship is based.

Each of us lives life with a wholeness that is at odds with the way scholars often dissect the human experience. Anthropologists, psychologists, literary critics, and political scientists (to name just a few) study only discrete parts of our existence. The result is a rather arbitrary collection of disciplinary boundaries enshrined not only in specialized publications but also in university academic departments and in professional organizations.

As a scholarly enterprise, the study of history necessarily crosses these boundaries of knowledge in order to provide a comprehensive view of the past. Over the last few years, social and cultural historians have reached across the disciplines to understand the history of the British North American colonies and the United States in all its fullness. Unfortunately, much of that scholarship, published in specialized monographs and journals, remains inaccessible to undergraduates. Consequently, instructors often face choices that are not very appealing – to ignore the recent scholarship altogether, assign bulky readers that are too detailed for an undergraduate audience, or cobble together packages of recent articles that lack an overall contextual framework. The individual volumes of this series, however, each focus on a significant topic in American history, and bring new, exciting scholarship to students in a compact, accessible format.

The series is designed to complement textbooks and other general readings assigned in undergraduate courses. Each editor has culled particularly innovative and provocative scholarly essays from widely scattered books and journals, and provided an introduction summarizing the major themes of the essays and documents that follow. The essays reproduced here were chosen because of the authors' innovative (and often interdisciplinary) methodology and their ability to reconceptualize historical issues in fresh and insightful ways. Thus students can appreciate the rich complexity of an historical topic and the way that scholars have explored the topic from different perspectives, and in the process transcend the highly artificial disciplinary boundaries that have served to compartmentalize knowledge about the past in the United States.

Also included in each volume are primary texts, at least some of which have been drawn from the essays themselves. By linking primary and secondary material, the editors are able to introduce students to the historian's craft, allowing them to explore this material in depth; and draw additional insights – or interpretations contrary to those of the scholars under discussion – from it.

Jacqueline Jones
Brandeis University

Acknowledgments

The editors and publishers gratefully acknowledge the following for permission to reproduce copyright material, which is here listed in alphabetical order of author:

Ira Berlin, "The Plantation Generations of African Americans": Reprinted by permission of the publisher from *Many Thousands Gone: The First Two Centuries of Slavery in North America* by Ira Berlin, pp. 95–108, Cambridge, Mass.: The Belknap Press of Harvard University Press, Copyright © 1998 by the President and Fellows of Harvard College.

Ira Berlin, Barbara J. Fields, Steven F. Miller, Joseph P. Reidy, and Leslie S. Rowland, "The Destruction of Slavery in the Confederate Territories": From *Slaves No More: Three Essays on Emancipation and the Civil War*, by Ira Berlin, Barbara J. Fields, Steven F. Miller, Joseph P. Reidy, and Leslie S. Rowland, New York and Cambridge: Cambridge University Press, 1992. Copyright Cambridge University Press 1992. Reprinted with the permission of Cambridge University Press.

Kathleen M. Brown, "Masters and Mistresses in Colonial Virginia": From *Good Wives, Nasty Wenches, and Anxious Patriarchs: Gender, Race, and Power in Colonial Virginia* by Kathleen Brown. Published for the Omohundro Institute of Early American History and Culture. Copyright

© 1996 by the University of North Carolina Press. Used by permission of the publisher.

Charles East (ed.), "Sarah Morgan Defends Slavery against Lincoln's Plan for Emancipation": From *The Civil War Diary of Sarah Morgan*, ed. Charles East, Athens and London: University of Georgia Press, 1991. Copyright 1991 by the University of Georgia Press, Athens, Georgia.

Drew Gilpin Faust, "Confederate Woman in the Crisis of the Slaveholding South": From *Mothers of Invention: Women of the Slaveholding South in the American Civil War*, by Drew Gilpin Faust. Copyright © 1996 by the University of North Carolina Press. Used by permission of the publisher

Don E. Fehrenbacher, "Slavery and Territorial Expansion": From *The Slaveholding Republic: An Account of the United States Government's Relations to Slavery* by Don E. Fehrenbacher and Ward M. McAfee, copyright © 2001 by Oxford University Press, Inc. Used by permission of Oxford University Press, Inc.

John Hope Franklin and Loren Schweninger, "The Impact of Runaway Slaves on the Slave System": From *Runaway Slaves*, by John Hope Franklin and Loren Schweninger, copyright © 1999 by John Hope Franklin and Loren Schweninger. Used by permission of Oxford University Press, Inc.

Eugene D. Genovese, "The Slaveholders' Dilemma Between Bondage and Progress": From *The Slaveholders' Dilemma: Freedom and Progress in Southern Conservative Thought, 1820–1860* by Eugene D. Genovese, Columbia: University of South Carolina Press, 1992.

Paul Goodman, "Abolitionists and the Origins of Racial Equality": From Paul Goodman, *Of One Blood: Abolitionism and the Origins of Racial Equality*, Copyright © 1998, The Regents of the University of California.

Walter Johnson, "Paternalism and Exploitation in the Antebellum Slave-Market": Reprinted by permission of the publisher from *Soul by Soul: Life Inside the Antebellum Slave Market* by Walter Johnson, pp. 19–30, 102–16, Cambridge, Mass.: Harvard University Press, Copyright © 1999 by the President and Fellows of Harvard College.

Peter Kolchin, "Slavery and the American Revolution": From *American Slavery, 1619–1877* by Peter Kolchin. Copyright © 1993 by Peter Kolchin. Reprinted by permission of Hill and Wang, a division of Farrar, Strauss and Giroux, LLC.

Philip D. Morgan, "Two Infant Slave Societies in the Chesapeake and the Lowcountry": From *Slave Counterpoint: Black Culture in the Eighteenth-Century Chesapeake and Lowcountry* by Philip D. Morgan. Copyright © 1998 by the University of North Carolina Press. Used by permission of the publisher.

Mark M. Smith, "Debating the Profitability of Antebellum Southern Agriculture": From *Debating Slavery: Economy and Society in the Antebellum American South* by Mark Smith, New York: Cambridge University Press, 1998. Copyright The Economic History Society 1998. Reprinted with the permission of Cambridge University Press.

Brenda E. Stevenson, "Slave Marriage and Family Relations in Antebellum Virginia": From *Life in Black and White: Family and Community in the Slave South* by Brenda E. Stevenson, copyright © 1996 by Brenda Stevenson. Used by permission of Oxford University Press, Inc.

Marli F. Weiner, "Plantation Mistresses' Attitudes toward Slavery in South Carolina": From *Mistresses and Slaves: Plantation Women in South Carolina, 1830–80* by Marli F. Weiner. Copyright 1998 by Board of Trustees of the University of Illinois. Used with permission of the University of Illinois Press.

The publishers apologize for any errors or omissions in the above list and would be grateful to be notified of any corrections that should be incorporated in the next edition or reprint of this book.

Introduction

Slavery and emancipation are essential fields of study for any student of American history. The United States was born as a slaveholding republic, and it took a civil war which caused more than 600,000 deaths to transform the nation into a permanently free country. The fact that the issue of slavery was at the heart of the Civil War and that emancipation occurred only as a consequence of its outbreak has led the editors of the present volume to consider the experiences of slavery and emancipation as inextricably linked to one another. For this reason, the present collection of documents and essays includes the events from the fall of Fort Sumter to the aftermath of emancipation as part of the same historical thread which began with the arrival in 1619 of the first Africans in Jamestown. Peter Kolchin's recent synthesis, *American Slavery, 1619–1877*, has convincingly shown the need to treat the entire history of the "peculiar institution" and the aftermath of its demise as a whole. To a certain extent, we see this reader as an ideal companion to Kolchin's book, even though we have assembled the documents and readings in such a way that it can serve as a text for courses on slavery and emancipation without the need for additional material.

The first four chapters of the book cover the first two centuries of the slavery experience. The story begins with the famous letter in which James Rolfe described the arrival of "twenty odd Negroes" in Virginia, but is soon complicated by the flow of seventeenth-century laws and statutes which restricted the freedom of blacks and sealed their fate as an enslaved work force both in the Chesapeake and in the South Carolina low country. Philip Morgan's excerpt in this section summarizes various strands of old and recent scholarship and compares similarities and differences with regard to the origins of slavery in the two regions (chapter 1). The most important consequence of the South's reliance on an African work force was the forced migration of thousands of people – such as Olaudah Equiano – who were enslaved and whose descendants gave origin to a distinctive African American population and culture. By the eighteenth century, slavery had already acquired many of the characteristics which we normally associate with the antebellum period. As Ira Berlin has shown, it was the "plantation generation" of African American slaves that made possible with its forced labor the economic revolution that transformed the southern colonies into major producers of tobacco and rice (chapter 2). The plantation revolution, in turn, led to the firm establishment of an elite which adopted an ideology characterized by both the kind of patriarchal ideal shared by planters such as William Byrd II of Westover and by the entrepreneurial attitude manifested by other planters such as Landon Carter. Kathleen Brown's contribution shows how the key to the planter class's success in maintaining its hold on southern society from the seventeenth century onward was in its continuous regeneration through intermarriage (chapter 3).

In the last decades of the eighteenth century, slavery underwent a deep economic, social, and political crisis, which threatened to annihilate the institution. In a short excerpt from his synthetic text, Peter Kolchin shows how social, economic, and religious arguments joined together to condemn the inefficiency, backwardness, and cruelty of a slave system which had enjoyed universal support for several centuries, but was now criticized by renowned personalities such as Thomas Jefferson. The Revolutionary War, during which both American and British officers – such as Lord Dunmore – took advantage of the slaves' will to fight for their freedom, caused further disruption and accelerated the movement toward manumission. Even though this early thrust toward emancipation gradually waned in the South, by 1804 slavery was outlawed in every state north of the Mason–Dixon line (chapter 4).

The largest part of the present volume includes eight chapters on slavery in the antebellum South and focuses especially on social aspects of both the world of the planters and the world of the slaves. Our point of departure for the history of the antebellum South is an analysis of the unparalleled economic expansion related to cotton cultivation. This expansion allowed a revival of the moribund institution of slavery through widespread accumulation of wealth in the newly settled areas of the Old Southwest, as external observers such as Joseph Baldwin and Frederick Law Olmsted clearly argued in their writings. In recent years, studies of the economics of antebellum slavery have increased exponentially and, in some cases, have even overturned previously held assumptions. However, as Mark Smith's excerpt shows, the main historiographic debate continues to be between the South-as-non-capitalist view held by the Marxist-oriented works written by the early Eugene Genovese and his followers and the South-as-capitalist view held by neoclassical economic historians such as Robert Fogel and Stanley Engerman. Though the next generation of southern historians is likely to attempt to find a middle ground between the two positions, at present most scholars regard the two views as diametrically opposed to one another (chapter 5).

In the central chapters of this collection we treat the world of the planters, the life of the plantation mistresses, and the master–slave relationship as three topics closely related to, and part of, the ideology of exploitation which informed the southern elite's relations with both family members and slaves. The planter elite's complex world view included among its most important elements the concept of honor as a normative set of rules – exemplified by John Lyde Wilson's *Code Duello* – and the arguments in defense of slavery – well represented by reactionary sociologist George Fitzhugh (chapter 6). Within the boundaries of the precise norms of conduct which dominated the elite's world, women's behavior was subject to constant regulation and repression; this was due to the existence of an elaborate set of conventions imposed upon them by the patriarchal system – as both Adele Petigru and Mary Chesnut were well aware (chapter 7). At the same time, patriarchal relations within the family – with the head of the household as the central figure – served as a metaphor for social relations at large, and especially for relations between the master and his slaves; no one exemplified these ideas better than James Henry Hammond and Charles Manigault, two prominent planters who behaved both as absolute despots and as condescending parents in the treatment of their bondsmen (chapter 9).

In the study of the ideology of the master class, Eugene Genovese's early writings are still fundamental readings for any scholar of the antebellum South. Several of his assumptions have been radically revised and seriously challenged by studies such as James Oakes's *The Ruling Race* – which pointed out and explored the capitalist ideology of small and medium slaveholders as opposed to large planters – but Genovese's overall framework, though slightly tarnished, has not been replaced by any alternative model. His complex view of the Old South as a pre-capitalist society in which planters' paternalism functioned as the elite's ideological means of exercising "hegemony" over an enslaved African

American working class has been refined by a host of recent works, including Genovese's own extended essay, *The Slaveholders' Dilemma*, a particularly perceptive and insightful explanation of the ideology at the heart of the planter elite's pro-slavery culture (chapter 6).

Though preceded by the enormously influential work of scholars such as Anne Firor Scott and Catherine Clinton, Elizabeth Fox-Genovese's studies of the plantation household have performed a similar role to Eugene Genovese's writings in regard to the scholarship on the plantation mistresses. Yet, a large number of recent monographs, such as the one by Marli Wiener on different aspects of the lives of elite women, has dramatically changed our view of female social roles and activities. Indeed, we have come to understand that it is virtually impossible to think about patriarchal relations within the family and in society as two distinct and separate spheres, since the most recent scholarship has demonstrated their fundamental connections in the minds of small and large slaveholders (chapter 7).

Few issues, though, have generated more scholarship than the master–slave relationship. Eugene Genovese's particular view of paternalism has been challenged by several recent studies which have documented and analyzed the particularly exploitative character of the business of slavery. Books such as William Dusinberre's *Them Dark Days* have distanced themselves both from Genovese's interpretive framework and the ideas of neoclassical economic historians such as Fogel and Engerman, who supported the view of a substantial harmony of firm-like relations between masters and slaves. However, some of the best recent scholarship – such as Walter Johnson's *Soul by Soul* on the antebellum slave market – has built upon Genovese's fundamental argument about the centrality of paternalism and the way the ideology permitted a two-way process of interaction and bargaining between masters and slaves. By focusing on the relatively neglected topic of the slave market, Johnson was able to examine the precise workings and internal contradictions within paternalism to produce fresh insight and understanding (chapter 8).

Since the historiographic revolution of the 1970s, slave life has consistently been one of the most popular topics among scholars of the antebellum South. In the 1970s, the combined analysis of nineteenth-century slave narratives – such as Frederick Douglass's autobiography – and George Rawick's re-edition of 1930s interviews with ex-slaves (from which we have taken the excerpt by Tempie Herndon) supported a new wave of scholarship. In the 1980s and 1990s, though the wide framework of the everyday life of bondsmen on the plantations had been outlined in popular works by John Blassingame, Eugene Genovese, and Herbert Gutman, there were still several unexplored areas which became the object of detailed study. Among these, scholarship on slave women and slave families has produced some of the most interesting work. Pioneered by Deborah Grey White's *Ar'n't I a Woman?*, which was the first full-scale treatment of the subject, the analysis of female slaves' lives in the antebellum South has reached a level of sophistication well represented by Brenda Stevenson's *Life in Black and White*. In this highly acclaimed and controversial work – from which we have taken an excerpt – Stevenson contends that masters and slaves lived in separate worlds and that the few contacts between them were determined by the violent and exploitative nature of the business of slavery (chapter 9).

Until recently, two of the most neglected – though immensely important – areas of slave life were resistance and rebellion. Apart from Genovese's *From Rebellion to Revolution* and occasional references to resistance activities in the surveys of slave life mentioned above, little else was available in terms of solid scholarship. The fact that few rebellions occurred in the antebellum South and that only one – led by Nat Turner in 1831 – was successful left historians with little room for the study of organized resistance. Yet, in the past few years, scholars have looked back at the fragmented evidence on resistance activities among southern slaves and have assigned increasing importance to episodes such as the one which Frederick Douglass recounts in his autobiography about his fight with the brutal slave-breaker Mr. Covey. Indeed, in the first full-scale scholarly study of slave runaways, from which we have taken an excerpt, John Hope Franklin and Loren Schweninger have shown how day-to-day resistance, of which running away was the most extreme form, had a profound impact on the slavery system and on the masters' attitudes toward slavery as a whole (chapter 10).

It is virtually impossible to understand how the slaveholders' defense of slavery transformed into the political ideology of southern nationalism and ultimately led to secession and Civil War without taking into account and analyzing the contemporaneous birth of an intransigent movement for the immediate abolition of slavery in the northern states. There is little doubt that William Lloyd Garrison was the heart and soul behind the 1830s wave of Abolitionist efforts; both the famous 1831 "I Will Be Heard" excerpt from his newspaper *The Liberator* and the 1833 *Declaration of Sentiments of the American Anti-Slavery Society* testify to the depth of his view, which held that slavery was a sin in the eyes of God and a violation of the principles of the Declaration of Independence. Yet, scholars have always noted the Abolitionists' patronizing attitudes toward blacks and have tended to echo the charge, first leveled by Frederick Douglass, of an inherent hypocrisy within the white Abolitionist movement. Paul Goodman's posthumous study, from which we have taken an excerpt, has successfully managed to correct some previously held assumptions and has shown how Abolitionists strongly believed, implemented, and fought for racial equality and equal opportunities and treatment of blacks and whites (chapter 11).

Even though a minority, Abolitionists had a significant influence on public opinion and, through this influence, contributed a great deal in creating the necessary background for the emergence of a committed antislavery movement in politics. Certainly by the late 1820s and 1830s, at the time of the Nullification Crisis in South Carolina, southerners such as John C. Calhoun saw that the federal government was divided over the issue of protecting southern agricultural interests and the slave economy. Yet, the issue of slavery truly came to occupy the center of national attention only with the acquisition of vast western territory after the Mexican War, as the article written by Free-Soil Democrat Walt Whitman and reproduced here shows. The famous "House Divided" speech given by Republican Abraham Lincoln ten years later shows how, by 1858, the conflict between the expansion of slavery and the expansion of free labor in the West had reached a point of no return. Lincoln's speech, however, also shows how, during the antebellum period, the interests of slaveholders had been protected by the federal government and through federal measures. A similar argument is also at the center of Don Fehrenbacher's recent work, from which we have taken an excerpt, on the history of the relation between slavery and the American Republic and the analysis of the causes of the Civil War (chapter 12).

Seen from this perspective, it hardly comes as a surprise that the slaveholders of South Carolina – the same state in which the Nullification Crisis had raged – decided to secede when a Republican president committed to antislavery, though not to abolition, was elected in 1860. Though South Carolina was soon joined by the states of the Deep South – which formed the Confederate States of America – it was only after southern soldiers conquered the federal garrison at Fort Sumter, in Charleston harbor, that the rest of the South seceded as well; the excerpt by Mary Chesnut well describes the mixture of passions, from joy to fear, that this event provoked in the heart of most southerners. Not long after, the war that the slaveholders had begun to preserve slavery started to prove long and costly. As the second year of fighting came to a close and stalemate prevailed on the battlefield, talk about emancipating the slaves began to be heard in the North. Needless to say, most southerners – such as Sarah Morgan, a Louisiana mistress whose words form one of the documents in this collection – considered this an absurd idea conceived by ignorant northern statesmen. Yet, as slaveholders, their sons, and their overseers left for the war in increasing numbers, both because of the high rate of casualities and the enforcement of conscription, more and more mistresses were left alone to take care of the slaves. Drew Gilpin Faust's study, from which we have taken a particularly insightful excerpt, shows that the mistresses' struggle "to do a man's job" on the plantations radically changed their ideas about the patriarchal assumptions governing female behavior (chapter 13).

The Emancipation Proclamation, which became effective from 1 January 1863, had a cataclysmic effect on the already fragile economy and society of the Confederacy. Though justified by Lincoln as little more than a war measure valid only within enemy territory, the proclamation permanently transformed the nature of the conflict into a war for the destruction of slavery. As the excerpt by Ira Berlin and the other scholars belonging to the *Freedom Project* shows, slaves had contributed a great deal to this shift, forcing the issue of emancipation by turning up in Union camps and fleeing their plantations in order to join the war effort against their former masters. The Emancipation Proclamation also paved the way for African Americans to enlist in regiments of their own, don the Union blue uniforms, and serve in companies such as the famous 54th Massachusetts under Robert Gould Shaw. The call to arms published by Frederick Douglass in his newspaper, and reproduced here, clearly demonstrates the importance of the enlistment of northern free blacks in the Union army as a means to show to the world that African Americans could fight for liberation of their southern brethren. On the other hand, the statement of the anonymous 'Colored Man' that follows shows the contradictions of Union policy, which on the one hand was nominally committed to emancipation, whilst on the other hand continued to be far more ambiguous on the issue of African Americans' enlistment (chapter 14).

In spite of the transformation of the Civil War into a war for black liberation, the full dismantling of the slavery system and the making of a legal apparatus designed to protect the rights of the freed people took several years to achieve during the postwar period, or Reconstruction; in fact, the status of the freedmen became the object of a political tug-of-war between Congress, dominated by radical Republicans, and President Andrew Johnson, who was eventually impeached because of his lenient policy toward the post-Confederate South. Yet, by 1870, after the passage of the Thirteenth, Fourteenth, and Fifteenth Amendments, not only had the abolition of slavery been legally sanctioned, but black civil rights and adult male enfranchisement had been legally guaranteed. The new opportunities provided by the new legislation included, among the most important, freedom of mobility and education. Yet, the most important issue for African Americans in the South was the ownership of land. The federal government's failure to address this issue caused the freed people to remain under the economic control of their former masters; therefore, it is fair to say that in this respect Reconstruction was a missed opportunity or, in the words of Eric Foner, an "unfinished revolution."

All in all, if we take a long view of the entire course of events that led from slavery to emancipation and Reconstruction, we can distinguish four revolutionary moments in the history of the South: two such moments emerged out of economic and social revolutions which gave birth to, and then reinforced, the slavery system, while the other two arose from political and social revolutions which shook the foundations of slavery and eventually led to its collapse. The first economic and social revolution occurred when tobacco and rice became staple crops in the Chesapeake and in the South Carolina low country at the end of the seventeenth century; the so-called plantation revolution also gave birth to the first slave society in the South, meaning a society in which slavery was at the center of social life and economic activity. A similar "plantation revolution" occurred at the beginning of the nineteenth century, when cotton became the main staple crop cultivated in the South, regenerating the slavery system and creating a new class of slaveholders in the Old Southwest. In between these two economic revolutions, the American Revolution – a political and social movement – with its ideas of freedom and equality and its criticism of the old order based on hierarchy and discrimination, threatened to annihilate the system of human bondage. The upheaval caused by the disruptive effect of democratic ideas was equal to the one caused by the impact of the war itself in which the American colonists fought for their freedom from the British. A similar upheaval, in ideological and material terms, occurred during the Civil War, which in many respects was a true second American Revolution. Once again, and even more than in the eighteenth century, ideas of freedom and equality circulated and gained credence. In complete contrast with the fundamental tenets of the slavery system, these beliefs helped transform a war that had begun with conservative intent into a revolutionary movement for the destruction of a system of human bondage. However, unlike what took place after the American Revolution, when constitutional compromises ended up protecting the legality of slavery, the Civil War led to definitive abolition – a fact which was officially sanctioned by the Thirteenth Amendment to the Constitution, ratified in 1865. In this perspective, this second American Revolution, though left unfinished at the end of Reconstruction, was part of a much larger and enduring historical process. It is a process that did not reach its next defining moment till the post-World War II civil rights movement forced the passage of the 1965 Civil Rights Act. As a process whereby Americans come to terms with race and attempt to make good the promises of their first revolution, it remains ongoing today.

Further reading

Boles, J. B., *Black Southerners, 1619–1869* (Lexington, Ky.: University Press of Kentucky, 1985).

Boles, J. B. and Nolen E. T. (eds.), *Interpreting Southern History: Historiographical Essays in Honor of Sanford W. Higginbotham* (Baton Rouge: Louisiana State University Press, 1987).

Campbell, D. C. and Rice, K. S. (eds.), *Before Freedom Came: African American Life in the Antebellum South* (Richmond: Museum of the Confederacy and University Press of Virginia, 1991).

Cooper, W. J. and Terrill, T. E., *The American South: A History* (New York: McGraw-Hill, 1999).

Escott, P., Goldfield, D., McMillen S. and Turner, E. (eds.), *Major Problems in the History of the American South*, vol. 1: *The Old South*, 2nd edn. (New York: Houghton Mifflin, 1999).

Goodheart, L. B. et al. (eds.), *Slavery in American Society* (Lexington, Mass.: D. C. Heath, 1992).

Harris, J. W. (ed.), *Society and Culture in the Slave South* (London: Routledge, 1992).

Kolchin, P., *American Slavery, 1619–1877* (New York: Hill & Wang, 1993).

Miller, R. M. and Smith J. D. (eds.), *Dictionary of African American Slavery* (Westport, Conn.: Praeger Publishers, 1997).

Mullin, M. (ed.), *American Negro Slavery: A Documentary History* (Columbia, SC: University of South Carolina Press, 1976).

Parish, P. J., *Slavery: History and Historians* (New York: Harper & Row, 1989).

Rose, W. L. (ed.), *A Documentary History of Slavery in North America* (New York and London: Oxford University Press, 1976).

Smith, M. M., *Debating Slavery: Economy and Society in the Antebellum American South* (New York: Cambridge University Press, 1998).

Smith, M. M. (ed.), *The Old South* (Oxford: Blackwell, 2000).

1
Colonial Origins: Race and Slavery

Introduction

In 1606, King James authorized the joint-stock Virginia Company to found a colony in present-day Virginia, which the settlers called Jamestown. In the first winter, Jamestown's residents rapidly declined from 105 to 38; the fledgling colony survived only because of the help of the local Indians, whose chief was named Powhatan. However, after Powhatan's death in 1622, war broke out and continued until the 1640s. During this period, the mortality rate in Virginia was extremely high. Thousands died from disease and Indian warfare. Those who survived used the abundant availability of land to grow crops. In 1616, John Rolfe started to grow tobacco, a plant that the Indians smoked, and shipped it to Europe. From this point on, Virginia's fortune as a colony became linked to tobacco production.

Several of the settlers who came to Virginia between the 1640s and the 1660s were younger sons of the English landed gentry or members of the aristocracy who had fled from England, where they could not rise in wealth and influence. In Virginia, they formed a substantial upper class and behaved like a local titled aristocracy; soon they started to grow tobacco on large plantations, where they put both indentured servants and slaves to work. Indentured servants were poor white men and women who had sold themselves for the price of the passage to America. Depending on the terms of their indentures, they were bound by a contract to work for a master for 10 to 20 years in harsh exploitative conditions. In 1676, Nathaniel Bacon led a rebellion of indentured servants, small farmers, and slaves against the Virginian planter elite. Bacon managed to burn Jamestown and threaten the elite, but shortly afterwards Governor Berkeley subdued the rebels and hanged 33 of them.

The first Africans arrived in Virginia aboard a Dutch ship in 1619. During the following 75 years, most of the Africans who arrived in the Chesapeake were "seasoned": they came from the English Caribbean, where they had already adjusted to the new disease environment and learned some English. However, from about 1680, planters began to rely on slaves coming directly from Africa, both because they were cheaper and because they were less likely to bond together and cause trouble. By 1680, special laws – the slave codes – established lifetime slavery, limited the rights of slaves and free blacks, discouraged masters from freeing slaves, and prescribed severe corporal punishments for rebels. They were followed by even more restrictive codes in the early eighteenth century.

The very first settlers in the Carolinas were successful Barbadian planters who acquired land in the coastal region of South Carolina in the 1660s and moved there with their "seasoned" slaves. In the last third of the seventeenth century, South Carolinians made several attempts to find a suitable crop for the low country environment. They eventually found it in rice, which some of the recently imported African slaves knew how to plant, cultivate, harvest, and thresh, since they had worked with this crop in their homelands. Rice soon became the main staple crop grown in the low country, and rice exports made the port-city of Charleston wealthy. The planting of rice required an initial outlay of substantial capital, because the crop required sophisticated irrigation works. Consequently, only already wealthy individuals, such as the emigré Barbadian planters, could enter the rice business. Rice planters soon formed the distinctive elite of a society which had been based on inequalities of race and class from the start.

From its very early days, South Carolina had a majority black population, both slave and free. Whether coming from Barbados or from Africa, slaves provided rice planters with a suitable workforce for the rice fields. The areas of rice cultivation were mostly swamps infested with malaria and mosquitoes during half of the year. No white person could live there during the summer season; enslaved Indians had been unable to survive in the rice swamps as well. Only Africans proved able to resist the harsh conditions, and hence they made a decisive contribution to the low country's booming rice economy. Already by 1690, slave codes similar to those in Virginia restricted the freedom of any person of color and sanctioned the lifetime enslavement of Africans. They were followed by harsher codes in 1696, 1712, and 1742.

Further reading

Berlin, I., *Many Thousands Gone: The First Two Centuries of Slavery in North America* (Cambridge, Mass. and London: The Belknap Press of Harvard University Press, 1998).

Breen, T. H. and Innes, S., *"Myne Owne Ground": Race and Freedom on Virginia's Eastern Shore, 1640–1676* (New York: Oxford University Press, 1980).

Chaplin, J. E., *An Anxious Pursuit: Agricultural Innovation and Modernity in the Lower South* (Chapel Hill: University of North Carolina Press, 1993).

Eltis, D., *The Rise of African Slavery in the Americas* (New York: Cambridge University Press, 1999).

Jordan, W., *White Over Black: American Attitudes toward the Negro, 1550–1812* (Chapel Hill: University of North Carolina Press, 1968).

Littlefield, D. C., *Rice and Slaves: Ethnicity and the Slave Trade in Colonial South Carolina*, 2nd edn. (Urbana: University of Illinois Press, 1991).

Morgan, E., *American Slavery, American Freedom: The Ordeal of Colonial Virginia* (New York: Norton, 1975).

Vaughan, A. T., *The Roots of American Racism* (New York: Oxford University Press, 1995).

Wood, B., *The Origins of American Slavery: Freedom and Bondage in the English Colonies* (New York: Hill & Wang, 1997).

Wood, P. H., *Black Majority: Negroes in Colonial South Carolina from 1670 through the Stono Rebellion* (New York: Knopf, 1974).

The First Blacks Arrive in Virginia (1619)

The first Africans arrived in North America with the expeditions of the sixteenth-century Spanish explorers Panfilo de Narvaez, Francisco Vasquez de Coronado, and Hernando de Soto. As early as 1565, there was already a population of more than a hundred Africans concentrated in the Spanish settlement of St. Augustine, Florida. However, the landing of 20 Africans at Jamestown, Virginia, in 1619, marked the start of a chain of events that led to the formation of the largest black community outside Africa and the most successful slave society in North America. The document describing the arrival of this first group of Africans in Jamestown is a letter written by Virginian planter John Rolfe to Sir Edwyn Sandys. In the letter, Rolfe casually describes the selling of "20 and odd Negroes" by "a Dutch man of Warr," a ship probably engaged in piracy against the Spanish empire in the Caribbean. The letter does not provide any specific detail, and its importance lies mainly in its being the earliest known reference to the presence of Africans in the Chesapeake.

About the latter end of August, a Dutch man of Warr of the burden of a 160 tunes arrived at Point-Comfort, the Commandors name Capt Jope, his pilott for the West Indies one Mr Marmaduke an Englishman. They mett with the Trer in the West Indyes and dtermyned to hold consort shipp hetherward, but in their passage lost one the other. He brought not any thing but 20 and odd Negroes, which the Governor and Cape Marchant bought for victualle (whereof he was in greate need as he pretended) at the best and easyest rate they could. He hadd a lardge and ample Comyssion from his Excellency to range and take purchase in the West Indyes.

(John Rolfe to Sir Edwyn Sandys, January 1619/20)

Source: Willie Lee Rose (ed.), *A Documentary History of Slavery in North America* (New York and London: Oxford University Press, 1976), p. 15

Slavery Becomes a Legal Fact in Virginia (17th-Century Statutes)

The first generation of African slaves in the Chesapeake coexisted with a large number of white indentured servants; until the 1630s legal statutes made little distinction between the two. Starting in the 1630s, however, the law increasingly discriminated between different categories of unfree labor. At the same time, a corresponding hardening of racial barriers led to the passage of laws such as the 1630 statute forbidding white men from having sexual relations with black women. By the 1670s, the expression "negroe slaves" – which characterizes the 1680 Act on Negroes Insurrection – had replaced more ambiguous terms such as "negro servants" or simply "negars." The change in terminology reflected a much more dramatic change in labor conditions; by 1640, Africans were enslaved for life. As the Chesapeake became a primary center of tobacco production and the flow of indentured servants from Europe decreased, black legal rights rapidly deteriorated. The 1662 Act defined the status of black children according to the free or enslaved condition of their mother, while the following 1667 Act declared that baptism of slaves did not exempt them from bondage. As the black population increased, so the colonial authorities passed an increasing number of laws like the 1680 Act in order to prevent slave insurrections and punish runaways and "other slaves unlawfully absent."

[1630]

September 17th, 1630. Hugh Davis to be soundly whipped, before an assembly of Negroes and others for abusing himself to the dishonor of God and shame of Christians, by defiling his body in lying with a negro; which fault he is to acknowledge next Sabbath day.

(*Statutes 1:146*)

[1662] Act XII Negro womens children to serve according to the condition of the mother

Whereas some doubts have arrisen whether children got by any Englishman upon a negro woman should be slave or ffree, *Be it therefore enacted and declared by this present grand assembly*, that all children borne in this country shalbe held bond or free only according to the condition of the

Source: Willie Lee Rose (ed.), *A Documentary History of Slavery in North America* (New York and London: Oxford University Press, 1976), pp. 16–22

mother, And that if any christian shall committ ffornication with a negro man or woman, hee or shee soe offending shall pay double the ffines imposed by the former act.

(*Statutes 2:170*)

[1667] Act III An act declaring that baptisme of slaves doth not exempt them from bondage

Whereas some doubts have risen whether children that are slaves by birth, and by the charity and piety of their owners made pertakers of the blessed sacrament of baptisme, should by vertue of their baptisme be made ffree; *It is enacted and declared by this grand assembly, and the authority thereof*, that the conferring of baptisme doth not alter the condition of the person as to his bondage or ffreedome; that diverse masters, ffreed from this doubt, may more carefully endeavor the propagation of christianity by permitting children, though slaves, or those of greater growth if capable to be admitted to that sacrament.

(*Statutes 2:260*)

[1680] Act X An act for preventing Negroes Insurrections

Whereas the frequent meeting of considerable numbers of negroe slaves under pretence of feasts and burialls is judged of dangerous consequence; for prevention whereof for the future, *Bee it enacted by the kings most excellent majestie by and with the consent of the generall assembly, and it is hereby enacted by the authority aforesaid*, that from and after the publication of this law, it shall not be lawfull for any negroe or other slave to carry or arme himselfe with any club, staffe, gunn, sword or any other weapon of defence or offence, nor to goe or depart from of his masters ground without a certificate from his master, mistris or overseer, and such permission not to be granted but upon perticuler and necessary occasions; and every negroe or slave so offending not haveing a certificate is aforesaid shalbe sent to the next constable, who is hereby enjoyned and required to give the said negroe twenty lashes on his bare back well layd on, and soe sent home to his said master, mistris or overseer. *And it is further enacted by the authority aforesaid* that if any negroe or other slave shall presume to lift up his hand in opposition against any christian, shall for every such offence, upon due proofe made thereof by the oath of the party before a magistrate, have and receive thirty lashes on his bare back well laid on. *And it is hereby further enacted by the authority aforesaid* that if any negroe or other slave shall absent himself from his masters service and lye hid and lurking in obscure places, comitting injuries to the inhabitants, and shall resist any person or persons that shalby any lawfull authority be imployed to apprehend and take the said negroe, that then in case of such resistance, it shalbe lawfull for such person or persons to kill the said negroe or slave soe lying out and resisting, and that this law be once every six months published at the respective county courts and parish churches within this colony.

(*Statutes 2:481–2*)

South Carolina Restricts the Liberty of Slaves (1740)

From its very early days, South Carolina had a black majority. Consequently, white anxiety ran higher than in any southern region and resulted in the erosion of rights of all the persons of color, especially after the mid-1720s, when imports of African slaves reached 1,000 per year. A special "Negro Watch" was established in Charleston in 1721 to confine blacks found in the streets after 9 p.m. At the same time, the colonial militia organized patrols which controlled the movement of blacks in rural areas. In 1739, newly imported slaves from Angola started the Stono Rebellion. They managed to kill 30 whites before they were eventually captured and executed by planters. Thereafter, white South Carolinians lumped together all blacks, considering them dangerous to white society, and further tightened the restrictions on both slaves and free blacks, as the 1740 statute shows. Together with limitations on personal rights, the statute includes long sections in which the slaves are forbidden to bear arms and gather or travel together.

I. *And be it enacted,*... That all negroes and Indians, (free Indians in amity with this government, and negroes, mulattoes and mustizoes, who are now free, excepted,) mulattoes or mustizoes who now are, or shall hereafter be, in this Province, and all their issue and offspring, born or to be born, shall be, and they are hereby declared to be, and remain forever hereafter, absolute slaves....

XXIII. *And be it further enacted* by the authority aforesaid. That it shall not be lawful for any slave, unless in the presence of some white person, to carry or make use of fire arms, or any offensive weapons whatsoever, unless such negro or slave shall have a ticket or license, in writing, from his master, mistress or overseer, to hunt and kill game, cattle, or mis-

---

Source: Paul Escott and David Goldfield (eds.), *Major Problems in the History of the American South*, vol. 1: *The Old South*, 1st edn. (Lexington, Mass.: D. C. Heath, 1991), pp. 47–8.

chievous birds, or beasts of prey, and that such license be renewed once every month, or unless there be some white person of the age of sixteen years or upwards, in the company of such slave, when he is hunting or shooting, or that such slave be actually carrying his master's arms to or from his master's plantation, by a special ticket for that purpose, or unless such slave be found in the day time actually keeping off rice birds, or other birds, within the plantation to which such slave belongs, lodging the same gun at night within the dwelling house of his master, mistress or white overseer. . . .

XXXII. *And be it further enacted* by the authority aforesaid. That if any keeper of a tavern or punch house, or retailer of strong liquors, shall give, sell, utter or deliver to any slave, any beer, ale, cider, wine, rum, brandy, or other spirituous liquors, or strong liquor whatsoever, without the license or consent of the owner, or such other person who shall have the care or government of such slave, every person so offending shall forfeit the sum of five pounds, current money, for the first offence. . . .

XXXIV. And *whereas*, several owners of slaves have permitted them to keep canoes, and to breed and raise horses, neat cattle and hogs, and to traffic and barter in several parts of this Province, for the particular and peculiar benefit of such slaves, by which means they have not only an opportunity of receiving and concealing stolen goods, but to plot and confederate together, and form conspiracies dangerous to the peace and safety of the whole Province; *Be it therefore enacted* by the authority aforesaid. That it shall not be lawful for any slave so to buy, sell, trade, traffic, deal or barter for any goods or commodities, (except as before excepted,) nor shall any slave be permitted to keep any boat, perriauger or canoe, or to raise and breed, for the use and benefit of such slave, any horses, mares, neat cattle, sheep or hogs, under pain of forfeiting all the goods and commodities which shall be so bought, sold, traded, trafficked, dealt or bartered for, by any slave, and of all the boats, perriaugers or canoes, cattle, sheep or hogs, which any slave shall keep, raise or breed for the peculiar use, benefit and profit of such slave. . . .

XXXVII. And *whereas*, cruelty is not only highly unbecoming those who profess themselves christians, but is odious in the eyes of all men who have any sense of virtue or humanity: therefore, to refrain and prevent barbarity being exercised towards slaves, *Be it enacted* by the authority aforesaid. That if any person or persons whosoever, shall wilfully murder his own slave, or the slave of any other person, every such person shall, upon conviction thereof, forfeit and pay the sum of seven hundred pounds, current money, and shall be rendered, and is hereby declared altogether and forever incapable of holding, exercising, enjoying or receiving the profits of any office, place or employment, civil or military, within this Province. . . .

XXXVIII. *And be it further enacted* by the authority aforesaid. That in case any person in this Province, who shall be owner, or shall have the care, government or charge of any slave or slaves, shall deny, neglect or refuse to allow such slave or slaves, under his or her charge, sufficient cloathing, covering or food, it shall and may be lawful for any person or persons, on behalf of such slave or slaves, to make complaint to the next neighboring justice, in the parish where such slave or slaves live or are usually employed....

XLIII. And *whereas*, it may be attended with ill consequences to permit a great number of slaves to travel together in the high roads without some white person in company with them; *Be it therefore enacted* by the authority aforesaid, That no men slaves exceeding seven in number, shall hereafter be permitted to travel together in any high road in this Province, without some white person with them....

XLV. And *whereas*, the having of slaves taught to write, or suffering them to be employed in writing, may be attended with great inconveniences; *Be it therefore enacted* by the authority aforesaid, That all and every person and persons whatsoever, who shall hereafter teach, or cause any slave or slaves to be taught, to write, or shall use or employ any slave as a scribe in any manner of writing whatsoever, hereafter taught to write, every such person and persons, shall, for every such offence, forfeit the sum of one hundred pounds current money.

XLVI. And *whereas*, plantations settled with slaves without any white person thereon, may be harbours for runaways and fugitive slaves; *Be it therefore enacted* by the authority aforesaid, That no person or persons hereafter shall keep any slaves on any plantation or settlement, without having a white person on such plantation or settlement.

Two Infant Slave Societies in the Chesapeake and the Lowcountry

Philip D. Morgan

In *Slave Counterpoint*, Philip Morgan analyzes and compares black life and culture in the eighteenth-century Chesapeake and the South Carolina low country; his analysis focuses upon the similarities and differences between the

---

Philip D. Morgan, *Slave Counterpoint: Black Culture in the Eighteenth-Century Chesapeake and Lowcountry* (Chapel Hill: University of North Carolina Press, 1998), pp. 1–23.

experiences of the slaves in the two regions. In this excerpt, Morgan shows how different historical conditions gave rise to two different types of slave societies with a number of common characteristics. In the late seventeenth century, Virginia had a fully fledged plantation economy based on a long-standing tradition of tobacco cultivation; at the same time, the colony's still flexible slave statutes allowed for a significant population of free blacks. South Carolina, on the other hand, was a relatively new colony, but one with an already closed slave society. Moreover, South Carolina's planter class was still searching for a suitable crop for plantation agriculture. As the end of the seventeenth century approached, Virginia passed increasingly stricter laws on manumission, while South Carolina's plantation economy became fully identified with the cultivation of rice.

By the late seventeenth century, Virginia had a plantation economy in search of a labor force, whereas South Carolina had a labor force in search of a plantation economy. A tobacco economy for decades, Virginia imported slaves on a large scale only when its supply of indentured servants dwindled toward the end of the century. By the time Virginia began to recruit more slaves than servants, a large white population dominated the colony. In fact, before the last decade of the seventeenth century, Virginia hardly qualified as a slave society. Only by the turn of the eighteenth century did slaves come to play a central role in the society's productive activities and form a sizable, though still small, proportion of its population. In 1700, blacks formed just a sixth of the Chesapeake's colonial population. By contrast, South Carolina was the one British colony in North America in which settlement and black slavery went hand in hand. From the outset, slaves were considered essential to Carolina's success. With the Caribbean experience as their yardstick, prospective settlers pointed out in 1666 that "thes Setlements have beene made and upheld by Negroes and without constant supplies of them cannot subsist." Even in the early 1670s, slaves formed between one-fourth and one-third of the new colony's population. A slave society from its inception, South Carolina became viable only after settlers discovered the agricultural staple on which the colony's plantation economy came to rest. By the turn of the century, then, the Chesapeake was emerging as a slave society; the Lowcountry, a slave society from its inception, was just emerging as a productive one.[1]

In spite of this fundamental difference, both infant slave societies shared several characteristics. In both societies, seasoned slaves from the Caribbean predominated among the earliest arrivals; early on, the numbers of black men and women became quite balanced; many slaves spent much of their time clearing land, cultivating provisions, rearing livestock, and working alongside members of other races; race relations were far more fluid than they later became. All of these similarities point toward a high degree of assimilation by the slaves of the early Chesapeake and Lowcountry. Many slaves arrived speaking English, could form families and have children (more readily than white servants, for example), worked at diverse tasks, and fraternized with whites both at work and at play.

Nevertheless, as the seventeenth century drew to a close, differences began to outweigh similarities. The Chesapeake imported quite large numbers of Africans long before the Lowcountry; and, by the 1690s, the region had many more slave men than women, whereas the Lowcountry boasted more equal numbers of men and women than ever before – and for many decades thereafter. If these differences seem to point toward a more Africanized slave culture in the Chesapeake than in the Lowcountry, other dissimilarities incline in a different direction and were ultimately more decisive in shaping the lives of blacks in the two regions. Slaveowners in Virginia put most of their new Africans to planting tobacco on small quarters, usually surrounded by whites, whereas their counterparts in South Carolina, though still experimenting with many agricultural products, grouped their slaves on somewhat larger units with little white intrusion. Furthermore, the Lowcountry always was – and increasingly became – a far more closed slave society than the Chesapeake. Lowcountry slaves had less intimate contact with whites and constructed a more autonomous culture than their Chesapeake counterparts.

The origins of the earliest black immigrants to the Chesapeake and Lowcountry were similar. Most came, not directly from Africa, but from the West Indies. Some might have only recently arrived in the islands from their homeland and a few were probably born in the Caribbean, but most were seasoned slaves – acclimatized to the New World environment and somewhat conversant with the ways of whites. Some came with Spanish or Portuguese names; others with some understanding of the English language. . . . Both Lowcountry and Chesapeake received a somewhat gentle introduction, as it were, to New World slavery. Neither experienced a massive or immediate intrusion of alien Africans.

By the late seventeenth century, however, Africans began to arrive, especially in the Chesapeake. From the mid-1670s to 1700, Virginia and Maryland imported about six thousand slaves direct from Africa, most arriving in the 1690s. While the Chesapeake's slave population was being transformed by a predominantly African influx, the Lowcountry did not undergo the same process for another twenty or so years. In the year 1696 the first known African slaver reached South Carolina; a constant trickle of Africans became commonplace only about the turn of the century.

The structures of these two societies' slave populations, much like their origins, were initially similar. By the 1660s in the Chesapeake and by the 1690s in the Lowcountry, a rough balance had been achieved between slave men and women. Although men outnumbered women among the earliest black immigrants to both regions, women apparently outlived men. Moreover, some of the children born to the earliest immigrants reached majority, also helping to account for the relative balance between men and women. When, in 1686, Elizabeth Read of Virginia drew up her will, she mentioned twenty-two slaves: six men, seven women, five boys, and four girls. Twelve of these slaves had family connections: there were three two-parent families and two mothers with children. An incident involving a free black of Northampton County illuminates a typical Chesapeake slave household at this stage of development. On the eve of the New Year of 1672, William Harman, a free black, paid a visit to the home quarter of John Michael. Harman spent part of the evening and parts of the following two days carousing with Michael's slaves, who numbered at least six adults, three men and three women, only one of whom had been newly imported. The rest had been living with their master for ten years or more.

By the last decade of the seventeenth century, however, Harman would have found it harder to find such a compatible group. By this time, many Chesapeake quarters included at least one newly imported African. In addition, most plantations could no longer boast equal numbers of men and women, because the African newcomers were predominantly men and boys. In fact, evidence from a number of Chesapeake areas during the 1690s indicates that men now outnumbered women by as much as 180 to 100. The impact of this African influx was soon felt. Before 1690, one Virginian planter had boasted of his large native-born slave population; by the first decade of the eighteenth century, another Virginian despairingly found "noe increase [among his blacks] but all loss." In 1699, members of the Virginia House of Burgesses offered an unflattering opinion of these new black arrivals, referring to "the gross barbarity and rudeness of their manners, the variety and strangeness of their languages and the weakness and shallowness of their minds." Prejudice aside, these legislators were responding to the increased flow of African newcomers.[2]

Even as the Africans started arriving, Chesapeake planters put their slaves to more than just growing tobacco. Ever since 1630, when Virginia's tobacco boom ended, the colony's planters had gradually begun to diversify their operations. They farmed more grains, raised more livestock, and planted more orchards. Pastoral farming in particular gained impetus during the last few decades of the seventeenth century when the Chesapeake tobacco industry suffered a prolonged depression. Some planters devoted more attention to livestock than ever before, and large herds of cattle became commonplace. Slaves were most certainly associated with this development. In late-seventeenth-century Charles County, Maryland, there were more cattle in the all-black or mixed-race quarters than in those composed solely of whites....

The diversified character of the youthful South Carolina economy owed little to the fluctuating fortunes of a dominant staple and more to the harsh realities of a pioneer existence. Many slaves spent most of their lives engaged in basic frontier activities – clearing land, cutting wood, and cultivating provisions. If late-seventeenth-century South Carolina specialized in anything, it was ranch farming – the same activity into which some Chesapeake planters were diversifying. Indeed, some Virginians took advantage of the opportunities presented by the nascent colony. In 1673, Edmund Lister of Northampton County transported some of his slaves out of Virginia into South Carolina. Presumably they had already gained experience, or displayed their native skills, in tending livestock, because Lister sent them on ahead to establish a ranch. The extensiveness of this early cattle ranching economy became apparent when South Carolinians took stock of their defensive capabilities. In 1708, they took comfort in the reliance that could be placed on one thousand trusty "Cattle Hunters."[3]

The multiracial composition of the typical work group suggests yet another similarity between Chesapeake and Lowcountry. In both societies in the late seventeenth century, blacks more often than not were to be found laboring alongside members of other races. The South Carolina estate of John Smyth, who died in 1682, included nine Negroes, four Indians, and three whites. All sixteen undoubtedly worked shoulder to shoulder at least some of the time.... Similarly, in late-seventeenth-century Virginia, white servants and slaves – both Indian and black – often worked side by side. An incident involving William Harman, the free black already encountered, underscores the lengths to which work time cooperation extended. In the summer of 1683, Harman's neighbors came to assist him in his wheat harvest. As was the custom, once the task was accomplished, they relaxed together, smoking pipes of tobacco in Harman's house. Nothing unusual in this pastoral scene, one might surmise, except that those who came to aid their black neighbor were whites, including yeomen of modest means and well-connected planters. Harman was not, of course, a typical black man, but his story proves that blacks and whites of various stations could work together, even cooperate, in the late-seventeenth-century Chesapeake.[4]

In spite of these similarities, the economic situations of these two societies diverged. By the late seventeenth century the Chesapeake possessed a fully fledged plantation economy. No matter what the level of diversification of a late-seventeenth-century Chesapeake estate, therefore, most slaves were destined to spend the bulk of their time tending tobacco. There were some all-black quarters; accordingly, a few slaves acted as foremen, making decisions about the organization of work, the discipline of the laborers, and the like. However, most slaves simply familiarized themselves with the implements and vagaries of tobacco culture. Seventeenth-century South Carolina, by contrast, was a colony in search of a plantation economy. Experiments were certainly under way with rice, which was first exported in significant quantities in the 1690s. In June 1704, one South Carolina planter could bemoan the loss of a Negro slave because the season was "the height of weeding rice." This was still a pioneer economy, however, with no concentration on one agricultural product. Indeed, if South Carolinians were "Graziers" before they were "planters," they were just as much "lumbermen," too. About the turn of the century, a South Carolinian wrote to an English correspondent extolling the virtues of a particular tract of land. If only the proprietor had "twelfe good negroes," the writer asserted, "he could get off it five Hundred pounds worth of tarr yearly."[5] . . . South Carolinians might have been thinking in terms of large profits and sizable labor forces from the first, but, as yet, these were not to be derived from any single agricultural staple.

In one final area – the flexibility of early race relations – the Chesapeake and Lowcounty societies also resembled each other. The once-popular view that the earliest black immigrants in the Old Dominion were servants and not chattels is no longer tenable. Rather, from the outset, the experience of the vast majority of blacks in early Virginia was slavery, although some were servants and even more secured their freedom. In fact, the status of Virginia's blacks seems singularly debased from the start, evident in their impersonal and partial identifications in two censuses dating from the 1620s; their high valuations in estate inventories, indicating lifetime service; the practice of other colonies, most notably Bermuda, with which Virginia was in contact; and early legislation, such as a Virginia law of 1640 that excepted only blacks from a provision that masters should arm their households – perhaps the first example of statutory racial discrimination in North American history – or an act of 1643 that included black, but not white, servant women as tithables.

In spite of the blacks' debased status, race relations in early Virginia were more pliable than they would later be, largely because disadvantaged blacks encountered a group of whites – indentured servants – who could claim to be similarly disadvantaged. Fraternization between the two arose from the special circumstances of plantation life in early Virginia. Black slaves tended to live scattered on small units where they were often outnumbered by white servants; more often than not, the two groups spoke the same language; the level of exploitation each group suffered inclined them to see the others as sharing their predicament. In short, the opportunity, the means, and the justification for cooperation between black slaves and white servants were all present. Racial prejudice, moreover, was apparently not strong enough to inhibit these close ties.

Not only did many blacks and whites work alongside one another, but they ate, caroused, smoked, ran away, stole, and made love together. In the summer of 1681, a graphic example of white–black companionship occurred in Henrico County. One Friday in August, Thomas Cocke's "servants" were in their master's orchard cutting down weeds. The gang included at least two white men, who were in their midtwenties and presumably either servants or tenants, and at least three slaves. After work, this mixed complement began drinking; they offered cider to other white visitors, one of whom "dranke cupp for cupp" with the "Negroes." One of the white carousers, Katherine Watkins, the wife of a Quaker, later alleged that John Long, a mulatto belonging to Cocke, had "put his yard into her and ravished" her; but other witnesses testified that she was inebriated and made sexual advances to the slaves. She had, for instance, raised the tail of Dirke's shirt, saying "he would have a good pricke," put her hand on mulatto Jack's codpiece, saying she "loved him for his Fathers sake for his Father was a very handsome young Man," and embraced Mingo "about the Necke," flung him on the bed, "Kissed him and putt her hand into his Codpiece." Thus, a number of white men exonerated their black brethren and blamed a drunken white woman for the alleged sexual indiscretion. If this was sexism, at least it was not racism.[6]

Black and white men also stood shoulder to shoulder in more dramatic ways. In 1640, six servants belonging to Captain William Pierce and "a negro" named Emanuel belonging to Mr. Reginald stole guns, ammunition, and a skiff and sailed down the Elizabeth River in hopes of reaching the Dutch. Thirty years later, a band of white servants who hoped to escape their Eastern Shore plantations and reach New England put their faith in a black pilot as a guide. In 1676, black slaves and white servants joined together in a striking show of resistance. With Nathaniel Bacon dead and his rebellion petering out, one of the last groups to surrender was a mixed band of eighty blacks and twenty white servants. . . . This willingness to cooperate does not mean that white laborers regarded blacks as their equals; it may connote only a temporary coalition of interests. Nevertheless, the extent to which whites, who were exploited almost as ruthlessly as blacks, could overlook racial differences is notable. Apparently, an approximate social and economic (as opposed to legal) parity sometimes outweighed inchoate racial prejudices.[7]

The flexibility of race relations in the early Chesapeake is illustrated most dramatically in the incidence of interracial sex. At first glance, this might seem an odd proposition, for surely interracial sex is largely synonymous with sexual exploitation – particularly of black women. Abuse of slave women undoubtedly occurred in the early Chesapeake, as in all slaveowning societies. At the same time, the evidence of sexual relations between the races suggests that choice, as much as coercion, was involved – as might well have been the case for Katherine Watkins. For one thing, much recorded miscegenation in early Virginia was, not between white men and black women, but between black men and white women. Many white female servants gave birth to mulatto children. The only realistic conclusion to be drawn from this evidence – and Virginia's ruling establishment was not slow to see it – was that "black men were competing all too successfully for white women." In addition, many black women shared relationships of mutual affection with white servant men, and many of their mulatto children were the offspring of consensual unions.... Finally, there were a number of marriages between blacks and whites in the early Chesapeake. In 1671, for example, the Lower Norfolk County Court ordered Francis Stripes to pay tithes for his wife, "shee being a negro." Occasionally, even a male slave was able to engage the affections of a white woman....[8]

The access slaves had to freedom is a third area that reveals the flexibility of race relations in the early Chesapeake. Some slaves were allowed to earn money; some even bought, sold, and raised cattle; still others used the proceeds to purchase their freedom. This phenomenon may be attributable, in part, to the Latin American background of some of the earliest black immigrants. Perhaps they had absorbed Iberian notions about the relation between slavery and freedom, in particular that freedom was a permissible goal for a slave and self-purchase a legitimate avenue to liberty. Perhaps they persuaded their masters to let them keep livestock and tend tobacco on their own account in order to buy their freedom. Perhaps, however, some of the first masters of slaves were somewhat unsure about how to motivate their new black laborers and assumed that rewards, rather than sheer coercion, might constitute the best tactic.... Finally, the confusion that reigned in early Virginia concerning the legal status of the new black immigrants created other paths to liberty: some seventeenth-century Chesapeake slaves even sued for freedom in colonial courts.... [W]hatever their origins and precise numbers (which were certainly small), free blacks in late-seventeenth-century Virginia seem to have formed a larger share of the total black population than at any other time during slavery. In some counties, perhaps a third of the black population was free in the 1660s and 1670s.

And, once free, these blacks interacted with their white neighbors on terms of rough equality. At least through the 1680s, Virginians came close to envisaging free blacks as members or potential members of their community. Philip Mongon, a Northampton County free black and former slave, was certainly a full participant in the boisterous, bawdy, and competitive world that was seventeenth-century Virginia. Mongon arrived in Virginia as a slave in the 1640s. While still a slave, he entertained and harbored an English runaway maidservant. Early in 1651, now a free black, he arranged to marry a white woman, a widow. Perhaps the marriage never took place, for, if it did, his bride soon died, and Mongon took a black woman as his wife. However, his contacts with white women were not over: in 1663, he was charged with adultery and with fathering an illegitimate mulatto child whose mother was an unmarried white woman. Mongon gave security for the maintenance of the child. Like many a lower-class white, Mongon was not always deferential to his erstwhile superiors. Accused of hog stealing in 1660, he was able to prove his innocence, but then elicited a fine for his "presumptious actions" in throwing some hogs' ears on the table where the justices presided. . . . He stood up for his rights, as in 1681, when he claimed six hundred pounds of tobacco for dressing the meat for his landlord's funeral dinner. Relations with his neighbors occasionally descended into outright friction. He came to court in 1685 to confess that he "had most notoriously abused and defamed my most loveing friends and neighbours John Duparkes and Robert Jarvis." Two years later, Mongon was a member of an interracial fracas. One Sunday, a number of whites, both tenant farmers and yeomen, both husbands and wives, came to Mongon's house. After much "drinking and carousing as well without doors as within," some of the men began to victimize one of the tenant farmers present. Both Mongon and his son as well as a number of his guests joined forces to inflict a severe beating on the hapless man. Surely seventeenth-century Virginia could claim the pugnacious, truculent, and enterprising Philip Mongon as one of its very own.

The most celebrated free black family, the Johnson clan, also met with little apparent discrimination. Their activities and opportunities seem not much different from their fellow white planters'. They owned land, paid taxes, and acquired servants and slaves. They went to court, signed legal documents, served as witnesses, and transacted openly with white planters. They not only borrowed money from but extended credit to whites. Although they were excluded from military duties, they might well have voted and served on juries.

The fluidity and unpredictability of race relations in early Virginia gradually hardened into the Anglo-American mold more familiar to later generations. The cooperation between white servants and blacks began to dissolve as the numbers of white servants declined and slaves increased. Moreover, a greater distance between lower-class whites and blacks inevitably arose as more and more black newcomers arrived direct from Africa, unable to speak English and utterly alien in appearance and demeanor. As T. H. Breen has put it, "No white servant in this period, no matter how poor, how bitter or badly treated, could identify with these frightened Africans." There was, of course, more to this distancing than natural antipathies. The Chesapeake ruling establishment did all it could to foster the contempt of whites for blacks. Legislation enacted in the late seventeenth century was designed specifically to this end: no black was to "presume to lift up his hand" against a Christian; no Christian white servant was to be whipped naked, for nakedness was appropriate only for blacks; the property of servants was protected, whereas slaves' property was confiscated.[9]

Legislation was not the only way in which this separation occurred. At midcentury, Lancaster County Court appointed Grasher, a black man, to whip offenders who were almost exclusively white, an action that certainly strained good feelings between blacks and lower-class whites. More than a generation later, an Accomac County planter enlisted his mulatto slave Frank to help beat a white maidservant who was ill and not pulling her weight. At about the same time, a white tenant farmer of neighboring Northampton County invented a scheme to take advantage of the worsening climate for free blacks. He told Peter George, manumitted just six years earlier, that "there was a law made that all free Negroes should bee slaves againe." He promised to look after George's property – three head of cattle and hogs – and encouraged him, by providing his cart, to leave the colony. Three years later, George returned to Virginia and successfully brought suit to recover his livestock. More significant than George's small victory was the growing constriction of status and opportunities for free blacks, a transition that prompted whites of modest means to exploit their black neighbors.[10]

In these and other ways, the slaveowning planter class of late-seventeenth-and early-eighteenth-century Virginia attempted to drive a wedge between servants and slaves, whites and blacks. They were undeniably successful. As slaves grew more numerous in the work force, claims to English customary rights, such as reasonable amounts of food, adequate clothing, and observance of holidays, could more easily be ignored. Onerous work, harsh punishment, and rudimentary conditions became associated primarily with black laborers. . . . A stigma was doubtless attached to working in the fields alongside or near slaves: some servants even agreed to longer terms to avoid such work. Resistance to authority now came largely from blacks, not from the mixed groups of earlier years. At the same time, the authorities were not reticent in proclaiming the new dangers, thereby fostering a sense of caste consciousness among all whites.

Nowhere were Virginia's rulers more assiduous in separating the races than in the realm of sex. In 1662, they passed a law doubling the fine for interracial fornicators. Almost thirty years later, Virginia took action to prevent all forms of interracial union by providing that any white man or woman who married a black, whether bond or free, was liable to permanent banishment, and by laying down fines and alternative punishments for any white woman who engaged in illicit relations with blacks. This legislation can be ascribed to practical, moral, and religious concerns; but, in part at least, it sprang from deeper anxieties. In Winthrop Jordan's words, the legislators lashed out at miscegenation "in language dripping with distaste and indignation." A Maryland law of 1664 referred to interracial unions as "shamefull Matches" and spoke of "diverse free-born English women . . . disgrac[ing] our nation"; Virginia legislators in 1691 denounced miscegenation and its fruits as "that abominable mixture and spurious issue."[11] This legislation reflected a desire to cordon off the "white, Christian" community – and particularly its female sector. Though never completely successful, the laws gradually had the desired effect, and voluntary interracial sexual relations occurred much less frequently after the turn of the century.

A strenuous attempt to limit the numbers of free blacks began in 1691, when the Virginia assembly forbade masters from freeing slaves unless they were willing to pay for their transportation out of the colony. . . . Furthermore, manumissions after 1691 tended to be conditional rather than absolute. . . . With few additions to their numbers, the proportion of free blacks in the total black population declined. Their numbers had always been small: by the third quarter of the seventeenth century, the celebrated and intensively studied free colored population of Virginia's Eastern Shore totaled no more than fifty individuals. But even some of these pulled up stakes in the middle to late seventeenth century, no doubt because of the growing hostility they faced. Those who remained might cling to freedom, but only as a pariah class. Poverty, landlessness, and dissociation from whites increasingly constituted their lot. Occasional amicable relations between free blacks and whites were perhaps still possible, but such associations had to be conducted more furtively than before. By the turn of the century, Virginia, like all the other mainland plantation colonies, was set to become a closed slave society. There was to be no room for an intermediate body of freedpersons.

South Carolina was never at any time an open slave society. And yet seventeenth-century Lowcountry society also had more flexible race relations than its eighteenth-century successor. By comparison with seventeenth-century Virginia, early South Carolinian race relations scarcely seem flexible, but, in the overall history of Lowcountry slave society, the first thirty or so years of slavery constitute something of a privileged era, a time when relations between the races contained an element of spontaneity and unpredictability that they subsequently lost. White servants and black slaves resided on the same plantations in early South Carolina, ... black newcomers might labor like hired hands. Servants and slaves traded with one another, leading the colony's legislators to pass laws against the practice in 1683, 1687, and again in 1691. In play, as in work, blacks participated rather fully in early Lowcountry life – to the point that their involvement in the trade for strong liquors elicited official displeasure in 1693. In politics, as in leisure, black involvement led one observer to protest that, in the elections for the assembly in 1701, "Strangers, Servants, Aliens, nay Malatoes and Negroes were Polled."[12] ...

The degree of cooperation between blacks and lower-class whites was far more attenuated in the Lowcountry than in the Chesapeake – and this, of course, applied to interracial sexual relations as in other spheres. The reason was simple: South Carolina never had a substantial class of white indentured servants. There was therefore little basis for the anxieties about the sexual preferences of white servant women that existed in the Chesapeake. Furthermore, South Carolina had fewer nonslaveholding whites than the Chesapeake and therefore less need or occasion to encourage caste consciousness by outlawing interracial marriages. In the Lowcountry, as in the plantation societies of the West Indies, the yawning social chasm between most whites and most blacks bred a self-confidence about the unthinkability of interracial marriage that was absent in the Chesapeake. Whereas interracial marriage did not have to be prohibited, open concubinage between male planters and female slaves could be treated more casually than elsewhere in North America, precisely because it presented less of a danger to fundamental social distinctions. Nevertheless, in spite of these social realities, sexual relations between whites and blacks probably occurred more frequently in the seventeenth than in the eighteenth century....

To compare the infant slave societies of the Chesapeake and the Lowcountry is, in essence, to engage in different ways of measuring time. In fact, three forms of historical time must be kept simultaneously in mind. First, the obvious youthfulness of these two seventeenth-century societies accounts for many of their shared features: both acquired their first slaves from the same places, race relations tended to be flexible in the early years, and whites and blacks often worked alongside one another. To make such a comparison is to employ the time scale common to all social organisms: they are born, develop, and die. What could be more natural, then, but to see the likenesses in these two societies in the youthful stages of their development?

Yet, fundamental differences arose from another facet of historical time – the sheer fact of precedence. Virginia was founded almost three-quarters of a century before South Carolina. From this perspective, to compare Virginia and South Carolina is to compare two societies that, in their historical trajectories, were moving in parallel paths but from different starting points. Virginia acquired slaves, imported Africans, and inserted them into a fully fledged plantation economy much earlier than did South Carolina. This comparison draws on the simplest, most basic form of historical time: the sheer fact of chronological precedence.

Another set of differences comes into view if historical time is conceived in one further way – not which society was founded first, but which was the more developed as a slave society. In this respect, turn-of-the-century Virginia was a late developer while its southern cousin was thoroughly precocious. To make this comparison is to measure these two societies, not by the implacable uniformity or fixed divisions of clock-and-calendar time, but by their internal rhythms. In this comparison, the rank order needs to be reversed, with South Carolina being placed ahead of Virginia, for, in 1700, the Lowcountry contained a much larger proportion of slaves and depended more fundamentally on slave labor than its Chesapeake counterpart.

The significance of this juggling act in temporalities lies in our being able not only to situate these two turn-of-the-century slave societies more clearly but also to see in what directions they were pointing. The similarities of youthfulness were most important in defining these two societies in their mid- to late-seventeenth-century phases. At this point, most blacks spoke English, worked alongside whites, and associated fairly easily with them. The cultural distinctions between the two races were muted. The black population was not generally numerous enough to provide the critical mass for autonomous cultural development. Many of the earliest blacks in both the Chesapeake and the Lowcountry assumed the customs and attitudes of their white neighbors and acquaintances.

Furthermore, the early emergence of an assimilationist culture among the slaves of both societies diminished, much more than might otherwise seem possible, the African influences that accompanied the later infusion of African immigrants. In other words, the recently arrived Africans were probably incorporated into an embryonic cultural system that, though creole, nevertheless approximated the Anglo-American model. Later arrivals faced a double challenge. They had to adjust not only to new surroundings but to the rules and customs already worked out by the earliest migrants. The first colonists acted as a "charter group," determining many of the terms under which the newcomers were incorporated.

But the contrasts that were soon evident between these two youthful societies, arising from the timing of their settlements and the rate of their social developments, point in a different direction by the end of the seventeenth century. In the Lowcountry, an assimilationist slave culture had little chance to put down roots before it was swept aside by a rising tide of African slaves. Although these growing numbers of Africans had to adapt to an embryonic cultural system, they swamped it more than they were incorporated within it. Moreover, from the first, Carolina blacks had more freedom to shape their culture than blacks had elsewhere on the North American mainland. Their numbers were not large in the seventeenth century, but most blacks lived in units made up of more than a few of their fellows; and, in the society as a whole, blacks always formed a significantly large proportion of the population. An important urban center that provided a key gathering place for Lowcountry slaves also emerged quickly. As early as 1698, South Carolina legislators took action against the "great numbers of slaves which do not dwell in Charles Town [who] do on Sundays resort thither to Drink Quarrel Curse Swear and pro[p]hane the Sabboth." The autonomy of the cowpen and the freedom of movement inherent in stock raising also contributed to the latitude early Carolina blacks enjoyed. It is not difficult to envisage these seventeenth-century Lowcountry slaves incorporating significant elements of their African past into an embryonic African American cultural system. This early Africanization gained momentum, of course, when the floodgates opened in the early eighteenth century and African immigrants poured into the region.[13]

In the Chesepeake, an assimilationist slave culture took much firmer root. To be sure, Africans began to enter the region in large numbers at least by the 1690s. But, in comparison with Lowcountry patterns, they were dispersed more widely, formed a much smaller proportion of the overall population, and for the most part were unable to constitute enclaves within an increasingly black countryside. Of course, they did not abandon their African heritage entirely. The Johnson clan of the Eastern Shore, for example, could hardly have behaved more like typical white settlers. And yet, in 1677, John Johnson, grandson of Anthony Johnson, "the patriarch of Pungoteague Creek," purchased a tract of land that he called "Angola." As T. H. Breen and Stephen Innes put it, "If the Johnsons were merely English colonists with black skins, then why did John, junior, name his small farm 'Angola'?" This small shred of evidence, the authors declare, suggests the existence of a deeply rooted, separate culture, a judgment that, although it likely goes too far, at least points to memories of a homeland being kept alive by at least one third-generation free black (and presumably others).[14]

There is also evidence, both for this clan and for other free black families, and by implication for slaves, of blacks seeking out other blacks. No doubt, the colony's earliest black residents wove webs of friendship and kinship through which they transmitted cultural values. Racial identity was not necessarily sacrificed even where blacks associated widely with whites. As early as 1672, Surry County "Negroes" were said "to mete together upon Satterdayes and Sundayes . . . to consult of unlawful p[ro]jects and combinations." Eight years later, Virginians discovered a "Negro Plott," hatched in the Northern Neck, which they again blamed on the relative autonomy of the black community, particularly "the great freedome and Liberty that has beene by many Masters given to their Negro Slaves for Walking on broad on Saterdays and Sundays and permitting them to meete in great Numbers in makeing and holding of Funeralls for Dead Negroes." Clearly, then, late-seventeenth-century Chesapeake blacks participated in their own social and cultural events.[15]

One way that late-seventeenth-century Chesapeake slaves transmitted values was through their naming patterns. Among the eighty-nine Virginia slaves that Lewis Burwell owned between 1692 and 1710, the vast majority became known at least to their master by English names. Nevertheless, one in nine Burwell slaves achieved something more distinctive: at least five men retained African names, two couples chose an African name for one of their children, and another three parents seem to have combined an English name with a West African naming principle – that is, the father's first name became the son's second name. In this way, African memories were not lost altogether.[16]

A further tantalizing glimpse of possible African influences derives from the decorated clay tobacco pipes produced in the early Chesapeake. Although most known pipe forms were either Native American or European in shape, all three major social groups in the region – Indians, Europeans, and Africans – seem to have made and decorated them. Although many of the decorative techniques (repeated patterns of dots or dashes known as pointillé and rouletted or white inlay) and motifs (hanging triangles, stars, and diamonds) might have been African in inspiration, they also can be traced in prehistoric Indian and European decorative arts traditions. Perhaps African slaves incorporated abstract designs and representational motifs drawn from their homelands, but most likely the pipes are evidence of a vibrant cultural syncretism in the seventeenth-century Chesapeake. A bone handle discovered at Utopia quarter along the James River in Virginia has been dated to the early eighteenth century, when a large community of Africans was transferred to the site. The bone handle is intricately carved in ways reminiscent of the abstract designs found on many Chesapeake pipes.

Overall, syncretism was more pronounced than African influence in the culture of early Chesapeake slaves, whereas the scales tipped in the other direction in the culture of early Lowcountry slaves. The emergence of an assimilationist cultural amalgam structured later developments in both regions, helping to explain the relative paucity (in New World terms) of African cultural features in eighteenth-century British North American slave life. But the Lowcountry slave world was, from the first, more autonomous than that of the Chesapeake. Carolinian slaves took advantage of this relative measure of latitude to shape a culture more in touch with memories of an African past than Chesapeake slaves could construct. By 1700, the paths on which these two slave societies were embarked had diverged; they moved even farther apart as time passed.

Notes

1 William L. Saunders (ed.), *The Colonial Records of North Carolina*, vol. 1 (Raleigh, NC, 1886), p. 150.

2 Richard Beale Davis (ed.), *William Fitzhugh and His Chesapeake World, 1676–1701* (Chapel Hill, NC, 1963) p. 175; Robert Bristow to John Grason, Sept. 15, 1707, Robert Bristow Letterbook, VSL [Virginia State Library]; W. Noel Sainsbury et al. (eds.), *Calendar of State Papers*, Colonial Series, *America and West Indies*, XVII, *1699* (London, 1908), p. 261.

3 *Boston News-Letter*, May 17–24, 1708, as quoted in Clarence L. Ver Steeg, *Origins of a Southern Mosaic: Studies of Early Carolina and Georgia* (Athens, Ga., 1975), p. 106.

4 Peter H. Wood, *Black Majority: Negroes in Colonial South Carolina from 1670 through the Stono Rebellion* (New York, 1974), pp. 54–5, 97.

5 Elizabeth Hyrne to Burrell Massingberd, Mar. 13, 1704, Massingberd Deposit, Lincolnshire County Archives, Lincoln, England; Thomas Smith to Burrell Massingberd, Nov. 7, 1705, Massingberd Deposit.

6 Warren M. Billings (ed.), *The Old Dominion in the Seventeenth Century: A Documentary History of Virginia, 1606–1689* (Chapel Hill, NC, 1975), pp. 161–3.

7 Ibid., p. 159; Accomac County Orders, 1671–1673, p. 95, as cited by J. Douglas Deal, *Race and Class in Colonial Virginia: Indians, Englishmen, and Africans on the Eastern Shore during the Seventeenth Century* (New York, 1993), p. 32; Edmund S. Morgan, *American Slavery, American Freedom: The Ordeal of Colonial Virginia* (New York, 1975), pp. 327–8.

8 Lorena S. Walsh, "'A Place in Time' Regained: A Fuller History of Colonial Chesapeake Slavery through Group Biography," in Larry E. Hudson, Jr., ed.,

Working toward Freedom: Slave Society and Domestic Economy in the American South (Rochester, N.Y., 1994), p. 5.

9 T. H. Breen, "A Changing Labor Force and Race Relations in Virginia, 1660–1710," in Breen, *Puritans and Adventurers: Change and Persistence in Early America* (New York, 1980), p. 145; William Waller Hening, *The Statutes at Large: Being a Collection of All the Laws of Virginia...*, 13 vols. (Richmond and Philadelphia, 1809–1823). vol. 2, p. 481, vol. 3, pp. 448, 459–60.

10 Lancaster County Deeds, I, 1652–1657, p. 213, as cited in Robert Anthony Wheeler, "Lancaster County, Virginia, 1650–1750: The Evolution of a Southern Tidewater Community" (Ph.D. diss., Brown University, 1972), p. 24; Accomac County Wills, 1682–1697, pp. 91a, 93a–96a, as cited in Deal, *Race and Class in Colonial Virginia*, pp. 103–4; Northampton County Orders and Wills, 1689–1698, p. 116, as cited in Deal, "A Constricted World: Free Blacks on Virginia's Eastern Shore, 1680–1750," in Lois Green Carr, Philip D. Morgan, and Jean B. Russo (eds.), *Colonial Chesapeake Society* (Chapel Hill, NC, 1988), pp. 281–4.

11 Winthrop D. Jordan, *White over Black: American Attitudes toward the Negro, 1550–1812* (Chapel Hill, NC, 1968), pp. 139, 79–80; Morgan, *American Slavery, American Freedom*, pp. 333–6; Kathleen M. Brown, *Good Wives, Nasty Wenches, and Anxious Patriarchs: Gender, Race, and Power in Colonial Virginia* (Chapel Hill, NC, 1996), pp. 197–201.

12 Thomas J. Little, "The South Carolina Slave Laws Reconsidered, 1670–1700," *South Carolina Historical Magazine*, (1993), pp. 92, 94, 98.

13 An Act for the Better Ordering of Slaves, no. 168, 1698, MSS Acts, SCDAH [South Carolina Department of Archives and History, Columbia].

14 T. H. Breen and Stephen Innes, "*Myne Owne Ground*": *Race and Freedom on Virginia's Eastern Shore, 1640–1676* (New York, 1980), pp. 17–18, 71–2.

15 Ibid., pp. 103–4, 83–8, 100–2; "Management of Slaves," *Virginia Magazine of History and Biography* (1899–1900), p. 314; H. R. McIlwaine et al. (eds.), *Executive Journals of the Council of Colonial Virginia*, vol. 1 (Richmond, Va., 1925), p. 86.

16 Walsh, "'A Place in Time' Regained," p. 5.

2
From African to African American: Slave Adaptation to the New World

Introduction

In "societies with slaves," slaveholdings were small and slave-owners were few, because slaves were marginal to the central productive process; slavery was simply one form of labor. In "slave societies," slavery was at the center of economic production, slaveholders were numerous, and those who aspired to enter the slaveholding class were the majority. The shift from a "society with slaves" to a full-fledged "slave society" in the colonial South was due to the discovery of crops – such as tobacco in the Chesapeake and rice in the South Carolina low country – that could command an international market; their production was monopolized by slaveholders, who consolidated their power and imported an ever growing number of slaves.

On the plantations, slaves had different experiences according to the places where they lived. In Virginia, they usually had little time for themselves, given the fact that tobacco growing was an exhausting, ongoing activity which filled most of the day. In the South Carolina low country, on the other hand, slaves worked according to the "task system," performing certain given tasks on a daily basis after which they had time for themselves. Children and female slaves often performed domestic tasks; in general, the treatment of domestic slaves was less harsh than that of field slaves.

Due to the relatively favorable living conditions in eighteenth-century mainland North America, the slave population, unique among those in the New World, increased substantially. Soon, a generation of American-born creole slaves came into being. The presence of these creole slaves eased the process of cultural adaptation of African-born slaves. Although they had lost a large part of their identity coming to America, in some regions – such as the Carolina low country – slaves were able to retain a substantial part of their language and culture.

However, even though they kept what they could of their African traditions, slaves were forced to adapt their culture to the New World and to their condition as bondspeople. Their language soon became intermixed with English, creating pidgin languages, such as Gullah. The same was true for religion; although they retained many of their old African beliefs, many slaves converted to Christianity, especially during the Great Awakening, and combined a surface of Christian practices with a deeper level of African worship and rituals. This process led to what John Blassingame has called the "Africanization of the South and the Americanization of the Slave": American-born slaves successfully adapted to the New World, eventually passing on to subsequent generations the memory of their origins in a new, syncretistic, African American culture.

Slave life was very brutal and led to an impressive number of cases of runaways from plantations, especially in the case of newly arrived slaves from Africa, who had yet not been broken, or "seasoned." However, the brutality of slavery was not exceptional in the early-eighteenth-century world. In general, any offence or challenge to public authority brought terrible punishments to common people, and torture and death were the norm. Slaves, whose grade on the social scale was even lower than that of common whites, were commonly mistreated, whipped, branded, tortured, and killed in the most inhuman way.

In spite of this, during the eighteenth century, a shift toward a more humane attitude to slave treatment took place. Several planters, prompted by a general shift in public opinion toward the condemnation of excessively cruel practices, began to move toward a paternalistic outlook. Increasingly, they provided for the well-being of their slaves out of self-interest. A large part of this transformation was due to the challenge brought by the Great Awakening to traditional concepts of authority and the emphasis on individuals' awareness of their sins – including mistreating slaves – in order to achieve salvation. Several planters went as far as indoctrinating their slaves with Christian beliefs in order to ease their own road to salvation by converting the heathens.

Further reading

Berlin, I., *Many Thousands Gone: The First Two Centuries of Slavery in North America* (Cambridge, Mass., and London: The Belknap Press of Harvard University Press, 1998).
Littlefield, D. C., *Rice and Slaves: Ethnicity and the Slave Trade in Colonial South Carolina*, 2nd edn. (Urbana: University of Illinois Press, 1991).
Morgan, P. D., *Slave Counterpoint: Black Culture in the Eighteenth-Century Chesapeake and the Lowcountry* (Chapel Hill: University of North Carolina Press, 1998).
Mullin, G. W., *Flight and Rebellion: Slave Resistance in Eighteenth-Century Virginia* (New York: Oxford University Press, 1972).
Sobel, M., *The World they Made Together: Black and White Values in Eighteenth-Century Virginia* (Princeton: Princeton University Press, 1987).
Thornton, J., *Africa and Africans in the Making of the Atlantic World, 1400–1800* (New York: Cambridge University Press, 1998).
Wood, P. H., *Black Majority: Negroes in Colonial South Carolina from 1670 through the Stono Rebellion* (New York: Knopf, 1974).
Wright, D. R., *African Americans in the Colonial Era: From African Origins through the American Revolution* (Arlington Heights, Ill.: Harlan Davidson, 1998).

A Runaway Ad from the *Virginia Gazette* (1767)

From the time of their first arrival in America, blacks tried to resist enslavement by running away. Slaves who arrived directly from Africa and had never experienced the harsh discipline of plantation labor were as likely to runaway as "seasoned" slaves who were brought from Britain's West Indian islands. The number of black runaways increased following the decrease in number of indentured servants and the consequent deterioration in the rights of African slaves. Between 1736 and 1776, in Virginia alone more than 1,500 runaway notices were published in newspapers. A typical notice in the *Virginia Gazette*, like the one below, provided the name and sex of the runaway slave, together with his or her distinctive physical features, and advertised a reward for anyone who captured the fugitive.

Source: *The Virginia Runaways Project* (University of Virginia) at Web Site: http: //www.wise.virginia.edu/history/runaways

Williamsburg, Jan. 14, 1766 [1767]

RUN from the Subscriber's plantation in Albemarle county, a tall slim Negro fellow, named GEORGE; he is marked in the face as the Gold Coast slaves generally are, had the usual clothing of labouring Negroes, and is supposed to be harboured at some of the plantations on Cary's creek, in Goochland county. Also run away from the subscriber's quarter called Westham, in Henrico county, another Negro fellow, named ROBIN: he is very tall slim and of a thin visage having lost some of his teeth; he formerly belonged to Col. Benjamin Harrison of Berkeley, and is supposed to be gone in the neighbourhood of his plantation on Nottoway river, where he formerly lived. Whoever will convey the former Negro to Mr. Lucas Powell in Albemarle, and the latter to William Walker at Westham, shall receive FORTY SHILLINGS for each of them, besides what is allowed by law. As I have been always tender of my slaves, and particularly attentive to the good usage of them, I hope wherever these fellows may be apprehended that they will receive such moderate correction as will deter them from running away for the future; and wherever any of my Negroes are taken up as runaways, I desire the favour of the magistrate, who may be applied to for a certificate, to order them back to their respective overseers, instead of sending them to me in this city, RO. C. NICHOLAS.

(*Virginia Gazette* (Purdie & Dixon), Williamsburg, January 15, 1767)

Olaudah Equiano Describes his Capture (1789)

Olaudah Equiano (1745–97) was born in the Ibo region of present-day Nigeria into a prosperous family of seven children; his father owned slaves himself. Intertribal warfare ravaged the area where Equiano lived, and African slave-traders were constantly looking for captives to kidnap and sell to Europeans. When he was 11, Equiano was kidnapped together with his sister, taken aboard a ship, and brought first to Barbados and then to Virginia. Sold into

Source: Olaudah Equiano, "The Interesting Narrative of the Life of Olaudah Equiano or Gustavus Vassa, the African, Written by Himself," in Henry Louis Gates, Jr. (ed.), *The Classic Slave Narratives* (New York: Penguin Books, 1987), pp. 25–31.

slavery and with his name changed to Gustavus Vassa, he eventually managed to regain his freedom and became a spokesman for British blacks in the 1780s. His description of the pain and horror of his capture by the slave-traders is a powerful recollection written by one of the few who survived to tell the tale.

I. . . . I have already acquainted the reader with the time and place of my birth. My father, besides many slaves, had a numerous family, of which seven lived to grow up, including myself and a sister, who was the only daughter. As I was the youngest of the sons, I became, of course, the greatest favourite with my mother, and was always with her, and she used to take particular pains to form my mind. I was trained up from my earliest years in the art of war: my daily exercise was shooting and throwing javelins; and my mother adorned me with emblems, after the manner of our greatest warriors. In this way I grew up till I was turned the age of eleven, when an end was put to my happiness in the following manner: – When the grown people in the neighbourhood were gone far in the fields to labour, the children generally assembled together in some of the neighbours' premises to play; and some of us often used to get up into a tree to look out for any assailant, or kidnapper, that might come upon us. For they sometimes took those opportunities of our parents' absence, to attack and carry off as many as they could seize. One day, as I was watching at the top of a tree in our yard, I saw one of those people come into the yard of our next neighbour but one, to kidnap, there being many stout young people in it. Immediately on this I gave the alarm of the rogue, and he was surrounded by the stoutest of them, who entangled him with cords, so that he could not escape till some of the grown people came and secured him.

II. But alas! ere long it was my fate to be thus attacked, and to be carried off, when none of the grown people were nigh. One day, when all our people were gone out to their work as usual, and only I and my sister were left to mind the house, two men and a women got over our walls, and in a moment seized us both; and without giving us time to cry out, or to make any resistance, they stopped our mouths and ran off with us into the nearest wood. Here they tied our hands, and continued to carry us as far as they could, till night came on, when we reached a small house, where the robbers halted for refreshment and spent the night. We were then unbound, but were unable to take any food; and being quite overpowered by fatigue and grief, our only relief was some sleep, which allayed our misfortune for a short time. The next morning we left the house, and continued travelling all the day. For a long time we had kept the woods, but at last we came into a road which I believed I knew. I had now some hopes of being delivered; for we had advanced but a little way before

I discovered some people at a distance, on which I began to cry out for their assistance; but my cries had no other effect than to make them tie me faster and stop my mouth; they then put me into a large sack. They also stopped my sister's mouth, and tied her hands; and in this manner we proceeded till we were out of sight of these people.

When we went to rest the following night, they offered us some victuals; but we refused it; and the only comfort we had was in being in one another's arms all that night, and bathing each other with tears. But alas! we were soon deprived of even the small comfort of weeping together. The next day proved one of greater sorrow than I had yet experienced; for my sister and I were then separated, while we lay clasped in each other's arms. It was in vain that we besought them not to part us; she was torn from me, and immediately carried away, while I was left in a state of distraction not to be described. I cried and grieved continually; and for several days did not eat any thing but what they forced into my mouth. At length, after many days' travelling, during which I had often changed masters, I got into the hands of a chieftain, in a pleasant country. This man had two wives and some children, and they all used me extremely well, and did all they could to comfort me; particularly the first wife, who was something like my mother. Although I was a great many days' journey from my father's house, yet these people spoke exactly the same language with us. This first master of mine, as I may call him, was a smith, and my principal employment was working his bellows, which were the same kind as I had seen in my vicinity. They were in some respects not unlike the stoves here in gentlemen's kitchens; and were covered over with leather, and in the middle of that leather a stick was fixed, and a person stood up and worked it, in the same manner as is done to pump water out of a cask with a hand pump. I believe it was gold he worked, for it was of a lovely bright yellow colour, and was worn by the women on their wrists and ankles.

I was there, I suppose, about a month, and they at length used to trust me some little distance from the house. I employed this liberty in embracing every opportunity to inquire the way to my own home: and I also sometimes, for the same purpose, went with the maidens, in the cool of the evenings, to bring pitchers of water from the springs for the use of the house. I had also remarked where the sun rose in the morning, and set in the evening, as I had travelled along: and had observed that my father's house was towards the rising of the sun. I therefore determined to seize the first opportunity of making my escape, and to shape my course for that quarter; for I was quite oppressed and weighed down by grief after my mother and friends; and my love of liberty, ever great, was strengthened by the mortifying circumstance of not daring to eat with the free-born children, although I was mostly their companion.

Venture Smith Describes his Childhood as a Domestic Slave (1798)

Domestic slavery in America dated from the time the first blacks arrived in Jamestown; household slaves performed a variety of different tasks, usually in the plantation Big House. Widespread common beliefs notwithstanding, only a relatively low percentage of slave women worked as domestic servants taking care of cooking and housekeeping. Slave children were used as domestic servants, performing small household chores, until they reached an age when they could start working in the fields. This excerpt from the 1798 biography of Venture Smith – a free black from New England who spent his early life in bondage – describes how, when he was a child, his master first assigned him household chores and then forced him to alternate these with much heavier outdoor tasks. Like many small slave-owners, Smith's master sought to squeeze the most labor out of the few slaves he owned. Venture Smith's resistance to this demanding regime and to other abuses led to his inevitable punishment.

The first of the time of living at my master's own place, I was pretty much employed in the house at carding wool and other household business. In this situation I continued for some years, after which my master put me to work out of doors. After many proofs of my faithfulness and honesty, my master began to put great confidence in me. My behavior to him had as yet been submissive and obedient. I then began to have hard tasks imposed on me. Some of these were to pound four bushels of ears of corn every night in a barrel for the poultry, or be rigorously punished. At other seasons of the year I had to card wool until a very late hour. These tasks I had to perform when I was about nine years old. Some time after I had another difficulty and oppression which was greater than any I had ever experienced since I came into this country. This was to serve two masters. James Mumford, my master's son, when his father had gone from home in the morning, and given me a stint to perform that day, would order me to do *this* and *that* business different from what my master directed me. One day in particular, the

Source: "A Narrative of the Life and Adventures of Venture, a Native of Africa but Resident above Sixty Years in the United States of America. Related by Himself," in *Documenting the American South* (University of North Carolina at Chapel Hill), pp. 15–16, at Web Site: http://docsouth.unc.edu/neh/venture.

authority which my master's son had set up, had like to have produced melancholy effects. For my master having set me off my business to perform that day and then left me to perform it, his son came up to me in the course of the day, big with authority, and commanded me very arrogantly to quit my present business and go directly about what he should order me. I replied to him that my master had given me so much to perform that day, and that I must therefore faithfully complete it in that time. He then broke out into a great rage, snatched a pitchfork and went to lay me over the head therewith; but I as soon got another and defended myself with it, or otherwise he might have murdered me in his outrage. He immediately called some people who were within hearing at work for him, and ordered them to take his hair rope and come and bind me with it. They all tried to bind me but in vain, tho' there were three assistants in number. My upstart master then desisted, put his pocket handkerchief before his eyes and went home with a design to tell his mother of the struggle with young VENTURE. He told her that their young VENTURE had become so stubborn that he could not controul him, and asked her what he should do with him. In the mean time I recovered my temper, voluntarily caused myself to be bound by the same men who tried in vain before, and carried before my young master, that he might do what he pleased with me. He took me to a gallows made for the purpose of hanging cattle on, and suspended me on it. Afterwards he ordered one of his hands to go to the peach orchard and cut him three dozen of whips to punish me with. These were brought to him, and that was all that was done with them, as I was released and went to work after hanging on the gallows about an hour.

The Plantation Generations of African Americans

Ira Berlin

In *Many Thousands Gone*, Ira Berlin follows the development of African American slavery from the first colonial settlements to the Revolutionary years. The focus of his work is as much on the varieties of slave experiences in different areas of the South as on the differences in slave adaptation from one generation

Ira Berlin, *Many Thousands Gone: The First Two Centuries of Slavery in North America* (Cambridge, Mass., and London: The Belknap Press of Harvard University Press, 1998), pp. 95–108.

to the next. In this excerpt, Berlin describes the characteristics of the second generation of slaves brought to North America; he calls it the "plantation generation." Slaves who belonged to the plantation generation witnessed the transformation of the southern colonies from societies with slaves to slave societies as a consequence of the plantation revolution based upon tobacco and rice cultivation. Plantation slavery became the most important factor in the southern economy and, as a consequence, slave life and labor conditions rapidly deteriorated. Violence – supported by the law – became common practice on the plantations, whilst planters' rule became inextricably linked to a racialized ideology of white supremacy over black slaves.

The first black people to arrive in mainland North America bore – or soon adopted – names like Anthony Johnson, Paulo d'Angola, Juan Rodrigues, Francisco Menéndez, and Samba Bambara. Although slaves, they established families, professed Christianity, and employed the law with great facility. They traveled widely and enjoyed access to the major Atlantic ports. Throughout the mainland, they spoke the language of their enslaver or the ubiquitous creole lingua franca. They participated in the exchange economies of the pioneer settlements and accumulated property, gaining reputations as knowledgeable traders and shrewd bargainers in the manner of creoles throughout the Atlantic littoral. A considerable portion of these first arrivals – fully one-fifth in New Amsterdam, St. Augustine, and Virginia's eastern shore – eventually gained their freedom. Some attained modest privilege and authority in mainland society.

Their successors were not nearly so fortunate. They worked harder and died earlier. Their family life was truncated, and few men and women claimed ties of blood or marriage. They knew – and wanted to know – little about Christianity and European jurisprudence. They had but small opportunities to participate independently in exchange economies, and they rarely accumulated property. Most lived on vast estates deep in the countryside, cut off from the larger Atlantic world. Few escaped slavery. Their very names reflected the contempt in which their owners held them. Most answered to some European diminutive – Jack and Sukey in the English colonies, Pedro and Francisca in places under Spanish rule, and Jean and Marie in the French dominions. As if to emphasize their inferiority, some were tagged with names such as Bossey, Jumper, and Postilion – more akin to barnyard animals than men and women. Others were designated with the name of some ancient deity or great personage like Hercules or Cato as a kind of cosmic jest: the more insignificant the person in the eyes of the planters, the greater the name. Whatever they were called, they rarely bore surnames, which represented marks of lineage that their owners sought to obliterate and of adulthood that they would not permit.

The degradation of black life in mainland North America had many sources, but the largest was the growth of the plantation, a radically different form of social organization and commercial production controlled by a new class of men whose appetite for labor was nearly insatiable. Drawing power from the metropolitan state, planters – who preferred the designation "masters" – transformed the societies with slaves of mainland North America into slave societies. In the process, they redefined the meaning of race, investing pigment – both white and black – with a far greater weight in defining status than heretofore.

While new to North America, such planters had a long and notorious history. Beginning in the twelfth century in the Levant, planters discovered a commodity – sugar – for which the demand was nearly limitless. After centuries of experimenting, they devised a new way to grow, process, and market this great fount of sweetness, and though the plantation remained identified with sugar, its techniques and organization were eventually extended to other commodities, such as tobacco, coffee, rice, hemp, and cotton. Sugar planters moved steadily across the Mediterranean, perfecting their organization and technology as they transformed, by turns, Cyprus, Crete, Sicily, southern Spain, and northern Africa. By the fifteenth century, they had entered the Atlantic, first in the Azores, then Madeira, the Canary Islands, and Cape Verde Islands, traveling south until they reached São Tomé, Fernando Po, and Principé in the Gulf of Guinea. From there, it was just a short step across the Atlantic, where by the late sixteenth century the plantation economy had become entrenched on the coast of Brazil. Although hardly a seamless process and not always a progressive one, the possibilities inherent in drawing together European capital, African labor, and American lands became manifest. During the following century, planters turned northward, to the Antilles and mainland North America.

Everywhere they alighted, planters transformed the landscape, creating new classes, remaking social relations, and establishing new centers of wealth and power. Armed with the power of the state and unprecedented agglomerations of capital, planters chased small holders from the countryside and monopolized the best land. To work their estates, they impressed or enslaved indigenous peoples or, in the absence of native populations, imported large numbers of servants or slaves, for sugar production was extraordinarily labor intensive.

Planters cared little about the origins, color, and nationality of those who worked the cane and processed its juices. When the locus of sugar production was on Cyprus and Crete, they employed – along with peoples native to those islands – white slaves transported across the Black Sea from southern and eastern Europe and black slaves transported across the Sahara from Africa. As the trade moved to São Tomé, Fernando Po, and Principé, planters used Africans imported from mainland Africa and Jews deported from Europe. In the New World, Native Americans and imported Africans were the planters' laborers of choice. When native populations withered under the onslaught of European conquest and disease, plantation slavery became African slavery....

The plantation revolution transformed all before it. But what distinguished the slave plantation from other forms of production was neither the particularities of the crop that was cultivated nor the scale of its cultivation. Many crops identified with the plantation – tobacco and cotton, for example – had been grown and would continue to be grown on small units with the labor of freeholders and their families, occasionally supplemented by wage workers, indentured servants, and even one or two slaves. The farmers who directed such mixed labor forces enjoyed considerable success, producing bumper crops at costs competitive with the largest holders.

The plantation's distinguishing mark was its peculiar social order, which conceded nearly everything to the slaveowner and nothing to the slave. In theory, the planters' rule was complete. The Great House, nestled among manufactories, shops, barns, sheds, and various other outbuildings which were called, with a nice sense of the plantation's social hierarchy, "dependencies," dominated the landscape, the physical and architectural embodiment of the planters' hegemony. But the masters' authority radiated from the great estates to the statehouses, courtrooms, countinghouses, churches, colleges, taverns, racetracks, private clubs, and the like. In each of these venues, planters practiced the art of domination, making laws, meting out justice, and silently asserting – by their fine clothes, swift carriages, and sweeping gestures – their natural right to rule. Although the grandees never achieved the total domination they desired, it was not for want of trying.

Planters worked hard at play, for they needed to distinguish themselves from those who simply worked hard. From the planters' perspective, slaves were labor and nothing more. While the slavemasters took to their sitting rooms, book-lined libraries, and private clubs to affirm their gentility, they drove their slaves relentlessly, often to the limits of exertion. Those who faltered faced severe discipline. In the process, millions died.

Such a regime had to rest upon force. Violence was an inherent part of slave society, playing a role quite different from the one it had played in a society with slaves. To be sure, the use of force and even gratuitous brutality was endemic in societies with slaves, especially the rough pioneer societies of the New World, with their disproportionate numbers of armed young men. But violence was not only common in slave societies, it was also systematic and relentless; the planters' hegemony required that slaves stand in awe of their owners. Although they preferred obedience to be given rather than taken, planters understood that without a monopoly of firepower and a willingness to employ terror, plantation slavery would not long survive. The lash gained a place in slave societies that was not evident in societies with slaves.

The planters' authority could not stand by force alone. Like every ruling class, the grandees legitimated their preeminence by the word – be it unspoken custom or written law. Indeed, the arrival of the planter class was generally followed by the creation or elaboration of some special judicial code. Behind these laws, however, stood complex and sophisticated ideologies. Planters understood themselves not as economic buccaneers exploiting the most vulnerable, or as social parasites living on the labor of others, but as metaphorical fathers to the plantation community. Such ideologies came easily enough, as they were an extension of the time-honored traditions that undergirded the governance of the household, workshop, church, and state and bore a close resemblance to the system of patronage so much in evidence in societies with slaves. But small differences made for large distinctions, as slaves in plantation regimes were not just another subordinate group whose continuing loyalty could be assured by some gratuity. Slaves in plantation societies were an extension of their owners' estate in ways they never were in societies with slaves. As the "fathers" of their vast plantation families, paternalists granted themselves the right to enter into the slaves' most intimate affairs, demanded the complete obedience due a father, and consigned slaves to a permanent childhood. This domestication of domination became a central element in shaping slave life.

There were other elements as well. Because slavery in mainland North America, as in the New World generally, was color-coded, novel notions of race accompanied the imposition of the plantation regime. To be sure, such new ideas were slow in developing in a world in which there were many other markers of difference. Nevertheless, slave societies – far more than societies with slaves – naturalized and rationalized the existing order through use of racial ideologies. *African* slavery was no longer just one of many forms of subordination – a common enough circumstance in a world ruled by hierarchies – but the foundation on which the social order rested. The structures of chattel bondage and white supremacy became entwined as they never had been in societies with slaves. Like plantation paternalism, the new racial ideologies distinguished slaves from all other subordinates. White supremacy demoted people of color not merely to the base of the life cycle as children, but to the base of civilization as savages.

Slaves understood these ideologies and employed them on their own behalf. When playing the part of loving children redounded to their advantage, they adopted the role. In 1774, upon his return from a transatlantic sojourn, planter Henry Laurens was greeted by Old Daddy Stepney with a "*full* Buss of my Lips," along with "the kindest enquiries over & over again... concerning Master Jacky Master Harry Master Jemmy."[1] Doubtless Old Daddy Stepney was pleased to see his owner and to express his concern for Laurens's children. But the effusive show of devotion demonstrated that two could play the paternalist game. The negotiation between master and slave was no less evident in Daddy Stepney's embrace than it was in the wrathful fury of a slave insurrectionist or the fawning deference of a slave supplicant. Daddy Stepney expected his embrace would be rewarded, and it was.

Generally, the interplay between master and slave was neither the "kindest enquiries" nor a "*full* Buss" on the lips. The glad smile and tight clasp masked a bitter contest whose seething animosities periodically exploded with volcanic force. Planters threatened and cajoled, pressing their slaves to greater exertion through a combination of intimidation and promises of better times. As long as slaveowners controlled the apparatus of coercion, slaves conceded what they could not resist. But such concessions should not be confused with assent. Slaves continued to struggle to take back piecemeal what their owners had appropriated at once. The contest of master and slave was a never-ending war in which the terrain changed frequently but the combatants remained the same. The struggle in slave society was no different than in societies with slaves, except that slaves labored at still greater disadvantage.

The slaves' disadvantage on the plantations of the New World was compounded by changes in the Old, for the plantation revolution transformed Africa just as it transformed the Americas. The sharp increase in demand for slaves during the eighteenth century – a demand to which mainland North American planters contributed just a small part – revolutionized west African society. Slaves, some of whom had previously been carried northward from the savannah across the Sahara Desert in caravans, moved south in ever greater numbers to the Guinea coast, spurring the development of the great slave trading ports of Mina, Whydah, and, farther south, Loango (and later Bonny, Lagos, and Cabinda). As they did, the economies of the African interior changed, and so did its politics. Slaving came to serve a different function, as ambitious African merchants and politicos constructed dynasties from the profits of slave trading. In west Africa, new men rose to chiefdoms and paramountcies, creating states like Asante, Dahomey, and Oyo which not only gained control of the interior but also extended their reach north to the savannah and south to the aptly named "slave coast." Farther to the

South, Kongo and Mbundu merchants subverted the old kingdoms, allowing the Portuguese to gain a foothold on the continent. New states arose as these merchants and their mercenary allies pushed deeper into the interior of central Africa.

As these predatory African slaving states grew in strength during the eighteenth century, the character of the men and women forcibly transported across the Atlantic also changed. Whereas condemned criminals, political prisoners, religious heretics, debtors, and others collectively denominated as "refuse" numbered large among the slaves drawn to mainland North America's societies with slaves, men and women innocent of crime except for being in the wrong place at the wrong time were hunted down for the purpose of sale to the great plantations. Especially commissioned armies and freelancing gangs, driven by the possibility of political aggrandizement and great wealth, moved deep into the interior of Africa, kidnapping millions of men and women and killing millions of others. The kidnappers sometimes became the kidnapped, and the line between predator and prey became slim indeed. Large traders on the coast pressured the small traders in the interior towns, who in turn pressed the still more marginal traders in the hinterland, shaving their profit, forcing the most vulnerable merchants into more desperate measures. It was a world in which no one was safe. Families without large lineages, villages without powerful patrons, and weak polities were hard hit. . . .

But even at the height of the slave trade, African slave raiders were not indiscriminate kidnappers. If marauding slave traders swept up princes and paupers alike, one distinction was not lost: the slave trade was highly selective with respect to sex. Although a few men might be enlisted into the very armies that captured them and ravaged their homeland, slave traders generally considered men too dangerous to keep in close proximity. Women captives, on the other hand, could be incorporated into their captor's household, and, like children of both sexes, they could be employed as agricultural workers and domestic servants – the traditional tasks that fell to women and children. A few might gain full status within the household, since accumulating wives and other dependents added to a man's power and prestige. However, most were put to work in agriculture, which expanded greatly – with some units equaling the size of New World plantations. Captive men thus became the prime candidates for deportation, a welcome coincidence from the traders' perspective, as "men and stout men boys," "none to exceed the years of 25 or under 10," were the objects of greatest demand in the New World.

Beyond the preference for adult men, almost all Africans were fair game. Nationality, religious beliefs, shared languages, and geographical propinquity counted for little, as slave captives were marched hundreds of miles from the interior to coastal factories. From these warehouses of humanity, the new moguls bartered away the captives' future and that of their posterity.

Although traders who operated the coastal factories also had little interest in distinguishing slaves by national, linguistic, or religious affiliations, the larger patterns of Atlantic commerce linked specific regions of Africa to specific regions of the Americas. Some three-quarters of the slaves transported from west central Africa went to Brazil; two-thirds of slaves shipped from the Bight of Biafra landed in the British Caribbean; half of those leaving Senegambia alighted in the French Caribbean. Such linkages allowed European sea captains, who frequently came armed with requests for specific peoples, to satisfy planter preferences for particular "nations." But even with these connections, meeting the planters' requirements was difficult in the competitive world of international slaving. First, the ethnic composition of the slaves in any oceanside entrepôt had little necessary relationship to the ethnicity or nationality of its hinterland. In the long march from the interior, a trek that could take months, slave traders conscripted men and women of many peoples into their sad coffles, so that the ships leaving any particular port rarely carried the peoples of a single nation or language group. Once at sea, moreover, slavers often made additional stops, first along the African coast and then in the Americas, where slaves were bought and sold, increasing the heterogeneity of their cargoes. Finally, the internal and transatlantic trade changed over time. The result was a patchwork of African origins in the New World. Even on a plantation where most Africans derived from a single port, slaves could be found from places as distant as Senegambia and Madagascar. If the slave trade was not random, its outcome often was.

But if neither planters in the Americas nor slave traders in Africa could fully control the commerce-in-person, the difference between newly arrived plantation slaves and those who had composed the charter generations was nonetheless striking. Atlantic creoles were cosmopolitans, for whom the Atlantic was a vast thoroughfare for commercial opportunity and a crucible for cultural interaction. The men and women drawn from the interior of Africa, by contrast, were provincials, for whom the Atlantic was a strange, inhospitable place, a one-way street to oblivion. Rather than broad connections with the Atlantic, it was deep roots in the village, clan, and household which shaped their world. Although their economies were complex, most enslaved Africans had been tied to the land as farmers or herdsmen. They lacked the linguistic range and cultural plasticity of the charter generations.... Whereas creoles – with their knowledge of the religions of the Atlantic rim – had demonstrated a willingness to incorporate Christianity into their system of belief, the men and women of the interior were loathe to accept the religion of their enslaver.

Captives taken from the interior also differed from the charter generations in another way, for if the Atlantic created unity, the interior spoke to divisions. Africa housed hundreds, perhaps thousands, of different "nations," whether defined by the languages they spoke, the religions they practiced, or the chieftains to whom they gave allegiance. Some were small states, hardly more than villages; others were great confederations extending over thousands of miles. The language, religion, domestic organization, aesthetics, political sensibilities, and military traditions that Africans carried from the interior to the plantations cannot be understood in their generality but only in their particulars, for the enslaved peoples were not Africans but Akan, Bambara, Fon, Igbo, or Mande.

If Africa provided few common experiences, enslavement did. Above all, plantation slaves – especially in the early years of the plantation revolution – were immigrants. The immigrant experience, with all the difficulties of displacement and readjustment, shaped the lives of new arrivals. But the movement of slaves from Africa to the Americas was no ordinary migration. The slave trade fractured the Atlantic, creating profound discontinuities in the lives of those transported to the plantations of the New World. Attended by extraordinary levels of coercion, the forced transfer of "saltwater" slaves proved deadly to many and traumatic to all. The creoles' transit from the periphery of the Atlantic – whether from Africa, Europe, or the Caribbean – to mainland North America, no matter how frightening and disorienting, had none of the nightmarish qualities of the Middle Passage which the mass of plantation slaves experienced. Slavers bound for the plantations of the New World stuffed their human cargoes tight between the creaking boards of vessels specially designed to maximize the speed of transfer. Slaves were forced to wallow in their own excrement and were placed at the pleasure of the crew. Although conditions improved on slave ships over time, death stalked these vessels, and more than one in ten Africans who boarded them did not reach the Americas. The survivors arrived in the New World physically depleted and psychologically disoriented. They were in a far poorer position to address the anarchic effects of long-distance migration than any other people who made the transatlantic journey.

With power and circumstance weighted against them, African slaves confronted planters who were certain that their prosperity depended upon the slaves' productivity. In time, saltwater slaves and their descendants shifted the balance of power, and in the process transformed themselves from Africans to African Americans. The growth of an indigenous slave population was a critical event in the history of the New

World. But the long, complicated process of transformation was already under way by the time the captives were taken from the coastal factories. When the captives boarded ship in Africa, they did not think of themselves as Africans. Their allegiance was to a family, clan, community, or perhaps – although rarely – state, but never to the continent itself. By the time they reached American shores, that had begun to change; as they disembarked, the process by which many African nations became one had already gained velocity. The construction of an African identity proceeded on the western, not the eastern, side of the Atlantic, amid the maelstrom of the plantation revolution.

New identities took a variety of forms, shaped – but not determined – by slavery. If slavery loomed large among the new realities that confronted captive Africans, many other circumstances also weighed heavily upon them. The obvious differences with members of the owning class could not conceal differences among the new arrivals. Some of these had their roots in Old World animosities. Competition, as well as cooperation, within the quarter compounded the remnants of ancient enmities, giving nationality or ethnicity an ever-changing reality and with it new meanings to Akan, Bambara, and Fon identity. In this changing world, nationality or ethnicity did not rest upon some primordial communal solidarity, cultural attribute, or common experience, for these qualities could be adopted or discarded at will. In the Americas, men and women identified as Angolans, Igbos, or Males frequently gained such identities not from their actual birthplace or the place from which they disembarked but because they spoke, gestured, and behaved like – or associated with – Angolans, Igbos, or Males.

For most Africans, as for their white counterparts, identity was a garment which might be worn or discarded, rather than a skin which never changed its spots. While the color coding of New World slavery placed some identities off-limits, Africans still had many from which they might choose. Choice, as well as imposition or birthright, determined who the new arrivals would be. Indeed, rather than transporting a primordial nationality or ethnicity to the New World, the arrival of Africans often became the occasion for the creation of nationality that had little salience in Africa. Igbos or Angolans who searched out their countrymen in the Americas may have made more of those connections in the New World than they did in the Old precisely because of their violent separation from their homeland.

Whatever the new identity Africans accepted, adopted, or created, the process was hardly assimilation, if for no other reason than that the world around them was so diverse and was changing so rapidly that no single ideal to which to assimilate existed. Instead, there were many ideals from which Africans could select – among themselves, among the members of the owning class, and, for many, among the Native American population. In short, identity formation for African slaves was neither automatic nor unreflective, neither uniform nor unilinear. Rather it was a slow process that proceeded unevenly and was often repeated as Africans were forcibly transferred from the Old World to the New.

The plantation revolution came to mainland North America in fits and starts. Beginning in the late seventeenth century in the Chesapeake, it moved unevenly across the continent over the next century and a half. In its wake, societies with slaves were transformed into slave societies. By the time the revolution had run its course, slave societies dedicated to cultivating tobacco in the Chesapeake, rice in lowcountry South Carolina, Georgia, and East Florida, sugar in the lower Mississippi Valley, and cotton across the breadth of the southern interior were the heart of mainland North America's economy and culture. Those areas not committed to plantation production, most prominently the North, became deeply enmeshed in the plantation economy as suppliers of capital, factorage, draft animals, food, technology, and – in the person of the plantation tutor – education, so much so that they took on the trappings of slave societies. Indeed, until urban-based manufacture eclipsed staple agriculture as a source of wealth during the nineteenth century, the plantation shaped society, economy, and politics throughout the mainland, as it did throughout the Atlantic.

As elsewhere, the emergence of slave societies in the North American mainland affected everyone, those who owned the vast estates, those who worked them, those who supplied them, and those who only wanted to avoid them. But it touched no one more deeply than African and African-American slaves. The degradation of black life that accompanied the plantation revolution on mainland North America put the charter generations – and other poor people – to flight. Those who did not escape the onrushing plantation regime shared the plight of the slaves imported to grow the great staples. But whether they fled the new regime or were incorporated into it, the creoles' history cast a long shadow over African-American life. Their economies and societies – the memory of their successes and the tragedy of their dispersion – would shape the evolution of slave societies.

As plantation production expanded and the planters' domination grew, slaves in mainland North America faced higher levels of discipline, harsher working conditions, and greater exploitation than ever before. Without question, members of the plantation generations worked longer, harder, and with less control over their own lives than did the members of the mixed labor force of slaves, servants, and wage workers who had preceded them....

If the plantation revolution escalated the level of exploitation and inaugurated a new, violent form of discipline, it also raised the level of resistance. The masters' gross violation of the ill-defined but nonetheless real boundaries of what might be imposed upon slaves elicited a vigorous response. The slaves' rejoinder took a variety of forms, from suicide to maroonage and from truancy to insurrection....

As in other slave societies in the Caribbean, mainland plantations devoted to staple production devoured labor. Unlike the largest agricultural units in societies with slaves, plantations required slaves not by ones and twos, the score, or even the dozens but by the hundreds, thousands, and eventually tens of thousands. But the Africanization of mainland slavery was neither a steady nor a uniform process. Of all the transatlantic slave routes between the eastern and western hemispheres, the one that transported Africans to the mainland North American colonies was the most indirect, producing heterogeneity that was perhaps unique in the Americas. In some places, Africanization took place within the course of a decade; in others, it was a century-long process. And once accomplished, the Africanization of slavery was not necessarily completed, as in time creoles – in the form of native-born African Americans – reasserted themselves, only to be replaced by a new wave of African arrivals. Reafricanization frustrates any notion of a linear progression from African to creole. It also suggests that the Africanization of plantation society was not a matter of numbers, as small groups who arrived early often had greater influence than the mass of late arrivals. In short, the Africanization of mainland North American slavery was not a matter of who arrived or even who arrived where, but who arrived where and when.

The peasants and pastoralists carried from the African interior to North American plantations confronted a host of new diseases and the harsh demands of staple production. Africans put to plantation production died by the thousands. Although slaves in mainland North America would be distinguished by their ability to reproduce themselves, few did so in the first generation. With their numbers weighted heavily toward men, the first arrivals struggled to form families and reconstruct the institutions that had guided life in their former homeland. The new circumstances depreciated the strategies that had been employed by the charter generations; linguistic fluency, church membership, and juridical knowledge provided no advantage to those condemned to plantation labor. Rather than try to integrate themselves into the larger European-American world by adopting the languages, religions, and ethos of their enslavers, the plantation slaves turned inward, making the plantation itself – the slaveholders' home – the site for a Reconstruction of African life. As elsewhere in the Americas, slaves made an African culture from their diverse memories of the Old World and the harsh realities of the New. As the plantation matured, *African* burial grounds, *African* churches, and eventually *African* academies appeared.

The name was of course significant, signaling an unprecedented joining together of African peoples. But that nascent culture was not of one piece, because the experiences of African people on the mainland was not of one piece. Rather, many different African "nations" emerged from the series of plantation revolutions that raked the continent between the late seventeenth and the early nineteenth centuries. . . . The character of these diverse nations of African descent depended upon the requirements of particular plantation staples, the terrain on which they were grown, the numbers of slaves imported and their origins, the nationality of the slaveowning class and its ideology, the character of the white nonslaveholding population and its numbers, and the commitment of metropolitan authorities and their interest in settlement. As a result, the African nations of the mainland followed different paths in the Chesapeake, the lowcountry, the North, and the lower Mississippi Valley. In some parts of mainland North America, Africans replaced Atlantic creoles, and the charter generations sank swiftly into historical oblivion. In other parts of the mainland, Atlantic creoles maintained their place, and the charter generations' influence extended into the late eighteenth century. . . .

Note

1 Quotation in *The Papers of Henry Lawrens*, ed. Philip M. Hamer, 1st edn. (Columbia, SC: University of South Carolina Press, [1968] 2000), x. 2–3.

3
The Formation of the Master Class

Introduction

Several members of the Virginian elite became tobacco planters and made fortunes selling the crop. This colonial elite combined characteristics of both European titled aristocracies and the self-made landed gentries of the New World who relied on the demand of the world economy for particular products, including tobacco. In the Chesapeake, the plantation revolution brought about by tobacco allowed the accumulation of immense fortunes, such as that of Robert "King" Carter, who owned 390 slaves in 48 different holdings, and even Thomas Jefferson and George Washington, who had, respectively, 187 and 216 slaves divided between their home plantations and several additional holdings. In colonial Virginia, tobacco planters earned special respect because of the difficulty and the risk involved in the cultivation of the crop. Tobacco cultivation required constant attention and direct supervision of the laborers during the tending and harvesting of the crop; at the same time tobacco prices had periodic fluctuations and, furthermore, tobacco had the disadvantage of depleting the soil after only three years. In order to counter the exhaustion of their prime acreage, planters looked for new lands and experimented with the cultivation of other crops such as wheat. Despite these efforts, they periodically suffered through particularly harsh agricultural crises.

The vast majority of southern whites did not posses the planters' wealth. Most were farmers or yeomen who had settled in the backcountry because of the abundance of land. They built their own houses, and sometimes they owned slaves, but their aspiration was to become part of the planter class. The yeomen were truly deferential toward planters, who considered them socially inferior and usually employed some of them as overseers on their plantations. Together with the planters, the elite included lawyers and merchants; these three groups dominated the political life of the colonial South as the leading elements in local governments and assemblies. The structure of the Church reflected the ranking of society, with the Anglican Church attached to the elite and dissenting Protestant churches popular among the lower classes.

Great planters wanted to imitate the English landed gentry and built their plantations with the idea that they were traditional gentlemen's seats. At the center of their plantations, they erected large Georgian-style mansions, two or three stories high, surrounded by gardens and streams, and with interiors that had colonnaded walls, molded ceilings, marble fireplaces, and grand staircases. Part of the gentleman's ideal was the sophistication of life reached through education. Therefore, many Virginia planters owned large collections of books that included the indispensable readings of the eighteenth-century educated classes, especially classical authors, philosophical treatises, and historical works.

In spite of these efforts at trying to appear like an Old World aristocracy, southern planters had the typical entrepreneurial spirit of the New World's rising classes. Their main concern was the business related to agriculture and slavery. Their wealth was inextricably attached to the cultivation of staple crops, and this factor gave them a particular sense of identity. This was especially the case with Virginia planters, who had what T. H. Breen has called a "tobacco mentality," a sense of belonging to a particular class of individuals whose material culture and public recognition revolved around the cultivation of tobacco. Foremost examples of planters with this outlook include Landon Carter and William Byrd II. Carter, in particular, demonstrates in his diary a complete identification with the figure of the tobacco planter and with the public recognition arising from successful tobacco cultivation.

The eighteenth-century South was a world in which planters exercised their power with unchallenged authority both in society at large and within the family. Eighteenth-century planters' families were strictly patriarchal: the fathers and heads of the family had absolute authority over their wives and children. Even though – as the century moved toward its second half – family relations became more affectionate, power relationships were still valued more than emotional attachment, and order was considered the basis of a perfect union. Wives could not challenge the authority of their husbands. In the case of marital choices for their daughters, planters were concerned with the acquisition of property and social status rather than personal preferences. Deference also ruled over the relationship between fathers and children. Children were expected to conform to the codified rules of behavior governing their class and requiring them to follow their fathers' decisions in matters of education and choice of life and career.

Further reading

Blake-Smith, D., *Inside the Great House: Planters' Family Life in Eighteenth-Century Chesapeake Society* (Ithaca, NY: Cornell University Press, 1980).

Breen, T. H., *Tobacco Culture: The Mentality of the Great Tidewater Planters on the Eve of Revolution*, 2nd edn. (Princeton: Princeton University Press, 2001).

Brown, K. M., *Good Wives, Nasty Wenches, and Anxious Patriarchs: Gender, Race, and Power in Colonial Virginia* (Chapel Hill: University of North Carolina Press, 1996).

Chaplin, J. E., *An Anxious Pursuit: Agricultural Innovation and Modernity in the Lower South* (Chapel Hill: University of North Carolina Press, 1993).

Isaac, R., *The Transformation of Virginia, 1740–1790* (Chapel Hill: University of North Carolina Press, 1982).

Kulikoff, A., *Tobacco and Slaves: The Development of Southern Cultures in the Chesapeake, 1680–1800* (Chapel Hill: University of North Carolina Press, 1986).

Olwell, R., *Masters, Slaves, and Subjects: The Culture of Power in the South Carolina Lowcountry, 1740–1790* (Ithaca, NY: Cornell University Press, 1998).

William Byrd II Describes the Patriarchal Ideal (1726)

Few planters could match William Byrd II in wealth and success. He was one of the largest slave-owners of his generation. With the profits from tobacco, he built one of the finest and largest mansions in colonial Virginia at Westover. In this excerpt, which he wrote in 1726, shortly before starting the construction of Westover, Byrd proclaimed proudly his independence and economic

Source: William Byrd II to Charles, Earl of Orrery, July 5, 1726, quoted in Rhys Isaac, *The Transformation of Virginia, 1740–1790* (Chapel Hill: University of North Carolina Press, 1982), pp. 39–40

prosperity and argued that they allowed him to have both animals and slaves to perform labor for him. Like other Virginia planters, he saw himself as a patriarch and benevolent master who took care of his family and dependents. However, he clearly perceived his status as both a blessing and a burden; in fact, according to the ethos of the time, as a member of the planter elite, he carried the obligation of looking after the life and health of his inferiors, administering punishments only when necessary.

I have a large Family of my own, and my Doors are open to Every Body, yet I have no Bills to pay, and half-a-Crown will rest undisturbed in my Pocket for many Moons together. Like one of the Patriarchs, I have my Flocks and my Herds, my Bond-men and Bond-women, and every Soart of trade amongst my own Servants, so that I live in a kind of Independence on every one but Providence. However this Soart of Life is without expence, yet it is attended with a great deal of trouble. I must take care to keep all my people to their Duty, to set all the Springs in motion and to make every one draw his equal Share to carry the Machine forward.

Landon Carter Describes the Business of Tobacco Planting (1770)

Growing tobacco was a difficult and demanding task which required exceptional skills and no small measure of luck. Poor management, improper technique, or crop failure could easily ruin the reputation of a planter. Unlike rice growing, tobacco planting required the constant presence of the planter in the fields, where he managed small groups of slaves, often together with the overseer. Colonel Landon Carter's diaries offer a detailed description of the kinds of tasks involved in tobacco planting; they also provide an example of the pride which tobacco planters took in directly managing their own plantations. One of the major problems caused by tobacco was soil depletion. By the time Landon Carter wrote this excerpt, planters had begun to experiment with crop diversification, and tobacco was starting to lose its central place in Virginia agriculture to wheat and other cereals.

Source: Jack Greene (ed.), *The Diary of Landon Carter of Sabine Hall, 1752–1778* (Charlottesville: University Press of Virginia, 1965), pp. 417–20; reprinted in Karen Ordahl Kupperman (ed.), *Major Problems in American Colonial History* (Lexington, Mass.: D. C. Heath, 1993), pp. 405–8

29. Tuesday

Yesterday I rode by my fork plantation to Coll. Tayloe's and if anybody could have seen the least sign of those scuds of rain that happened on Friday morning, friday night, and the Sprinkling Saturday in the night we must have discovered it. But excepting in the plant patch there did not appear the least moisture so that little profess that George who was setting Corn there had left off upon account of the dryness of the earth and had got to weeding his field.

As we rode round we had the opportunity of discovering the Tobacco ground which Coll. Tayloe had planted on friday. On horseback we could not see above 3 plants in the whole 30,000. I sent Nassau in. He walked deep in the rows but could not see one alive and it was it seems the general complaint on Sunday with every body that had planted that the ground worm had cut off most of that which stood.

We have this morning just such another little sprinkling which promised so much that really I had inclined to have some hills cut off as my plants at the fork are fine and large but I had scarce given my orders when I found occasion by the ceasing of the rain to send to the overseer to keep on dunging till it should rain to some purpose. Indeed it is a difficult matter to act because, though planting without rain might be done very well and the plants in a manner so covered with earth that the worms could hardly cut them under ground, yet with wet earth the Cover would bake and injure the plant....

30. Wednesday

Went to Mr. Ball's yesterday with Mr. Berkeley. A great prospect of rain but none as yet fallen which from the 6th of April 55 days including since the earth here has been blessed with any real moisture. It has mizzled, scudded, and sprinkled four times in the time once half an hour, once 15 minutes, once three minutes, and once perhaps 10 minutes, all of which did not even make moisture enough to hold out picking any thing of a plant patch. Nevertheless, having some very find plants at the fork, I ordered Lawson yesterday to get about 15,000 of them ready drawn to plant between 5 and dark in the way I pursued last year, that is, open the hills with my hand put the plant with its roots at full liberty, press the earth close round upon those roots up to the level of the hill, then bend the plant to the sunrise and lay a handful of dry dust over it to the tips of the leaves.

But Lawson stranger like to the time such a work might be done in did not get above 8,000 plants drawn and planted in the place designed.

This day finish covering in my dung upon the hill. The whole ground replenished to beyond the valley going to the Mill and about 9 rows in the wattled ground for which we must contrive and scrape our stubbs another day.

Set the people this day to turning the rest of the hills in the last year's Cowpen ground by the gate below to compleat that piece in order to be planted every night in the same manner if no rain falls. I believe the natural moisture of the earth perpetually rising will keep the plant alive till we may have rain and the covering prevent the attacks of the ground worm who never eat below the earth. If so, the hastiness of others has not put them in any forwardness before me. Mr. Ball told me his people wormed over the day before the 30,000 he had planted and got 8 measured quarts of worms and yesterday he himself took 8 worms out of the same ground and five off from many hills. . . .

It seems it took the fork gang all day yesterday setting the right hand corn field which is but one fourth of the ground they tend. The hemp wed out by Gardener Tom though very indifferently come up by means of the dry weather and I will fancy the badness of the seed for tutt was a Rascal in saving it. Lame Johnny has been 3 days weeding the flax and as he goes on will be three weeks but he says the young crab grass is coming much in it. We must take a day all hands to do this jobb at once.

We set in the Riverside Corn field tomorrow to hoe and set the corn if the ground [is] moistened.

31. Thursday

At last a mighty blizz of rain is come. It come on drop by drop from about dark last night so that we may reckon a full 30 days' dry weather in May and 24 in April.

I pursued my method of dry planting yesterday to the number of what my Overseer calls 15,000 but as he overreckoned the day before dry planting above 1,500 plants I have sent to have these counted.

My situation is such that, although I have more plants big enough, the ground I have cut off being of the stiffest land and quite mucky by the rain all night as I have no over abundance of plants I must run no chance of throwing them away in such a wet season.

Again as the hills I have turned is in the same stiff land it will evidently be making mortar of them to cut them of. Therefore the season must dry away more before I can venture upon that. Of course my hands can only go to setting Corn in my light fields till this season and its very moist effects shall abate. Then I must prepare a good stock of hills for dry planting or what moisture may happen and in particular turn all my hardest ground by which time I do suppose I shall have a great plenty of plants fit. But during this my river side corn field has all its lists to break up owing to the quantity I tend as well as the hardness of the Tobacco hills that I have turned and the vast heaps of dung I have buried. However I am in hopes the great breadth of the ridges which I hoed to plant Corn in will keep that from suffering or being in the least injured till those lists can be hoed and as the Fork are better than 3 parts done weeding I do imagine I shall have 6 of those hands at least to throw in and help out with this work very soon.

I receive this rain with prodigious pleasure. The earth dearly wanted it in all my cultivations as well as the old fields and every thing I hope will be benefited by it for my plant patches were all cleaned wed out.

Philip Fithian Visits Virginia's Planter Elite (1773–1774)

Philip Fithian was a New Jersey tutor who resided with Virginia planter Robert Carter III at his residence, Nomini Hall, in 1773–4. Fithian left us an early example of the travel accounts that later became ubiquitous in the American South. He was particularly interested in the social life and customs of the planter elite. He commented extensively on Virginia planters' sense of hospitality, their family life, pastimes, treatment of women, and religious ceremonies. Fithian's portrait of southern gentlemen and their families was generally sympathetic, though far from uncritical, especially with regard to slavery; he was specially struck by the wealth displayed at his host's mansion and, more generally, by the luxury and refinement of the planters with whom he became acquainted.

... Dr Franks is moving, he has lived in the House adjoining our School. The morning is fine, I rose by eight, breakfasted at ten, Miss Prissy & Nancy are to-Day Practising Music one on the Forte Piano, the other on the Guitar, their Papa allows them for that purpose every Tuesday, & Thursday. Ben is gone to the Quarter to see to the measuring the crop of Corn. On his return in the Evening, when we were sitting & chatting, among other things he told me that we must have a House-warming, seeing we have now got possession of the whole House – It is a custom

Source: Paul Escott and David Goldfield (eds.), *Major Problems in the History of the American South*, vol. 1: *The Old South*, 1st edn. (Lexington, Mass.: D. C. Heath, 1991), pp. 92–3

here whenever any *person* or *Family* move into a *House*, or repair a house they have been living in before, they make a *Ball* & give a Supper. . . .

. . . After considering a while I consented to go, & was dressed – we set away from Mr Carters at two; Mrs *Carter* & the young Ladies in the Chariot, Mrs Lane in a Chair, & myself on Horseback – As soon as I had handed the Ladies out, I was saluted by Parson *Smith*; I was introduced into a small Room where a number of Gentlemen were playing Cards, (the first game I have seen since I left Home) to lay off my Boots Riding-Coat &c – Next I was directed into the Dining-Room to see Young Mr *Lee*; He introduced me to his Father – With them I conversed til Dinner, which came in at half after four. The Ladies dined first, when some Good order was preserved; when they rose, each nimblest Fellow dined first – The Dinner was as elegant as could be well expected when so great an Assembly were to be kept for so long a time. – For Drink, there was several sorts of Wine, good Lemon Punch, Today, Cyder, Porter &c. – About Seven the Ladies & Gentlemen begun to dance in the Ball-Room – first Minuets one Round; Second Giggs; third Reels; And last of All Country-Dances; tho' they struck several Marches occasionally – The Music was a French-Horn and two Violins – The Ladies were Dressed Gay, and splendid, & when dancing, their Silks & Brocades rustled and trailed behind them! – But all did not join in the Dance for there were parties in Rooms made up, some at Cards; some drinking for Pleasure; some toasting the Sons of america; some singing "Liberty Songs" as they call'd them, in which six, eight, ten or more would put their Heads near together and roar, & for the most part as unharmonious as an affronted – Among the first of these Vociferators was a young Scotch-Man. Mr *Jack Cunningham:* he was nimis bibendo appotus; noisy, droll, waggish, yet civil in his way & wholly inoffensive – I was solicited to dance by several.

. . . I rose at eight – . . .

Breakfasted at half after nine. Mr Lane the other Day informed me that the *Anabaptists* in *Louden County* are growing very numerous; & seem to be increasing in afluence; and as he thinks quite destroying pleasure in the Country; for they encourage ardent Pray'r; strong & constant faith, & an intire Banishment of *Gaming, Dancing*, & Sabbath-Day Diversions. I have also before understood that they are numerous in many County's in this Province & are Generally accounted troublesome – Parson *Gibbern* has preached several Sermons in opposition to them, in which he has labour'd to convince his People that what they say are only whimsical Fancies or at most Religion grown to Wildness & Enthusiasm! – There is also in these counties one Mr Woddel, a presbiterian Clergyman, of an irreproachable Character, who preaches to the people under Trees in summer, & in private Houses in Winter, Him, however, the people in general dont more esteem than the Anabaptists Preachers; but the People of Fashion in general countenance, & commend him. I have never had an opportunity of seeing Mr *Woddel*, as he is this Winter up in the Country, but Mr & Mrs *Carter* speak well of him, Mr & Mrs *Fantleroy* also, & all who I have ever heard mention his Name....

Masters and Mistresses in Colonial Virginia

Kathleen M. Brown

In *Good Wives, Nasty Wenches, and Anxious Patriarchs*, Kathleen Brown investigates the role of gender and race in the creation of patriarchal ideology in colonial Virginia. She argues that gender and racial discrimination was instrumental to the rise of African American slavery and to the planter elite's claims to power within the family and in society. In this excerpt, Brown argues that Virginia's wealthy families maintained their grip over society through strategic intermarriages which gave sons a prominent political position and daughters economic security. Marriages were essential for the survival and continuous reassertion of the planter elite as the dominant class; therefore, during the period of courtship between future masters and mistresses, the reputation and finances of both families underwent close scrutiny. Planters used their wealth primarily to increase their landholdings and buy slaves. They also built elaborate houses which were at once the material expressions of their power and the symbols of their distinctiveness as an elite. Together with the practice of hospitality, planters' conspicuous consumption impressed foreign visitors while performing the vital function of reinforcing the elite's consciousness of itself as a ruling class.

The publication of Robert Beverley's *History and Present State of Virginia* in 1705 signified the dawning of a new self-consciousness among elite planters in Virginia. Throughout the text's wide-ranging discussions of Anglo-Indian relations, Bacon's Rebellion, African slavery, and colonial

Kathleen M. Brown, *Good Wives, Nasty Wenches and Anxious Patriarchs: Gender, Race, and Power in Colonial Virginia* (Chapel Hill: University of North Carolina Press, 1996), pp. 247–82.

politics, Beverley searched for an authoritative colonial voice. Acutely aware of his position as a gentleman and his distance from the sophisticated culture of London, he represented his homeland as an oversized English country estate that boasted a glorious history. He depicted himself as a "Native and Inhabitant of the Place" whose plain style contrasted sharply with the "*Fopperies*" of French travel accounts. Proclaiming at the outset of his history, "I am an *Indian*," Beverley identified with indigenous peoples, adopting a subordinate posture in relationship to English readers. Yet Beverley the Indian and the Indians who peopled the pages of his *History* were clearly not the same. The exoticism and innocence he ascribed to them allowed him to play the part of European sophisticate. With its self-conscious attempt to put Virginia on the map and into the annals of history, *The History and Present State of Virginia* provided compelling evidence of coalescing class interests and consciousness among Virginia's elite planters.[1]

With their wealth rooted in land, slaves, and tobacco – tangible evidence of the success of their immigrant fathers – native-born men coming of age between 1690 and 1730 became increasingly aware of their common economic and political interests and their identity as colonials. Their success was due in great measure to the legacy of Bacon's Rebellion and the changes in colonial society during the quarter-century after the conflict. The decimation of local Indian populations that resulted from the rebellion effectively reduced their actual proximity to Anglo-Virginian settlements, thereby increasing Indians' symbolic value to men like Beverley. Legal innovations – including the elaboration of racial categories, the tightening of restrictions on enslaved men, and new sanctions against white female sexual offenders – strengthened the institutional bases of white male authority. The white male public culture that subsequently blossomed during the early eighteenth century . . . celebrated the success of elite planters.

Beverley's family and personal history typified some of the patterns that were beginning to distinguish Virginia's elite planter class. Like many wealthy young men, Beverley spent his youth in England. Adulthood brought a return to Virginia and a renewed commitment to pursuing the genteel life within a colonial context. Beverley's marriage to Ursula Byrd, daughter of a Baconian opponent of his own staunch Berkeleyan father, testified to the consolidation of elite power through familial and political networks. Expressing their class position through the purchase of luxury items, slaves, fine clothing, and gracious houses, most elite young men of Beverley's generation distinguished themselves from their less wealthy neighbors both materially and culturally while competing from afar with their English counterparts. Unlike most of his peers, however, Beverley professed an antipathy to dependence upon

English commodities, a posture that paralleled his attempt to give Virginia a unique historical identity. . . .

Although not sharing his brother-in-law's renunciation of things English, William Byrd II similarly tried to make a mark on the political and social world of early-eighteenth-century London. When Byrd's wife, Lucy Parke Byrd, died of smallpox there in 1716, he feverishly pursued wealthy young women, political preferment, and prostitutes. During this time, he recorded sexually graphic and racist anecdotes in his commonplace book. Only after making peace with his political failures and his Virginia estate's lack of appeal for the fathers of London's most eligible women did Byrd return to Virginia to rebuild his father's house, turning it into a sturdy English-style brick mansion. Like his brother-in-law, Byrd subsequently fashioned his own identity as a colonial by writing a history of Virginia.

For the members of this generation of native-born elites, securing profitable political posts within the colony, living according to the rules of English gentlemanly conduct, and marrying into families of similar wealth and status became part of an effort to assert themselves as an English gentry in Virginia. When thwarted political ambitions and rejected marriage proposals made such Anglocentric pretensions impossible, men like Beverley and Byrd worked out their dilemmas of identity with fine plantation houses and quill pens, situating both their political battles and themselves within a glorified material and historical context. That this endeavor differed significantly from that of their mid-seventeenth-century counterparts, whose sullied honor could be recovered only by military engagement, reflects the new stability of Britain's empire and the gentrification of imperial culture. By the mid-eighteenth century, the young men who sought an education at the College of William and Mary and married the daughters of Virginia planters appear to have completed the psychological journey begun by Beverley and Byrd: they thought of themselves less as an English gentry in Virginia than as a Virginia gentry.

Marriage was vital to class formation and gentry identity. It was one of the primary means by which Virginia's planters maintained their dominance for the rest of the century. Through strategic intermarriages, wealthy families reaffirmed their social position and launched their sons in prominent political careers. Their daughters, meanwhile, gained economic security and a release from some of the manual labor that characterized the lives of less wealthy and enslaved women.

If marriage was the gateway to gentry status, it was also its testing ground. During courtship, a young man risked repudiation in his quest for self-affirmation and an advantageous match. Courtship also constituted a period of trial for his family, during which its fortunes would be judged by the courted woman and her parents. For an elite woman, however, courtship's liminality offered an unparalleled chance to intervene in the course of her own life and influence the men in it. A woman could reject a suitor, shattering fragile egos and blasting family pretensions. She might also influence her father to accept a man he would otherwise consider unworthy. Courtship was thus an unusual time in which the balance of power tipped briefly in favor of young women.

Courtship also brought together the usually distinct performances of male and female gentility. Different patterns of socializing and access to public spaces like courts and taverns distinguished the experiences of men and women who otherwise shared many of the material benefits of their class. Virginia's elite male planters participated in a robust and largely homosocial public culture that regularly provided men with opportunities to articulate their social relationships with other men. Elite women's public performances of gentility were not only fewer but heterosocial in nature: men as well as women attended church services, dances, and weddings.

An elite woman in eighteenth-century Virginia rarely engaged in public displays of status unless she was in the company of elite men. . . . An unaccompanied woman risked both her reputation and her safety when she ventured into male public spaces. Her negotiations of status with other women took place primarily in domestic settings. . . . Yet, despite this dependence on men to escort and mediate her public self, an elite woman remained capable of influencing male fortunes, particularly during the phase of her life spent in courtship.

Efforts by Virginia gentlemen to express their class position and contain the influence of women were visible in the landscape and architecture of plantation houses. Built during the second quarter of the eighteenth century as a consequence of the rising self-consciousness and economic might of a new generation of men, the stately brick homes of the colony's great planters also reflected growing gentry needs for distinction. The construction of Georgian edifices was, therefore, not simply the proud display of accumulated wealth and power but an anxious attempt to call attention to those privileges. A man's house revealed his vision of his place in the world as he wished it to be: it declared his cultural and economic ties to England, his preeminence in colonial society, and his authority over members of his household, including the slaves who generated his wealth.

The organization of space and labor within the plantation house complemented public performances of male gentility. The separation of work space from living space and the addition of new rooms designed for entertainment distanced elite women and men from the manual labor needed to run the household and affirmed their gentility. The work spaces cordoned off from the main house, moreover, were primarily *domestic* spaces – kitchens, laundries, and dairies – that had previously been coextensive with living space. By building separate quarters for this labor and assigning it to servant and slave women, the male planter defined his wife's place in the domestic landscape as that of a wife, mother, and hostess, duties that emphasized her relationship to him and denied independent sources of female identity. Although the invisibility of a woman's domestic labor confirmed her own class privilege, it ultimately conferred status upon her husband....

For elite men such as Beverley and Byrd, however, public affirmations of masculine identity and the creation of an equally affirming domestic landscape were not sufficient compensation for the insecurity of their position within the colony and the British empire.... With wives carefully shielded from public view and Indian men tamed by the appropriation of their masculinity, men like Beverley and Byrd pressed their claim to be genteel colonial patriarchs.

Material foundations

For most Chesapeake counties settled by 1668, the latter half of the seventeenth century and the early years of the eighteenth century brought greater economic stratification, a rapid growth in numbers of slaves, an increasing proportion of native-born Virginians, and equilibrium to the white sex ratio. By 1700 in Middlesex County, Virginia, 8 percent of free, male-headed families owned 62 percent of the wealth, whereas 33 percent owned less than 2 percent, a pattern that was also well under way in many other Tidewater counties. In the same county between 1668 and 1724, the number of native-born individuals leaped from 19 to 77 percent of the population. The diminishing pool of English laborers after 1660 also reduced the numbers of white immigrants entering the colony. These trends worked in tandem to create conditions ripe for capital accumulation. Through land speculation and the large-scale production of tobacco, wealthy planters and a few lucky newcomers weathered periods of low tobacco prices and exploited the growing demand for frontier lands.

The use of slave labor to produce tobacco was a major reason for the rapid changes in the distribution of wealth after 1700. Between 1700 and 1750, slave traders brought nearly 45,000 Africans to Virginia, causing the black population to surpass 100,000 by midcentury and resulting in a black majority in most Tidewater counties between the James and Rappahannock Rivers. Among the wealthy members of the Virginia House of Burgesses, the men who had first choice from the cargoes of

African laborers arriving in the Tidewater, slaveholding increased from a median of five slaves per legislator in the late seventeenth century to seven slaves by the 1720s. The number of nonslaveholders, meanwhile, also declined. . . .

The trend in slaveholding reflected both the spread of slavery throughout the Chesapeake and the growing economic power an elite class of planters derived from it. By the 1740s, more than half of the slaves in Virginia were living in holdings of more than ten people, although the average holding remained under five until after 1750 in most places. As both land and slaves were necessary capital for young men beginning their own households, the sons of wealthy planters entered adulthood with the greatest chance of success. Men from these families were usually well equipped to diversify into corn, wheat, and cloth production when the tobacco market became sluggish and to employ specialized laborers who provided the plantation with meat, fruit, and dairy products. Most important, these men established valuable patrimonies through land speculation, enabling their families to perpetuate economic and political prominence. . . .

By the end of the seventeenth century, elite white planters also increasingly dominated colonial politics. Although wealthy planters had always enjoyed ready access to local offices, exerting considerable sway over the colonial governor as members of the Council, it was not until the turn of the century that elite transatlantic and regional networks coalesced to create a powerful political interest group. Planters enhanced their own and their sons' fortunes through political appointments as customs collectors, naval officers, and, after 1730, as tobacco inspectors. . . .

During the 1730s and 1740s, the planter elite reached a new level of dominance over the politics and economy of the colony with the passage of the Virginia Inspection Act of 1730 and the successful suppression of opposition from small planters. Small and large planters alike had initially contested the act, which gave Governor William Gooch control over appointments to tobacco inspection posts. When Gooch relinquished this facet of his plan, most larger planters supported the act and filled the posts with men of their own choosing. The act was never popular with smaller planters, however, who rightly feared that inspection of their tobacco by wealthy men was an attempt to quash small producers like themselves whose allegedly low-quality leaves were believed to drive down prices. These small planters expressed their displeasure by burning warehouses in Lancaster, Northumberland, Falmouth, and King George Counties and behaving in a rowdy fashion at a militia muster in a district with a particularly corrupt inspector. The large planters held the day, however, and, in 1734, pushed through the renewal of the law for four more years. A third generation of elite planters thus remained powerful in the colony at midcentury through a combination of wealth, political posts, imperial connections, and marital alliances with other planter families.

Marriage

Although slaves, land, and political preferment constituted the main material foundations of gentry power, marriage knit families together and honed self-awareness as a class. It continued to be one of the surest ways for men with capital to maintain their place amid the colony's wealthy and powerful planters. During each courtship, family reputations and finances endured scrutiny. With so much at stake, parents and friends remained closely involved in marriage negotiations, offering advice, serving as go-betweens, and softening the blow of rejection.

Virginia planters cagily assessed each other's worth, not simply in terms of the value of estates but on the basis of vague credentials like family lineage, honor, and status. Philip Ludwell, Sr., a wealthy planter... revealed the intricacies of these evaluations in a letter to his son in 1707. Writing of Daniel Parke's alleged disapproval of his daughter's marriage to John Custis, Ludwell commented, "I take Custis [the groom] to be of as good extraction as Byrd or Park[e] himselfe." Ludwell's statement reflected a careful weighing of the ranks and worth of Custis and Byrd.... Drawing upon a vast store of knowledge about the "extraction" of Virginia's eligible bachelors, Ludwell expressed skepticism of Parke's supposed disappointment over the match.[2]

A slippery concept even in England, "extraction" was even more ambiguous for Virginia's gentlemen planters who, at the start of the eighteenth century, were only beginning to identify themselves as a class. Vast estates enabled individuals in Virginia to compensate for humble birth, allowing them to compete with men of more genteel origins for marriage partners and enter the ranks of elite planters. Courtship in Virginia thus entailed more than the usual risks of disappointment and humiliation because of uncertainty over the meaning of extraction in a colonial society.

The porous nature of colonial social hierarchies intensified the liminality of courtship, magnifying its capacity to render a young man temporarily vulnerable and a young woman briefly powerful. A daughter's appeals to a parent to look kindly upon a particular man's suit could increase the chances of its success, just as her apathy or animosity could ensure its failure. Capable of swaying parental decisions based on lineage, net worth, and economic prospects, a young woman might exert considerable influence over the choice of a marriage partner. As a result, the sinews of class formed by marital alliances also reflected her input....

Strategic marriage within the ranks of Virginia's planter class established several families and helped others to maintain their position for several generations. Although Robert "King" Carter is best known for building a fortune through shrewd deals and the ruthless management of estates, he was also the matchmaking "king" of early-eighteenth-century Virginia, a skill that contributed in no small measure to his success.... Carter advanced his career through two advantageous matches. By the time his children came of age, Carter was in a position to help them attract and win the wealthiest partners in the colony through generous marriage portions. Each son received a home plantation, several subsidiary landholdings, and the necessary slaves, livestock, and tools to make them profitable. Each subsequently married a woman who brought to the union considerable wealth and political connections....

"King" Carter's greatest accomplishment, however, may have been the marriages of his daughters. Daughters often proved a financial liability because of the need to provide sons-in-law with substantial marriage settlements. Carter appears to have facilitated these marital agreements with cash rather than property, with the result that his family cemented alliances with four of the wealthiest families in the colony – the Burwells, Pages, Harrisons, and Fitzhughs – without losing control over family lands. Carter deserved the epithet "King," then, not simply because of his business acumen or massive holdings of land and slaves but because he skillfully encouraged matches that strengthened both the patriarchal line of the Carter family through his sons and the family's connections to the colony's richest and most powerful citizens through his daughters.

In employing different strategies for settling his estate upon sons and daughters, Carter adeptly worked what one historian has called an "inheritance grid," the gendered laws and customs in which family name and estate were carefully protected and passed to sons. Yet Carter was also participating in the formation of a new grid, in which land and slaves needed to be used together to generate wealth in tobacco. Carter portioned out slaves, capital, and land in different amounts to each child to complement the material contribution of each child's spouse. Although female children adopted husbands' names and transferred paternal inheritances from their family of origin to that of their male children, they too needed to be adequately endowed with property (in the form of dower) both to attract a suitable mate and to ensure that as widows they could either remarry or live comfortably on their own.

Smoothly engineered marriages, lubricated by the disposition of generous settlements, required that children be able to distinguish appropriate marriage partners from frauds, rakes, and gold diggers. Although the timely intervention of a parent when a child seemed headed for a disadvantageous match undoubtedly protected many children from such dangers, the successful transmission from parent to child of standards of quality, breeding, and social position prevented planter children from straying too far from people their parents defined as their own kind. The replication of class values in a younger generation made it possible for children to choose their own spouses while still furthering the social and political goals of their parents. . . .

[M]others and fathers were concerned that . . . the marriages of their children should be "easie," allowing the child to live among the same sort of people with whom he or she had grown up and to enjoy similar material comforts. This marriage ethic was actively promulgated in the colony's print culture after 1736, appearing in the essays, poetry, and announcements of the *Virginia Gazette*. Fearing that his daughters would not be well provided for, William Byrd II discouraged several suitors, including cousin Daniel Custis, who came to express interest in Anne Byrd in July 1741. Byrd believed that his own falling out with John Custis, the suitor's father, would diminish the couple's chances of receiving a generous settlement. Byrd also ended a romance between his eldest daughter, Evelyn, and an English suitor he found unsatisfactory, despite his daughter's wishes to the contrary.[3] Byrd's stated concern – the material security of his daughters once they became the dependents of other men – was one with which many gentry fathers could have identified.

Parents normally intervened early in a courtship to inquire after the financial prospects of the young man or woman in question and to offer information that might improve a child's appeal to prospective lovers and in-laws. Jane Parke wrote to her estranged husband Daniel Parke in 1705 to learn details about her daughters' estates that would be crucial to their successful courtship, especially in the case of the eldest, who had already received an offer of marriage. She asked Parke pointed questions about his plans for his daughters' marriage portions because uncertainty over the location of land settlements (Parke had estates in both Barbados and Virginia) had become an obstacle to concluding the match. . . .

Routine parental inquiries into the finances of a prospective mate made early in the courtship were designed to prevent scandal or the defrauding of the family. . . .

Parents or married siblings might also intervene to protect a child from embarrassment or to offer practical advice when emotions threatened to lead them astray. Richard Lee received several letters in this vein from his married older brother John Lee concerning a series of unhappy courtships during the 1750s. John Lee wrote his brother in 1750 to wish him happiness and good luck in what he believed to be a nearly resolved courtship. He spurred Richard on with advice "not to be Cast down at any faint denials but Look upon them as Intices of Further pressing of a Tender heart which no Doubt will be prevailed on to yield." In John's reading of the courtship dance, a woman's refusals were mere form, signifying nothing authentic.[4] . . .

Elite young men and women involved in courtship seem to have been well aware of the social position of their potential mates and convinced of the role of wealth in making marriages "easie." . . . If emotion and economic calculation became unhinged, threatening to distort a young person's view of the importance of financial assets, parents and married siblings who knew better the "contingent expences that are inherent to marriage" offered practical advice and suggested more suitable objects for their affections. By the mid-eighteenth century, most members of the planter elite seem to have internalized the warning of John Lee's "worthy Unkle Presid[en]t [of the Council] Lee . . . that the first fall and ruin of familys and estates was mostly occasioned by imprudent matchs to Imbeggar familys and to beget a race of beggars."[5]

Elite planter families in Virginia continued to heed Uncle Lee's advice even as the eighteenth century drew to a close. Most of the one hundred wealthiest families in 1787 could boast a dense web of inter- and intrafamilial marital connections that dated back to the 1690s. Nearly one-fourth of the hundred bore the last name Armistead, Berkeley, Beverley, Burwell, Carter, Custis, Fitzhugh, Harrison, or Lee, and three others boasted a first name like Carter or Bassett, which indicated a prominent maternal line. As for the family of Robert "King" Carter, its visible patriarchal line was the best represented of any family, accounting for seven of the hundred; equally important, the marriages of several generations of Carter daughters and granddaughters to the sons of other prominent families had knit them into a class capable of sustaining its dominance during and after the Revolution.

Plantation households

Perhaps the most telling evidence of the emergent planter class was the appearance by the 1730s of brick dwellings and more elaborate wooden structures to house wealthy planters and their families. Often these houses were built to celebrate the marriage of individuals from prominent families. . . . Throughout the 1750s and 1760s, many other planters began married life in brick mansions that were constructed to celebrate their coming of age.

The landscaping of the plantation as well as the architecture and floor plans of the main house reflected a desire for dominance over both nature and society. Planters situated their mansion houses in commanding settings such as the bluffs above a river's banks. Such a location not only provided convenient access to waterways that were crucial for transporting goods and people but also gave the planter's dwelling a controlled and interpreted visibility that was flattering to his authority on the plantation as well as in the neighborhood, county, and colony. Terraced hills from the main house to the river's edge made the structure appear more imposing from the water. The house was also designed, however, to be impressive when approached from the road. After passing through an elaborate gateway, visitors entered the processional space of a long drive, at the end of which the main house became suddenly visible. Surrounding the mansion house were several small buildings known as "dependencies." Within these buildings, slaves lived and performed the domestic work necessary for the maintenance of the white family. Highly ordered, formal garden plots containing walkways filled with fruit trees, hedges, and flowering plants provided vivid evidence of the planter's ability to tame nature. In its overall landscape design, the plantation celebrated the triumph of the male planter over nature, his household, and colonial society.

By the mid-eighteenth century, planters had adopted a self-consciously European architectural style, characterized by a symmetrical, columned façade and a repetition of window units. Adapted from contemporary English high architecture, this Georgian style was compatible with the contradictions of a world view that was at once hierarchical and increasingly influenced by rationalism. No longer content with wooden dwellings that were vulnerable to fire and might need repair within a generation, a handful of planters turned to brick to build lasting monuments to their family's achievement of wealth and power. Although brick was more functional than wood in Virginia's stifling summer heat, it was also more expensive in a colony where wood was plentiful and skilled bricklayers and masons few. . . .

The colony's wealthiest planters expanded upon the one- or two-room design common in seventeenth-century Virginia homes to create two-story, multiroom mansions in which most rooms had specialized functions. Instead of entering immediately into the main living or sleeping area of the house, as they might still do in the homes of smaller planters, guests passed first into a hallway containing stairs to the second floor. This front hall offered the family greater privacy and separation from the outdoors and allowed them some means of withdrawing politely from "company." Specialized rooms for eating and entertaining were situated off the main hallway on the first floor, and, on the second floor family chambers were set off from the main activity of the house. . . .

Perhaps the most striking difference between these new planter mansions and their seventeenth-century counterparts was the reconfiguration of women's domestic work spaces to signify the racial, class, and gender dominance of the male planter. In the wealthiest households, service rooms such as the kitchen, laundry, milkhouse, and slave quarters were separated from the main house. Surrounding the mansion like the clustered buildings of a little village, these dependencies allowed the most strenuous and distasteful work of meal preparation, clothes laundering, and dairying to take place at a discreet distance from the white family's living quarters. Dependencies also separated the white family from the labor of slaves who made plantation life possible. Such a division of living and working space distinguished the wealthy planter's household from that of poorer planters, where men, women, and children shared the burden of agricultural and domestic tasks with servants and slaves who lived under the same roof.

The architecture of the largest houses called attention to a planter's ability to release his wife from manual labor, emphasizing her social and reproductive rather than economic roles. On large plantations, hired white and enslaved black women took over many of the tasks of food preparation, cooking, laundering, and child care that occupied both wives and their servants in smaller households. Lucy Parke Byrd, wife of William Byrd II, retained responsibility for overseeing the upkeep of the household, sewing, brewing beer or ale, managing and processing food supplies, and supervising kitchen staff. The bulk of her duties, however, revolved around bearing and raising children and making the household ready for guests. . . . Meanwhile, several women attended to running the household, caring for the Byrd children, and preparing meals: the slave woman Anaka and a white woman Byrd referred to as "Nurse" appear to have had primary responsibility for his children. Jenny, another slave, seems to have had general duties to maintain the household, and the slave Moll functioned as a cook. Although, throughout the eighteenth century, most black women remained engaged in agricultural tasks, an increasing number filled domestic posts in the largest plantation households as the century progressed, relieving planters' wives of much of the strenuous household labor and bringing black and white people into intimate contact under the roof of the mansion house.

The racial and gender division of duties that distanced white mistresses from the work of their slaves also released planter men from stenuous labor. William Byrd II, Robert "King" Carter, and Landon Carter left daily records of their letter writing, improving reading, visiting, card playing, political networking, and plantation management, but few descriptions of their own manual labor. Byrd and Carter walked or rode around plantation grounds, examined livestock, crops, and fences, and occasionally planted trees. So removed was elite planter life from the backbreaking work that characterized the daily routines of most white and black men in the colony that many were forced to take exercise in order to remain in good health. . . .

As a result of their mainly managerial function, wealthy planters enjoyed a very different perspective on the colony's notoriously intemperate weather than their laboring counterparts. Robert Beverley dismissed accounts of Virginia's unbearable summer heat with advice of a very class-specific nature aimed at an elite reading audience:

> Their Heat is very seldom troublesome, and then only by the accident of a perfect Calm, which happens perhaps two or three times in a year, and lasts but a few Hours at a time; and even that Inconvenience is made easie by cool Shades, by open Airy rooms, Summer-Houses, Arbors, and Grottos.

From the cool interiors of their brick houses, planters like Beverley interpreted summer deaths from heat stroke and malaria as the result of foolishness, not as the consequence of the need to toil outside.[6] . . .

Although the physical comforts of residence in a brick mansion were undoubtedly important in a colony where oppressive heat and disease claimed many victims each year, such a life also offered Virginia's young male planters many psychic benefits as well. Large houses, like conspicuous displays of wealth, clearly distinguished the colony's most elite men from ordinary planters, most of whom still inhabited two-room dwellings the size of a great planter's dependencies. As the master of such a household and owner of land and laborers, an elite planter enjoyed an assertion of will and identity unparalleled in a society where the family and household usually received much greater emphasis than the individual. Rooted firmly in familial, race, and class relations, Virginia planters' material and social representations of self were the bedrock of gentry masculinity. . . .

For young men educated in the classics and impressed by the simple grandeur of English gentry country life, rural plantations run by slaves and dominated by the brick mansion house were tangible proof of the colonial elite's legitimacy as a ruling class and historical connection to the patriarchs of old. More than one man documented his consciousness of the historical reverberations of plantation life by giving his home a Latin name, as Landon Carter did with Sabine Hall, or describing it as his personal arena for mastery, as William Byrd II did in 1726:

> Like one of the patriarchs, I have my flocks and my herds, my bond-men, and bond-women, and every soart of trade amongst my own servants, so that I live in a kind of independence on every one, but Providence. However tho' this soart of life is without expence yet it is attended with a great deal of trouble. I must take care to keep all my people to their duty, to set all the springs in motion, and to make every one draw his equal share to carry the machine forward.

Using a mechanical metaphor, Byrd not only reinforced the notion that nature and society were machines subject to human control but declared his affiliation with London's metropolitan culture and scientific community.[7] . . .

The male planter's individual and familial identities became more firmly tied to the physical site of the plantation with the celebration and observation of family events within the grounds of his estate. Weddings and births typically took place in the plantation house during the seventeenth and eighteenth centuries, eventually to be joined by funerals. At the turn of the century, elite families such as the Harrisons of Berkeley used the plantation house as a place for eating, drinking, and socializing before traveling to the churchyard to bury family members. By midcentury, gentry self-consciousness and generational continuity had given rise to family identities predicated upon a deep sense of place. The need for greater distinction than that provided by burial in a common church plot encouraged elite families to seek eternal rest on their own plantations. Some wealthy men, such as Charles Carter of Cleve, requested small funerals and burial on their own land near loved ones. . . .

As an older man living in England, Lancaster County planter Joseph Ball began to feel this tug of place quite urgently. In 1754, he instructed his cousin to

> go down to the Plantation where my Grandfather and mother liv'd and are buryed; and get the assistance of Hannah Dennis to show you as nigh as she can the spot where they are buryed; and let the hands skim the Ground over about four or five inches Deep; and if you come over the Graves you will find the Ground of a different colour. If you can find that, then stake it out at the four corners with sound Locust or Cedar stakes.

Ball wanted his cousin to be "sure to find it again" for he planned to "send a stone to put over them."[8] For planters whose estate grounds contained these family plots, family lineage and sense of place blended together to reinforce identities as landowners, masters of households, and gentlemen.

Hospitality

Despite planter claims about retiring, neither the mansion house nor its organization of household labor was intended for a privatized, intensely emotional family life. Rather, they served the very different purpose of affirming male authority and social position through sociability. The normal routine at William Byrd's Westover and Benjamin Harrison's Berkeley between 1709 and 1710, for example, was the entertainment of a steady stream of guests, even during the serious illness of family members. At such times of crisis, friends and neighbors might spend days and even nights with the afflicted family, sitting up with the invalid and comforting the parent or spouse....

The material comforts and organization of labor within the plantation house responded to social imperatives for entertaining guests. The food, drink, and implements on the table, the horses in the stable, and the interactions between the master, his family, and laborers all reflected the quality of the man whose social and familial self was represented by the great house. The honor of the elite male host thus depended in some measure on the liberality of his hospitality and the appearance of order in his household. His duties as host complemented his public roles as politician and neighbor, much as the architecture of his home mimicked that of public places such as churches and court-houses.

Although not the exclusive province of the planter elite, the ethos of hospitality reached its apogee in the gracious brick homes along the James, York, and Rappahannock Rivers.... William Hugh Grove, an English traveler to the colony in 1732, commented... that Virginia residents "are very Hospita[b]le, and in places where there are no Ordinarys you ride in where 2 brick Chimbles shew there is a spare bed and lodging and Welcome." Men who owned houses boasting two "brick Chimbles" were, of course, wealthy planters.[9]

Robert Beverley believed that the spirit of generosity transcended class divisions and that most Virginians were willing to expend their resources for the sake of guests. "Inhabitants are very Courteous to Travellers," he observed. "A Stranger has no more to do, but to inquire upon the Road, where any Gentleman, or good House-keeper Lives, and there he may depend upon being received with Hospitality." Of Virginia's gentry, Beverley claimed, "When they go abroad, [they] order their Principal Servant to entertain all Visitors, with every thing the Plantation affords." Poor planters, likewise, "who have but one Bed, will very often sit up, or lie upon a Form or Couch all Night, to make room for a weary Traveller, to repose himself after his Journey."[10] . . .

Wealthy male planters who traveled frequently and could summon the greatest resources for entertaining guests were most sensitive to the nuances of the material culture of hospitality and its implications for a man's reputation. During overnight stays in the homes of other planters, elite men continually evaluated their hosts. William Byrd II often recorded small glitches in the hospitality he received, implicitly comparing himself to his hosts. On at least two occasions, he found fault with the servants: once, an otherwise well-served dinner at Colonel Ludwell's was marred when "Ludwell's boy broke a glass." On a visit to his brother-in-law Custis, Byrd remarked laconically, "Here are the worst servants that ever I saw in my life." Men who could not provide company with good-quality beverages also received mention in Byrd's diary. He commented after a visit to his father-in-law, Colonel Duke, whose house had just been torn apart by a storm, "He had no drink good so that I was forced to drink thick cider."[11]

Like many of his planter peers, Byrd interpreted hospitality as the most visible indication of gentility and domestic authority. . . .

Although a wife's cooperation was necessary to making guests feel welcome, in Byrd's view hospitality reflected differently upon a woman than it did upon a man, revealing her proficiency at domestic tasks that the architecture of plantation mansions normally rendered invisible. Byrd usually credited men with the provision of necessaries like liquor, food, and fodder for horses but attributed domestic services to women. Cleanliness, sweet-smelling bed linen, and an abundance of fine food at the table revealed to visitors a plantation mistress's good character, even when such tasks were clearly being performed by female slaves and servants. While staying at the home of the wealthy Widow Allen of Isle of Wight County, Byrd commented, "She entertain'd us elegantly, and seem'd to pattern Solomon's Housewife if one may Judge by the neatness of her House, and the good order of her Family."[12] . . .

Although Byrd generally considered men responsible for providing food and shelter, he noticed and commended women's efforts to keep house and feed guests. . . .

Under ideal conditions, hospitality was an exchange between guest and host that reinforced the connections between a man's domestic and public selves. When he opened his house to a visitor, a planter invited comparison between his public reputation for wealth, power, and sophistication and the circumstances of his daily life. Family relationships, the management of servants, and even the carefully obscured domestic labors of wives became visible to guests. To ensure that this comparison was favorable, a great planter encouraged the recipients of his hospitality to interpret fancy accommodations as representative of the household's daily fare. Yet, because the transaction of hospitality required that a guest leave his host feeling flattered as well as well provisioned, a planter had to highlight the unique and honorific nature of the food and drink. . . .

Genteel accoutrements

After 1690, elite planters increasingly revealed their consciousness of social position through conspicuous consumption, purchasing furnishings and luxuries that were important to a routine of frequent entertainment. Generous hospitality required that planter houses be outfitted with chairs, tables, rugs, bedding, and tableware beyond the needs of most families in the colony. Monogrammed silver, fine china, and expensive silks that would have been beyond the means of many wealthy planters in the seventeenth century were, by the mid-eighteenth century, part of a highly ritualized and rich material culture that distinguished the wealthiest planters from their less prosperous neighbors. Such displays of luxury, moreover, symbolized the leisure and wealth made possible by slave labor and aligned Virginia's elite planters with their elite peers in England. William Fitzhugh, Robert "King" Carter, and William Byrd II periodically sent to England for these goods to grace their tables so they could entertain guests with an easy elegance. Other planters went to the trouble of researching family crests and coats of arms to decorate silverware and livery with appropriate and meaningful symbols and colors.

Fancy clothing constituted one of the most personal expressions of gentility. Wearing expensive imported garments, a planter could step out of the genteel environment of the plantation house – while traveling, for instance – yet still be recognized and treated as gentry. Wealthy colonial men shaved their heads and wore wigs after the turn of the century and tried to keep pace with changing styles in London. . . .

Exclusive social engagements related to colonial politics and other occasions such as plays, dances, and raffles provided elite men and women with opportunities to show off their finery. Although Robert "King" Carter reported to his London merchant that he had no need for the "fine gay cloke" sent to him several years earlier, claiming it was "fitter for an Alderman of London than a Planter of Virginia," other wealthy men seem to have relished dressing the part of the gentry. William Byrd II, who normally did not comment on male attire, noted on one festive evening in Williamsburg that "the President had the worst clothes of anybody there." The congregation of the colony's most politically prominent men provided Byrd with the chance to compare his own wardrobe favorably to that of his peers.[13]

Fashion held even greater significance and attraction for elite women, much to the annoyance of husbands and fathers who resented the time and money invested in female dress but who found, nonetheless, that the appearance of wives and daughters ultimately reflected on their own prestige.... By staying current with London fashions, elite women displayed their connections to the sophisticated culture of Europe, much as their husbands might show off a library or coach. Elite women were often responsible, moreover, for sponsoring the social events like balls and raffles that required elegant formal attire. Although gentlewomen did not wear these fancy clothes every day, the quality and style of most of their garments prohibited the kind of strenuous garden and field labor performed by ordinary white and enslaved black women, thus testifying to their release from strenuous agricultural work. Much as the plantation house obscured traces of domestic labors, elite women's costume signaled the wearer's ornamental value rather than her economic productivity, a message that confirmed not only her own gentility but also that of her husband.

Wealthy planters also displayed their status and cosmopolitan ties through elegant menus that set them apart from other Virginians. After 1700, many elite men and women enjoyed breakfasts that included chocolate, coffee, or tea, drinks to which they might have become accustomed while living in England. In the houses of these wealthy planters, guests drank to the monarch's health with wine, "drams" of liquor, or "strong water." In less well-to-do households, rum, brandy, or punch might suffice to provide an atmosphere of conviviality. The array of dishes on a planter's table also spoke volumes about his abilities as a host. Dinner at the house of a wealthy planter might include several meat dishes such as pork, beef, mutton, fowl, lamb, and fish. The meal itself would be washed down by wine at the wealthiest tables and beer or cider at those of ordinary planters.... Following dinner, male guests at an elite planter's house would follow him to his drawing room for more drinking, usually wine or syllabub, and tobacco smoking. The women, meanwhile, would retire to a separate room until the party reunited for games, more drinking, and conversation.

The material culture of hospitality reflected the class consciousness and cosmopolitan background of Virginia's planter elite. Throughout the eighteenth century, planters performed their wealth and status with imported props that were clearly beyond the means of most men in the colony. Revealing both a man's taste and the soundness of his finances, furniture, table settings, food, clothing, and well-dressed wives provided tangible evidence of gentility.

Travel and sociability

Whether their journeys took them across several counties or simply to the county courthouse, Virginians performed and reconstituted their gender and class identities as they traveled. With the exception of elite women, whose social contacts were circumscribed by gender, class position, and the organization of labor in their households, nonelite women and men of all classes frequently encountered each other in court, on the road, and in taverns. Travel and the social interactions incumbent upon it might mean different things, however, depending upon whether one was male or female, white or black, wealthy, subsisting, or impoverished. To travel alone, stay overnight at an inn, or attend a horse race entailed different risks for women than it did for wealthy planters. Whereas a gentleman might expect and find gratifying a certain degree of intimacy in encounters with people he considered his social inferiors, these same overtures might be deemed rude or presumptuous under other circumstances or if the lone traveler was an elite woman. Not all destinations were equally accessible to all travelers, moreover. Within male-dominated public spaces, men interacted in carefully scripted and ritualized ways, reenacting status distinctions that women expressed in domestic contexts through their clothing and labor.

In a society of far-flung rural settlements where travel was both frequent and extended, a person's mode of transportation reflected social and economic position and, for men, their masculinity and mastery. By the early eighteenth century, most elite planters distinguished themselves on the colony's dusty and poorly kept roads with fine horses and coaches that were used exclusively for the transportation of the white family and its guests. The quality of a man's riding mount was easily found out when he traveled with friends or lent his horse to a visitor. In their youth, elite men such as William Byrd II traveled by horseback when they went to visit neighbors or journeyed to the colonial capital to participate in the meetings of the Governor's Council. As an older man, Byrd traveled mainly in his coach or chaise. Female guests, relatives, and family members rode sidesaddle for short distances to visit friends, neighbors, and kin but might take the family's coach for extended trips. When Maria and Evelyn Byrd came to meet the family patriarch at the end of his dividing line adventure, they arrived in a sedan chair. . . .

Just as hospitality reflected upon the mistress and master of the house to different degrees, so, too, patterns of sociability varied by gender, class, and race. Social visits proceeded at a frantic pace for men like William Byrd II, who welcomed guests into his home nearly every day, sometimes several at a time. When not entertaining, Byrd was off on his horse to enjoy a drink or a meal at a friend's house. In light of his sporadic resolutions to enjoy a quieter life, his frenetic sociability seems to have had an almost addictive quality. Elite women enjoyed the leisure time to make frequent social calls but found the length and duration of their trips constrained by the difficulty of securing appropriate accommodations and by domestic responsibilities.... Hampered by the need to stay in respectable homes with friends and relatives rather than in public lodgings where they might suffer close contact with an unsavory stranger, elite women circumscribed their travels....

For a woman traveling the colony's highways and entering public spaces, freedom of movement came at considerable cost. If she was not clearly identifiable as the wife or daughter of a gentleman or if she traveled alone, a woman risked being deemed sexually available by the men she met. Her incursion into male homosocial spaces – taverns and, to a lesser degree, the colony's highways – signified that she lacked respectability.... [T]he greater a woman's social, racial, and actual distance from the patriarchal and protected world of the elite planter's family, the more likely she was to become fair game for any white man who caught her alone. Being alone was indeed one of the keys to a nonelite woman's vulnerability to other men....

Of nonelite people, slaves and servants had the least freedom of movement and leisure for visiting and could not count on the accommodations of public houses or wealthy friends. Risking the sanctions of masters and night watches, enslaved people traveled short distances in the evenings to visit neighboring plantations. These gatherings aroused the suspicion of white residents who usually spent the evenings drinking and letting down their guard. Enslaved men and women with spouses on distant plantations traveled weekly under the watchful eye of plantation masters. Joseph Ball sent instructions to the overseer of his Lancaster plantation that his slave Jo, for example, should not travel to see his wife more than once a month. The rest of the time, Ball insisted, Jo's wife must journey to him. Such constraints must have been extremely difficult for enslaved women, who were often responsible for children and extremely vulnerable while they traveled.

White men, in contrast, most fully enjoyed the prerogative of free movement on the king's highways and the convenience of readily available – albeit often unappealing – food and lodging at public houses and, if they were gentlemen, at planters' homes. The importance of travel to the business of growing and selling tobacco, participating in politics, and buying and protecting slave property meant that white men needed to move about unchallenged, making it quite likely that individuals of vastly different backgrounds might come into intimate contact. By scrutinizing each other's clothing, the quality of their horses if they had them, their military titles, their deportment, and their speech (which reflected education as well as place of birth), white men determined how to behave toward one another.

Male public culture

Virginia's white men enjoyed closer bonds than those afforded by bumping into each other on the highways or "pigging" together in the same bed. They participated in a common public and homosocial culture, marked by activities such as horse racing, cockfighting, wrestling, drinking, gambling, and events such as court days and militia musters. Such activities provided a ritualized outlet for competition between white propertyholders that stopped short of armed combat. Militia musters and court days, meanwhile, rearticulated social hierarchies by assigning different roles to white men according to their actual position as laborers, masters of households, propertyholders, or county officers.

The foundation underpinning these public displays of white male prowess was propertyownership. Propertied white men were entitled, even expected, to participate in public events while other men – the old, the very young, the infirm, the unfree – and women served as witnesses. Although spectatorship was itself a form of participation, it offered audiences only a limited means to complicate the social relationships being tested. No matter how it was resolved, the contest provided spectators and participants alike with a reassuring confirmation of male propertyowners' importance to the social order.

White men pitted themselves against each other in the representational form of horses, fighting birds, or the property backing a wager. They also competed in matches of strength, such as wrestling or footracing, and those of skill, including fiddling, archery, dancing, or card playing. None of these embodiments of self was far-fetched for elite men who depended upon material trappings and tangible signs of status to confirm their sense of social legitimacy. The intricacies of these contests, moreover, mimicked wealthy planters' daily "games" of playing the tobacco market or jockeying for political preferment. For nonelite white men, meanwhile, competitions of strength and skill offered an opportunity to flaunt manliness publicly in an arena in which the size of an estate did not always determine the victor. ... In all instances of competition, a white planter placed his social self at risk in the hopes that his position would be confirmed. To suffer defeat was to experience, at least briefly, a sense of social death that some might have considered as baneful as taking a loss on a tobacco crop or losing the favor of the colonial governor.

Events like horse races were not a complete free-for-all, however, in which all men competed as equals. Rather, white men tended to compete in somewhat homogeneous groups, with gentlemen gambling among themselves and guarding horse racing as an exclusive privilege. The size of the wagers effectively barred many nonelite men from participating in the betting that accompanied horse races or card games. During the late seventeenth century, moreover, laborers and artisans who owned little property were legally prohibited from racing horses. Although, by the eighteenth century, ordinary planters had made greater inroads into this culture, its origins lay in the wealth of the gentry, its growing self-consciousness as a class, and the competition of its members for social legitimacy. . . .

In contrast to horse races, militia musters represented an idealized version of elite male visions of the social order in which every man and his place were clearly evident from his title and all were subjected to an overarching and unambiguous military hierarchy. A wealthy planter such as Byrd would normally serve as commander in chief over the militia of the county. At the governor's order, the commander would muster the militia in a field for parades or in response to an alarm. Men of substance received commissions as officers; other propertied planters would form a troop of horses. Less well-to-do white men would comprise "a company of foot." Finally, free black men would appear unarmed and be required to play the bugle or drums. . . .

The militia muster's recapitulation of the social order has been read by some historians as a microcosm of society in eighteenth-century Virginia, but such a reading neglects to probe the nature and meaning of the distortion inherent in the muster. Although colonial Virginia was male-dominated, it was not an exclusively male society. Nonelite women appeared frequently in otherwise male public places, as did gentlewomen, although somewhat less frequently and accompanied by an appropriate escort. Gentlewomen, moreover, remained capable of rejecting offers of marriage, thereby foiling the plans of men who had laid their estates and themselves on the line. Rather than representing the realities of this social order in miniature, the militia muster conformed to a view of society in which elite men's authority and supremacy over other men was obvious, legitimate, and unchallenged by women. The muster, in other words, celebrated a world in which men ranked themselves against other men as individuals, unconnected to women. . . .

The public, homosocial nature of white male culture signified an important difference between the situations of men and women in the colony. Whereas white men negotiated both individual identities and male communality publicly – for example, by owning the most aggressive fighting bird but being able to gain prestige from it only by participating in an all-comers cockfight – white women did not have these means at their disposal. If they were wealthy, moreover, women's public appearances and domestic lives were constrained by the need to enhance a husband's prestige. Although they did appear publicly at occasions such as balls and weddings, these forays were carefully mediated by men, to whom the status conveyed by women's presence ultimately redounded....

There was no equivalent for white women of the homosocial public culture enjoyed by white men, an asymmetry that seems to have resulted from a combination of fears about unescorted female travel and constraints on women's access to public places. William Byrd II offered perhaps the best summary of elite men's desires to contain their women in an anecdote recorded in his commonplace book: "A woman should not appear out of her house, til she is old enough for people to enquire whose mother she is, and not so young as to have it askt, whose wife she is, or whose daughter."[14]

Byrd's commentary captured the reasons why a woman's public visibility was deemed so undesirable by men. When a woman appeared in public alone, her relationships to particular men – her father, her husband – became less apparent. Her ability to make men wonder "whose wife she is" threatened to disturb the scripting of male hierarchies. Female access to public space, moreover, compromised women's symbolic value to men, jeopardizing the fiction that men imprinted independently derived public identities upon the persons of their wives. Plantation architecture and the militia muster perpetuated this fiction, masking the very real dependence of male status upon successful alliances with women.

Only when she was past the age of courtship and childbearing, in Byrd's opinion, could a gentlewoman be granted the freedom to leave the house as she wished. At that point, she was no longer capable of offering contradictory or compromising images of her husband to public view. Byrd's advice to elite women reflected a male vision of control in which the erasure of women from public spaces and their containment in plantation houses protected both fragile male constructions of self and the carefully scripted communality of male public culture.

Notes

1 Robert Beverley, *The History and Present State of Virginia* (1705), ed. Louis B. Wright (Chapel Hill, NC, 1947), p. 9.

2 Philip Ludwell to his son, Oct. 20, 1707, Lee Family Papers, VHS [Virginia Historical Society, Richmond].

3 . . . William Byrd, *Another Secret Diary of William Byrd of Westover, 1739–1741, with Letters and Literary Exercises, 1696–1726*, ed. Maude H. Woodfin (Richmond, Va., 1942), p. 175.

4 Richard Bland Lee Papers, 1700–1825, July 6, 1750, p. 377, LC [Library of Congress].

5 See *Virginia Gazette*, Nov. 19, 1736, for the marriage of Ralph Wormeley, "a young Gentleman of a fine Estate," to the "celebrated Miss Salley Berkeley, a young Lady of Great Beauty, and Fortune."

6 Beverley, *History and Present State of Virginia*, ed. Wright, p. 299.

7 Marion Tinling (ed.), *The Correspondence of the Three William Byrds of Westover Virginia, 1684–1776* (Charlottesville, 1977), ii, p. 355.

8 Joseph Ball Letterbook, Colonial Williamsburg transcript, Williamsburg, Va., May 13, 1754, p. 138.

9 Stiverson and Butler (eds.), "Virginia in 1732," *Virginia Magazine of History and Biography*, 85 (1977), p. 30.

10 Beverley, *History and Present State of Virginia*, ed. Wright, p. 312.

11 William Byrd, *The Great American Gentleman: William Byrd of Westover in Virginia, his Secret Diary for the Years 1709–1712*, ed. Louis B. Wright and Marion Tinling (New York, 1963), pp. 69, 108, 407.

12 William Byrd, *William Byrd's Histories of the Dividing Line betwixt Virginia and North Carolina* (Raleigh, NC, 1929), pp. 33, 77.

13 Carter to James Bradley, May 22, 1731, Robert Carter Letterbook, 1728–31; Byrd, *Secret Diary*, ed. Wright and Tinling, p. 298.

14 William Byrd II Commonplace Book, 1722–1737, p. 50, VHS.

4
Slavery and the American Revolution

Introduction

During the eighteenth century, the ideas of the Enlightenment spread from Europe to America. Its basic principles condemned cruelty and emphasized natural rights, toleration of differences, political liberty, freedom of religion, and equality before the law. This influence was a decisive factor which – together with the Great Awakening – led to a significant improvement in the treatment of slaves. During the same period, capitalist ways of thinking about economies gained influence. According to classical capitalist thought, labor should be free, and labor relations were best based on the mutual agreement of consenting parties. Slavery violated all the basic tenets of classical capitalism, based as it was on coerced labor and violence. Partly for these reasons, slavery started to be seen as an economically inefficient system. At the same time, it seemed that slavery brought about a general degradation of society, since poorer whites appeared to absorb much of the "laziness" of slaves and exhibit an aversion to manual labor. The moral and the economic arguments against slavery formed an important background to the general contraction experienced by the South's slave system during the Revolutionary era.

When the Revolutionary War reached the South, a few planters, such as South Carolina's Colonel John Laurens, proposed enrolling slaves in the Patriot Army, promising freedom at the end of the war. In general, war brought widespread destruction, and British depredations led to a serious economic crisis, as properties were confiscated and discipline on plantations was lost. In 1775, Virginia governor Lord Dunmore promised freedom to all slaves ready to fight on the British side against the rebellious Americans. Although many slaves took the chance to flee, only a relatively small number joined the British Army.

Throughout the war, thousands of slaves seized the opportunity to run away, while their masters were away fighting the war and while there was a general disruption of the economic and social system. In the Chesapeake, the war dealt another blow to an economy already shaky because of the 1760s crisis in tobacco production. As a consequence, manumission rates increased, and restrictions on slave movement and employment eased considerably. Many slaves, who had earned the trust of their masters, were hired out for particular jobs, often those requiring a certain degree of skill, and thus broadened their horizons and experienced unprecedented freedom from white supervision.

After the Revolution, most white intellectuals were convinced that slavery was morally wrong and would eventually die out, especially if assisted by gradual measures designed to facilitate emancipation without provoking a sudden change in society. Several states in the upper South passed special laws easing manumission between the 1780s and the 1790s; thousands of blacks were freed in Delaware, Maryland, and Virginia. At the same time, by 1804, virtually every state in the North had provided for complete slave emancipation. The most important consequences of the adverse attitude toward slavery were the compromises reached by northern Congressmen with southern planters in the debate over the drafting of the Constitution. Congress established the year 1808 for the end of the importation of African slaves into the United States. However, in other respects, the Founding Fathers were extremely cautious and at times hypocritical with regard to slavery, avoiding use of the term in the Constitution, allowing masters to reclaim fugitive slaves, and accepting a compromise by which congressional representation of a slave counted as 3/5 of a free person, thereby increasing the power of southern states in Congress.

The ambivalent attitude of the Revolutionary and post-Revolutionary generation toward slavery can be seen in Thomas Jefferson. Like many of his generation, Jefferson took for granted that slaves belonged to an inferior race, but was always convinced that slavery was wrong, not because of the suffering it inflicted upon blacks, but rather because it was dangerous and deleterious for whites. After the Revolution, he was convinced that slavery was near extinction for economic and social reasons. However, when, in the early nineteenth century, he saw the South recovering from its economic crisis and the movement against slavery retreating, he abandoned his previous convictions and embraced a paternalistic position toward his slaves. In 1820, he declared about slavery, "we have the wolf by the ears and we can neither hold him, nor safely let him go. Justice is in one scale, and self-preservation in the other."

Further reading

Berlin, I., *Many Thousands Gone: The First Two Centuries of Slavery in North America* (Cambridge, Mass., and London: The Belknap Press of Harvard University Press, 1998).

Berlin, I. and Hoffman R. (eds.), *Slavery and Freedom in the Age of the American Revolution* (Charlottesville: University Press of Virginia, 1983).

Blackburn, R., *The Overthrow of Colonial Slavery, 1776–1848* (London: Verso, 1988).

Davis, D. B., *The Problem of Slavery in the Age of Revolution, 1770–1823* (Ithaca, NY: Cornell University Press, 1975).

Frey, S. R., *Water from the Rock: Black Resistance in a Revolutionary Age* (Princeton: Princeton University Press, 1991).

Klein, R. N., *Unification of a Slave State: The Rising of the Planter Class in the South Carolina Backcountry, 1760–1808* (Chapel Hill: University of North Carolina Press, 1990).

MacLeod, D. J., *Slavery, Race, and the American Revolution* (New York: Cambridge University Press, 1974).

Miller, J. C., *The Wolf by the Ears: Thomas Jefferson and Slavery* (New York: Free Press, 1977).

Wood, G., *The Radicalism of the American Revolution* (New York: Random House, 1992).

Lord Dunmore's Proclamation Freeing the Slaves in Virginia (1775)

From the outset, the Revolutionary War offered new possibilities of freedom for African American slaves. British officials intended to hit southern economy and society by disrupting the slave system. In 1775, after capturing Williamsburg, Governor Lord Dunmore issued a proclamation which freed all the slaves who joined the British Army. Therefore, the only slaves who were freed were the patriots' slaves, who passed to Britain, while the loyalists' slaves were left in bondage. In 1779, a subsequent proclamation by British Commander-in-Chief Sir Henry Clinton gave freedom to every slave – North and South – who joined the British Army. In spite of this, out of the 15,000 to 20,000 blacks who fled to the British side, only about 1,000 became British soldiers; the rest simply seized the opportunity to escape from their masters.

As I have ever entertained Hopes that an Accommodation might have taken Place between GREAT-BRITAIN and this colony, without being compelled by my Duty to this most disagreeable but now absolutely necessary Step, rendered so by a Body of armed Men unlawfully assembled, bring on His MAJESTY'S [Tenders], and the formation of an Army, and that Army now on their March to attack His MAJESTY'S troops and destroy the well disposed Subjects of this Colony. To defeat such unreasonable Purposes, and that all such Traitors, and their Abetters, may be brought to Justice, and that the Peace, and good Order of this Colony may be again restored, which the ordinary Course of the Civil Law is unable to effect; I have thought fit to issue this my Proclamation, hereby declaring, that until the aforesaid good Purposes can be obtained, I do in Virtue of the Power and Authority to ME given, by His MAJESTY, determine to execute Martial Law, and cause the same to be executed throughout this Colony: and to the end that Peace and good Order may the sooner be [effected], I do require every Person capable of bearing Arms, to [resort] to His MAJESTY'S STANDARD, or be looked upon as Traitors to His MAJESTY'S Crown and Government, and thereby become liable to the Penalty the Law inflicts upon such Offences; such as forfeiture of Life, confiscation of Lands, &c. &c. And I do hereby further declare all indentured Servants, Negroes, or others,

---

Source: Paul Escott and David Goldfield (eds.), *Major Problems in the History of the American South*, vol. 1: *The Old South*, 1st edn. (Lexington, Mass.: D. C. Heath, 1991), pp. 153–4

(appertaining to Rebels,) free that are able and willing to bear Arms, they joining His MAJESTY'S Troops as soon as may be, for the more speedily reducing this Colony to a proper Sense of their Duty, to His MAJESTY'S Leige Subjects, to retain their [Qui?rents], or any other Taxes due or that may become due, in their own Custody, till such Time as Peace may be again restored to this at present most unhappy Country, or demanded of them for their former salutary Purposes, by Officers properly authorised to receive the same.

GIVEN under my Hand on board the ship WILLIAM, off NORPOLE, the 7th Day of NOVEMBER, in the SIXTEENTH Year of His MAJESTY'S Reign.

DUNMORE.

(GOD save the KING.)

George Corbin's Manumission of Slaves by Will (1787)

One of the most important consequences of the American Revolution for slavery was the increase in the rate of manumissions. Until 1770, slaveholders could manumit – or legally free – their slaves only with the permission of the colonial assemblies. When the war started, several slave-owners manumitted their slaves in exchange for their enlistment in the Revolutionary militias. By the time the Revolution ended, practical circumstances and humanitarian concerns had combined to prompt an increasing number of slaveholders to free their slaves. Manumission reached its highest rates in the northern states, where slavery was abolished everywhere by 1804. In the South, manumission had its highest peak of popularity in the immediate post-Revolutionary period; then, it gradually waned.

Will of George Corbin, 25 September 1787*
Accomack County Deeds, No. 6, 1783–1788*

To all Christian People to whom these presents shall come, Greeting Know Ye that I George Corbin . . . for divers good Causes and Consider-

Source: *Primary Source Documents from the Collections at the Library of Virginia Compiled for Educational Use* (The Library of Virginia, 1997–8) at Web Site: http://www.lva.lib.va.us/k12

ations me hereunto moving but more Especially from Motives of Humanity, Justice, and Policy, and as it is Repugnant to Christianity and even common Honesty to live in Ease and affluence by the Labour of those whom fraud and Violence have Reduced to Slavery; (altho' sanctifyed by General consent, and supported by the law of the Land) Have, and by these presents do manumit and set free the following Persons. James, Betty Senior, Jenny Senior, Joshua, son, Betty Junior, Bob, Jarry, Spencer, Levin [Sevin?], Abel, Peter, Parker, Lithco, Alicia, Hannah, Amey, Esther, Jenny Junior, Sue, Bob, Liddia, and Will; and that the Identity of the aforesaid persons may in future be better known, and thereby their Right to freedom firmly secured, I do hereby affix to Each and every one of them the Sirname of Godfree Have and I do hereby for myself my heirs, Executors, and Administrators relinquish all my right or Title of in and unto the Persons aforesaid and their increase forever...; Reserving only to myself... the power of holding the Young ones who are under lawful age in such manner only as negroes born free.

(excerpt)

Thomas Jefferson Expresses his Unease over Slavery (1794)

No document better illustrates the ambiguous attitude of the post-Revolutionary generation toward slavery than Thomas Jefferson's *Notes on the State of Virginia*. As the most prominent revolutionary ideologue and a large planter owning more than 200 slaves, Jefferson understood better than anybody the contradiction between the ideals of the young American Republic and the existence of slavery. He personally disliked the institution and opposed it on moral grounds. Yet, as this excerpt shows, like many of his contemporaries, he harbored a profound racial prejudice against African Americans; he thought of them as lazy, unintelligent compared to whites, and inclined "to participate more of sensation than reflection." In the end, he thought that the best solution to the problem of the presence of slaves in America was to free them and return them to Africa, where they could not corrupt white society and customs.

Source: Thomas Jefferson, *Notes on the State of Virginia* (Philadelphia: Matthew Carey, 1794), pp. 187, 198–210, 236–8

[...] The first difference which strikes us is that of colour. Whether the black of the negro resides in the reticular membrane between the skin and scarf-skin, or in the scarf-skin itself; whether it proceeds from the colour of the blood, the colour of the bile, or from that of some other secretion, the difference is fixed in nature, and is as real as if its seat and cause were better known to us. And is this difference of no importance? Is it not the foundation of a greater or less share of beauty in the two races? Are not the fine mixtures of red and white, the expressions of every passion by greater or less suffusions of colour in the one, preferable to that eternal monotony, which reigns in the countenances, that immoveable veil of black which covers all the emotions of the other race? Add to these, flowing hair, a more elegant symmetry of form, their own judgment in favour of the whites, declared by their preference of them, as uniformly as is the preference of the Oranootan for the black women over those of his own species. The circumstance of superior beauty, is thought worthy attention in the propagation of our horses, dogs, and other domestic animals; why not in that of man? Besides those of colour, figure, and hair, there are other physical distinctions proving a difference of race. They have less hair on the face and body. They secrete less by the kidnies, and more by the glands of the skin, which gives them a very strong and disagreeable odour. This greater degree of transpiration renders them more tolerant of heat, and less so of cold, than the whites. Perhaps too a difference of structure in the pulmonary apparatus, which a late ingenious (* 1) experimentalist has discovered to be the principal regulator of animal heat, may have disabled them from extricating, in the act of inspiration, so much of that fluid from the outer air, or obliged them in expiration, to part with more of it. They seem to require less sleep. A black, after hard labour through the day, will be induced by the slightest amusements to sit up till midnight, or later, though knowing he must be out with the first dawn of the morning. They are at least as brave, and more adventuresome. But this may perhaps proceed from a want of forethought, which prevents their seeing a danger till it be present. When present, they do not go through it with more coolness or steadiness than the whites. They are more ardent after their female: but love seems with them to be more an eager desire, than a tender delicate mixture of sentiment and sensation. Their griefs are transient. Those numberless afflictions, which render it doubtful whether heaven has given life to us in mercy or in wrath, are less felt, and sooner forgotten with them. In general, their existence appears to participate more of sensation than reflection. To this must be ascribed their disposition to sleep when abstracted from their diversions, and unemployed in labour. An animal whose body is at rest, and who does not reflect, must be disposed to sleep of course. Comparing them by their faculties of memory, reason, and imagination, it appears to me, that in memory they are equal to the whites; in reason much inferior, as I think one could scarcely be found capable of tracing and comprehending the investigations of Euclid; and that in imagination they are dull, tasteless, and anomalous.... [N]ever yet could I find that a black had uttered a thought above the level of plain narration; never see even an elementary trait of painting or sculpture. In music they are more generally gifted than the whites with accurate ears for tune and time, and they have been found capable of imagining a small catch (* 2). Whether they will be equal to the composition of a more extensive run of melody, or of complicated harmony, is yet to be proved. Misery is often the parent of the most affecting touches in poetry. – Among the blacks is misery enough, God knows, but no poetry. Love is the peculiar oestrum of the poet. Their love is ardent, but it kindles the senses only, not the imagination.... It is not their condition then, but nature, which has produced the distinction. – Whether further observation will or will not verify the conjecture, that nature has been less bountiful to them in the endowments of the head, I believe that in those of the heart she will be found to have done them justice. That disposition to theft with which they have been branded, must be ascribed to their situation, and not to any depravity of the moral sense. The man, in whose favour no laws of property exist, probably feels himself less bound to respect those made in favour of others. When arguing for ourselves, we lay it down as a fundamental, that laws, to be just, must give a reciprocation of right: that, without this, they are mere arbitrary rules of conduct, founded in force, and not in conscience: and it is a problem which I give to the master to solve, whether the religious precepts against the violation of property were not framed for him as well as his slave? And whether the slave may not as justifiably take a little from one, who has taken all from him, as he may slay one who would slay him? That a change in the relations in which a man is placed should change his ideas of moral right and wrong, is neither new, nor peculiar to the colour of the blacks. Homer tells us it was so 2600 years ago....

But the slaves of which Homer speaks were whites. Notwithstanding these considerations which must weaken their respect for the laws of property, we find among them numerous instances of the most rigid integrity, and as many as among their better instructed masters, of benevolence, gratitude, and unshaken fidelity. – The opinion, that they are inferior in the faculties of reason and imagination, must be hazarded with great diffidence.... I advance it therefore as a suspicion only, that the blacks, whether originally a distinct race, or made distinct by time and circumstances, are inferior to the whites in the endowments both of body and mind. It is not against experience to suppose, that different species of the same genus, or varieties of the same species, may possess different qualifications. Will not a lover of natural history then, one who views the gradations in all the races of animals with the eye of philosophy, excuse an effort to keep those in the department of man as distinct as nature has formed them? This unfortunate difference of colour, and perhaps of faculty, is a powerful obstacle to the emancipation of these people. Many of their advocates, while they wish to vindicate the liberty of human nature, are anxious also to preserve its dignity and beauty. Some of these, embarrassed by the question "What further is to be done with them?" join themselves in opposition with those who are actuated by sordid avarice only. Among the Romans emancipation required but one effort. The slave, when made free, might mix with, without staining the blood of his master. But with us a second is necessary, unknown to history. When freed, he is to be removed beyond the reach of mixture . . .

. . . There must doubtless be an unhappy influence on the manners of our people produced by the existence of slavery among us. The whole commerce between master and slave is a perpetual exercise of the most boisterous passions, the most unremitting despotism on the one part, and degrading submissions on the other. Our children see this, and learn to imitate it; for man is an imitative animal. This quality is the germ of all education in him. From his cradle to his grave he is learning to do what he sees others do. If a parent could find no motive either in his philanthropy or his self-love, for restraining the intemperance of passion towards his slave, it should always be a sufficient one that his child is present. But generally it is not sufficient. The parent storms, the child looks on, catches the lineaments of wrath, puts on the same airs in the circle of smaller slaves, gives a loose to his worst of passions, and thus nursed, educated, and daily exercised in tyranny, cannot but be stamped by it with odious peculiarities. The man must be a prodigy who can retain his manners and morals undepraved by such circumstances. And with what execration should the statesman be loaded, who permitting one half the citizens thus to trample on the rights of the other, transforms those into despots, and these into enemies, destroys the morals of the one part, and the amor patriae of the other. For if a slave can have a country in this world, it must be any other in preference to that in which he is born to live and labour for another: in which he must lock up the faculties of his nature, contribute as far as depends on his individual endeavours to the evanishment of the human race, or entail his own miserable condition on the endless generations proceeding from him. With the morals of the people, their industry also is destroyed. For in a warm climate, no man will labour for himself who can make another labour for him. This is so true, that of the proprietors of slaves a very small proportion indeed are ever seen to labour. . . .

Slavery and the American Revolution

Peter Kolchin

Peter Kolchin's *American Slavery, 1619–1877* is a survey of the slave experience from the arrival of the first blacks in the Chesapeake in 1619 to Reconstruction; its focus is on the transformations that slavery underwent as an institution and on the consequent changes in the master–slave relationship. A particularly strong part of Kolchin's synthetic work is dedicated to the colonial and Revolutionary periods. In this excerpt, Kolchin argues that for the first time during the Revolutionary era slavery became a serious social issue, because of both the influence of Enlightenment ideas and classical capitalism and the antislavery attitude of dissenting religious denominations such as the Quakers. The Revolutionary rhetoric of liberty and the disruptions of the Revolutionary War further challenged an economic and social system which many educated members of the elite considered on the verge of extinction. The antislavery momentum had its most important consequence in the abolition of slavery in every northern state by 1804.

I

The Revolutionary era witnessed the first major challenge to American slavery. Almost overnight, it seemed, an institution that had long been taken for granted came under intense scrutiny and debate: critics questioned its efficacy and morality, proponents rushed to its defense, and thousands of slaves took advantage of wartime turmoil to flee their bondage. Tangible results of this challenge included the abolition of slavery in the North, a sharp increase in the number of free blacks in the upper South, and the ending of the African slave trade. Despite these developments, however, slavery in the Southern states emerged from the agitation of the era largely unscathed. Indeed, for all the talk of natural rights, manumission, and abolishing imports from Africa, the slave population of the new nation in 1810 was more than twice what it had been in 1770.

II

Until the middle of the eighteenth century there was little questioning in the colonies – or anywhere else, for that matter – of slavery. For centuries,

Peter Kolchin, *American Slavery, 1619–1877* (New York: Hill & Wang, 1993), pp. 63–92.

a wide range of social thinkers had seen the institution as fully compatible with human progress and felicity. Aristotle, Thomas Aquinas, and John Locke differed from one another in many ways, but the three, proponents respectively of reason, Christian theology, and liberty, agreed in finding slavery an acceptable part of the social order. In the seventeenth and early eighteenth centuries, only a handful of thinkers in the British colonies dared challenge this long-standing consensus; the most notable early criticism of slavery came from the pen of Massachusetts judge Samuel Sewall, whose cautious pamphlet *The Selling of Joseph* (1700) elicited an immediate and forceful rebuttal (*A Brief and Candid Answer*) from merchant-politician John Saffin. This was, however, an isolated exchange that made little impression upon contemporaries, few of whom bothered either to defend or to attack slavery. Largely taken for granted, the institution was simply not much of an issue for the white colonists.

Where slavery did compel attention, it was almost always over pragmatic considerations involving the utility of particular policies, not the morality of human bondage. The first substantial movement in defense of slavery occurred in newly settled Georgia, where for a variety of practical reasons – chief of which was concern that the Spanish in Florida would incite slave revolt among their neighbors to the North – an act of 1735 barred slaves from the colony; proponents of slavery, who stressed the necessity of black labor for the prosperity of the semitropical colony, carried the day by 1750, when the prohibition was lifted. Other colonies, however, worried about the threat to security posed by too many slaves. As planter William Byrd II noted in 1736, in praising Georgia's prohibition on slavery, too many slaves produced "the necessity of being severe," for "numbers make them insolent" and their "base Tempers require to be rid with a tort Reign, or they will be apt to throw their Rider." Lamenting that "this is terrible to a good naturd Man," Byrd opined that "the farther Importation of them in Our Colonys should be prohibited lest they prove as troublesome and dangerous everywhere, as they have been lately in Jamaica."[1] Precisely such fears – supplemented by the desire to raise money – prompted several colonies to pass import duties on slaves, beginning in the 1690s.

In the Revolutionary era, slavery for the first time became a serious social issue. Relatively few people called for its immediate abolition, but many, including some slave owners, expressed real concern over its morality as well as its utility. This questioning of slavery, even when it did not lead to clear-cut support for universal emancipation, represented a significant departure from the general neglect of the subject that had previously prevailed. The challenge to an established institution in turn elicited vigorous protests from those convinced that their interests, and the social fabric in general, were being recklessly threatened.

A variety of factors converged, beginning in the third quarter of the eighteenth century and accelerating during the Revolutionary War, to produce this development. Perhaps most basic was a fundamental shift that occurred in the middle decades of the eighteenth century, under the influence of the Enlightenment thought that flourished among Western European and American intellectuals, in attitudes toward cruelty, rights, fair play, and toleration of differences: in short, how human beings should treat one another. Because of this pervasive shift, these years must be regarded as a kind of watershed, separating the modern from the pre-modern eras. Seventeenth-century settlers in the colonies – and usually their children as well – lived in a world that took for granted stocks and tongue-borings, religious proscriptions, fear of witches, and savage repression of the lower orders. The Founding Fathers who led the American Revolution spoke instead of natural rights, political liberty, freedom of religion, and equality before the law. In this new intellectual climate, the treatment, and even the ownership, of slaves became a pertinent subject.

Especially significant were changing notions of what constituted legitimate treatment of those who were poor, weak, or different. A new concern for humane treatment – symbolized by the stricture in the Eighth Amendment to the United States Constitution against "cruel and unusual punishments" – led to a sharp decrease in the use of corporal punishment on free adults. Although this decrease did not extend to slaves (or children), heightened attention to the mistreatment of slaves was evident both among outsiders shocked by the barbarities they witnessed and among resident masters concerned with the lives of their people. This opposition to the physical mistreatment of slaves did not necessarily lead to opposition to slavery itself; indeed, in the antebellum years, accentuating the humane treatment of slaves became a prime concern of the peculiar institution's defenders, who believed that by softening slavery they would render it more secure. Still, attention to treatment was a necessary first step in the overall challenge to slavery, because it involved the questioning of established practices; once begun, it was not always clear where such questioning would stop.

Take South Carolina planter and merchant Henry Laurens, whose letters during the 1740s and 1750s were filled with straightforward business comments on the buying and selling of Africans: "please to observe that prime People turn to best Account here," he wrote his supplier in 1757, that "the Males [are] preferable to the Females & that Callabars are not at all liked with us when they are above the Age of 18, Gambias or Gold Coast are prefer'd to others, Windward Coast next to them." By 1763, however, expressing qualms that were increasingly prevalent among others of his generation, Laurens had decided that he "would rather not pursue the African Trade" (although he did not immediately cease participating in it). Later in the year he went further still, agreeing with a Moravian missionary who had written to him complaining that children whose parents owned slaves grew up lazy; Laurens responded that he "wished that our economy & government differ'd from the present system but alas – since our constitution is as it is, what can individuals do?"[2] Within a few years, in action highly atypical of whites in labor-hungry South Carolina, Laurens had moved beyond this cautious disquiet over slavery and decided that individuals could, in fact, make a difference; in 1779, he and his son John, both active Patriots, promoted an unusual (and ultimately unsuccessful) scheme to enroll in the Revolutionary army three thousand slaves who would be freed at the end of the war.

Among intellectuals, a spreading belief in human malleability sparked questions about the grounds for enslaving Africans. In the seventeenth century, English thinkers (on both sides of the Atlantic) had been struck by what they considered the savagery of Africans, and in the first half of the eighteenth century, many white Americans had come to see blacks as innately depraved, fit only for slavery. In the second half of the eighteenth century, however, growing awareness of the cultural diversity of peoples, accompanied by intense interest in the question of human nature, spawned new thinking on the question of black "depravity." Perhaps it was their slave status that created slave-like behavior, rather than the behavior that justified the status; if so, blacks removed from slavery would no longer act like slaves. Because discovery of talented blacks could confirm this environmentalist hypothesis, poet Phillis Wheatley and mathematician Benjamin Banneker received considerable attention during the late eighteenth century; even Thomas Jefferson, who had more doubts than many of his contemporaries about the intellectual potential of blacks and who dismissed Wheatley as a mediocre poet, was impressed by Banneker. "I am happy to be able to inform you that we have now in the United States a negro...who is a very respectable Mathematician," the Virginian wrote the Marquis de Condorcet in 1791. "I shall be delighted to see these instances of moral eminence so multiplied as to prove that the want of talents observed in them is merely the effect of their degraded condition, and not proceeding from any difference in the structure of the parts on which intellect depends."[3]

The spread of capitalism, and the new "dismal science" of economics that it spawned, contributed significantly to the questioning of slavery. Slavery lacked a basic ingredient of capitalism: the free hire of labor through mutual agreement of consenting parties. Substituting the physical coercion of the lash for the economic coercion of the marketplace, slavery thus did violence to the central values implicit in capitalist relations. While most late-eighteenth-century merchants only dimly perceived (or did not perceive at all) the conflict between slavery and a capitalist world view, the logic of belief in free trade and the freedom of the individual to succeed – or fail – on the basis of one's own efforts inexorably led to challenges to slavery's legitimacy. Early political economists – including Adam Smith, whose book *The Wealth of Nations* (1776) remained for decades the most influential justification of the principles underlying capitalism – believed that slavery, by preventing the free buying and selling of labor power and by eliminating the possibility of self-improvement that was the main incentive to productive labor, violated central economic laws; like government regulation of wages, prices, and interest rates, slavery constituted an artificial restraint of trade.

The view that slavery was immoral because it violated fundamental economic law – which eighteenth-century thinkers almost invariably elevated to either natural or divine law – was especially prevalent among the Quakers, who in both Britain and America took the lead first in opposing slavery and then in organizing abolitionist groups to combat it. A small sect dominated by hardworking businessmen "distinguished by their mercantile wealth and above all by their entrepreneurial leadership," Quakers rejected religious authority in favor of an "Inner Light" that would guide each individual to religion and morality; by the 1760s, most had come to view slavery as unethical. To Quakers, the slave represented the diametric opposite of the dependable, orderly, and industrious worker that they strove to create. As prominent Quaker abolitionist John Woolman put it, explaining his response in 1757 to a Virginian who insisted that blacks were too slothful to be free, "I replied, that free Men, whose Minds were properly on their Business, found a Satisfaction in improving, cultivating, and providing for their Families; but Negroes, labouring to support others who claim them as their Property, and expecting nothing but slavery during Life, had not the like Inducement to be industrious."[4] Among Quakers, more than among any other group, environmentalism combined with a capitalist world view and religious sensibilities to produce principled opposition to slavery.

More widespread was the related view that slavery was inefficient and socially degrading to society at large. The germs of the "free labor" critique of slavery that would be fully developed in antebellum years were already present in diverse strains by the middle of the eighteenth century. Planters as different as William Byrd II and Thomas Jefferson joined outside observers in worrying that growing up with slaves made white Southerners lazy, haughty, and overbearing. Others feared that white children would absorb the "brutish" behavior of the blacks who surrounded them and become degraded themselves. But it was the harmful economic impact of slavery that seemed most obvious of all. Planters had long lamented what they considered the slovenly work habits of their slaves, who needed to be coaxed and chided, bribed and beaten to engage in their everyday labor, and in times of pique they had wondered aloud whether plantation management was worth the effort. During the second half of the eighteenth century, such concern was exacerbated in the upper South by the crisis in the tobacco economy.

Economic hardship proved especially conducive to questioning established relations, including slavery; indeed, many outside observers, and some Southerners as well, blamed slavery itself for the economic hardship. New Jersey–born minister-in-training Philip Fithian, who spent 1773–74 in Virginia tutoring the children on Robert Carter III's Nomini Hall plantation, was no abolitionist, but he was convinced that slavery degraded the manners, morals, and work habits of whites and blacks alike. When he broached the subject of "Negroes in Virginia" with Carter's wife (whom he greatly admired), he was pleased to find that "she esteems their value at no higher rate than I do." They agreed that if the slaves were sold, the money loaned out, and the land allowed to lie uncultivated, "the bare Interest of the price of the Negroes would be a much greater yearly income than what is now received from their working the Lands." Fithian's conclusion was pointed: "How much greater then must be the value of an Estate here if these poor enslaved Africans were all in their native desired Country, & in their Room industrious Tenants, who being born in freedom, by a laudable care, would not only inrich their Landlords, but would raise a hardy Offspring to be the Strength & the honour of the Colony."[5]

New religious developments provided a final source of anti-slavery thought. It is not always easy to isolate religious from other motivation in the second half of the eighteenth century, because people so commonly phrased other sentiments in religious terms; a thin line, for example, frequently separated economic law from natural law or divine law in the rhetoric of the time. Nevertheless, it is clear that the religious revivals that began with the Great Awakening in the 1740s and spread through much of the South in the 1770s and 1780s had a major impact on thinking about slavery. Not only did evangelical Christians show a new interest in the souls of the slaves, but they also often displayed real anguish about slavery itself. Especially in the upper South, Methodists and Baptists, who stressed humility, submission, and the equality of all souls before God, seemed ready during the last quarter of the eighteenth century to follow the Quakers into anti-slavery agitation.

Before the outbreak of the Revolutionary War, then, slavery had emerged for the first time as a major issue. Although diverse strains of thought had converged to produce this development, they were in a broad sense related to each other. On both sides of the Atlantic, the third quarter of the eighteenth century saw a remarkable growth of intellectual activity among educated gentlemen – and a much smaller number of ladies – convinced that they represented the dawn of a bright new era. These gentlemen thought, wrote, and exchanged information about an extraordinary range of subjects, from the orbiting of planets and the taxonomy of animal species to human nature and ideal forms of government. Maintaining that the key to progress lay in reason, they questioned established beliefs, such as the divinity of Christ, and established institutions, such as monarchy and hereditary privilege. It is hardly surprising that these modern Renaissance thinkers also questioned slavery.

In America, these were also the men who led the movement for independence and have often been referred to as Founding Fathers. Usually members of the colonial elite, they included lawyers such as John Adams and self-educated artisan-intellectuals such as Benjamin Franklin and Thomas Paine. In the South, however, they were most often wealthy planters. An extraordinary generation of planter-politicians – historian Clement Eaton termed it the "great generation" – led the American states to independence, created a new government, and dominated that government during its early years. Although they ranged from Maryland to Georgia, they were most concentrated in Virginia; one thinks immediately of George Washington, Thomas Jefferson, James Madison, and Patrick Henry (all among the largest slave owners of their day) but could easily add others, such as George Mason and Edmund Randolph. Although these leaders were part of an international community of intellectual-statesmen that even before the outbreak of the American Revolution had come to challenge the legitimacy of slavery, that Revolution would soon lead them to push their challenge substantially further.

III

The Revolutionary War had a major impact on slavery – and on the slaves. Wartime disruption undermined normal plantation discipline, and division within the master class offered slaves unprecedented opportunities that they were not slow in grasping. The Revolution posed the biggest challenge the slave regime would face until the outbreak of the Civil War some eighty-five years later; indeed, it appeared for a while as if the very survival of slavery in the new nation was threatened.

The British wasted little time in reaching out to the slaves as potential allies against the American rebels. On November 7, 1775, Virginia's Governor John Murray, Earl of Dunmore, issued a proclamation offering freedom to all slaves who would bear arms against the rebellion.

Throughout the South, the offer raised understandable panic among slaveholders already fearful for the loyalty of their slaves; "if the Virginians are wise," noted Washington, "that arch traitor... Dunmore should be instantly crushed."[6] Similar concern was evident farther south; three months earlier, Patriots in Charleston had hanged and burned a free black harbor pilot suspected of helping slaves flee to British ships.

As this incident suggests, despite varying responses Americans were unable to come up with a satisfactory way of blunting the British appeal to their slaves. Virginia planter Robert Carter III warned his people that a British victory would result in their being sold into a far more oppressive slavery in the West Indies. A very different approach came from South Carolina Colonel John Laurens, who for both idealistic and pragmatic reasons proposed enrolling up to five thousand slaves in the Patriot army, with freedom promised for them at the war's end; the proposal – scaled back to three thousand slaves – won the eventual endorsement of the colonel's prominent father, Henry Laurens, but was defeated by the South Carolina legislature early in 1782. Some slaves did serve in the Patriot army: Maryland specifically authorized slave enlistments, and several states (North and South) allowed slaves to serve in place of their masters, usually with informal promises of subsequent freedom; New York offered freedom to slaves in return for three years of military service, with a compensatory land bounty to be paid to their owners. Small numbers of *free* blacks served in all states except South Carolina and Georgia, and a few bondsmen enlisted, pretending to be free. Most slaves, however, saw little reason to believe that the War for Independence was their war; it was important to them because it provided many with a new opportunity to escape their own thralldom, not because it pitted the forces of freedom against those of despotism.

Unable or unwilling to compete with the British for the loyalty of their slaves, Southern masters struggled to preserve a threatened way of life. In the Chesapeake region, British depredations of 1775, 1777, and 1781 intensified the existing economic crisis and induced some planters to flee with their slaves to the security of the backcountry or to Kentucky and Tennessee. Wartime destruction was greater still in the South Carolina and Georgia low country. First loyalist planters saw their property plundered by rebel forces; many Tories were able to evacuate their slaves to safer locales (including the West Indies), but others lost some or all of their holdings. Patriots suffered a similar fate after the British captured Savannah in 1778 and Charleston in 1780, and many of the loyalists returned – temporarily, it turned out – to reclaim their slaves. (Some of these slaves wound up fighting the Patriots. At least forty-seven blacks served the British in a Hessian regiment; others worked as scouts, guides, and laborers.)

The destruction, confusion, and loss of authority that accompanied the war provided slaves with numerous opportunities to escape bondage. The absence of able-bodied white males and the proximity of enemy forces produced an abrupt decline in discipline on many farms and plantations throughout the South; slaves were emboldened, and masters complained of a breakdown of order and deference. No mass uprising of slaves occurred in the United States during the American Revolution, the way it did in Saint Domingue during the French, for American slaves lacked the overwhelming numerical advantage enjoyed by their Haitain cousins. Tens of thousands of slaves did, however, take advantage of the wartime disruption to run away. The fugitives faced varying fates.

Dunmore's proclamation unleashed massive flight among slaves in the upper South. On June 25, 1776, nine of Landon Carter's slaves, whom he denounced as "accursed villains," ran away at night, "to be sure," the planter guessed, "to L[or]d. Dunmore"; later he heard a rumor that minutemen shot and killed three of the fugitives. In part because the British governor lacked a land base after December 1775, only a relatively small number of slaves – the usual estimate is eight hundred – reached his forces, and most of these died from disease (especially smallpox); when Dunmore's fleet left the Potomac on August 6, 1776, it carried with it some three hundred fugitive slaves. But these represented only a small fraction of the slaves who had fled, and slaves continued throughout the war to seize any opportunity to run away. Jefferson's "Farm Book" lists some thirty slaves of his who escaped in 1781, with various descriptions such as "joined enemy" or "caught smallpox from enemy & died."[7] Most fugitives fled individually or in very small groups, to avoid detection, but the turmoil and weakened authority that accompanied the Revolution made possible, for the last time until the Civil War, coordinated escapes of whole families and larger groups as well. Upon occasion the population of entire plantations, including all eighty-seven slaves owned by John Willoughby in Norfolk County, Virginia, ran away.

Because disruption was even greater in the lower South, so, too, was opportunity for flight. The scope of both is evident in testimony at the 1807 inventory of a deceased South Carolina planter's estate explaining why his slaves had decreased in number from 172 in 1776 to 132 in 1789: 64 slaves had disappeared one night in 1779, and there followed "years of general . . . calamity, . . . in which all but the particular friends of the British thought themselves fortunate if they could raise provisions, and save their negroes from being carried off."[8] When British forces evacuated Savannah and Charleston at the end of the war, some ten thousand blacks accompanied them. An uncertain future awaited them (and the thousands more removed from New York City): some died, some gained their freedom, and others wound up as slaves elsewhere (usually in the British West Indies).

Estimates vary on the number of people who escaped slavery during the Revolution. Allan Kulikoff has recently suggested that about five thousand slaves from the Chesapeake area and thirteen thousand from South Carolina reached the British, with smaller numbers from North Carolina and Georgia, for a total of some 5 percent of all Southern blacks. (These would have constituted considerably more than 5 percent of black adults and of black males, however, since young adult males were disproportionately represented among the fugitives.) But this figure represents only the tip of the iceberg. Many other slaves fled their owners but did not go over to the British. The extent of the loss to slave owners in the lower South is indicated by the sharp decline between 1770 and 1790 in the proportion of the population made up of blacks (almost all of whom were slaves): from 60.5 percent to 43.8 percent in South Carolina and from 45.2 percent to 36.1 percent in Georgia. Philip D. Morgan has estimated that during the Revolution, South Carolina lost about 25,000 slaves (or about 30 percent of the state's slave population) to flight, migration, and death. When one adds to these imprecise estimates the slaves who were freed by emancipation in the North and private manumissions in the South, one can begin to see the magnitude of the jolt the Revolution provided to American slavery.

The Revolutionary era also brought significant changes to the lives of slaves who did not run away, as both masters and bondspeople strove to make sense of radically new conditions. Some, especially in the North and the upper South, received (or were promised) their freedom (see section IV). Increased autonomy also characterized the daily lives of the majority of Southern blacks who remained slaves. This autonomy took strikingly different forms, however, in the upper and lower South.

In the Chesapeake region, the war dealt an added blow to the already faltering tobacco economy and thus accentuated the surplus of slaves. Slack demand for slaves had many consequences, ranging from the proliferation of private manumissions to the cessation of African imports, but one of the most important was a relaxation in the severity of the slave regime and increased opportunity for individuals – especially males – to escape field work and engage in skilled occupations. In Maryland, according to historian Lorena S. Walsh, "ordinary field hands spent more time in self-sufficient activities such as gardening, hunting, and fishing," while agricultural diversification led to a proliferation of new jobs. "By the end of the century many men were performing a greater variety of tasks," she concluded, "and even on large plantations they sometimes worked on special projects by themselves or with only one or two mates and not always under constant supervision."[9] This relaxation was also facilitated by the increasingly creole character of upper South slaves, whose behavior no longer seemed so "outlandish" to whites as did that of Africans. The largely acculturated slave population enjoyed considerably more "breathing space" than had Africans whose breaking in was thought to require careful supervision of every move.

Slaves who earned the trust of their masters often received increased freedom to dispose of their "spare" time. Those with particular skills were sometimes allowed to hire themselves out, contracting on their own and paying their masters a fixed weekly fee from their earnings, the remainder of which they kept. Far more common were slaves whose masters, having too many hands, hired them out for odd jobs or seasonal work. Although slaves who were hired out were not necessarily treated better than those who were not – hirers had less direct financial incentive than did owners to take good care of their laborers – slave hiring provided slaves with new experiences, contacts (white and black), and knowledge, and broadened their horizons. Trusted slaves visited friends and relatives on nearby holdings and also increasingly interacted with whites in the revival meetings that converted whites and blacks alike to evangelical Christianity. Increased freedom of action for slaves went hand in hand, ironically, with growing contact between white and black.

This loosening of controls in no way implies that slaves had come to accept their servitude, except in the sense that they made the best of the circumstances in which they found themselves. They continued to run away, with fugitives now for the first time having the prospect of securing freedom in the North. And the Gabriel Prosser conspiracy of 1800, a carefully planned but abortive uprising in which thousands of blacks were to attack Richmond, shows the potential for armed rebellion in even the most trusted, "acculturated" slaves. In a number of ways the Prosser uprising, nipped in the bud after being revealed to authorities by a black informer, bears the mark of the Revolutionary age, for if the uprising's planning was facilitated by the easy association and relaxed controls prevalent at the time, its leaders seem to have been influenced by the era's rhetoric of liberty. Perhaps too much should not be made of the conspirators' ideology. Blind hatred of slavery – and of those responsible for it – motivated participants far more than abstract theories of the social good; as one recruit coolly stated, "I could kill a white man as free as eat." Still, a number of reports indicated that the rebels had planned to spare Quakers, Methodists, and Frenchmen because they were "friendly to liberty."[10] Clearly, many black Virginians were aware of the "outside" world – and of the contradiction between the "liberty" their masters invoked and the slavery they practiced.

Slave autonomy in the lower South manifested itself very differently. The coastal low country of South Carolina and Georgia was dominated by a black majority – with a heavy African component – who often saw little of their owners. In two ways the Revolution acted to accentuate this distinctive pattern. Wartime disruption and the military obligations of whites increased the existing tendency toward owner absenteeism and further isolated the slave population from white Southerners; as one historian put it, "wartime anarchy created a power vacuum in the countryside that allowed slaves to expand their liberty."[11] A postwar surge in slave arrivals from Africa, prompted in part by a conscious effort to make up for the heavy wartime losses and in part by a determination to secure as many laborers as possible while the federal government still tolerated the importation of slaves, reinforced this black isolation and sharply differentiated the low country from the Chesapeake, where the turn of the nineteenth century was a time of growing cultural interaction between white and black. During the late eighteenth century, notable features of low-country slave life – owner absenteeism, slave isolation, the task system, the internal slave economy – became more pronounced, even as Gullah took root as the embodiment of the region's cultural distinctiveness.

The Revolutionary era, in short, saw the further differentiation of upper from lower South, although increased slave autonomy characterized both sections. In the Chesapeake region, an overwhelmingly creole slave population lived in close physical and cultural contact with whites, many of whom exercised relatively loose control over their slaves and expressed heightened concern for their physical and spiritual well-being. In the coastal region of the lower South, most blacks lived in a world of their own, largely isolated from whites, and developed their own culture and way of life; into this world poured tens of thousands of Africans imported in a last surge by labor-hungry planters anxious to beat the anticipated cutoff of the slave trade in 1808. Although these regional distinctions would persist in the nineteenth century, the contrast between upper South and lower South would never be so great as it was during the years immediately following the War for Independence.

IV

The Revolutionary era also saw an increasing gap between the South as a whole, where slavery survived the challenge to its legitimacy and remained firmly entrenched, and the North, where slavery gradually gave way to freedom, albeit a severely restrictive freedom. Because the Revolution was waged for "liberty," and generated an enormous amount of rhetoric about despotism, tyranny, justice, equality, and natural rights, it inevitably raised questions about slavery, questions that seemed all the more pertinent in view of the determined efforts of slaves to gain their own freedom, and it is no accident that the United States was the first country to take significant (although ultimately limited) action against the peculiar institution. Patriots commonly denounced the "slavery" they suffered at the hands of the British, and insisted that they would rather die than remain slaves; although there was considerable hyberbole in this rhetoric – clearly Patriots did not believe that they were slaves in the same sense their own chattels were – the irony of fighting a war for liberty at the same time that they held one-third of their own population as slaves was not lost upon them. They might not have liked the way British Tory author Samuel Johnson phrased the matter when he asked rhetorically, "How is it that we hear the loudest *yelps* for liberty among the drivers of negroes?" but they were acutely aware of the problem.[12]

Whites in the Revolutionary era were by no means united on the question of slavery. A few Americans became abolitionists, arguing for the immediate and unconditional freeing of all slaves; although abolition societies emerged in the South as well as the North, they were heavily dominated by Quakers and became progressively rarer as one moved farther south. Others took action to end their own association with what they regarded as an immoral practice, providing freedom for their slaves either immediately or (like George Washington) in their wills. Even among the great majority of slave owners who never freed their slaves, however, there was widespread unease about an institution that seemed backward and unenlightened. Many agreed with Thomas Jefferson that slavery was wrong, both for moral and practical reasons, and would if properly curtailed suffer a gradual and peaceful death.

Indeed, the Founding Fathers took a series of steps designed to bring about slavery's gradual demise. As children of the Enlightenment, they typically abjured hasty or radical measures that would disrupt society, preferring cautious acts that would induce sustained, long-term progress; rather than a frontal assault on the peculiar institution, they favored a strategy of chipping away at it where it was weakest. Still, there seemed reason to believe – although time would ultimately prove otherwise – that these acts had contained American slavery and put it on the road to gradual extinction.

Much of the action on slavery during the Revolutionary era occurred at the state level. In the upper South, the state legislatures of Virginia, Maryland, and Delaware revised their laws on manumission, making it easier during the 1780s and 1790s for masters to free their bondspeople. (From 1723 to 1782, private acts of manumission had been illegal in Virginia.) In those states (and to a lesser extent in North Carolina and in the new state of Kentucky), prompted by both principled opposition to slavery and a reduced demand for labor stemming from the downturn in tobacco cultivation, growing numbers of slave owners took advantage of the new laws to free some or all of their slaves. Some masters manumitted only a few select favorites; others, such as George Washington, John Randolph, and Robert Carter III, provided in their wills for the freedom of all their slaves, thereby securing emotional benefit without suffering financial loss. (Legal complications, however, prevented most of Randolph's and Carter's slaves from ever receiving their freedom, and Washington lacked the legal authority to free the numerous "dower Negroes" belonging to his wife, Martha, from a previous marriage; of 277 Washington slaves, 124 belonged to George at the time of his death in 1799, while 153 belonged to Martha.) A smaller number of slaveholders – often Quakers – followed to the end the logic of their antislavery convictions and freed all their slaves immediately. Acts of private manumission freed thousands of blacks in the upper South following the Revolution, and for the first time, especially in Delaware and parts of Maryland, seemed to threaten the very survival of slavery; in Delaware, three-quarters of all blacks were free by 1810 (see section V, below).

Farther north, state action was more decisive. Because slaves in the Northern states formed only a small proportion of the population and constituted a minor economic interest, abolishing the peculiar institution in an era that celebrated liberty and natural rights proved relatively easy, although often painfully slow. During the three decades following the outbreak of the Revolutionary War, every Northern state initiated complete slave emancipation. The process varied considerably. In some states, emancipation was immediate: the Vermont constitution of 1777 prohibited slavery, and soon thereafter Massachusetts courts, reacting to a series of freedom suits brought by blacks themselves, interpreted that state's constitution as outlawing slavery, too; as the state's chief justice put it in 1781, "there can be no such thing as perpetual servitude of a rational creature."[13] In most Northern states, however, especially those with a significant slave population, emancipation was gradual, so as to provide as little shock to society (and the masters' pocketbooks) as possible. According to Pennsylvania's law of 1780 – the first of five gradual-emancipation acts passed by Northern states – all future-born slaves would become free at age twenty-eight. New York's law of 1799 freed future-born boys at age twenty-eight and girls at twenty-five; New Jersey's act of 1804 (the last emancipation act of a Northern state) was similar, but provided that boys would receive freedom at age twenty-five and girls at twenty-one. Because these gradual-emancipation laws freed no one actually in bondage at the time of their passage, and freed children subsequently born into slavery only when they reached adulthood, the North contained a small number of slaves well into the nineteenth century. By 1810, however, about three-quarters of all Northern blacks were free, and within a generation virtually all would be.

Complementing the abolition acts of individual Northern states was legislation by Congress to restrict the geographical scope of slavery. Because the western territories were largely unsettled (except by Indians), the movement to prohibit the spread of slavery there did not challenge vested interests in the same way that the movement to abolish slavery in existing states did, and received considerable support from those convinced that slavery, although wrong, could not be immediately ended in the South. In 1784, a bill drafted by Jefferson, which would have barred slavery from all the western territories after 1800, was defeated by a single vote. Three years later, the Northwest Ordinance did abolish slavery in a vast area north of the Ohio River known as the Northwest Territory, including the present states of Ohio, Indiana, Illinois, Michigan, and Wisconsin.

The African slave trade, viewed as deplorable even by many defenders of slavery, was also the object of considerable legislation, at both the state and the national level. Widespread opposition to the trade in the North and upper South led the second Continental Congress to pass a resolution opposing slave imports in 1776, and a number of states (including Virginia in 1778) banned such imports on their own. In the upper South, economic depression sharply reduced the demand for new slaves, and the happy convergence of economic interest with principle easily carried the day. Farther south, however, in South Carolina and Georgia, planters suffered from an acute shortage of labor and bitterly resisted what they considered the hypocritical efforts of those who now had enough slaves suddenly to force others to do without.

Although advocates of the slave trade represented a small minority among the Founding Fathers, they were powerful enough to force a compromise on the question at the Constitutional Convention of 1787: the new Constitution prohibited Congress from outlawing the slave trade for twenty years. During this period, labor-hungry planters in the lower South imported tens of thousands of Africans; indeed, more slaves entered the United States between 1787 and 1807 than during any other two decades in history. Still, the general understanding among those who were politically active was that Congress would abolish the slave trade at the end of twenty years, an expectation that was borne out by congressional legislation passed in 1807 and taking effect in 1808. In their usual cautious, roundabout manner, the Founding Fathers succeeded in ending the importation of Africans to the United States; many believed, incorrectly, that this ending would doom slavery in the United States as well.

The Constitutional Convention showed the Founding Fathers at their most cautious with respect to slavery. In drafting the Constitution, they carefully avoided the word "slavery," resorting to a variety of euphemisms such as "other persons" and "person[s] held to service or labor." At the same time, they acceded to slaveholding interests by recognizing the right of masters to reclaim fugitives and by unanimously accepting a compromise formula whereby for purposes of congressional representation a slave would count as three-fifths of a free person, thereby substantially augmenting the political power of the Southern states. In the future, both supporters and opponents of slavery would wrap themselves in the Constitution and claim to be expressing the views of the Founding Fathers. In fact, although most of the decisions taken by the delegates at the Constitutional Convention represented compromises rather than clear-cut victories for pro-slavery or anti-slavery forces, on balance the Constitution bolstered slavery by throwing the power of the federal government behind it.

Still, to many informed Americans in the 1790s, time seemed to be on the side of reason, reform, and progress. The Northern states were in the process of abolishing slavery within their borders. Congress had acted to guarantee that the Northwest would be forever free. The laws of several Southern states had been changed to facilitate private manumissions, and hundreds of slave owners in the upper South were taking advantage of these laws to free some or all of their chattels. And although importation of new slaves remained legal in South Carolina and Georgia, a compromise had been worked out that would end such importation in 1808. In short, a moderate opponent of slavery – like many of the Founding Fathers – had good grounds for being cautiously optimistic. Slavery appeared to be in full retreat, its end only a matter of time.

V

The Revolutionary and post-Revolutionary years saw the emergence, for the first time, of a large community of free blacks. They escaped slavery in a variety of ways, ranging from state-enacted emancipation in the North to private manumissions and flight in the South. Some in the upper South were the beneficiaries of sweeping acts by individual slaveholders who, prompted by newly felt moral qualms, freed all their bondspeople; others were objects of selected manumissions by less idealistic masters – most commonly in the upper South but also in the lower South – of particular favorites (including their own children); others still, especially in the border states, were discharged from bondage because they were old and no longer able to perform useful labor. Slaves who were able to earn money could sometimes purchase their own freedom. Fugitives escaped slavery by fleeing to the North, especially from the border states of Maryland, Delaware, and Kentucky, and by blending with free blacks in cities such as Baltimore and Charleston.

In addition, during the 1790s and 1800s, hundreds of free, light-skinned refugees from Saint Domingue entered the United States, concentrating in Charleston, Savannah, and New Orleans, much to the alarm of local whites.

In sheer numbers, the growth of the free black population was staggering. Although statistics on free blacks before the Revolution are lacking, it is clear that there were few; as late as 1782, only about 1,800 out of 220,582 black Virginians – less than one percent – were free. Between 1780 and 1810, however, the number of free blacks in Virginia surged, reaching 12,766 (4.2 percent) in 1790 and 30,570 (7.2 percent) by 1810. In the United States as a whole, the number of free blacks rose to 59,466 (7.9 percent of all blacks) in 1790 and 186,446 (13.5 percent) in 1810. Over half these free blacks were concentrated in the upper South, where more than 10 percent of all blacks were free by 1810. As a proportion of the black population, however, free blacks were most numerous in the North; by 1810 three-quarters of Northern blacks were free, and by 1840 virtually all were. In the lower South, by contrast, the number of free blacks grew far more modestly, from 1.6 percent of the black population in 1790 to 3.9 percent in 1810. At the latter date in South Carolina and Georgia, only about 2 percent of all blacks were free. . . .

It was this post-Revolutionary beginning that provided the basis for the South's free black population in the antebellum period, for after 1810, few slaves were freed. The proportion of blacks who were free grew slightly in the upper South, from 10.4 percent in 1810 to 12.8 percent in 1860, primarily because of a surge of manumissions in Delaware, which by the mid-nineteenth century had become virtually a free state, and in Maryland, which, as historian Barbara J. Fields has shown, was threatening to do so; in 1860, 91.7 percent of Delaware's and 49.1 percent of Maryland's black population was free. In the lower South, by contrast, the proportion of free blacks decreased after 1810, as state after state passed new laws restricting manumission and harassing those who had been manumitted, and after 1840 the absolute number decreased as well. By 1860, only 1.5 percent of Deep South blacks were free, and half of these lived in Louisiana. In Mississippi, free blacks constituted only 0.2 percent of the population. The great majority of free blacks in the antebellum South were descendants of those who received their freedom between 1780 and 1810.

There were significant regional variations in the status and character of the free black population, both between North and South and within the South. Northern blacks, although free, were objects of both legal discrimination and vicious hostility. Excluded from most public schools, denied the right to vote (except in Maine, Vermont, New Hampshire,

Massachusetts, and – if they could meet a property requirement – New York), forbidden by (sporadically enforced) law from entering many states, jeered at and at times physically attacked by whites who refused to work with them or live near them, blacks quickly came to appreciate the difference between freedom and equality. Although their legal rights were usually greater than those of free blacks in the South, and a few of them achieved wealth and prominence, most Northern blacks were relegated to menial occupations such as day laborers and domestic servants. They constituted a highly urban population: more than three-fifths lived in cities at a time when fewer than one-fifth of all Americans did.

Although there were relatively few free blacks in the deep South, their condition was, ironically, in many respects better than that of those in the upper South. An unusually high proportion of them were elite people of "color" – neither physically nor mentally black – who set themselves apart from the mass of slaves. This was especially true of descendants of French and Spanish colonists who lived along the Gulf of Mexico and called themselves "Creoles" to indicate their ancestry. (White descendants of the French and Spanish commonly referred to *themselves* as "Creoles" and refused to use the term to apply to people of African origin. . . .) In Mobile, Pensacola, and especially in New Orleans, these light-skinned Creoles prided themselves on their wealth, breeding, heritage, and membership in exclusive organizations such as Mobile's Creole Fire Company Number 1 and New Orleans' octoroon balls. Refugees from Saint Domingue brought similar attitudes with them when they settled in New Orleans, Savannah, and Charleston.

The free black population in the lower South, unlike that in the North or upper South, was overwhelmingly light-skinned; in 1860, the census categorized about three-quarters of lower-South free blacks (and more than four-fifths of those in Louisiana) as mulattoes. A majority of these "free colored" were, like their cousins in the North, urban dwellers, although the South was, overall, overwhelmingly rural. Although most of them could hardly be termed wealthy – and many supported themselves through a variety of menial occupations including day labor, domestic service, and prostitution – they occupied many skilled positions, and held a near monopoly on some important service occupations such as barbering. A significant minority, both urban and rural, *were* wealthy. In Louisiana's Natchitoches Parish a colony of free Creoles, descended from an eighteenth-century French settler and an African slave, grew and flourished until by 1860 it contained 411 persons who owned 276 slaves; equally remarkable was the free South Carolina family whose patriarch, cotton gin maker and planter William Ellison, owned 63 slaves in 1840.

The position of elite free blacks in the deep South was never secure, but because they were few in number and seemed so different from the mass of slaves – a difference they strove to accentuate – they usually received at least grudging toleration from prominent whites whose favor they strove to curry. In southern Louisiana especially, but to a lesser extent elsewhere along the Gulf Coast as well as in Charleston and Savannah, many whites followed a practice common in much of Latin America but rare in most of the United States of distinguishing between mulattoes, especially their own sons and daughters, and blacks. As a Louisiana judge ruled in 1850, in allowing a free Negro to testify against whites, many of the state's free population were "respectable" as well as "enlightened by education, and the instances are by no means rare in which they are large property holders... such persons as courts and juries would not hesitate to believe under oath."[14]

The vast majority of the South's free blacks, however – about 85 percent – lived under very different circumstances in the upper South. They were darker, poorer, less urban, and less educated than those farther south; only about one-third were mulattoes or resided in cities. They typically lived on the margins of society, as farmhands, casual laborers, and occasionally small landowners, shunned by most whites and isolated from most slaves. Those who lived in cities – Baltimore and Washington, D.C., contained most of the region's urban free blacks – worked as domestics, day laborers, factory hands, and artisans and usually lacked the elitist pretensions evident in the lower South. Where they were able, they often fraternized with (and sometimes married) slaves.

Wherever they lived, free blacks faced hardship, persecution, and physical insecurity, all of which grew after 1850 as the Fugitive Slave Act increased the risk in the North of being kidnapped into slavery and concerted action in the South threatened more stringent enforcement of existing restrictive legislation; in the deep South, free blacks were sometimes pressured into enslaving themselves to masters of their own choice, and the free black population actually declined. Faced with such implacable white hostility, free blacks turned increasingly inward to their own community organizations, the most important of which were the independent "African" churches that emerged in the 1780s and 1790s; in Philadelphia, for example, the Free African Society, a quasi-religious organization founded in 1787 by former slaves Richard Allen and Absalom Jones, spawned a number of churches, the most influential of which was Allen's Bethel Church, which in 1816 expanded to form the African Methodist Episcopal Church. Overwhelmingly Baptist and Methodist, African churches flourished openly in major cities of the North and were sometimes tolerated in the urban South. Free blacks also set up schools for their children (usually clandestinely in the South) and formed a wide variety of mutual-aid associations to provide members with benefits such as burial and insurance.

During the crisis of the 1850s, free blacks not only turned inward but also increasingly looked outward, as some concluded that white America would never provide a hospitable environment and viewed with increasing favor the prospect of emigration to Liberia. Although only a small number of blacks actually moved to Africa, the heightened interest in emigration was a sign of the growing pessimism that gripped many free blacks during the 1850s, for emigrationist sentiment has always been a key index of black attitudes toward white America, rising during times of particular hardship and receding during periods of hope and progress.

Most free blacks, however, rejected the notion of emigrating to Africa, for they saw themselves as (and indeed were) quintessentially American and looked upon Africa as a distant and savage land. (The idea of sending blacks "back" to Africa drew more support from whites who sought to remove a thorn in the side of the slave regime or to "purify" America than from blacks who sought to improve their status.) In the North, they fought for their own rights by holding "colored conventions" in which they promoted common interests and cautiously demanded equal treatment, and they worked as abolitionists to promote the rights of those blacks still in slavery; in 1829, David Walker stirred (and in some cases alarmed) free blacks throughout America with his "incendiary" booklet *An Appeal to the Colored Citizens of the World*, in which he denounced slavery as a crime against humanity and called for its violent overthrow. Despite all the disabilities they faced, even in the South free blacks were sometimes able, as historian Loren Schweninger has recently demonstrated, to acquire impressive quantities of wealth, often with the help of particular whites who acted as their sponsors and protectors. Although most free blacks in the South remained propertyless, one of every six rural family heads in Maryland and Virginia owned land in 1860, and one in seven urban families in the upper South owned real estate.

However oppressive "freedom" was for blacks in America, it remained far preferable to slavery. Blacks made this preference clear when they "voted with their feet": tens of thousands put themselves in mortal peril to escape slavery, but virtually none voluntarily gave up freedom for bondage.

VI

Despite the hopes aroused during and immediately after the American Revolution, Southern slavery survived the era intact. The reform spirit had never spread very far in the lower South, where most slave owners seemed far more concerned with securing additional African laborers before the 1808 deadline than with the moral ambiguities of holding humans in bondage. And in the upper South, the kind of moderate questioning of slavery that was so pervasive in the 1770s and 1780s declined during the 1790s and early 1800s, as a new orthodoxy increasingly took hold of the region. During the Revolutionary era, the South was home to much of the most liberal social thought in America, as the "great generation" wrestled with the problem of slavery, challenged traditional religious doctrine, and championed a republicanism that when pushed to its Jeffersonian limits had a strong egalitarian thrust. During the post-Revolutionary years, however, the South began a retreat from this liberalism, a retreat that would in the antebellum years leave the section the undisputed home of conservatism.

As in the growth of Revolutionary-ear liberalism, a number of factors helped bring about its decline. A reaction against the more radical tendencies present in the American Revolution – spurred in part by revulsion over the excesses of the French Revolution – increasingly led statesmen in the new nation to espouse a conservative strand of republican thought that emphasized protection of property and order rather than equality. (In the Declaration of Independence, Jefferson had substituted "life, liberty and the pursuit of happiness" for John Locke's "life, liberty and property.") By the time of his death in 1809, Thomas Paine, that fiery exponent of republican egalitarianism who had at one time captured the imagination of a fledgling nation struggling against despotism and privilege, was widely reviled as a radical and an infidel; the former hero died in obscure poverty, his funeral attended by only six persons, including a Quaker and two blacks.

A similar trend was evident in Southern religion. Revolutionary-era Southerners had been among the least orthodox of Americans. Calvinist-oriented Northerners had long derided Southerners for not taking their religion seriously enough; Presbyterian tutor Philip Fithian, who spent 1773–74 on the plantation of Robert Carter III, filled his diary with scathing comments about the perfunctory nature of religious behavior among Virginia Anglicans. During the Revolutionary era, this tendency toward religious moderation was supplemented by a new challenge to established tenets that took the dual forms of a rational questioning of Christian faith epitomized by the Deism that captivated many gentry intellectuals, and of an evangelical recommitment to that faith that brought with it an egalitarian emphasis on the equality of all souls, white and black, before God. The 1790s and 1800s, however, saw a sharp reversal of this trend toward religious unorthodoxy, as Deism – and reason in general – lost its appeal to white Southerners, at the same time that evangelical Christianity lost much of its egalitarian thrust. Baptism and Methodism continued their advance throughout the South, but their message was no longer tinged with anti-slavery overtones. Indeed, during the antebellum years, the Southern churches would become bulwarks of the peculiar institution, and Southern religious spokesmen would lead the way in developing arguments in its behalf.

Economic considerations reinforced this new conservatism. If the tobacco crisis that gripped much of the Chesapeake region had facilitated moderate opposition to slavery, Southern economic expansion in the early nineteenth century had the opposite effect, for people are much less likely to question an institution when they are making money from it hand over fist than when they are suffering from hard times. Although tobacco never fully recovered its position of dominance in the upper South, and conditions in much of the Chesapeake remained depressed until the 1830s, the South as a whole experienced substantial economic growth, based primarily on a surge in the planting of cotton. This surge brought a sharp increase in demand for labor at precisely the same time that the importation of new slaves was being ended, and therefore resulted in a substantial increase in slave prices throughout the South. Ironically, ending the slave trade may have strengthened the commitment of Southern whites to slavery, both by putting upward pressure on slave prices and by removing the most easily identifiable barbarity associated with the slave regime.

The changing intellectual climate of the post-Revolutionary South had a major impact on attitudes toward slavery. Whereas many well-intentioned Southerners in the 1780s could legitimately believe that slavery had been placed on the road to gradual extinction and that "enlightened" sentiment would gradually become more and more opposed to the peculiar institution, a generation later it was clear that this was not to be. Not only did natural population growth among slaves mean that Southern slavery could, unlike slavery elsewhere in the New World, continue to flourish even after African imports were cut off; Southern white opinion moved steadily away from the moderate, rational questioning of slavery shown by many of the Founding Fathers. If these leaders abandoned much of their youthful liberalism, their children revealed little of the moral ambivalence and few of the doubts their parents felt about slavery. The Revolutionary-era challenge to slavery proved to be a short-lived phenomenon.

This development may be clearly illustrated by examining Thomas Jefferson's changing attitude toward slavery. Jefferson never renounced his belief that slavery was wrong, but as he aged he abandoned his youthful conviction that it could readily be abolished. In his original draft of the Declaration of Independence, rejected as too inflammatory by the Continental Congress, he had denounced George III for foisting slavery on the colonies, noting that that monarch "waged cruel war against human nature itself, violating the most sacred right of life and liberty in the persons of a distant people who never offended him." Unlike many others of his generation, however, Jefferson harbored serious doubts that blacks' "depravity" could be attributed entirely to their slave status, and he expressed strong views on what he considered their innate racial characteristics. In his celebrated *Notes on the State of Virginia* (written in 1781–82 and published in 1785), he argued that blacks were physically unattractive – maintaining that they displayed a "preference" for whites "as uniformly as is the preference of the Oranootan for the black woman over those of his own species" – stressed their deficiency in reasoning, and proclaimed that "in imagination they are dull, tasteless, and anomalous."

Jefferson's opposition to slavery always rested more on the harm it did to whites than on the harm it did to blacks, and after the Revolution he grew increasingly cautious in his criticism of the peculiar institution, increasingly concerned about the perils of too reckless an assault on the very basis of the South's social fabric. By 1805, although still believing that anti-slavery sentiment was on the rise, Jefferson admitted that he had "long since given up the expectation of any early provision for the extinguishment of slavery among us." Nine years later, forced to concede that emancipation sentiment was not spreading among the next generation, he had abandoned hope for any near-term end to slavery, contenting himself instead with advocating humane treatment of its victims: "My opinion has ever been that, until more can be done for them, we should endeavor, with those whom fortune has thrown on our hands, to feed & clothe them well, protect them from ill usage, require such reasonable labor only as is performed voluntarily by freemen, and be led by no repugnancies to abdicate them, and our duties to them. The laws do not permit us to turn them loose, [even] if that were for their good."

Even this retreat to benevolent stewardship did not, however, represent Jefferson's ultimate position. By 1819, he had come to identify almost wholly with the defense of Southern "rights" against those who would limit the spread of slavery into Missouri. Espousing the casuistic doctrine that the expansion of slavery would actually weaken the institution, by bringing about its "diffusion," the Sage of Monticello in his more honest moments expressed the Southern dilemma with brutal frankness: "We have the wolf by the ears," he declared in 1820, "and we can neither hold him, nor safely let him go. Justice is in one scale, and self-preservation in the other."[15]

Lacking Jefferson's introspective ambivalence, most Southern whites came to accept slavery as a legitimate if not yet necessarily desirable institution, and the early nineteenth century saw a general hardening of sentiment on the subject. As evangelical Protestants made their peace with the peculiar institution, active support for abolitionism was more and more confined to Quakers, who represented a tiny fraction of the population; 78 percent of the leaders of the North Carolina Manumission Society in the 1790s were Quakers. Panicky reaction to the Saint Domingue revolution of the 1790s and Gabriel Prosser's abortive uprising of 1800 dealt a further blow to what remained of Southern abolitionist sentiment – and organization – among non-Quakers; by the early nineteenth century, abolitionism was virtually nonexistent in the deep South and increasingly limited in the upper South to small pockets of dissenters on the fringes of society.

Private manumissions, by which thousands of blacks had received their freedom in the 1780s and 1790s, also declined precipitously in the nineteenth century (although they never ceased altogether). Concern for order, property rights, and their own economic security exceeded interest in the rights of their slaves among all but the most exceptional slave owners; even Jefferson failed to free his slaves, either during his lifetime or upon his death. Changing attitudes toward manumission were evident not only in the behavior of individuals but also in the actions of state legislatures, which, one after another, beginning with South Carolina in 1800, moved to restrict the slaves' access to freedom. Although state laws varied slightly, those in the lower South typically barred private manumissions without legislative approval, and those in the upper South (such as Virginia's act of 1806) required newly freed blacks to leave the state or face reenslavement. Laws expelling free blacks were not always strictly enforced, but they sent the clear message that most Southern whites regarded the existence of free blacks in their midst as a troublesome anomaly; the only proper status of blacks in white society was that of slave.

Formal defense of slavery did not yet reach the crescendo that it would during the late antebellum period, but here, too, the trend was clear. If the Revolutionary era saw the first sustained attack on slavery in the South, that attack was met by the first sustained defense of it; what is more, whereas the attack was feeble and short-lived, the defense would prove remarkably hardy and persistent. Most early arguments in defense of slavery were tentative and practical and lacked the later boastful assertions that slavery provided the best possible form of social organization. Still, many of the racial, religious, and paternalistic arguments that would flourish during the three decades before the Civil War were already evident in embryonic form during the late eighteenth century.

Five pro-slavery petitions, signed by 1,244 persons and presented to the Virginia legislature in 1784 and 1785, asserted that emancipation was "exceedingly *impolitic*" because it would produce "Want, Poverty, Distress, and Ruin to the Free Citizen"; they also appealed to property rights, however, proclaimed that slavery was best for the slaves, pointed to biblical precedent, and warned of "the Horrors of all the Rapes, Murders, and Outrages, which a vast Multitude of unprincipled, unpropertied, revengeful, and remorseless Banditti are capable of perpetrating."[16]

Indeed, the Revolution clearly served to accentuate two themes that would be central to Southern white thought in the antebellum years. One was the racial component in the defense of slavery. Although the Revolution did not immediately democratize American society, it produced an egalitarian republicanism that posed a severe problem for those who would defend slavery: if all men were created equal, how could some hold others in bondage? As Duncan J. MacLeod and other scholars have pointed out, the only logical answer to this question (aside from replying that they could not) was to assert that those held as slaves were somehow so different from free Americans that they were not entitled to the same rights and privileges. Because race was the most easily identifiable difference, it became an increasingly important justification for slavery; the assumption that blacks were not fit for freedom was crucial to the defense of slavery in an era of liberty and equality. Although arguments for the innate inferiority of blacks to whites were not fully elaborated until later, a new racism was one of the ironic byproducts of Revolutionary-era republicanism.

Equally problematical – and significant for the future – was the reconciliation of liberty and slavery, terms that in other times and places have seemed to be diametric opposites. The concept of liberty, like that of rights, assumes for most present-day readers, as it did for most antebellum Northerners, an abstract character. Its origin and early usage, however, were often much more specific and were related to custom, tradition, and interest: just as slaves commonly viewed as theirs by right the little privileges that were extended to them (such as the "rights" to cultivate garden plots and enjoy certain holidays), so, too, colonists put great stock in the "English liberties" they enjoyed by tradition, and viewed the abrogation of those liberties as signs of monarchical despotism.

Although the Revolution fostered an abstracted sense of rights – specific "liberties," enjoyed by specific groups, became a generalized "liberty" belonging to all – many Southerners continued to use the term in the older sense. According to this usage, infringing on their right to own slaves was a violation of their liberty. In this manner, Southerners in the antebellum period were able to portray themselves as both ardent defenders of slavery (that is, of blacks) and equally ardent proponents of liberty (that is, their own). To many Northerners, the simultaneous defense of liberty and slavery seemed patently hypocritical. To defenders of slavery, however, the right to own slaves was *their* most important liberty (the meaning of which came close to the right to pursue one's own interest); indeed, they insisted that to deprive them of the right to own slaves would be to subject them to slavery (just as the Patriots had argued that the British, in infringing on their traditional liberties, were subjecting them to slavery).

Although formal articulation of these arguments was still in its infancy at the beginning of the nineteenth century, it was clear that Southern slavery had survived the multiple threats it faced during the Revolutionary era and, like steel tempered by fire, had emerged from that era stronger than ever. Before the Revolution, Southern whites had generally taken slavery for granted. The Revolutionary ferment, both physical and intellectual, forced them to grapple with the question of slavery's morality and utility and, after a brief period of uncertainty, left them far more committed to the peculiar institution than they had previously been. With emancipation in the North, slavery became ever more deeply identified with the South, Southern interests, and the Southern way of life. The next time Southern whites fought for their "liberty," it would be explicitly for their rights as slave owners.

Notes

1 William Byrd II to the Earl of Egmont, 1736, in Elizabeth Donnan (ed.), *Documents Illustrative of the History of the Slave Trade to America* (4 vols., New York, 1969; orig. pub. 1930–5), vol. 4, pp. 131–2.
2 Laurens letters, January 7, 1757, February 15, 1763, and March 19, 1763, in *The Papers of Henry Laurens*, ed. Philip M. Hamer (3 vols., Columbia, SC, 1968–72), vol. 2, p 402; vol. 3, pp. 259–60, 373–4.
3 Jefferson to Condorcet, August 30, 1791, in *Thomas Jefferson's Farm Book with Commentary and Relevant Extracts from Other Writings*, ed. Edwin Morris Betts (Princeton, NJ, 1953), p. 11.
4 David Brion Davis, *The Problem of Slavery in the Age of Revolution, 1770–1823* (Ithaca, NY, 1975), pp. 237–8; John Woolman, *The Journal with Other Writings of John Woolman* (London, 1910), p. 54.
5 *Journal & Letters of Philip Vickers Fithian, 1773–1774: A Plantation Tutor of the Old Dominion*, ed. Hunter Dickinson Farish (Charlottesville, Va., 1968), p. 92.
6 Quoted in Gerald W. Mullin, *Flight and Rebellion: Slave Resistance in Eighteenth-Century Virginia* (New York, 1972), p. 132.

7 *The Diary of Colonel Landon Carter of Sabine Hall, 1752–1778*, ed. Jack P. Greene (2 vols. in 1, Charlottesville, Va., 1965), pp. 1051, 1052; *Thomas Jefferson's Farm Book*, p. 29.

8 Helen Tunnicliff Catterall (ed.), *Judicial Cases Concerning American Slavery and the Negro* (5 vols., New York, 1968; orig. pub. 1926–37), vol. 2, pp. 290–1.

9 Lorena S. Walsh, "Rural African Americans in the Constitutional Era in Maryland, 1776–1810," *Maryland Historical Magazine*, 84 (Winter 1989), pp. 336, 337.

10 Both quotations are from G. W. Mullin, *Flight and Rebellion: Slave Resistance in Eighteenth-Century Virginia* (New York, 1972), pp. 145, 158.

11 Philip D. Morgan, "Black Society in the Lowcountry, 1760–1810," in Ira Berlin and Ronald Hoffman (eds.), *Slavery and Freedom in the Age of the American Revolution* (Charlottesville, Va., 1983), p. 110.

12 Quoted in Davis, *The Problem of Slavery in the Age of Revolution*, p. 275.

13 Quoted in Edgar J. McManus, *Black Bondage in the North* (Syracuse, NY, 1973), p. 165.

14 Catterall (ed.), *Judicial Cases*, iii. 601.

15 Quotations are from John Chester Miller, *The Wolf by the Ears: Thomas Jefferson and Slavery* (New York, 1977), p. 8; Thomas Jefferson, *Notes on the State of Virginia* (New York, 1964), pp. 133, 134; Jefferson to William A. Burwell, January 28, 1805, in *Thomas Jefferson's Farm Book*, p. 20; Jefferson to Edward Coles, August 25, 1814, ibid., p. 39; Miller, *The Wolf by the Ears*, p. 241.

16 Fredrika Teute Schmidt and Barbara Ripel Wilhelm (eds.), "Early Proslavery Petitions in Virginia," *William and Mary Quarterly*, 30 (January 1973), pp. 139–40.

5
The Growth of the Cotton Kingdom

Introduction

After the tobacco boom of the seventeenth and eighteenth centuries, widespread soil depletion and frequent economic crises plagued the Chesapeake. Prime tobacco planting had moved from areas close to the coast, where wheat replaced it, to the interior. Rice continued to be a prosperous business in coastal Georgia and South Carolina, but the crop responsible for the South's economic recovery at the beginning of the nineteenth century was cotton. In 1793, Eli Whitney invented the cotton gin, a machine which mechanically separated the fiber, called lint, from the seed. The invention accelerated and made cheaper the production of short-staple cotton in the up-country. Concurrent with Whitney's invention was an increase in demand for cotton from the textile mills of England and northeastern America. In 1800, cotton production stood at 73,000 bales; by 1860, it had reached 4.5 million bales. Cotton suited both large- and small-scale cultivation. Planted in the spring, the plants were tended until cotton bolls ripened and opened in the fall; then it was picked, ginned, and packed in bales. A production boom pushed hundreds of farmers and impoverished planters to settle the "Old

Southwest," leaving depleted areas together with their slaves and, in the process of migration, causing the dissolution of thousands of slave families. Other upper South masters sold their slaves to the labor-hungry planters of the cotton "black belt," fueling an internal slave trade which flourished until the Civil War.

A dual pattern characterized the economy of the antebellum South. On the one hand, plantations and farms produced staple crops for commercial agriculture and long-distance trade. The expansion of cotton into the interior Piedmont area had put the world of the plantations – which were mainly near coasts and navigable rivers – in contact with the inland farms. Both planters and farmers who engaged in long-distance trade were slave-owners; slavery was embedded in a society with a large white farming population, since half of the farm operators owned slaves. On the other hand, at the periphery of the cotton belt, a large non-slaveholding yeomanry owned land but participated only marginally in the market, since commercial agriculture and trade were hindered by poor transportation and limited access to market facilities. They grew foodstuffs for their own consumption and raised fowl and livestock. The corn and cereal crops they raised were minor parts of their economic life; these were bartered for other goods or exchanged on the internal market.

There were few cities and few factories in the South compared to other more industrialized regions; cities were small by European standards, having fewer than 50,000 inhabitants, except for Baltimore in Maryland, Saint Louis in Missouri, and New Orleans in Louisiana. These urban centers were poorly connected by an underdeveloped railroad system and by few canals and navigable rivers. The cities on the coast functioned primarily as markets for agricultural products, where merchants – called factors – acted as middlemen selling slave-produced staples on the world market. Factors who were successful in handling planters' business often became planters themselves.

There is a long-standing argument between those historians who believe that slavery retarded southern economic development and those who think that it was a profitable economic system. Marxist and neo-Marxist historians maintain that slavery prevented the South from industrializing and from developing a strong, fully capitalist economy like the one in the North. Furthermore, they maintain, slavery weakened the South by giving rise to an economy wholly dependent on the demand for cotton by the more industrialized regions of the world. Neoclassical economic historians, on the other hand, argue that slavery was a very advanced and profitable agricultural system, where cotton production was conducted according to the same rules of economic behavior adhered to by modern business firms. Consequently, the South did not need a more industrialized economy, since it would have added little to its economic strength.

Whatever position one takes, it is clear that the slave economy was inextricably linked to unfree labor and to plantation agriculture; therefore, it was by definition an economic system which left very little room for industrialization and urbanization. Even if it had a much more complex economic profile than historians previously believed, antebellum southern agriculture still depended in large measure for its economic health upon worldwide demand for cotton. Moreover, cotton production could expand only with new land and additional slaves – clearly, there were structural limits, both geographical and political, to this sort of expansion.

Further reading

Bateman, F. and Weiss, T., *A Deplorable Scarcity: The Failure of Industrialization in the Slave Economy* (Chapel Hill: University of North Carolina Press, 1981).

Fogel, R. W., *Without Consent or Contract: The Rise and Fall of American Slavery* (New York: Norton, 1989).

Fogel, R. W. and Engerman, S. L., *Time on the Cross: The Economics of American Negro Slavery* (Boston: Little, Brown, and Company, 1974).

Fox-Genovese, E. and Genovese, E. D., *Fruits of Merchant Capital: Slavery and Bourgeois Property in the Rise and Expansion of Capitalism* (New York: Oxford University Press, 1983).

Genovese, E. D., *The Political Economy of Slavery: Studies in the Economy and Society of the Slave South* (New York: Vintage, 1965).

Shore, L., *Southern Capitalists: The Ideological Leadership of an Elite, 1832–1855* (Chapel Hill: University of North Carolina Press, 1986).

Smith, M. M., *Debating Slavery: Economy and Society in the Antebellum South* (New York: Cambridge University Press, 1998).

Tadman, M., *Speculators and Slaves: Masters, Traders, and Slaves in the Old South* (Madison: University of Wisconsin Press, 1989).

Wright, G., *The Political Economy of the Cotton South: Households, Markets, and Wealth in the Nineteenth Century* (New York: Norton, 1978).

Joseph Baldwin on Society in Alabama and Mississippi (1835–1837)

In the early nineteenth century, the area of cotton production expanded rapidly from its original center in up-country South Carolina and Georgia to Alabama and Mississippi. Several travelers' accounts and contemporary documents describe the movement of settlers to what used to be called the "Old Southwest." This passage by Joseph Baldwin succeeds in conveying the idea of frontier society that characterized these early western settlements. Baldwin mentions, critically, the treaties whereby the Native American tribes were forced to cede their lands. He sees these as opening the way to a mass migration of merchants, speculators, and planters-in-the-making attracted by the seemingly unlimited possibilities for profit. In fact, largely because of land speculation, the settlers of the "Old Southwest" were hit particularly hard by the economic depression of 1837.

In trying to arrive at the character of the South-Western bar, its opportunities and advantages for improvement are to be considered. It is not too much to say that, in the United States at least, no bar ever had such, or so many: it might be doubted if they were *ever* enjoyed to the same extent before. Consider that the South-West was the focus of an emigration greater than any portion of the country ever attracted, at least, until the golden magnet drew its thousands to the Pacific coast. But the character of emigrants was not the same. Most of the gold-seekers were mere gold-diggers – not bringing property, but coming to take it away. Most of those coming to the South-West brought property – many of them a great deal. Nearly every man was a speculator; at any rate, a trader. The treaties with the Indians had brought large portions of the States of Alabama, Mississippi and Louisiana into market; and these portions, comprising some of the most fertile lands in the world, were settled up in a hurry. The Indians claimed lands under these treaties – the laws granting preemption rights to settlers on the public lands, were to be construed, and the litigation growing out of them settled, the public lands afforded a field for unlimited speculation, and combinations of purchasers, partnerships, land companies, agencies, and the like, gave occasion to much difficult litigation in after times. Negroes were brought

---

Source: Paul Escott and David Goldfield (eds.), *Major Problems in the History of the American South*, vol. 1: *The Old South*, 1st edn. (Lexington, Mass.: D. C. Heath, 1991), pp. 245–7

into the country in large numbers and sold mostly upon credit, and bills of exchange taken for the price; the negroes in many instances were unsound – some as to which there was no title; some falsely pretended to be unsound, and various questions as to the liability of parties on the warranties and the bills, furnished an important addition to the litigation: many land titles were defective; property was brought from other States clogged with trusts, limitations, and uses, to be construed according to the laws of the State from which it was brought: claims and contracts made elsewhere to be enforced here: universal indebtedness, which the hardness of the times succeeding made it impossible for many men to pay, and desirable for all to escape paying: hard and ruinous bargains, securityships, judicial sales; a general looseness, ignorance, and carelessness in the public officers in doing business; new statutes to be construed; official liabilities, especially those of sheriffs, to be enforced; banks, the laws governing their contracts, proceedings against them for forfeiture of charter; trials of right of property; an elegant assortment of frauds constructive and actual; and the whole system of chancery law, admiralty proceedings; in short, all the floodgates of litigation were opened and the pent-up tide let loose upon the country. And such a criminal docket! What country could boast more largely of its crimes? What more splendid rôle of felonies! What more terrific murders! What more gorgeous bank robberies! What more magnificent operations in the land offices! Such... levies of black mail, individual and corporate! Such superb forays on the treasuries, State and National! Such expert transfers of balances to undiscovered bournes! Such august defalcations! Such flourishes of rhetoric on ledgers auspicious of gold which had departed for ever from the vault! And in INDIAN affairs! – the very mention is suggestive of the poetry of theft – the romance of a wild and weird larceny! What sublime conceptions of super-Spartan roguery! Swindling Indians by the nation! (*Spirit of Falstaff, rap!*) Stealing their land by the township! (*Dick Turpin and Jonathan Wild! tip the table!*) Conducting the nation to the Mississippi river, stripping them to the flap, and bidding them God speed as they went howling into the Western wilderness to the friendly agency of some sheltering Suggs duly empowered to receive their coming annuities and back rations? What's Hounslow heath to this? Who Carvajal? Who Count Boulbon?

And all these merely forerunners, ushering in the Millennium of an accredited, official Repudiation; and IT but vaguely suggestive of what men could do when opportunity and capacity met – as shortly afterwards they did – under the Upas-shade of a perjury-breathing bankrupt law! – But we forbear. The contemplation of such hyperboles of mendacity stretches the imagination to a dangerous tension. There was no end to the amount and variety of lawsuits, and interests involved in every complication and of enormous value were to be adjudicated. The lawyers were compelled to work, and were forced to learn the rules that were involved in all this litigation.

Many members of the bar, of standing and character, from the other States, flocked in to put their sickles into this abundant harvest. Virginia, Kentucky, North Carolina and Tennessee contributed more of these than any other four States; but every State had its representatives.

Consider, too, that the country was not so new as the practice. Every State has its peculiar tone or physiognomy, so to speak, of jurisprudence imparted to it, more or less, by the character and temper of its bar. That had yet to be given. Many questions decided in older States, and differently decided in different States, were to be settled here; and a new state of things, peculiar in their nature, called for new rules or a modification of old ones. The members of the bar from different States had brought their various notions, impressions and knowledge of their own judicature along with them; and thus all the points, dicta, rulings, offshoots, quirks and quiddities of all the law, and lawing, and law-mooting of all the various judicatories and their satellites, were imported into the new country and tried on the new jurisprudence.

After the crash [a sharp recession] came in 1837 – (there were some *premonitory fits* before, but *then* the *great convulsion* came on) – all the assets of the country were marshalled, and the suing material of all sorts, as fast as it could be got out, put into the hands of the workmen. Some idea of the business may be got from a fact or two: in the county of Sumpter, Alabama, in one year, some four or five thousand suits, in the common-law courts alone, were brought; but in some other counties the number was larger; while in the lower or river counties of Mississippi, the number was at least double. The United States Courts were equally well patronized in proportion – indeed, rather more so. The white *suable* population of Sumpter was then some 2,400 men. It was a merry time for us craftsmen; and we brightened up mightily, and shook our quills joyously, like goslings in the midst of a shower. We look back to that good time, "now past and gone," with the pious gratitude and serene satisfaction with which the wreckers near the Florida Keys contemplate the last fine storm.

It was a pleasant sight to professional eyes to see a whole people let go all holds and meaner business, and move off to court, like the Californians and Australians to the mines: the "pockets" were picked in both cases. As law and lawing soon got to be the staple productions of the country, the people, as a whole the most intelligent – in the wealthy counties – of the rural population of the United States, and, as a part, the *keenest* in all creation, got very well "up to trap" in law matters; indeed, they soon knew more about the delicate mysteries of the law, than it behooves an honest man to know.

James Henry Hammond on Agriculture in Virginia (1841)

James Henry Hammond (1807–64) was a prominent planter and statesman from up-country South Carolina. He owned a large plantation of about 7,000 acres at Silver Bluff, where his 147 slaves grew mainly cotton, which he shipped to the port of Savannah, Georgia, for sale on the world market. Like many South Carolina planters, Hammond was hit particularly hard by the crisis in the cotton market that accompanied the economic depression of 1837. As this entry from Hammond's diaries makes clear, the consequences of the depression were still felt in South Carolina in 1841. Interestingly, Hammond compares the situation of his native state with the condition of Virginia, which was afflicted by a long-term crisis in tobacco production. The crisis had prompted some planters – among them Edmund Ruffin – to resort to fertilizers, such as marl, in order to allow the soil to recover from the exhaustion caused by years of tobacco cultivation. However, the results seem to have been less than promising, given Hammond's description of the improvement to Virginia land as "imaginary."

[Columbia] 12 Feb. [1841]

The most important news of the day is the third suspension and supposed failure of the U.S. Bank of Penna. It resumed specie on the 15 Jan. and suspended on the 4 Feb., having during the interval paid out nearly 6 millions of dollars. This Institution for a long time sustained the highest reputation abroad and raised that of the U.S. to a high eminence. Even the withdrawal of the Gov. deposits in 1834 and the subsequent expiration of its charter from the U.S. and renewal of it by the State of Penn. did not affect it seriously in point of credit. When the crisis of 1837 occurred, it came forward to relieve the country by throwing into circulation an immense amount of post notes, payable in London at 12 months. To meet them it had to purchase cotton largely, and was an

Source: Carol Bleser (ed.), *Secret and Sacred: The Diaries of James Henry Hammond, a Southern Slaveholder* (Oxford and New York: Oxford University Press, 1988), pp. 32–3

immense loser on it. It also speculated, largely in State stock, which, in the embarrassed state of the finances of the world, proved to be a dead weight on their hands. These things have destroyed it – if, as is pretty generally believed, it is bankrupt. It is computed that 2 millions will be lost by it in S.C. The shock I fear will be severely felt in Europe by those who have an interest in American securities and will bring down American credit there below its present low ebb. In a country town like this it produces little or no effect. Money is already as scarce here as it can well be. The Banks discount scarcely anything but drafts for 60 days and those sparingly. At the last discount day at the Br. Bank, $100,000 were offered and only $7,000 discounted. Yet prices are fair. Prime cotton will bring 11¢, corn 56¢, fodder 1.25, fowls 5 to the dollar, and surloin of beef 12¢. It has been excessively cold to day. I am yet in great hurry and confusion, and find myself getting "fixed" but slowly. Dined with [David] McCord to day. Small party to Dr. Carter of Virginia – a common sort of man. He told me that in Virginia now planters realized nothing except from raising slaves and the increase in the value of their lands in consequence of improvements from marling [fertilizing with deposits rich in calcium carbonate, typically from oyster shells] and increase of population. I suspect the rise in lands is rather imaginary and that on the whole the wealth of Virginia does not increase more than that of the oldest countries. Such, I fear, will soon be the case with So.Ca. when the culture of cotton will be abandoned in consequence of its fall in price. The current expenses of raising cotton here on our fair lands is 5¢ per lb., and values of our negroes at $300 round, and on land at $10 per acre, we must get 10¢ nett to realize 7 per ct per annum, leaving out the increase of negroes. Dr. C[arter] said that the small farmers on the wheatlands made $100 nett per hand he thought. This is very light wages and can only be done, I imagine, by small farmers who own no more slaves than they overlook with their own eyes. Slaves can be worked in large gangs only on rice, cotton, and sugar estates, where the operations are regular and systematic for whole seasons, and the owner is not required to be present daily and hourly.

The weather is very cold. It has for a month been very inclement. I have seldom known in this country so long a spell of wet weather, except occasionally in July or August, last year for instance. An eclipse of the moon took place a few days ago and eclipses always bring extraordinary seasons.

Frederick Law Olmsted on the Profitability of Cotton (1861)

Among the accounts written by travelers who visited the antebellum South, none had more influence on public opinion both in the North and in Europe than the ones penned by Frederick Law Olmsted (1822–1903), who was later to achieve fame as the nation's foremost landscape architect. Olmsted originally published the accounts of his travels throughout the South in the 1850s as a correspondent to *The New York Times*. In 1861, as the Confederacy seceded and the country plunged into civil war, he compiled a two-volume re-edition of his newspaper reports, to which he added some additional material; his aim was to help find an explanation for what he called "the present crisis" by relating it to the distinctive features of southern society and economy. Borrowing the expression "Cotton Kingdom" from a famous speech by James Henry Hammond, he used it as the title of his work, a book in which cotton certainly plays a prominent part. In this excerpt, Olmsted summarizes the reasons behind the profitability of cotton agriculture and the benefits it extolled upon a relatively small – but powerful – class of planters.

...The area of land on which cotton may be raised with profit is practically limitless; it is cheap; even the best land is cheap; but to the large planter it is much more valuable when held in large parcels, for obvious reasons, than when in small; consequently the best land can hardly be obtained in small tracts or without the use of a considerable capital. But there are millions of acres of land yet untouched, which if leveed and drained and fenced, and well cultivated, might be made to produce with good luck seven or more bales to the hand. It would cost comparatively little to accomplish it – one lucky crop would repay all the outlay for land and improvements – if it were not for "the hands." The supply of hands is limited. It does not increase in the ratio of the increase of the cotton demand. If cotton should double in price next year, or become worth its weight in gold, the number of negroes in the United States would not increase four percent. unless the African slave-trade were re-established. Now step into a dealer's "jail" in Memphis, Montgomery, Vicksburg, or New Orleans, and you will hear the mezzano

Source: Arthur M. Schlesinger (ed.), *The Cotton Kingdom: A Traveller's Observations on Cotton and Slavery in the American Slave States* by Frederick Law Olmsted (New York: Alfred A. Knopf, 1953), pp. 13–17

[muezzin] of the cotton lottery crying his tickets in this way: "There's a cotton nigger for you! Genuine! Look at his toes! Look at his fingers! There's a pair of legs for you! If you have got the right sile and the right sort of overseer, buy him, and put your trust in Providence! He's just as good for ten bales as I am for a julep at eleven o'clock." And this is just as true as that any named horse is sure to win the Derby. And so the price of good labourers is constantly gambled up to a point, where, if they produce ten bales to the hand, the purchaser will be as fortunate as he who draws the high prize of the lottery; where, if they produce seven bales to the hand, he will still be in luck; where, if rot, or worm, or floods, or untimely rains or frosts occur, reducing the crop to one or two bales to the hand, as is often the case, the purchaser will have drawn a blank. . . .

The whole number of slaves engaged in cotton culture at the Census of 1850 was reckoned by De Bow to be 1,800,000, the crops at 2,400,000 bales, which is a bale and a third to each head of slaves. This was the largest crop between 1846 and 1852. Other things being equal, for reasons already indicated, the smaller the estate of slaves, the less is their rate of production per head; and, as a rule, the larger the slave estate the larger is the production per head. The number of slaves in cotton plantations held by owners of fifty and upwards is, as nearly as it can be fixed by the Census returns, 420,000. . . .

A similar calculation will indicate that the planters who own on an average two slave families each, can sell scarcely more than three hundred dollars' worth of cotton a year, on an average; which also entirely agrees with my observations. I have seen many a workman's lodging at the North, and in England too, where there was double the amount of luxury that I ever saw in a regular cotton-planter's house on plantations of three cabins.

The next class of which the Census furnishes us means of considering separately, are planters whose slaves occupy, on an average, seven cabins, lodging five each on an average, including the house servants, aged, invalids, and children. The average income of planters of this class, I reckon from similar data, to be hardly more than that of a private of the New York Metropolitan Police Force. It is doubtless true that cotton is cultivated profitably, that is to say, so as to produce a fair rate of interest on the capital of the planter, on many plantations of this class; but this can hardly be the case on an average, all things considered.

It is not so with many plantations of the next larger class even, but it would appear to be so with these on an average. That is to say, where the quarters of a cotton plantation number half a score of cabins or more (which method of classification I use that travellers may the more readily recall their observations of the appearance of such plantations, when I think that their recollections will confirm these calculations), there are usually other advantages for the cultivation, cleaning, pressing, shipping, and disposing of cotton, by the aid of which the owner obtains a fair return for the capital invested, and may be supposed to live, if he knows how, in a moderately comfortable way. The whole number of slave-holders of this large class in all the Slave States is, according to De Bow's Compendium of the Census, 7,929, among which are all the great sugar, rice, and tobacco-planters. Less than seven thousand, certainly, are cotton-planters. . . .

Debating the Profitability of Antebellum Southern Agriculture

Mark M. Smith

In *Debating Slavery*, Mark Smith analyzes the current debate over the economic profitability of slavery and its implications for antebellum southern society. Smith's work pays particular attention to the impact of the plantation economy on different classes of southerners – planters, yeomen, and slaves. In this excerpt, he summarizes the "contours of the debate" and shows how both the South-as-non-capitalist view – held by Marxist historians – and the South-as-capitalist view – held by neoclassical economists – have strengths and weaknesses related to the scholars' particular assumptions and methods of inquiry. Several recent studies have done much to demolish some of these assumptions and have complicated the picture of the slave economy and society that the two schools of thought once offered; however, they have not resolved the issue of the profitability of antebellum southern slavery in favor of either position.

Even at its height in the first half of the nineteenth century, Americans debated slavery. Was it a profitable, progressive, and healthy institution? If so, for whom? For slaveholders in particular? For non-slaveowners? For slaves? For the southern economy generally? Was the Old South an acommercial region, populated by premodern slaveowners and less than diligent slaves? The constitutional abolition of slavery in the United States in 1865 did not end this debate. Similar and sometimes identical

Mark M. Smith, *Debating Slavery: Economy and Society in the Antebellum American South* (New York: Cambridge University Press, 1998), pp. 1–14, 60–70.

questions concerning the economic and social character of antebellum southern slavery still inform modern historical debates which have raged with increasing volume and occasional acrimony in the twentieth century. Today, southern slavery is among the most hotly discussed topics in writings on American history and southern history generally....

Before sketching the outlines of these debates, it is perhaps helpful first to say a few words about the history of the Old South and, second, to suggest why the debate over slavery has been so important to Americans generally and to historians of the American South in particular.

Describing the slave South has proven easier than labeling it. Scholars continue to disagree on the origins of race-based southern slavery and several historians rightly caution that the growth and subsequent legal entrenchment of slavery during the colonial period of American history was highly contingent on time and place. There is, however, general agreement that by the end of the seventeenth century, racial slavery in the American colonies was recognized socially and endorsed legally....

By the end of the eighteenth century, the slave-based plantation system was beginning to define the southern cultural, social, political, and economic landscape. Just as plantation slavery was becoming ensconced in the South, however, it was dissipating in the North where climate and geography proved unfriendly to plantation labor and a growing recognition that the principles of the American Revolution were at odds with human bondage was beginning to take hold.... By contrast, slavery expanded in the South. Its existence was increasingly sanctioned through law, and the holding of slaves was important for southern whites' definition of personal freedom....

...Most historians agree that the plantation system was central to southern economic and social identity. Spreading from the Tidewater regions and Maryland in the seventeenth century, from their inception plantations produced tobacco for the international market. In the eighteenth century especially, the plantation system spread further south to the Carolinas and Georgia where slave labor was used to cultivate rice and indigo. In this period, plantation slavery was perceived by planters to be both profitable and racially desirable....

Although southern slaves could be found in a variety of occupations in both urban and rural areas, the typical late eighteenth-century slave lived and worked on the plantation. This was even truer with the westward expansion of the plantation system after the 1790s. The invention and subsequent spread of the cotton gin in and after 1793 profoundly affected the nature of southern slavery. In the first instance, the gin enabled planters to cultivate large tracts of short staple cotton. Lands west of the Atlantic coast with their rich soils, ample rainfall, and minimum of 200 frostless days a year proved ideal for growing the crop and the plantation system fingered its way west into Alabama, Mississippi, and eastern Texas in the opening decades of the antebellum period, 1800–1860. Planters in the lowcountry of South Carolina and Georgia continued to cultivate other staple crops like rice and long staple Sea Island cotton, tobacco was still grown in Virginia and North Carolina, and sugar became a staple of the Louisiana plantation economy. But the gin and the industrial revolution in New England and Britain, whose burgeoning textile manufactures consumed southern short staple cotton at a seemingly unquenchable rate, had unleashed the cotton boom which was to dominate the South's economy and plantation system up until the outbreak of the Civil War in 1861. More than ever, antebellum southern planters found themselves tied to the demands and vagaries of an international economy. Antebellum cotton replaced eighteenth-century tobacco as the South's main export staple and, in the process, provided slaveholders with a firm economic foundation for their slave society.

The second impact of the westward spread of cotton and the plantation system was the increase in the demand by planters for slave labor. From roughly 700,000 slaves in 1790 the South became home to just under 4 million bondpeople by 1860. In this period, putatively paternal masters sent to and traded to the West roughly 835,000 slaves with the aid of an increasingly sophisticated internal slave trade and improvements in transportation. Most of this growth took place between 1808, when the United States banned the further importation of slaves, and 1860, when the slave population had more than tripled. In this respect, southern slavery was unique, for, unlike other nineteenth-century slave societies which were dependent on the continued importation of chattels, southern slavery was able to sustain itself.

The consequences of this self-sufficiency were important for shaping antebellum plantation life. Cognizant that the future of their slave society depended on the natural reproduction of their workforce, antebellum planters became increasingly paternalistic toward their slaves and encouraged the formation of slave families and slaves' instruction in a rather slanted version of Christianity. These developments inevitably affected slaves. The natural reproduction of southern slaves helped equalize the sex ratio, which in turn contributed toward the formation of strong, sustainable slave families. Without fresh infusions of African slaves after 1808, antebellum slaves also became increasingly American-born and hence African American in their cultural propensities. By the 1830s, then, the slave–master relationship, buttressed by the economic imperatives of an export-oriented plantation system, undergirded by closer black–white interaction, and premised on slaveholders' cultural need to see themselves as masters of capital and guardians of chattels, had become firmly entrenched in the American South. . . .

But the last thirty or so years of the antebellum period, while demonstrating the economic and social vitality of the South's peculiar institution, also witnessed slavery's undermining from within and without. The aborted Denmark Vesey slave uprising in Charleston, South Carolina in 1822 and the bloody Nat Turner insurrection of 1831 in Southampton County, Virginia exposed the fallacy of masters' conviction that their bondpeople were content and happy. Slaveholders' subsequent clamp-down on the non-work activities of slaves and on urban free blacks from the 1830s onwards only added fuel to a blistering moral and essentially sectional critique of southern slavery by northern abolitionists. . . .More damning still was the growing criticism among northern wage labor advocates who contended that, regardless of its immorality, slavery was an archaic, inefficient institution, inferior to northern free wage labor. . . .

In grappling with [these] problems, historians of southern slavery have explicitly or implicitly aligned themselves with . . . one of two broadly defined schools of historical and scholarly thought. The first may usefully be considered as the school which aims to show that the Old South was a non-capitalist, unprofitable, and largely inefficient society. The second camp argues the opposite: as a market-oriented, staple-exporting economy the South was essentially profitable, slave labor was efficient, and hence the region was capitalist.

The South-as-non-capitalist school of thought contends that southern slaveholders were an acommercial class: that they had an aversion to making money for its own sake, that slavery was an unprofitable economic enterprise for the individual slaveowner and for the southern economy generally, and that slaves, horribly exploited though they were, were often able to preserve much of their own culture and identity. For some historians, the absence of wage labor under slavery meant that capitalism could not flourish in the South and that this absence necessarily created a class of planters who were very much like feudal lords. . . .

With the exception of historians like Ulrich B. Phillips (1918), much of the work that stresses the pre-capitalist nature of southern slavery has been written by historians who are of a Marxian persuasion. They believe that the distinguishing characteristic of capitalism is the existence of free wage labor – the freedom of laborers to sell their labor power on an open market for a wage. There are, of course, gradations within this Marxian interpretation, even within the work of the same historian. Eugene D. Genovese, the doyen among historians of the slave South, for example, has modified his earlier position, in which he described slaveholders as having an "aversion to profit" and being anti-commercial, to one which allows that masters may have wanted to make money but were prevented from so doing by the resistance of their slaves, by being only *in* and not *of* the capitalist Atlantic marketplace, and by only *appearing* to be modern.[1] Still, whatever these revisions and modifications, it remains clear that Marxist historians like Genovese . . . think that because the slave South was not premised on the use of *free wage* labor, because masters saw themselves more as benevolent paternalists rather than as exploitative capitalists, because masters viewed their chattels as cultural and social accouterments and not embodiments of economic capital, the region was necessarily destined to remain non-capitalist in a nation that was becoming capitalist through its increasing reliance on factory production and free wage labor. Therefore, distinctively southern masters must have fought the Civil War to preserve their cultural, social, and political identity which was premised on, and inextricably tied to, the ownership of property in the form of black slaves.

The South-as-capitalist school takes the opposite position on many of these issues. This so-called neoclassical school "rejects the more orthodox Marxian assumption that free wage labor is a *sine qua non* of genuinely capitalist enterprise."[2] Masters, so the argument goes, were very similar if not identical to northern and, indeed, European capitalists. True, they did not employ free labor on their plantations. But the way slaveholders organized their workforce, the way they treated their bondpeople, their heavy involvement in the market economy, and their drive for economic profit made them much more capitalist than historians like Genovese are willing to concede. This school of thought often, though not necessarily, employs statistical models and recruits exhaustive numerical data to support its position. This data is used to argue that slavery as both an individual business and as an economic system was profitable for slaveholders and the southern economy alike. Into this school, one may also fit works which stress the dehumanizing effects of slavery on African American slaves. According to this interpretation, the capitalist imperatives of slavery as a labor system stripped slaves of remnants of African culture and turned them into conventional industrial workers imbued with a Protestant work ethic that made them work hard and efficiently, very much like workers in the free wage labor, capitalist North.

These, then, are the contours of a debate and a brief outline of the two categories into which many social and economic historians of the Old South fall. . . .

Any discussion of how best to characterize the nature of southern slavery must at some point address the slippery and elusive question of profitability. To this end, [what follows is] premised on the distinction made by Harold Woodman and others between slavery as a business and slavery as a system.[3] Although the two were intimately linked, for the purposes of historical analysis it is useful to consider slavery as a business and as a system discretely. The former evaluates slavery from the microeconomic level, that is, from the plantation.

Before discussing either the macro or micro efficiency and profitability of slavery, it is worth noting what historians mean when they talk about efficiency and profitability. Unfortunately, there is often little definition of these terms. Historians sometimes write as though there existed an absolute level of profitability for which planters strove. Other times, questions of efficiency and profitability are improperly conflated. After all, as Peter Parish points out: "Profitability and efficiency are not quite the same thing. Profit may result, and often does result, from efficiency, but it may also arise from other causes – ruthless and extravagant exploitation of forced labor or virgin land or natural resources, or a monopoly or near-monopoly position as supplier of a product in urgent demand."[4] Even apparently simple measures of profitability – whether planters made enough money to satisfy their own predictions of a reasonable return on their investment – are plagued with problems. Some years were good, others bad and some masters were never happy no matter how much money they made. The problems multiply when profitability is measured counter-factually, i.e. could the planter have made more money if he had invested his resources in free instead of slave labor? Historians use these various measures and terms often implicitly in their analyses. With the possible exception of historians who compare the profitability of plantations to profits from contemporary factories and industries in free labor societies, it is often difficult to know which measures they are using and when. With these perhaps irreconcilable problems in mind, it is nevertheless clear that the question of profitability and efficiency has divided historians into distinct camps.

Agricultural and capitalized labor, crops, and profits

Here we consider Genovese's now classic statement that no matter how hard slaveholders tried to make their agricultural labor work well and efficiently, the nature of paternalism and the resistance of slaves necessarily produced a poor and inefficient form of agricultural labor. Against this claim, Fogel and Engerman examined the impact of the reward and punishment system employed by masters and concluded that, depending on the masters' individual concerns, slaves were able to labor efficiently on a day-to-day basis. Because of its seminal importance, the work of Ralph Anderson and Robert Gallman concerning the slave as a form of capitalized labor is also considered in detail. They challenge Genovese's notion that the division of labor on southern plantations was immature and underdeveloped. Nothing could be farther from the truth, they contend, since the nature of capitalized labor means that all hands must be employed at all times. Their research suggests that, as far as planters themselves were concerned, there was an efficient and appropriate allocation of labor on southern plantations.[5]

Genovese premises his argument by drawing on the views of contemporary observers of the South. A British economist, John Elliott Cairnes, and a pro-slavery, progress-minded Virginia slaveholder, Edmund Ruffin, contended that "the slave was so defective in versatility that his labor could be exploited profitably only if he were taught one task and kept at it."[6] As southern soil became depleted during and after the 1830s, slaves, if they were to be profitable plantation laborers, would have to be educated and trained, which, as Genovese argues, was a prospect anathema to planters who feared that skilled bondpeople would become dangerous subversives. Hence, slaves worked well below their capabilities and in turn rendered southern plantations unprofitable businesses.

Moreover, Genovese contends, there were other reasons behind slaves' low productivity, the nature and content of their diet being among the most important. "The slave usually got enough to eat," he contends, "but the starchy, high-energy diet of cornmeal, pork, and molasses produced specific hungers" which although giving slaves the appearance of good health was nevertheless insufficient "to ensure either sound bodies or the stamina necessary for sustained labor." Genovese counsels that slaves' low caloric intake and poor diet was not a product of masters' cruelty:

> The limited diet was by no means primarily a result of ignorance or viciousness on the part of masters, for many knew better and would have liked to do better. The problem was largely economic. Feeding costs formed a burdensome part of plantation expenses. Credit and market systems precluded the assignment of much land to crops other than cotton or corn. The land so assigned was generally the poorest available, and the quality of foodstuffs consequently suffered.[7]

Even if planters had managed to institute efficient divisions of labor on plantations, . . . the consequences would have been slight since their slave workers had neither the incentive nor the sheer physical stamina to work as efficiently or as long as slaveholders wanted. Hence, to get slaves to work, planters relied on an admixture of small incentives and frequent physical punishments, or threats thereof. But there were risks attendant on both methods of inducing greater labor. Incentives, after all, were often transmuted into customary rights by slaves and so could lose their inducement value. Promises of extra rations, time off, and miscellaneous benefits might work in the short run but would lose their efficacy in the long run. When masters attempted to extract greater labor by threatening to withdraw customary rights, such as visiting privileges or a scheduled Saturday night dance, they usually encountered such fierce protests by slaves that masters were drawn into protracted debates about their authority to withdraw these rights and were, in the process, diverted from their original efforts to increase productivity. As such, "sooner or later masters fell back on the whip." But problems arose here too. After all, scarred slaves would lose their value. If paddles instead of whips were used to punish refractory or dawdling slaves, wounds would be less likely but excoriation and accusations of barbarism from northern abolitionists would doubtless ensue. For Genovese, physical punishment was the preferred weapon in the slaveholders' arsenal even if it was used grudgingly. Although whipping an individual slave could serve to discourage infractions by others, for many slaveholders whipping was the last resort, but a frequent one, since nothing else seemed to get bondpeople to work. As Genovese put it: "The typical master went to his whip often – much more than he himself would usually have preferred."[8] For Genovese, then, a variety of factors conspired to render plantations at the micro level inefficient and unprofitable.

The argument that plantations were profitable businesses is often associated with the neoclassical view of slavery which gained widespread currency thanks primarily to the work of Lewis Cecil Gray in 1933. Gray's exhaustive examination of antebellum southern agriculture convinced him that plantation slavery was a "capitalist type of agricultural organization in which a considerable number of unfree laborers were employed under unified direction and control in the production of a staple crop." The system was capitalist because "the value of slaves, land, and equipment necessitated the investment of money capital," which in turn encouraged "a strong tendency for the planter to assume the attitude of the business man in testing success by a ratio of net money income to capital invested."[9]

This position has been given further credence by work which compares antebellum slave labor practices with the principles of scientific management advocated by theorists of industrial capitalism.... According to this interpretation, antebellum masters and late nineteenth-century industrial capitalists agreed that workers, both free and slave, shared a tendency to work lazily when they could.... The techniques that planter and industrialist employed to direct this labor, moreover, were very similar. In both instances, work was routinized and repetitively mechanical so that mistakes could be kept to a minimum. The plantation task system, for example, reduced everything to a predictable and precise system which made each slave responsible for a particular piece of work. While some historians prefer to stress the autonomy that the task system afforded slaves, . . . the system also increased the authority of the slaveholder who could match a particular piece of work with a particular slave. The planter could then punish or reward accordingly. Where the task system proved an inappropriate monitor of slave work, masters, again like industrial capitalists, stifled imminent resistance and rebellion by giving workers a vested stake in the plantation enterprise, primarily by granting them small compensations and garden plots of their own. . . . Should incentives and rewards fail, then planters would punish tardy or reluctant workers. Again, the parallels with free wage labor are apparent: under slavery the whip was used to punish; under freedom, fines were the preferred means of correction. Capitalist and planter, then, used punishments, incentives, and labor routines in very similar ways and worked from a common premise that laboring classes generally were indolent and incompetent and that their labor needed to be directed for them.

It has also been argued that southern plantations may be compared usefully to modern businesses. Like the businessman or factory manager, planters aimed to make profits. To that end they arranged the running of their plantations along rational lines, adopted modern business management techniques, and exploited economies of scale. According to Jacob Metzer, planters were the only agricultural producers who had workforces of sufficient size to enable them to take advantage of economies of scale. The plantation owner aimed to maximize his profits by employing an overseer or manager of labor and by attempting to persuade him to look to the long-term maximization of plantation output. Overseers, however, tended to undermine planters' efforts at profit maximization because they were paid fixed wages and received bonuses for short-term increases in cash crops. As a result, many planters assumed the dual role of planter-overseer in the Old South. Hands-on masters, argues Metzer, were successful at rationalizing the operations of their plantations. They instituted precise and efficient divisions of labor so that the best cotton pickers, like young women, were used and that the right slave was always assigned the appropriate job. . . . [P]lanters managed to routinize plantation labor independently of seasonal variations; . . . they achieved a high level of labor coordination and control; and . . . they successfully rendered the antebellum plantation a modern business by maximizing profit and exploiting economies of scale.[10]

Time on the Cross . . . also presented evidence to support the contention that plantations were profitable businesses. Fogel and Engerman attempted to take Genovese to task, particularly on the question of slaves' dietary intake. In characteristically emphatic and flamboyant style, Fogel and Engerman broached the diet issue thus: "The belief that the typical slave was poorly fed is without foundation in fact."[11] Historians had been misled as to the true nature and content of slaves' diets, they contended, because they had relied on the necessarily incomplete and sketchy records concerning food allowances contained in plantation diaries and overseers' records. Such documents were intended simply to outline the "major features" of plantation operations and since many foods were seasonal the true range and variety of food that was allocated to bondpeople was not reflected in such records. Fogel and Engerman's reading of alternative documents revealed that slaves ate an astounding variety of foods, some of which bondpeople grew themselves in their own time or acquired through hunting and fishing. Based on their analysis of manuscript schedules of the 1860 census returns, Fogel and Engerman computed "the average amounts of eleven of the principal foods consumed by slaves who lived on the large plantations of the cotton belt." By their own estimation, Fogel and Engerman's findings were "astounding." Although they based their findings on about 80 percent of the caloric intake of slaves, they discovered that the energy value of slaves' diet "exceeded that of free men in 1879 by more than 10 percent." More impressively still, the average slave diet "was not only adequate, it actually exceeded modern (1964) recommended daily levels of the chief nutrients. On average, slaves exceeded the daily recommended level of proteins by 110 percent, calcium by 20 percent, and iron by 230 percent." These findings, combined with their other arguments concerning the high standard of slave housing, clothing, and medical care, convinced Fogel and Engerman that slaves were fed more than enough high quality food to enable them to work long and productive hours.[12] . . .

Slaves, then, in Fogel and Engerman's opinion, were fed enough food of sufficient caloric and nutritional quality to enable them to work hard and efficiently. But was this in itself a guarantee that they would? . . . Fogel and Engerman believed that southern slaves were imbued with very much the same work ethic that free laborers putatively embraced. As such, slaveholders did not need to whip their bondpeople as often as Genovese believed to get them to work. Instead, slaves responded to incentive and reward systems established by planters and thereby rendered plantation labor orderly, efficient, and profitable. . . .

It is, of course, perfectly possible for Genovese to concede that slaves did respond positively to rewards and incentives, that their diet was of sufficient quantity and quality for them to work efficiently, and for him to still maintain that slave labor was inefficient. After all, Genovese made the astute and largely economic point that because "slavery requires all hands to be occupied at all times" and because the requisite "extensive division of labor cannot readily develop in slave economies" southern planters, by virtue of slavery and its reliance on agriculture, could not make the fullest use of their labor year round. There would, in Genovese's opinion, be slack periods when staples were in the process of growing and when slaves would remain relatively idle.[13] Superficially, Genovese's argument has much to recommend it: slave labor was devoted to the cultivation of staples which necessarily did not require the same intensity of labor year round. Because he had bought labor for life, the planter, unlike the employer of wage labor, could not readily lay off workers during slack periods. Slaveholders, then, must have been losing money on their investment for some part of the year and, as such, whatever profit they did make could have been greater had they abandoned plantation agriculture.

Ralph Anderson and Robert Gallman have challenged Genovese's implicit assumption that slaveholders were unable to keep slaves occupied at all times. Slaves, in their opinion, are best viewed as "fixed capital" or "capitalized labor." This indeed meant that the slaveholder could not lay off workers during slack periods of plantation work. Their largely economic analysis of the agricultural activities of nine plantations from all the major staple producing regions of the South preceding 1840, however, suggests that the "full use of the labor force in each season of the year was assured... by the adoption of a diversified output." Regardless of the type of staple produced, slaveholders managed to dovetail different types of labor "that fit together to produce a full work year for the labor force." Slaveholders, including slaveowning yeomen, did this by growing food or directing their slaves to construction work or clearing land during the lull periods when plantation staples required little attention. As Anderson and Gallman explained: "planters did press to use their labor fully, during all seasons of the year, and this led them to adopt a diversified pattern of output. This should not be surprising. The costs of allowing labor to idle simply outweighed the benefits of single-minded concentration on one product."[14] Although planters were forced to intensify their labor in order to diversify, the point that Anderson and Gallman stress is that diversification reflected the planters' essentially rational character – that they put their economic interests before the physical well-being of their slaves. Paternalism did nothing to diminish planters' steadfast pursuit of profit.

Jacob Metzer agrees. By vertically integrating various aspects of plantation labor, masters managed to avoid wasting time. In months when cotton growing required little labor, masters reallocated potentially idle labor to growing food crops and in so doing ensured that plantations were not only self-sufficient units but that labor was never underemployed. So too with the potentially idle labor of, say, crippled slaves, who were allocated jobs which did not require physical stamina or strength but rather a dexterous skill. The ability of masters to diversify plantation activities meant that all slaves were employed in some capacity at all times and this was most obviously manifest in the training of plantation slave artisans. Moreover, notes Metzer, skilled slave artisans were less likely to run away than free workers were to change jobs which suggests that the planters' investment in training the slave was rational and profitable.

Other studies support Metzer's position. Gavin Wright, for example, has pointed out that since masters invested most of their capital in slaves and not in land – since they were laborlords first and landlords second – planters naturally sought to increase output per hand rather than yield per acre.[15] According to John F. Olson, planters were successful in this endeavor. Even though slaves worked fewer hours per year than free workers, North and South, bondpeople "worked 94 percent more (harder) each hour."[16] By giving slaves longer breaks during the hottest seasons, by carefully ascertaining the appropriate length of rest periods, planters encouraged their slaves and, indeed their livestock, to work more efficiently and intensively per work hour than free laborers. A subtle, involved, and sophisticated amalgam of whip, incentive, and considered and monitored work breaks, then, succeeded in getting slaves to work diligently, efficiently, year round. Hence, even the physically delicate, such as pregnant slave women, were kept in the field until very late in their term. While it is not altogether clear if this practice was particularly sensible (slave birth weights were sometimes small as a result and infant mortality among slaves was relatively high) it is nevertheless compelling, if unpalatable, evidence of the slaveholders' drive for profit in their plantation businesses. Therefore, in an absolute sense, plantations were sufficiently profitable businesses to wed slaveholders to slave-based plantation agriculture. But was slavery as an economic system healthy for the southern economy generally?

Notes

1 See Eugene D. Genovese, *The Political Economy of Slavery: Studies in the Economy and Society of the Slave South* (New York: Vintage, 1965); Eugene D. Genovese and Elizabeth Fox-Genovese, *Fruits of Merchant Capital: Slavery and Bourgeois Property in the Rise and Expansion of Capitalism* (New York: Oxford University Press, 1983); Eugene D. Genovese, *The Slaveholders' Dilemma: Freedom and Progress in Southern Conservative Thought* (Columbia, SC: University of South Carolina Press, 1992).

2 Shearer Davis Bowman, *Masters and Lords: Mid-19th-Century U.S. Planters and Prussian Junkers* (New York: Oxford University Press, 1993), p. 93.

3 Harold Woodman, "The Profitability of Slavery: A Historical Perennial," *Journal of Southern History*, 29 (1963).

4 Peter Parish, *Slavery: History and Historians* (New York: Harper & Row, 1989), p. 44.

5 Robert William Fogel and Stanley L. Engerman, *Time on the Cross: The Economics of American Negro Slavery* (Boston: Little, Brown, 1974); Ralph V. Anderson and Robert E. Gallman, "Slaves as Fixed Capital: Slave Labor and Southern Economic Development," *Journal of American History*, 64 (1977).

6 John Elliot Cairnes, *The Slave Power: Its Character, Career, and Probably Designs: Being an Attempt to Explain the Real Issues Involved in the American Context* (New York, 1862).

7 Genovese, *Political Economy of Slavery*, pp. 43, 44–6.

8 Eugene D. Genovese, *Roll, Jordan, Roll: The World the Slaves Made* (New York: Vintage, 1976), p. 64.

9 Lewis Cecil Gray, *History of Agriculture in the United States to 1860*, 2 vols., (Washington, DC: Carnegie Institute, 1933), vol. 1, p. 302.

10 Jacob Metzer, "Rational Management, Modern Business Practices, and the Economies of Scale in the Ante-Bellum Southern Plantations," *Explorations in Economic History*, 12 (1975).

11 Fogel and Engerman, *Time on the Cross*, p. 109.

12 Ibid., pp. 111–15.

13 Genovese, *Political Economy of Slavery*, p. 49.

14 Anderson and Gallman, "Slaves as Fixed Capital," pp. 31, 32.

15 Gavin Wright, *The Political Economy of the Cotton South: Households, Markets, and Wealth in the Nineteenth Century* (New York: Norton, 1978).

16 John F. Olson, "Clock Time Versus Real Time: A Comparison of the Lengths of the Northern and Southern Agricultural Work Years," in *Without Consent or Contract: The Rise and Fall of American Slavery: Technical Papers*, ed. Robert William Fogel and Stanley L. Engerman, vol. 1 (New York: Norton, 1992).

6
The World of the Planters

Introduction

The large planters lived in colonnaded mansions, called "big houses," which were both their families' residences and the administrative centers of the plantations. Nearby, a smaller building usually housed the overseer, who was for all purposes the authority in charge of labor performance and the management of slaves. In many respects, the plantation functioned as an agricultural enterprise, since its existence revolved around the production of crops for sale on the market. However, the plantation's economic efficiency depended not just on the management of the workforce, but also on the planter's knowledge of agricultural techniques. Several planters realized that they needed to understand more about agriculture in order to keep up with domestic and foreign competition; this was especially true in the area of soil depletion, which was caused by both tobacco and cotton cultivation. Therefore, they promoted agricultural progress and sought to diffuse agricultural knowledge through specialized societies and journals.

Whether effectively managing their slaves or acquainting themselves with new agricultural techniques, planters were engaged in a search for the best way to realize a profit from their operations. For this reason, neoclassical economists have argued that they acted in entrepreneurial fashion. However, Marxist historians have pointed out that the planters' interest in agricultural progress stopped short of eliminating slavery as an institution. Crop diversification and improved agricultural techniques could lead to only partial recovery from the kind of soil depletion brought about by tobacco and cotton monoculture. The only way planters could survive as a class in economic and social terms was by reproducing the slave system of the South in new fertile lands in the West, and this inevitably led to conflict with the expanding free-labor North.

The World of the Planters

Therefore, left with no alternative for their survival as a class, planters tried to justify as best they could the economic and social advantages of the system that gave them power; they increasingly refined the intellectual defense of human bondage through a pro-slavery argument. After the revival of the abolitionist movement in the 1830s, the pro-slavery argument became an exercise that engaged the best minds of the South. Planters felt threatened by the growth of aggressive antislavery sentiment in the North, and they looked for increasingly sophisticated explanations and justifications for the existence of a system which many considered barbaric and inhuman. Among the most important pro-slavery ideologues was George Fitzhugh, a Virginia planter who wrote two important treatises in which he argued that, compared to industrial workers, slaves were better treated and better fed. According to Fitzhugh, industrial workers, unlike slaves, were condemned to a life of misery and exploitation in the cities, where factories employed them and left them starving after they were too old and decrepit to continue employment.

In the mind of the planters, slavery was closely linked with honor. Men of honor were those who adhered to a code of behavior based on personal worth and recognition of social position within the community. Honor implied respect from others and among equals; offences were often resolved with duels. The essence of honor was personal autonomy. Autonomy, freedom, and self-sufficiency were values that characterized the political sphere, while dependency, forced submissiveness, and lack of power were characteristics of slaves and all the individuals who were barred from political participation. Slave ownership ennobled and enhanced one's status and independence, because it provided an instrument with which to exercise power, not over the slaves alone, but over those without means. Politics, then, was simply an arena in which peers – men of honor – were rivals for public acclaim and power. Organized parties, elaborate bureaucracies, heavy taxes, and state power were threats to autonomy, freedom, and self-sufficiency – the qualities that planters linked to honor. Honor was such a pervasive force that, together with owning slaves, it was the other key defining element that cut across the regional divisions of the master class of the antebellum South.

Further reading

Allmendiger, D. F., *Ruffin: Family and Reform in the Old South* (New York: Oxford University Press, 1990).

Dusinberre, W., *Them Dark Days: Life in the American Rice Swamps* (New York: Oxford University Press, 1996).

Faust, D. G., *James Henry Hammond and the Old South: A Design for Mastery* (Baton Rouge: Louisiana State University Press, 1982).

Faust, D. G. (ed.), *The Ideology of Slavery* (Baton Rouge: Louisiana State University Press, 1981).

Genovese, E. D., *The Slaveholders' Dilemma: Freedom and Progress in Southern Conservative Thought, 1820–1860* (Columbia, SC: University of South Carolina Press, 1992).

Genovese, E. D., *The World the Slaveholders Made: Three Essays in Interpretation* (New York: Vintage, 1969).

Greenberg, K. S., *Honor and Slavery* (Princeton: Princeton University Press, 1996).

Greenberg, K. S., *Masters and Statesmen: The Political Culture of American Slavery* (Baltimore: Johns Hopkins University Press, 1985).

Morris, C., *Becoming Southern: The Evolution of a Way of Life, Warren County and Vicksburg, Mississippi, 1770–1860* (New York: Oxford University Press, 1995).

Oakes, J., *The Ruling Race: A History of American Slaveholders* (New York: Alfred A. Knopf, 1982).

Oakes, J., *Slavery and Freedom: An Interpretation of the Old South* (New York: Alfred A. Knopf, 1990).

Smith, M. M., *Mastered by the Clock: Time, Slavery, and Freedom in the Antebellum American South* (Chapel Hill: University of North Carolina Press, 1997).

Tise, L. E., *Pro-slavery: A History of the Defense of Slavery in America, 1701–1840* (Athens: University of Georgia Press, 1988).

Wyatt-Brown, B., *Southern Honor: Ethics and Behavior in the Old South* (New York: Oxford University Press, 1982).

Young, J. R., *Domesticating Slavery: The Master Class in South Carolina and Georgia, 1670–1830* (Chapel Hill: University of North Carolina Press, 1999).

John Lyde Wilson's Rules of the Code of Honor (1838)

The pervasiveness of honor as an organized code of rules for the behavior of the master class emerges clearly from this document. John Lyde Wilson was a South Carolinian who wrote one of the most popular handbooks setting out the rules of dueling. Nowhere more than in aristocratic South Carolina was dueling more widespread among gentlemen planters. As several scholars have argued, dueling was a highly ritualized activity which focused upon the staging of conflict resolution within the elite through a spectacular – and often deadly – performance. Gentlemen engaged in duels when they were challenged by their equals to defend their honor. This happened – as Wilson's *Code Duello* makes clear – when they believed they had been insulted or offended. The code bound them to proceed through detailed rules and, after sending a note to their adversary and choosing their seconds, they were to engage in armed confrontation with specified kinds of weapons.

CHAPTER I. THE PERSON INSULTED, BEFORE CHALLENGE SENT

1. Whenever you believe you are insulted, if the insult be in public, and by words or behavior, never resent it there, if you have self-command enough to avoid noticing it. If resented there, you offer an indignity to the company, which you should not.

2. If the insult be by blows or any personal indignity, it may be resented at the moment, for the insult to the company did not originate with you. But although resented at the moment, yet you are bound still to have satisfaction, and must therefore make the demand.

3. When you believe yourself aggrieved, be silent on the subject, speak to no one about the matter, and see your friend who is to act for you, as soon as possible.

4. Never send a challenge in the first instance, for that precludes all negotiation. Let your note be in the language of a gentleman, and let the subject matter of complaint be truly and fairly set forth, cautiously avoiding attributing to the adverse party any improper motive.

Source: John Lyde Wilson, *The Code of Honor, or, Rules for the Government of Principals and Seconds in Duelling* (Charleston, SC: James Phinney, 1838), pp. 91–9

5. When your second is in full possession of the facts, leave the whole matter to his judgment, and avoid any consultation with him unless he seeks it. He has the custody of your honor, and by obeying him you cannot be compromitted.

6. Let the time of demand upon your adversary after the insult be as short as possible, for he has the right to double that time in replying to you, unless you give some good reason for your delay. Each party is entitled to reasonable time to make the necessary domestic arrangements, by will or otherwise before fighting.

7. To a written communication you are entitled to a written reply, and it is the business of your friend to require it.

CHAPTER VI. WHO SHOULD BE ON THE GROUND

1. The principals, seconds, and one surgeon and one assistant surgeon to each principal, but the assistant surgeon may be dispensed with.

2. Any number of friends that the seconds agree on, may be present, provided they do not come within the degrees of consanguinity mentioned in the seventh rule of Chapter 1.

3. Persons admitted on the ground are carefully to abstain by word or behaviour, from any act that might be the least exceptionable, nor should they stand near the principals or seconds, or hold conversations with them.

CHAPTER VIII. THE DEGREES OF INSULT, AND HOW COMPROMISED

1. The prevailing rule is, that words used in retort, although more violent and disrespectful than those first used, will not satisfy – words being no satisfaction for words.

2. When words are used, and a blow given in return, the insult is avenged, and if redress be sought, it must be from the person receiving the blow.

3. When blows are given in the first instance and returned, and the person first striking be badly beaten or otherwise, the party first struck is to make the demand, for blows do not satisfy a blow.

4. Insults at a wine table, when the company are over-excited, must be answered for; and if the party insulting have no recollection of the insult, it is his duty to say so in writing, and negative the insult. For instance, if a man say, "you are a liar and no gentleman," he must, in addition to the plea of the want of recollection, say: "I believe the party insulted to be a man of the strictest veracity and a gentleman."

5. Intoxication is not a full excuse for insult, but it will greatly palliate. If it was a full excuse, it might well be counterfeited to wound feelings, or destroy character.

6. In all cases of intoxication, the seconds must use a sound discretion under the above general rules.

7. Can every insult be compromised? is a mooted and vexed question. On this subject no rules can be given that will be satisfactory. The old opinion, that a blow must require blood, is not of force. Blows may be compromised in many cases. What those cases are, must depend on the seconds.

George Fitzhugh on the Benefits of Slavery (1857)

Virginian George Fitzhugh (1806–81) was, doubtless, the most original pro-slavery advocate. Born into one of the oldest families of Virginia planters, Fitzhugh left the family estate to practice law and contributed a stream of articles to southern newspapers such as the *Richmond Enquirer* and *De Bow's Review*. In 1854, he published *Sociology for the South, or The Failure of Free Society*, the first of two works in which he vigorously defended agricultural slavery, arguing against the benefits of industrial freedom. His other work was *Cannibals All!, or Slaves without Masters*, published in 1857, from which this excerpt is taken. Fitzhugh's central idea was that slavery was "a benign and protective institution" which benefited blacks, since they were treated far better than free white laborers in industrial cities and factories. Industrial laborers were worked and starved to death by greedy capitalist bosses; black slaves, on the other hand, were well fed by their benevolent masters, who gave them shelter and freed them from "the curse of liberty."

The world at large looks on negro slavery as much the worst form of slavery; because it is only acquainted with West India slavery. Abolition never arose till negro slavery was instituted; and now abolition is only directed against negro slavery. There is no philanthropic crusade attempting to set free the white slaves of Eastern Europe and of Asia.

Source: C. Vann Woodward (ed.), *Cannibals All! or Slaves without Masters* (Cambridge, Mass., and London: The Belknap Press of Harvard University Press, 1996; orig. pub. 1960), pp. 199–206

The world, then, is prepared for the defence of slavery in the abstract – it is prejudiced only against negro slavery. These prejudices were in their origin well founded. The Slave Trade, the horrors of the Middle Passage, and West India slavery were enough to rouse the most torpid philanthropy.

But our Southern slavery has become a benign and protective institution, and our negroes are confessedly better off than any free laboring population in the world.

How can we contend that white slavery is wrong, whilst all the great body of free laborers are starving; and slaves, white or black, throughout the world, are enjoying comfort?

We write in the cause of Truth and Humanity, and will not play the advocate for master or for slave.

The aversion to negroes, the antipathy of race, is much greater at the North than at the South; and it is very probable that this antipathy to the person of the negro, is confounded with or generates hatred of the institution with which he is usually connected. Hatred to slavery is very generally little more than hatred of negroes.

There is one strong argument in favor of negro slavery over all other slavery: that he, being unfitted for the mechanic arts, for trade, and all skillful pursuits, leaves those pursuits to be carried on by the whites; and does not bring all industry into disrepute, as in Greece and Rome, where the slaves were not only the artists and mechanics, but also the merchants.

Whilst, as a general and abstract question, negro slavery has no other claims over other forms of slavery, except that from inferiority, or rather peculiarity, of race, almost all negroes require masters, whilst only the children, the women, the very weak, poor, and ignorant, &c., among the whites, need some protective and governing relation of this kind; yet as a subject of temporary, but worldwide importance, negro slavery has become the most necessary of all human institutions.

The African slave trade to America commenced three centuries and a half since. By the time of the American Revolution, the supply of slaves had exceeded the demand for slave labor, and the slaveholders, to get rid of a burden, and to prevent the increase of a nuisance, became violent opponents of the slave trade, and many of them abolitionists. New England, Bristol, and Liverpool, who reaped the profits of the trade, without suffering from the nuisance, stood out for a long time against its abolition. Finally, laws and treaties were made, and fleets fitted out to abolish it; and after a while, the slaves of most of South America, of the West Indies, and of Mexico were liberated. In the meantime, cotton, rice, sugar, coffee, tobacco, and other products of slave labor, came into universal use as necessaries of life. The population of Western Europe, sustained and stimulated by those products, was trebled, and that of the North increased tenfold. The products of slave labor became scarce and dear, and famines frequent. Now, it is obvious, that to emancipate all the negroes would be to starve Western Europe and our North. Not to extend and increase negro slavery, *pari passu*, with the extension and multiplication of free society, will produce much suffering. If all South America, Mexico, the West Indies, and our Union south of Mason and Dixon's line, of the Ohio and Missouri, were slaveholding, slave products would be abundant and cheap in free society; and their market for their merchandise, manufactures, commerce, &c., illimitable. Free white laborers might live in comfort and luxury on light work, but for the exacting and greedy landlords, bosses and other capitalists.

George Cary Eggleston Remembers the Aristocratic Life in Antebellum Virginia (1875)

George Cary Eggleston (1839–1911) descended from a prominent Virginian family whose members had fought in the American Revolution. His father Joseph instilled in him the passion for Virginia's culture of honor and aristocratic way of life. Though initially troubled by the presence of slavery, Eggleston grew to embrace the prevalent view that it was a fundamentally good institution and an essential part of southern society. In 1861, when war broke out, Eggleston enlisted in the Confederacy. After the Confederate defeat, he moved to the North, where he published his Civil War memoirs in an attempt to correct northern misunderstandings of the South and foster sympathy for his homeland. In this excerpt, Eggleston describes life in antebellum Virginia, focusing on the planter elite. His main concern was to explain why Virginia was a conservative aristocratic society preoccupied with the pride derived from family names, to which the honor and reputation of gentlemen were inextricably linked.

It was a very beautiful and enjoyable life that the Virginians led in that ancient time, for it certainly seems ages ago, before the war came to turn

Source: George Cary Eggleston, *A Rebel's Recollections* (Baton Rouge: Louisiana State University Press, 1996; orig. pub. 1905), pp. 27–33

ideas upside down and convert the picturesque commonwealth into a commonplace, modern state. It was a soft, dreamy, deliciously quiet life, a life of repose, an old life, with all its sharp corners and rough surfaces long ago worn round and smooth. Everything fitted everything else, and every point in it was so well settled as to leave no work of improvement for anybody to do. The Virginians were satisfied with things as they were, and if there were reformers born among them, they went elsewhere to work changes. Society in the Old Dominion was like a well-rolled and closely packed gravel walk, in which each pebble has found precisely the place it fits best. There was no giving way under one's feet, no uncomfortable grinding of loose materials as one walked about over the firm and long-used ways of the Virginian social life.

. . . The Virginians were born conservatives, constitutionally opposed to change. They loved the old because it was old, and disliked the new, if for no better reason, because it was new; for newness and rawness were well-nigh the same in their eyes. . . .

But chief among the causes of that conservatism which gave tone and color to the life we are considering was the fact that ancient estates were carefully kept in ancient families, generation after generation. If a Virginian lived in a particular mansion, it was strong presumptive proof that his father, his grandfather, and his great-grandfather had lived there before him. There was no law of primogeniture to be sure by which this was brought about, but there were well-established customs which amounted to the same thing. Family pride was a ruling passion, and not many Virginians of the better class hesitated to secure the maintenance of their family place in the ranks of the untitled peerage by the sacrifice of their own personal prosperity, if that were necessary, as it sometimes was. To the first-born son went the estate usually, by the will of the father and with the hearty concurrence of the younger sons, when there happened to be any such. The eldest brother succeeded the father as the head of the house, and took upon himself the father's duties and the father's burdens. Upon him fell the management of the estate; the maintenance of the mansion, which, under the laws of hospitality obtaining there, was no light task; the education of the younger sons and daughters; and last, though commonly not by any means least, the management of the hereditary debt. The younger children always had a home in the old mansion, secured to them by the will of their father sometimes, but secure enough in any case by a custom more binding than any law; and there were various other ways of providing for them. If the testator were rich, he divided among them his bonds, stocks, and other personal property not necessary to the prosperity of the estate, or charged the head of the house with the payment of certain legacies to each. The mother's property, if she had brought a dower with her, was usually portioned out among them, and the law, medicine, army, navy, and church offered them genteel employment if they chose to set up for themselves. But these arrangements were subsidiary to the main purpose of keeping the estate in the family, and maintaining the mansion-house as a seat of elegant hospitality. So great was the importance attached to this last point, and so strictly was its observance enjoined upon the new lord of the soil, that he was frequently the least to be envied of all.

The Slaveholders' Dilemma between Bondage and Progress

Eugene D. Genovese

In *The Slaveholders' Dilemma*, Eugene Genovese argues that the elite of the antebellum South perceived itself as modern and progressive in spite of the fact that southern intellectuals and politicians defended slavery; in fact, southern slaveholders thought of slavery as an indispensable guarantee of the "freedom necessary for progress." As Genovese explains in this excerpt, the slaveholders' dilemma lay in their simultaneous support of the necessity of both slavery and freedom for economic advancement and social modernization. The writings of some of the finest pro-slavery economists and social analysts – such as Thomas Roderick Dew, George Tucker, and George Fitzhugh – show clear indications of their ambiguous attitude toward definitions of freedom and progress. Especially southern theologians, such as James Henry Thornwell, argued that slavery was "the only safe, secure indeed, Christian foundation of freedom"; yet they knew that wherever freedom had expanded, slavery had been eradicated.

The mainstream of modern Western thought has cast slavery and progress as irreconcilable opposites, insisting that slavery impeded progress by restricting the freedom of every individual to contribute to society through the pursuit of self interest. Slavery, if we are to credit its adversaries, threatened the very identity of the American republic, according its virtue and retarding its development. Even the growing demand for rapid economic development through a program of free soil,

Eugene D. Genovese, *The Slaveholders' Dilemma: Freedom and Progress in Southern Conservative Thought, 1820–1860* (Columbia: University of South Carolina Press, 1992), pp. 10–45.

free labor, and free men elided moral and material progress, tying the fate of the one to the unfolding of the other. The War for Southern Independence appeared to confirm this reading and to embody the triumph of moral and material progress over the forces of stagnation and reaction.

The war, in sealing the triumph of the North over the South, also sealed the triumph of the association of freedom and progress over an alternate reading. If the seeds of the irreconcilable opposition between slavery and progress, like the seeds of the unquestioning association of progress with freedom, were sown in the American, French, and Haitian Revolutions, their blossoming was not immediately assured. The slaveholding intellectuals, clerical and lay, took radically different ground, arguing for an understanding of freedom and progress as grounded in – not opposed to – slavery as a social system.

Edmund Morgan has demonstrated that the slaveholders of colonial Virginia espoused slavery as the necessary foundation of individual freedom and republican virtue and saw themselves as the principal champions of both. David Brion Davis has demonstrated that important strands of Euro-American thought came to challenge the prevalent notion that slavery impeded progress and to conclude that, under certain conditions, slavery in fact generated progress. Despite the inestimable contributions of these and other learned historians, the southern slaveholders' discrete understanding of the precise interrelation of slavery, freedom, and progress remains to be explored.[1]

The southern intellectuals devoted a large number of books, pamphlets, and articles in lay and religious journals to these subjects. The answer they offered, notwithstanding variations of considerable political importance, contained a big surprise. For they viewed freedom, not slavery, as the driving force in human progress, moral and material. They based their defense of slavery on a prior defense of freedom, which they identified as the dynamic in a world progress the cause of which they claimed as their own. Freedom, in their view, could not be extended to all, but it could be extended to increasing numbers and could be expected to result in a better life for those who remained subservient. They thereby invoked slavery as a positive force that grounded the social order required to support the freedom necessary for progress. The slaveholders presented themselves to themselves and to the world as the most reliable carriers of the cause of progress in Western civilization, and they presented their social system as the surest and safest model for a worldwide Christendom that sought to continue its forward march.

The slaveholders had no greater success than others, before or since, in defining "progress," but they settled, as most others have, for a common-sense notion of a steady and irreversible advance in the material conditions of life for the masses as well as for the elites. However qualified their recognition of moral progress, the slaveholders displayed deep ambivalence toward that material progress which the overwhelming majority of them saw as inevitable: Literally, they loved and hated it. They embraced it on balance partly because they did see it as inevitable, and partly because they welcomed the leisure, knowledge, and comfort it brought. Like most traditionalist conservatives in Europe, they wanted to guide and temper social change, to slow it down so as to avoid destructive effects. Unlike the traditionalist conservatives in Europe, they thought they had found the means in the organization of social relations on a slaveholding basis.

In the eyes of foreign critics, by no means all or even most of whom were abolitionists, the slaveholders of the Old South qualified as reactionaries who were desperately clinging to a retrogressive social system in an age of accelerating economic, social, and intellectual development. Northerners, Britons, continental Europeans, and Latin Americans shook their heads at the existence of a backward yet politically powerful regional regime embedded in an economically dynamic, politically radical . . . republic poised to challenge for world power. The long list of such critics included not only radicals, democrats, and liberals of all stripes, but many high Tories, high churchmen, and other conservatives who shared the slaveholders' grave reservations about the vast changes that were occurring in the wake of the industrial and French revolutions.

Many of these conservatives, to one extent or another, carried into the nineteenth century the attitudes associated with, say, Samuel Johnson during the eighteenth. Even most of those who expressed sympathy for the Confederacy did so because they hated the bourgeois radicalism of the North, valued the conservatism and aristocratic tone of the South, and considered the race question intractable, not because they supported slavery in principle. More often than not . . . they hoped that the South would find a way to shed slavery and thereby rid itself of a moral incubus and the principal encumbrance to the material well-being required to sustain national independence.

The slaveholders saw themselves differently. Southern intellectuals, political leaders, and ordinary slaveholders, as their numerous diaries and personal papers attest, regarded themselves as progressive men and as active participants in the material and moral march of history. They saw themselves as men who sought an alternate route to modernity. . . .

The dilemma inherent in the slaveholders' contradictory ideas of progress, freedom, and slavery emerges most clearly in the work of Thomas Roderick Dew of Virginia (1802–1846), whose remarkable literary output ranged well beyond his famous review of the debates in the Virginia legislature over emancipation. As president of the College of William and Mary and a professor of history, political economy, moral philosophy, and other subjects, he devoted much of his career to an interpretation of the development of Western civilization.[2] . . .

Dew embraced "progress" with as much enthusiasm as any man of his day. If anything, his enthusiasm far exceeded that of other southern writers. Those who rose to prominence after his death especially displayed an ambivalence Dew largely had avoided. He reveled in the advances in learning, economic production, transportation, communications, even in morals, and he recognized the self-generating power of science and technology. Simply put, life was becoming qualitatively better for an ever-increasing number of men and women, and the root of this welcome progress lay in the expansion of individual freedom. Man, released from servitude and superstition, promoted enterprise, innovation, cultural improvement – in a word, progress. Western civilization stood alone among the great civilizations of the world in having found a way to break the cycle of flowering, stagnation, and decay by liberating the individual to pursue his own destiny within a Christian culture that provided a bulwark against the moral degeneration that marked previous epochs. . . .

For Dew, God provided harmony in nature and gave man the freedom of will to follow its laws. The sinful aspect of man's nature remained a serious impediment, but by devising free institutions he could promote the appropriate ways and means. His progress depended upon his socially secured freedom to pursue his own happiness in tandem with that of others. The necessary social security depended upon property rights, which had to be guaranteed by a state that protects the individual's right to dispose of his own property with as few restrictions as possible. To meet this responsibility the state must be firmly governed by propertied individuals under a constitution that restrains them from using their power at the expense of other propertied individuals; that is, it must be republican, democratic, and egalitarian.

Dew recognized democracy and egalitarianism only in the limited sense that applied to propertied individuals. He had no patience with the sweeping Jeffersonian formulations of the Declaration of Independence. He recognized neither the equality of races nor of individuals beyond that appropriate to the political life of those who owned property or, at least, respected its claims. Moral, intellectual, and material progress depended upon the special talents of superior individuals whose contributions depended on their release from drudgery. The progress of Western civilization has been spurred by the expansion of a freedom made possible by a class stratification that released some men to cultivate their talents. The expansion of the realm of freedom has generated economic and technological progress that has permitted the further expansion of freedom by reducing the amount of labor time necessary for the production of leisure. Freedom has become available to increasing numbers of men, whose combined efforts have resulted in an ever-quickening of progress. The course of progress and of freedom has remained upward and onward.

But could it continue? The laws of political economy, which Dew carefully studied and taught, pointed toward an unfolding tragedy. Dew pondered the ramifications of the Ricardian theories of rent, diminishing returns to agriculture, and the falling rate of profit, and he accepted Malthus's grim law of population. He concluded... that sooner or later... the cost of free labor would fall below that of slave labor and thereby inspire a widespread emancipation of slaves, as it had inspired the emancipation of the European serfs at the end of the Middle Ages. In short, the logic of Dew's political economy pointed toward the end of slavery.

George Tucker, unlike Dew, felt no trepidations. He concluded that slavery had no future and counseled the North to end its agitation and let the laws of political economy do their work. Tucker, arguably the ablest political economist in the United States and a man of generally humane temperament, easily swallowed the implications of the scenario: Slavery would disappear because the cost of free labor would fall and the living standards of laborers would sink to a subsistence level under a system that offered little or no protection during the periodic plunges well beneath that level. The great mass of mankind would have to live not only with poverty and brutal exploitation but with the threat of starvation.

Dew gagged. He regarded the outcome as morally unacceptable, as did the pro-slavery divines, who bemoaned it regularly in sermons, publications, and lectures to the academy and college courses many of them taught. No Christian should be asked to live with it. Perhaps worse, the outcome was politically an invitation to catastrophe. Dew did not believe that the laboring classes would submit. He took the measure of the French Revolution and the even greater radicalism that it opened the floodgates to....

Erudite, deeply thoughtful, and temperamentally optimistic,... Dew delineated the dilemma. The very political and intellectual freedom that lay at the heart of all freedom produced and could only be sustained by economic freedom. Dew, who supported laissez-faire and denounced state interference in the market, recognized economic freedom as the special dynamic of material progress. But he feared that the story would end badly wherever the laws of the market were permitted to apply to labor-power – wherever free labor prevailed.

At the risk of distorting Dew's subtle and elegantly crafted analysis, we may reduce it to a few propositions. Freedom generated progress, which permitted a vast expansion of freedom. The extension of freedom to the economy, upon which all material progress has rested, meant submission to laws of economic development that condemned the laboring classes to unprecedented exploitation, immiseration, and periodic starvation. At the same time the historical unfolding of those laws required the extension of republican liberties that could not wholly, if at all, be denied to the laborers who had been removed from the security of their servile status and declared free men. Faced with unbearable privations, they would rise . . . in insurrection. Worse, the intellectual freedom essential to all progress, including economic progress, was inexorably extruding every possible kind of utopian and demagogic scheme, which the revolution in communications was carrying to the desperate masses.

Like every other slaveholding intellectual, Dew denied that the laboring classes could consolidate a revolution and maintain power. They could, however, provoke anarchy and deprive the propertied classes of their power to rule. In the event, the capitalists, in particular, would turn to military despots, who would offer a minimum cradle-to-grave security to the laboring masses while protecting the propertied classes. But in so doing, the despots would have to destroy much of the intellectual, political, and economic freedom of the propertied classes. They would therefore undermine progress.

Dew ended by holding up the social system of the South as a model for a future world order. Only slavery or personal servitude in some form could guarantee republican liberties for the propertied, security for the propertyless, and stability for the state and society. Hence Dew faced a two-pronged dilemma: . . . Steady progress remained his great ideal; progress depended upon a regime of self-expanding freedom; a regime of self-expanding freedom provoked social conflicts that undermined it; and only the worldwide restoration of slavery could restore social stability and civilized order. What then of the self-generating progress that constituted the glory of Western civilization? The free market, once extended to labor-power, must end in perpetual civil war or the installation of despotism, but progress depended upon the extension of that very free market. Dew believed that the West faced a stark choice: It could continue a headlong progress that threatened to end in social catastrophe; or, it could effect a worldwide restoration of a servitude that threatened the end of civilization's progressive momentum. With a heavy heart he chose slavery, order, and stability.

His optimistic nature may well have led him to hope that material progress would continue, if at a much slower pace – that slavery, which he saw as the surest social foundation of republican liberty, would leave enough room for freedom of thought to do its work. After all, did not the South have a society free enough to participate in the progress of civilization? The problem nonetheless remained: Virtually all the great achievements associated with the extraordinary progress of the modern world had sprung from the free-labor economies, and it did so for reasons he elaborated as well as anyone in his work on political economy.

The dilemma had a second prong. The slave system of the South faced a relentless foe, determined to settle accounts with it. If Dew read the course of Western Europe accurately, the bourgeois countries would soon have to reinstitute their own forms of slavery and thereby end their criticism of the South. But what of the North? Dew saw the North on the same road that Britain and Europe were treading. But its great territorial expansion and peculiarly favorable social conditions promised to forestall the dreaded outcome for centuries. Dew recognized the increasing hostility to slavery in the North and feared a confrontation. If the North, with its dynamic economy and potentially greater military might, forced the issue, the South faced poor prospects. Besides, even if the South did secede successfully, two hostile regimes would face each other across a gun-bristling border. How could republican freedom on either side survive under such conditions?

Dew took unionist ground and counseled the South to resist provocations and eschew rash moves. His argument had many echoes among the unionists of the South. But again, the problem remained. If the North had centuries before it had to face its own social question and reassess its attitude toward southern slavery, it might very well become – indeed was rapidly becoming – more belligerent and determined to force a showdown. How could the South prepare itself economically and militarily without destroying the very fabric of its social system? Military might depended upon that vaunted economic progress which the free-labor system excelled in generating. Dew had an elegant formula: progress through a widening freedom based upon slavery. But as he well knew, if war came, formulaic elegance would not likely prove a match for the big battalions, and, as he himself showed in fleshing out the formula, the big battalions were likely to be on the side of the enemy.

In making the relation of progress to freedom and slavery the centerpiece of his life's work, Dew was focusing on the problem that increasingly was engaging the attention of thoughtful southerners. With few exceptions the lay and clerical intellectuals, in tandem with their fellow slaveholders, accepted both moral and material progress as the primary tendency in human history and as the unfolding of God's providence. But with varying degrees of emphasis they also recognized human conflict as inherent in that tendency, identifying the innate needs and egocentric practices of individuals as simultaneously its source and its social manifestation. . . .

At this level of abstraction the slaveholders' view of progress could be accommodated . . . within the mainstream of modern liberal thought and its bourgeois-conservative variant. Even the special attention to racial stratification and the presumed right of a superior race to enslave an inferior offered nothing new or startling. So long as the slaveholders restricted their defense of social stratification, including slavery, to scriptural justification, legal sanction, historical ubiquity, and economic imperatives, they did not break decisively with the mainstream of transatlantic thought, and especially did not break with its bourgeois-conservative right flank. True, by the nineteenth century liberal thought generally condemned slavery on moral as well as economic grounds, but much bourgeois-conservative thought either did not or so qualified the moral condemnation as to draw its political teeth.

The dizzying outcome of the Mexican War, with its enormous territorial annexations, the projection of American power into the Pacific, and the discovery of gold in California, deepened the sense of progress, indeed of rapid progress, as the controlling law of modern civilization. Military considerations emerged as critical. In a world of aggressive nation-states and rival social and political systems, each participant had to keep abreast of the spiraling revolution in technology and economic performance or risk its life. One event after another taught the same lesson. . . . Material progress would continue, whatever the wishes of those who lamented its pernicious effects. For slaveholders, as for the rest of humanity, the message was clear: Keep pace or die.

From self-proclaimed reactionaries like George Fitzhugh to such self-proclaimed progressives of Young America as Edwin DeLeon, pro-slavery southerners of every ideological hue invoked the rhetoric of human progress, sometimes with excruciating pomposity. Georgia and the South, exclaimed Whig and pro-slavery militant John M. Berrien in 1838, must progress under the banner "Onward! Onward!" The no less militantly pro-slavery Joseph A. Lumpkin, Chief Justice of the Supreme Court of Georgia, concurred, insisting that "the standstill doctrine must be forsaken, and forward, forward, be henceforth the watchword." The course of industrial progress cannot be arrested, he argued, and the slave system of the South must accommodate itself or disappear. "My motto," preached the Reverend Abednego Stephens of Nashville, "is – Upward – Onward!"[3]

Only a bit less flamboyantly, the famed oceanographer Matthew F. Maury of Virginia wrote Senator W. A. Graham of North Carolina in 1850, "Improvement and decay are alternatives. Nothing in the physical world is permitted to be in a state of rest and preservation too. When progress ceases, ruin follows. The moral world is governed by the same iron rule. Upward and onward, or downward and backward are the conditions which it imposes upon all individuals, societies, and institutions." Maury agreed with those who, like Rep. John H. Savage of Tennessee, viewed slavery as an essential element in the progress not only of the South but of the United States and the world. "With the possession of slaves," Savage told the House of Representatives in 1850, "the progress of this country has been onward and upward, with a power so mighty and a flight so rapid as to leave no doubt upon my mind but that the approving smiles of Providence have rested upon us." Calls to bold action normally invoked such language. Thus Francis W. Pickens, the wartime governor of South Carolina, exhorted in 1860: "You are obliged to go forward. You must increase, and the moment you stand still, it will be the law of your destiny to decay and die."[4] . . .

Those who have read the slaveholders' voluminous diaries, letters, and personal papers must surely be struck by their celebration of the southern people as modern, forward-looking men and women, but also by their alarm at a world that was changing too fast and not entirely for the better. . . . In particular, a belief in God and the deep piety that characterized many of the slaveholders – that "older religiousness of the South," as Richard Weaver called it – made them simultaneously hopeful, skeptical, and fearful that the modern world would suffer the fate of Sodom at the hands of the God of Wrath.[5]

The musings of Everard Green Baker, a planter of Panola, Mississippi, had parallels across the South. An admirer of Dr. Johnson, . . . he approvingly quoted a letter to Mrs. Thrale from the Hebrides, dutifully citing the appropriate passage in Boswell's *Life*. "Life," Dr. Johnson had written, "to be worthy of a rational being, must be always in progression, we must purpose to do more or better than in times past." Some months later Baker formulated his own view on the sinful nature of man: "strong & aspiring seeking to rise above the terrestrial greatness of all former beings like itself, & striving with that subtle intellect to peer into things which the wisdom of the great Creator has seen fit to shut out from mortals . . . ."[6]

Nothing in Baker's papers suggests that he saw a contradiction between the two thoughts he entered in his diary or that he fretted over the tension. His Christianity, as expounded by the southern divines and integrated into the worldview of his community, taught him that the tension would prove creative so long as southern society adhered to the laws of God. The enemy was not progress, which was God's gift to his beloved children, but the cult of progress, which, as Baker observed, strove to project man to the center of the universe and to make man, not God, the measure of all things. . . .

If Baker had read William Gilmore Simms's *Woodcraft*, he would have had no trouble in grasping the point of a conversation between Captain Porgy and Sergeant Millhouse, who was offering to become his overseer. Porgy complained, "I was always one of that large class of planters who reap thistles from their planting." Millhouse replied:

> That's because you never trusted to luck, cappin. You was always a-thinking to do something better than other people, and you wouldn't let nater [nature] alone. You was always a-hurrying nater, tell you wore her out; jest like those foolish mothers who give their children physic – dose after dose – one dose fightin agin the other, and nara one gitting a chance to work. Now, I'm a-thinking that the true way is to put the ground in order, and at the right time plant the seed, and then jest lie by, and look on, and see what the warm sun and the rain's guine to do for it. But you, I reckon, warn't patient enough to wait. You was always for pulling up the corn to see if it had sprouted; and for planting over jest when it was beginning to grow. I've known a-many of that sort of people, preticklarly among you wise people, and gentlemen born. It ain't reasonable to think that a man kin find new wisdom about everything; and them sort of people who talk so fine and strange, and sensible in a new way, about the business that has been practised ever since the world begun, they're always over-doing the business and working against nater. They're quite too knowing to give themselves a chance.
>
> That's philosophy, Millhouse.
>
> No, cappin, 'taint philosophy, but it's might good sense.[7]

A typical if unusually amusing illustration of the tension in southern thought over the very idea of progress in its relation to freedom came from Oxford, Georgia, in 1855. The Reverend William S. Sasnett, wishing to instruct his Methodist brethren on the responsibility of the church to keep up with the times, published a book on "progress," which he opened by declaring, "The development of the popular element peculiar to modern times, favored by the remarkable facilities for enterprise and expansion, has given, in the present day, signal activity to the spirit of progress." Immediately, he added a sentence he doubtless did not intend as a contribution to southern wit: "Progress, so far as it involves simply the ideas of alteration, modification, amendment, even as applied to Methodism, is not necessarily an evil." Change, Sasnett explained, "is not necessarily to be resisted," for when subordinated to "thought and virtue, it is the glory of the age." He attacked government interference with that private initiative which constituted the great spur to progress, but expressed horror at the secular and infidel ideology that was being spawned by the initiative he was supposedly celebrating.[8]

Even George Fitzhugh agreed that the last two thousand years had exhibited "an aggregate of improvement." He hailed the slave South as a "bulwark against innovation and revolution" – "the sheet anchor of our institutions, which the restless and dissatisfied North would soon overturn, if left to govern alone." Yet in the very same article he complained, "Tide-water old fogyism retains its dogged do-nothing spirit." The conservative Virginia tidewater, he observed, opposed "railroads, canals, daily mails, and other modern innovations."[9] . . .

As J. D. B. DeBow and others complained, Fitzhugh loved paradoxes, loved to shock, loved to put-on-the-dog. But he also took himself seriously and meant to instruct. The intrinsically paradoxical nature of progress constituted his subject. "All civilization," he wrote, "consists in the successful pursuits of the mechanic arts. The country is most civilized which most excels in them." None of which prevented Fitzhugh from warning that the extension of railroads and other such wonders would reduce Virginia to the status of Ireland or the West Indies unless subjected to a wise, conservative regulation that controlled them in the interests of the prevailing slave society.[10]

For Fitzhugh . . . material progress carried the promise of a better life, and, besides, it was inevitable. At issue was its rate and especially its specific content, for the dizzying rate made possible by the self-revolutionizing social and economic system of the transatlantic world threatened to unravel the fabric of civilization. Hence Fitzhugh's infuriatingly paradoxical rhetoric: "Slavery has truly become aggressive, ingressive, and progressive. It is the most distinguishing phenomenon of the reactionary conservative movement of our day." And again: "Let us show to the world that we, slaveholders, are the only conservatives; ready to lead a salutary reaction in morals, religion, and government; that we propose not to govern society less, but to govern it more."[11]

Few in the South could accept Fitzhugh's demand for increased state power, although many more might have if they had had the patience to follow his dialectics and smile at his irony. But then, sophisticated intellectuals and the less reflective country folk may well have intuitively espied Fitzhugh's backing-and-filling. Most southerners seem to have taken for granted that progress depended precisely on the individual freedom they claimed for themselves and agreed that only slavery could discipline individual freedom and thereby render progress morally wholesome and socially safe. But at that very moment transatlantic society, by dispensing with slavery and extending freedom to the laboring classes, was achieving unprecedented progress without the moral and social safeguards. Could, in fact, a modern slave society compete with such a rival in the all-out struggle that increasing numbers saw as just beyond the horizon?

As slave society slowly evolved from its origins in the seventeenth century to its flowering in the nineteenth . . . its political class and intelligentsia increasingly recognized the challenge and continued to hope that it could meet the expected test of strength. Articulating the worldview of the slaveholding class and, if more problematically, of the yeomanry and the middle classes of the towns, this impressive intelligentsia struggled to reconcile the claims of freedom and the legitimacy of slavery, and to find in their organic social relations a blueprint for ordered progress. On the relation of slavery to individual freedom and to moral and material progress, as on other matters of capital importance, a consensus emerged, notwithstanding its being wracked by the tensions, ambiguities, and quarrels that mark every worldview and social consensus.

In this case the tensions, ambiguities, and quarrels had a special root and quality that derived from a need to reconcile slavery with both freedom and progress. Ultimately, that reconcilitation proved impossible, and much of the intellectual, ideological, and political warfare that constantly threatened to disrupt the consensus and unravel the worldview stemmed directly from its impossibility. At the heart of the boldest and most widely embraced of the projected solutions lay explosive contradictions that at last exposed a political dilemma and provoked a headlong plunge into uncharted and forbidding waters.

The contradictions especially signaled the southern intellectuals' determination to claim the Western tradition while criticizing the direction it was taking in Europe and the North, and while advancing their own vision of a healthy modernity. Every talented southern thinker proposed his own solution. The nature of moral progress and of the moral dimension of material progress – distinct if related issues – loomed large at the outset. Virtually all insisted that freedom and moral progress had to be understood not simply as the product of recent political developments, but as rooted in Christianity. The advent of Christianity had propelled the moral progress of mankind, and the spirit and doctrines of Christianity could be read backward in time to demonstrate moral tendencies in pre-Christian civilizations, most notably the Greek. The erudite even saw God's providence in such non-Western and non-Christian civilizations as those of China and India. How else, after all, should Protestants interpret the advent and spread of Christianity, the Reformation, and the missionary work that was going forward in Asia and Africa?

In this perspective, recent material progress was spreading moral progress, or so they interpreted the growth of the Christian missions to heathen lands. The wonders of the industrial revolution were having an especially powerful effect in the innovations in transportation and communications, which were carrying the Word of God to the four corners of the earth. . . . Southerners, like northerners, generally identified the

United States as the modern age's divinely favored nation and saw its rapid rise toward world power as evidence of its Christian mission. That rise revealed God's anointing of a chosen and Christian people. The freedom of the individual, the preachers cried out in unison, was Christ's gift to mankind. The doctrine of the immortality of the soul in the light of the Atonement made man a responsible moral agent and released his energies to perfect his being.

The concept of moral progress nonetheless remained troubling. "The progress of Christianity," Albert Taylor Bledsoe reiterated after the war, "is the progress of man."[12] But if sin and depravity plagued mankind, as Bledsoe believed, then men might not progress to the point at which most, much less all, would be saved. . . .

William F. Hutson of South Carolina expressed the ambivalence toward moral progress as well as anyone. As revolution was setting Europe afire in 1848, he wrote: "The history of the last seventy years has been a series of startling changes, and at the same time, of precocious and hot house growth, in art, science and politics – Europe, for the most part, has been a battle field; revolution has followed revolution so fast, that steam presses can hardly chronicle the shifting lines of states." Art and science, he continued, have rendered space "a mere mathematical term," and civilization has almost reached the refinements of ancient Rome. But toward what end? "What is the advantage we possess over the past? To the rich, have been added comforts, and appliances unknown to our fathers; but are the mass better fed? – better clothed? – happier? – more contented? – even freer?" Hutson saw an unfolding social crisis in Europe, which the United States could not long avoid. As for the qualitative dimension of moral progress, he summed up the dominant southern attitude: "In religion and morals, we doubt all improvements, not known to certain fishermen who lived eighteen hundred years ago."[13]

Henry William Ravenel of South Carolina, a respected botanist and unionist, offered reflections upon the secessionist hysteria of 1861 that, ironically, a host of secessionists might easily have agreed with while drawing opposite political conclusions:

> What a commentary does this spectacle afford upon the boasted civilization of the nineteenth century! It is too sad proof that with all the progress made in the *Arts* and *Sciences* – with all the writings of learned men upon *Civil Liberty*, and *Political Rights* – upon *Moral and Intellectual Philosophy* – with all the great *improvements* in *manufactures* and *material prosperity*, mankind are no better now than at any previous time – the evil passions of our fallen state are just as prominent and as easily brought into exercise as in those earlier times that we, in our self-sufficiency have called the *dark*

> *ages*. Nations like individuals become arrogant with power, and Might becomes Right. Egypt, Babylon, Ninevah, Persia, Rome have all learned the lesson, but we cannot profit by their example. We are working out our destiny. Deo duce.[14]

For Ravenel, as for Hutson, any rash assumptions about moral progress would have to contend with the inescapable evidence of the society about them: If the quality of moral life was the standard, then progress was hard to find. The southern divines, who did their best to discourage the hubris that claimed qualitative moral progress, evinced a strong, if little noticed, millennialism, although a millennialism largely shorn of the tendency to engage the church in campaigns for social reform. . . .

The revolutionary upheavals in Europe, which began with the great revolution of 1789 and surged in 1830 and especially 1848, seized their imaginations. Individual divines differed as to which of the seals of *Revelation* was being opened, but they agreed that the Terror of 1793 and the June Days of 1848 marked the early stages of the prophesied cataclysm. In the wake of the working-class rising in Paris in 1848 and the radical turn in the European revolutions, the sober and politically sensitive Thornwell went scurrying back to *Revelation*, convinced that he was seeing the unfolding of its great prophecy.[15] In 1850 the *Tennessee Baptist* proclaimed that the European revolutions had ushered in the prophesied final battle of the nations. The Methodist Samuel Davies Baldwin, in his popular books *Armageddon* and *Dominion* and in extensive lecture tours with his colleague F. E. Pitt, interpreted the revolutions of 1848 as the "great earthquake" (*Revelation*, 16:18) that would usher in the final struggle. He predicted that the imminent battle of Armageddon would take place in the Mississippi Valley, not the Middle East, and related the expected triumph of American armies over European to the Second Coming of Christ.[16]

Not much imagination was required to translate this thinking into an interpretation of the slaveholders' confrontation with abolitionism as a war of Christ against Antichrist. Especially after the Mexican War, Thornwell and the most learned, temperate, and unionist of the southern divines . . . repeatedly proclaimed the confrontation with abolitionism as one between a Christian people and the Antichrist. Yet before the War southern millennialism evinced a pronounced cheerfulness that would be replaced after Appomatox by the desperate hope that God would yet deliver his chosen southern people in a worldwide catastrophe. So long as the power of the Christian slaveholders waxed and especially as the prospects of a great new Christian southern nation loomed, the divines could see God's goodness manifested in the material and moral progress of Western civilization.

In that cheerful spirit the Reverend Benjamin Morgan Palmer of Charleston . . . cried out in 1816, in a sermon aptly entitled "The Signs of the Times": "It seems as if everything [is] conspiring together in the moral and religious world and a multitude of things in the political world to introduce a new and better state."[17] In subsequent years the principal spokesmen of all the denominations read the signs of the times as a process of moral regeneration and material advancement that would hasten the millennium.

The study of history reinforced the prophecies of Scripture. Southern colleges encouraged the reading of d'Aubigné's history of the Reformation, which enjoyed wide circulation among the slaveholders and often turned up in their private libraries and accounts of the books they were reading. They read it as evidence of the progress of both Christianity and of social and political order. Even the great history of the fall of the Roman Empire by the religious skeptic Edward Gibbon became popular in the South, where it was read for moral instruction despite its denigration of Christianity. For did not the barbarian invasions and the rise of Islam reveal the opening of the Seven Seals?

Here too, the slaveholders' ambivalence toward material progress and the political dilemma it implied became apparent. As Christians, they saw moral progress in history in the wake of the "good news" of Jesus, however much one generation of divines after another stressed the inherent sinfulness of men, warned against backsliding, and thundered about God's wrath against a world too much of which resisted the message. And never had the good news spread so rapidly as at that very moment, carried by missionaries on the wings of a breathtaking revolution in transportation and communications and backed up by unprecedented military might. Yet that very industrial revolution was encouraging, with a no less unprecedented ferocity, a cult of scientism and an accompanying infidelity. New doctrines dared to raise man to the place reserved for God and thereby threatened moral decay and assaulted church and state, divinely ordained family and social relations, and God Himself.

Caveats notwithstanding, the slaveholders did place great weight on the quantitative progress of morality and did see material progress as its handmaiden. They thus linked Protestant Christianity to economic liberalism and political republicanism, much as a host of bourgeois liberals did. But in the slaveholders' perspective, slavery or, more precisely, the several forms of personal servitude, provided the necessary foundation for a society that could sustain a Christian social order and guarantee individual freedom for those who deserved and were competent to wield it. They acknowledged that the greater the extent to which the individual found himself free to pursue his own destiny, the greater his contribution to the economic progress on which the pace, although not the content, of moral progress depended. And in this spirit they joined their liberal adversaries at home and abroad in embracing the claims of freedom as developed in classical political economy as well as in the emerging arguments for freedom of thought.

The southerners' warm praise of the benefits of freedom and progress have led many able historians, reviewing these and other matters, to attribute to the slaveholders a basically bourgeois worldview to which they merely tacked on an opportunistic defense of slave property and racial stratification. These historians have found irresistible the invitation to conflate the slaveholders' searing ambivalence with the kind of moral objections to the social devastation attendant upon unregulated capitalist development that were being heard in London, Paris, New York, and Boston, as well as in Charlottesville and Williamsburg, Columbia and Charleston. . . . They err, for the slaveholders, unlike conservatives in the North and abroad, explicitly identified the free-labor system itself as the source of the moral evils and forged a critique that struck at its heart. With varying degrees of boldness, one after another came to view the freedom of labor as a brutal fiction that undermined the propertied classes' sense of responsibility for the moral and material welfare of society.

Despite similarities, only some of the important features of the reigning sensibility and worldview of the Old South may be assimilated to the broad current of conservatism that acted as a counterpoint to the increasingly dominant liberalism of the transatlantic world. In the North, in Britain, and most strikingly on the Continent, conservatives reacted forcefully against the high social costs of the industrial revolution, against radical-democratic and egalitarian social and political creeds, against secularization and the no less dangerous emergence of liberal theologies, and against the insidious pressures toward repudiation of church and family, authority and hierarchy, order and tradition. But for most, even their harshest critiques of the consequences of progress and individual freedom remained grounded in a fundamental acceptance of the reigning capitalist socioeconomic system. Some European and northern conservatives did assail capitalism itself, but they did so as isolated intellectuals who had been stripped of the social base on which the slaveholders stood.

The great divergence of southern thought from northern and transatlantic bourgeois thought, including its bourgeois-conservative variant, appeared in the confrontation with the specific nature of freedom and its implications for the present and future, most significantly the condition of laborers. Even the advocates of the extreme pro-slavery argument – of slavery as the natural and proper condition of all labor, regardless of race – understood freedom to entail a good deal more than their own claims to freedom as a privileged and preferred status. They acknowledged individual freedom as the motor force of a providential and potentially good historical progress. They simultaneously insisted that slavery afforded the best foundation for a free society.

The slaveholders' reaction against the ravaging consequences of bourgeois social relations had its counterparts in the radical-democratic and socialist onslaught of the Left and the nostalgia, lament, and harsh political response of the traditionalist Right, both of which condemned the moral irresponsibility and political corruption of the bourgeoisie. Unlike the radical democrats and socialists but very much like both traditionalist and bourgeois conservatives, the slaveholders feared the intrusion of the lower classes into politics and loathed the egalitarian doctrines that made it possible. Even when the slaveholders themselves invoked egalitarian rhetoric, . . . they implicitly, and often explicitly, suggested that equality and democracy could not be sustained outside a class-stratified system or its functional racial equivalent.

Thus at a first but deceptive glance, every southern denunciation of political radicalism, infidelity, and moral decay had its northern equivalent. . . .

The break of southern conservativism away from northern in theology and ecclesiology accompanied the break in political theory. Partly as a reflection of a growing theological and ecclesiastical rift, the social conservatism of the southern divines diverged sharply from that of the northern divines. The theological, ecclesiastical, and sociopolitical conservatives of the North were steadily retreating in the face of the rise of Unitarianism in New England and of assorted forms of liberalism in the principal denominations. Meanwhile, orthodoxy continued to hold sway in the South.

The southern churches slowly drifted apart from the northern over theology and ecclesiology and by no means only over slavery, for the northern churches were moving, if haltingly and in intense internal struggle, toward more liberal positions on original sin, human depravity, and the role of the laity. For immediate purposes, that larger sectional cleavage, notwithstanding its enormous importance, may be left aside. More directly relevant and illuminating was the growing estrangement of the theologically orthodox and socially conservative southerners from those northern conservatives who were trying to arrest the liberal trend in their own churches. . . .

The issues concerned theology and ecclesiology first and foremost and cannot be reduced to a projected ideological reflex of sociopolitical differences. Nor was the slavery question, in its direct political manifestation, the problem, for the northern conservatives condemned the abolitionists, opposed intervention in southern affairs, defended southern state rights, and, in general, resolutely insisted that the church must render unto Caesar that which is Caesar's. Theologically, they conceded the main southern argument that the Bible sanctioned slavery, which therefore could not be condemned as sinful, as *malum in se*. Slavery, in their view, was strictly a civil, a political, question on which the church could take no position.

In broader perspective, the slavery question did lie at the root of the growing sectional antagonism within the conservative clerical fold.... The conservative divines, North and South, agreed that infidelity and social and political radicalism were on the ascendant – that the barbarians were at the gates. They agreed that abolitionism was a Trojan horse for all other detestable isms. They agreed that the fate of slavery should be left to the discretion of the white people of the South. They agreed on more. But they disagreed radically on the nature of a proper Christian social order and of the place of slavery within it.

The argument of the southern divines against the northern conservative divines took many forms, with variations and nuances, and it exhibited different degrees of political tartness. In the end it reduced to one point that brooked no compromise. And that point was made by the outstanding figures in all denominations....

The point came to this: You northern conservatives share our revulsion against growing infidelity and secularism, against the rapid extension of the heresies of liberal theology, against the social and political abominations of egalitarianism and popular democracy, against the mounting assault on the family and upon the very principle of authority. You share our alarm at the growing popularity of the perverse doctrines of Enlightenment radicalism and the French Revolution – the doctrines of Voltaire, Rousseau, Paine. You share our fears for the fate of Western civilization. Yet you fail to identify the root of this massive theological, ecclesiastical, social, and political offensive against Christianity and the social order: the system of free labor that breeds egotism and extols personal license at the expense of all God-ordained authority. You fail to see that only the restoration of some form of personal servitude can arrest the moral decay of society. Indeed, you mindlessly celebrate free labor as a model and urge us to adopt it. In truth, the South stands virtually alone in the transatlantic world as a bastion of Christian social order because it rests upon a Christian social system. If, as you say, the world needs a social and moral order at once progressive yet conservative, dynamic yet regulated, republican yet immune to democratic demagogy, then our system, not yours, must be looked to as a model.

Thus the southern divines masterfully combined theological and socioeconomic arguments. Theologically, Calvinists and Arminians a like took a hard line on original sin and the depravity of man at a time when the mainstream churches of the North were retreating into rosier views of human nature and winning astonishing doctrinal concessions even from most northerners who claimed to be orthodox. The southerners developed an interdenominational social theory that stressed obedience to constituted authority, beginning with that of the male head of family and household, and they especially stressed the ubiquity and necessity of class stratification. At the same time they insisted, in a way completely different from that of northern conservatives, upon the moral duty of Christians to be their brothers' keepers.

Rejecting the kind of social reformism that was becoming popular in the North even among many conservatives, the southern divines insisted upon the solemn duty of the privileged classes to assume direct, personal responsibility for those whose labor supported society. Their rhetoric of family values had its northern equivalent, but with a decisive difference. In southern doctrine the family meant the extended household, defined to include "servants" – dependent laborers. The familiar expression, "my family, white and black," far from being a propagandistic ploy, expressed the essence of a worldview. For good reason Abraham loomed as the principal Old Testament figure among the slaveholders, much as Moses did among the slaves. Abraham was, in their oft-expressed view, simultaneously a great slaveholder and God's favored patriarch of a household that included his many slaves.

From theology the southern divines frequently passed to political economy, which they readily invoked in their books and sermons and in their lectures to the college classes in Moral Philosophy. And with a handful of exceptions, the divines taught the generally required courses in Moral Philosophy. They accepted the principles of classical political economy, much as their northern counterparts did, but they broke decisively in their attitude toward the free-labor system itself. They refused to accept the outcome of Ricardian theories of rent, profit, wages and capital accumulation and Malthusian theory of population, which separately and together predicted the steady immiseration of the laboring classes. They were as ready as the northerners to accept the "laws" of political economy as operative in the market, but... they did not agree that immiseration exceeded the control of man. Jesus had said that the poor we would always have with us; he did not say that we ought to tolerate starvation and brutality. The system itself, after all, could be changed.

The southern divines' understanding of Christianity forbade a fatalistic capitulation to such monstrous laws and instead pointed them toward an alternate social system that functioned with more humane laws of its own. Sounding like Dew but with a greater sense of urgency, Thornwell and Armstrong, among others, insisted that the very horror of the laws of political economy could only end in proletarian revolution, anarchy, and a collapse into despotism unless the bourgeois societies assumed responsibility for their laborers through some form of "Christian slavery."

Joseph LeConte, one of the South's most distinguished scientists, summed up the argument in a lecture to the senior class of South Carolina College. A devout Presbyterian, he spoke primarily in secular accents, but the publication of his lecture in the prestigious *Southern Presbyterian Review* should occasion no surprise. By the 1850s such articles by both divines and laymen were readily receiving sanction in the leading religious journals. LeConte argued that sociology must be made scientific through the study of the natural sciences and the use of the comparative method in the study of human institutions. And he concluded:

> No one, I think, who has thoroughly grasped the great laws of development, or practised the method of comparison, will find any difficulty in perceiving that free competition in labor is necessarily a transition state; that, as a permanent condition, it is necessarily a failure; and that the alternative must eventually be between slavery and some form of organized labor, circumstances, perhaps beyond our control, determining which of these will prevail in different countries.[18]

The arguments were often ingenious and the presentations masterly, but the dilemma constantly resurfaced. Notwithstanding all caveats, qualifications, and ambivalence, the slaveholders, lay and clerical, sophisticated and simple, did want to preserve freedom, conventionally if ambiguously defined, and they did want to see progress continue. They extolled freedom as the source of progress. . . . Yet they insisted upon slavery as the only safe, secure, indeed Christian foundation for freedom, while they could not deny that the material progress they celebrated flowed from the performance of the societies that were not merely expanding freedom but eradicating slavery. Since those societies, in the view of American slaveholders as well as of European socialists, were failing and doomed to extinction; since for the slaveholders socialism was neither desirable nor possible; since some form of personal slavery would soon be the order of the day in Europe – how could progress be sustained? And more ominously, how could the slave South, notwithstanding its claims to moral superiority, stand against an aggressive North that had all the material advantages made possible by an unbridled free economy?

Notes

1 Edmund Morgan, *American Slavery, American Freedom: The Ordeal of Colonial Virginia* (New York: Norton, 1975); David Brion Davis, *Slavery and Human Progress* (New York: Oxford University Press, 1984). . . .

2 The following discussion is drawn from Eugene Genovese, *Western Civilization through Slaveholding Eyes: The Social and Historical Thought of Thomas Roderick Dew* (New Orleans: The Graduate School of Tulane University, 1986)[Ed.].

3 John M. Berrien quoted in Stephen F. Miller, *The Bench and Bar of Georgia: Memoirs and Sketches*, 2 vols. (Philadelphia: J. B. Lippincott, 1858), 1, p.54; Joseph H. Lumpkin, "Industrial Regeneration of the South," *DeBow's Review*, n.s., 5 (1852), p. 43; Rev. A. Stephens, *Address before the Academic Society of Nashville University on the Influence of Institutions for High Letters on the Mental and Moral Character of the Nation, and the Obligations of Government to Endow and Sustain Them* (Nashville, Tenn.: B. K. McKennie, 1938), p. 25.

4 Matthew F. Maury to W. A. Graham, Oct. 7, 1850, in J. G. deRoulhac Hamilton and Max R. Williams, Jr. (eds.), *The Papers of William Alexander Graham*, 7 vols. (Raleigh, NC: State Department of Archives and History, 1957–84), iii. 409; Savage quoted in Arthur Alphonse Ekirch, *The Idea of Progress in America, 1815–1860* (New York: Columbia University Press, 1944), p. 236; Pickens quoted in William W. Freehling, *The Road to Disunion: Secessionists at Bay, 1776–1854* (New York: Oxford University Press, 1990), p. 461.

5 Richard M. Weaver, "The Older Religiousness of the South," in George M. Curtus III and James J. Thompson, Jr. (eds.), *The Southern Essays of Richard M. Weaver* (Indianapolis: Liberty Press, 1987), pp. 14–27.

6 Everard Green Baker Diary, July 22, 1858, and March 13, 1859, in the Southern Historical Collection of the University of North Carolina.

7 W. Gilmore Simms, *Woodcraft; or, Hawks about the Dovecote. A Story of the South at the Close of the Revolution*, new rev. edn (New York: Lovell, Coryell & Co., n.d.), p. 189.

8 William J. Sasnett, *Progress: Considered with Particular Reference to the Methodist Episcopal Church, South*, ed. T. O. Summers (Nashville, Tenn.: Southern Methodist Publishing House, 1855), pp. 7, 8, 61–4, 120, 135.

9 George Fitzhugh, "The Valleys of Virginia – the Rappahannock," *DeBow's Review*, 26 (March 1859), p. 275.

10 Fitzhugh, "Make Home Attractive," *DeBow's Review*, 28 (June 1860), p. 625.

11 Fitzhugh, "Slavery Aggressions," *DeBow's Review*, 28 (Feb. 1860), pp. 133, 138.

12 Quoted in John Joyce Bennett, "Albert Taylor Bledsoe: Social and Religious Controversialist of the Old South" (Ph.D. diss., Duke University, 1972), p. 49.

13 William F. Hutson, "The History of the Girondists, or Personal Memoirs of the Patriots of the French Revolution," *Southern Presbyterian Review*, 2 (1848), p. 398; [*idem*], "Fictitious Literature," *Southern Presbyterian Review*, 1 (1847), p. 78.

14 Arney Robinson Chiles (ed.), *The Private Journal of Henry William Ravenel, 1859–1887* (Columbia: University of South Carolina Press, 1947), p. 67.

15 Thornwell to Matthew J. Williams, July 17, 1848, in B[enjamin] M. Palmer, *The Life and Letters of James Henley Thornwell* (Richmond, Va.: Whittet & Shepperson, 1875), pp. 309–11.

16 Samuel Davies Baldwin, *Armeggedon; or, The United States in Prophecy* (Nashville, Tenn.: E. Stevenson and F. A. Owen, 1845); [*idem*], *Dominion; Or, the Unity and Trinity of the Human Race; with the Divine Constitution of the World, and the Divine Rights of Shem, Ham, and Japheth* (Nashville, Tenn.: E. Stevenson and F. A. Owen, 1858); Pamela Elwyn Thomas Colbenson, "Millennial Thought among Southern Evangelicals, 1830–1860" (Ph.D. diss., Georgia State University, 1980), esp. pp. 1, 12–14, 28, 49, 70–5, and p. 137 for the quotation from the *Tennessee Baptist.*

17 Quoted in Colbenson, "Millennial Thought," p. 1.

18 Joseph LeConte, "The Relation of Organic Science to Sociology," *Southern Presbyterian Review*, 13 (1860), p. 59.

7
Life within the Big House

Introduction

The nineteenth century was an era in which southern society was based on clear, codified rules of behavior; social expectations pressured individuals so that they would follow these norms and rules. This was particularly true for southern elite women, who were expected to follow a path of which one of the main goals was to find a prestigious, wealthy planter to marry. After marriage, they would run the plantation household as mistresses and give birth to several children. From the moment they commenced their education, elite women were taught how to be pleasant and refined so as to attract the attention of potential husbands. Consequently, female education was largely aimed at transforming girls into the refined ladies that men expected. Courtship took place in restricted places and circumstances. Young men and women could meet at church, at a ball, or at the homes of friends and relatives; these were considered safe locations because social interaction would take place amongst young men and women from the same social class.

Elite women experienced their most intense moments of independence during courtship, since they might have several men competing for their attention, and to a certain extent they could feel in control of their lives. However, all this vanished after marriage, because married women were expected to enjoy little of the social scene; their world was supposed to be confined to their homes and their husbands. Receiving attention from other men risked dishonor, since women's honor was measured according to their absolute faithfulness and submissiveness to their husbands. When it actually came to choosing a husband, the choice was almost always restricted to friends and relatives; most often, women would marry a cousin or a very close family friend.

Once married, plantation mistresses had a hard life ahead of them, not least because of the pressure upon them to bear multiple children, so that several heirs could inherit the planter's fortune and carry his name in society. Childbearing was a difficult and dangerous business. Often plantations were located in unhealthy areas, because of the necessities of the crop, and were isolated and far from any doctor. In plantations located near swamps, pregnant women were likely to contract malaria. Continuous childbearing brought a general exhaustion of energy in many mistresses, so that a number of them ran the risk of dying quite young if they were not exceptionally strong. Childbearing, however, enhanced the prestige of married women to such an extent that those who were married and did not have children were treated with less respect, almost as if they had not fulfilled their role in society.

Often mistresses were alone on the plantation because husbands were away managing other properties or taking care of business. Often, this meant that the mistress needed to oversee the running of the plantation and direct the overseer, a difficult task that required learning how to command respect from both slaves and the overseer himself. During their husbands' absences, mistresses spent days – or weeks – alone with the household slaves, tending to the back-breaking work of keeping the household in order through the daily duties of washing, cleaning, and food preparation. Since they shared these responsibilities with the household female slaves, mistresses necessarily developed close (though unequal) relations with them. In fact, several recent studies have gone so far as to argue that a special bond of affection developed between mistresses and female slaves due to their common fate as women oppressed by men and confined to the domestic realm of the Big House. However, relations between mistresses and slave women were exceedingly complex. One important factor complicating their relationship was the fact that many masters had illicit sexual relations with their slaves. In consequence, it is very difficult to assess the mistress–slave relationship. Even though mistresses and female slaves could feel close, because both felt exploited and oppressed as women, the mistress always regretted the presence of female slaves on the plantation, because she knew that her husband or sons were likely to have sexual affairs with them.

Further reading

Bynum, V., *Unruly Women: The Politics of Social and Sexual Control in the Old South* (Chapel Hill: University of North Carolina Press, 1992).

Cashin, J. (ed.), *Our Common Affairs: Texts from Women in the Old South* (Baltimore: Johns Hopkins University Press, 1996).

Clinton, C., *The Plantation Mistress: Woman's World in the Old South* (New York: Pantheon Books, 1982).

Fox-Genovese, E., *Within the Plantation Household: Black and White Women of the Old South* (Chapel Hill: University of North Carolina Press, 1988).

Friedman, J. E., *The Enclosed Garden: Women and Community in the Evangelical South, 1830–1900* (Chapel Hill: University of North Carolina Press, 1985).

Kierner, C. A., *Beyond the Household: Women's Place in the Early South, 1770–1835* (Ithaca, NY: Cornell University Press, 1998).

McMillen, S. G., *Southern Women: Black and White in the Old South* (Arlington Heights, Ill.: Marlan Davidson, 1992).

Pease, J. H. and Pease, W. H., *A Family of Women: The Carolina Petigru in Peace and War* (Chapel Hill: University of North Carolina Press, 1999).

Scott, A. F., *The Southern Lady: From Pedestal to Politics, 1830–1930*, 2nd edn. (Chicago: University of Chicago Press, 1990).

Stevenson, B., *Life in Black and White: Family and Community in the Slave South* (New York: Oxford University Press, 1996).

Stowe, S. M., *Intimacy and Power in the Old South: Ritual in the Lives of the Planters* (Baltimore: Johns Hopkins University Press, 1987).

Wiener, M. F., *Mistresses and Slaves: Plantation Women in South Carolina, 1830–1880* (Urbana and Chicago: University of Illinois Press, 1998).

Wyatt-Brown, B., *Southern Honor: Ethics and Behavior in the Old South* (New York: Oxford University Press, 1982).

Adele Petigru Allston is Reminded of the Mistress' Duties by Her Aunt (ca. 1830s)

Adele Petigru was a daughter of a relatively obscure up-country farmer and a sister of renowned Charleston lawyer James Louis Petigru. She was a typical Charleston belle, courted by many because of both her beauty and her family connections. Her brother arranged for her to meet one of his clients, Robert Allston, a prestigious rice planter who owned more than 100 slaves and was a member of the South Carolina House of Representatives. After their wedding in 1828, Robert and Adele moved to Robert's plantation at Chicora Wood, in the South Carolina low country, where Adele felt overwhelmed by the task of managing a multitude of slaves. Robert's Aunt Blythe came to her rescue and helped her to understand the responsibility involved in being a plantation mistress and the importance of faithfully discharging the duties attached to this role. Robert's and Adele's daughter, Elizabeth Allston Pringle, reported the story in her recollections entitled *Chronicles of Chicora Wood.*

Mamma told me that once she had said in a despairing voice to her:

"But, auntie, are there no honest negroes? In your experience, have you found none honest?"

"My dear, I have found none honest, but I have found many, many trustworthy; and, Adèle, when you think of it, that really is a higher quality....

My mother exclaimed: "Oh, my dear auntie, I do not see how I can live my whole life amid these people! I don't see how you have done it and kept your beautiful poise and serenity! To be always among people whom I do not understand and whom I must guide and teach and lead on like children! It frightens me!"

Aunt Blythe laid her hand on my mother's hand and said: "Adèle, it is a life of self-repression and effort, but it is far from being a degrading life, as you have once said to me. It is a very noble life, if a woman does her full duty in it. It is the life of a missionary, really; one must teach, train, uplift, encourage – always encourage, even in reproof. I grant you it is a life of effort; but, my child, it is *our life*: the life of those who have the great responsibility of owning human beings. We are responsible before our Maker for not only their bodies, but their souls; and never must we

---

Source: Elizabeth Allston Pringle, *Chronicles of Chicora Wood* (Atlanta, Ga.: Cherokee Publishing Company, 1922), pp. 76–8

for one moment forget that. To be the wife of a rice-planter is no place for a pleasure-loving, indolent woman, but for an earnest, true-hearted woman it is a great opportunity, a great education. To train others one must first train oneself; it requires method, power of organization, grasp of detail, perception of character, power of speech; above all, endless self-control. That is why I pleaded with my dear sister until she consented to send Robert to West Point instead of to college. Robert was to be a manager and owner of large estates and many negroes. He was a high-spirited, high-tempered boy, brought up principally by women. The discipline of four years at West Point would teach him first of all to obey, to yield promptly to authority; and no one can command unless he has first learned to obey. It rejoices my heart to see Robert the strong, absolutely self-controlled, self-contained man he now is; for I mean to leave him my property and my negroes, to whom I have devoted much care, and who are now far above the average in every way, and I know he will continue my work; and, from what I see of you, my child, I believe you will help him."

Rosalie Roos Describes Courtship in Charleston (1854)

One of the most interesting and least-known documents on antebellum southern society is a series of letters written by Rosalie Roos (1823–98). Born in Sweden, in 1851 Roos traveled to the United States, where she hoped to earn a living on her own. For five years she lived in South Carolina, where she worked as a teacher at Limestone High School and then as an instructor to the children of Edward Peronneau, a wealthy rice planter. During her years with the Peronneau family, Roos observed the customs of the South Carolina aristocracy from within. Like many Europeans, she was disturbed by the presence of slavery and puzzled by the strange mixture of freedom and repression which characterized the treatment of southern women. In this excerpt, Roos gives vent to her critical feelings in commenting on the customs and expectations of belles and beaux at social outings in Charleston.

Source: Carl L. Anderson (ed.), *Travels in America 1851–1855 by Rosalie Roos* (Carbondale and Edwardsville: Swedish Pioneer Historical Society/Southern Illinois University Press, 1982), p. 122

The young ladies usually have a "beau" (cavalier), whose duty it is to make himself as agreeable as possible, offer his arm to his fair one (the young ladies are called "belles") if she wishes to stroll on the piazza, escort her to a chair or sofa if she prefers to sit, supply her with the refreshments she desires, fan her occasionally if it is warm, and finally, accompany her home. The older ladies, of whom relatively few are seen attending such parties, receive these attentions from the host and hostess. Strangely enough, the young ladies and the young gentlemen converse little or not at all with their friends but are almost exclusively devoted to their beau or belle and this right out in the open, no fault being found with it. It is quite usual to ask a young girl who has just come home from a party, "Who was your beau for the evening?" If there is a lady there who is a stranger and has been somehow taken notice of, she usually does nothing other than sit still in the place she has first taken while the host, hostess, or others of her acquaintance present gentlemen to her who sit down next to her and converse for a while, one after the other. In the event there is a piano, those ladies who can play are selected for the sacrifice and entertain the company by taking their turn at it for a while. More often than not, however, the music is below average.

The pleasures of society are based wholly on tête-à-tête and flirtation, for the young girls do not trouble to make conversation among themselves, and do not think they have had a good time unless they have had beaux. Dancing is not usual except at balls; games and diversions do not exist. The American usually converses more easily than does the Swede, and in the company of an interesting and entertaining cavalier the evening can pass pleasantly, but in the opposite case, it turns into a litany.

Mary Chesnut Describes the Effects of Patriarchy (1861)

In the years after the Civil War, several southern women published memoirs and recollections of their lives in the Old South; many of these volumes became popular best-sellers. However, none of them achieved the fame of Mary Boykin Chesnut's *A Diary from Dixie*, originally published in the 1880s. Chesnut (1823–86) wrote her recollections in the form of a diary of a

---

Source: C. Van Woodward (ed.), *Mary Chesnut's Civil War* (New Haven and London: Yale University Press, 1981), pp. 27–31

Confederate woman during the eventful years 1861–5. However, she went far beyond the simple retelling of events by sprinkling her manuscript with pointed comments on the condition of women and their relation to the slave system in the South. As the wife of prominent up-country politician, James Chesnut, she was in contact with several South Carolinian planters and their families. Through her acquaintances and her personal experiences, Mary Chesnut became highly critical of both slavery and the patriarchal system. In this famous excerpt, she argued that both slavery and patriarchy encouraged men to have adulterous relations with their female slaves.

March 18, 1861

I did Mrs. Browne a kindness. I told those women that she was childless now, but that she had lost three children. I hated to leave her all alone. Women have such a contempt for a childless wife. Now they will be all sympathy and kindness. I took away "her reproach among women."

We came along (Sunday) with a Methodist parson – also a member of the Congress. Someone said he was using his political legs – his pulpit feet would not move on a Sabbath day.

A man claimed acquaintance with me because he has married an old school-girl friend of mine.

"At least, she is my present wife."

Whispered the Light Brigade, "Has he had them before or means he to have them hereafter?" We had no time to learn. But one parson friend gravely informed us, "If he is the man I take him to be, he has buried two."

One of our party ≪Mr. C≫ so far forgot his democratic position toward the public as to wish aloud, "Oh, that we had separate coaches, as they have in England. That we could get away from these whiskey-drinking, tobacco-chewing rascals and rabble." All with votes!! Worse, all armed. A truculent crowd, truly, to offend. But each supposed he was one of the gentlemen to be separated from the other thing.

The day we left Montgomery, a man was shot in the street for some trifle. Mr. Browne was open-mouthed in his horror of such ruffianlike conduct. They answered him, "It is the war fever. Soldiers must be fierce. It is the right temper for the times cropping out."

There was tragedy, too, on the way here. A mad woman, taken from her husband and children. Of course she was mad – or she would not have given "her grief words" in that public place. Her keepers were along. What she said was rational enough – pathetic, at times heartrending.

Then a highly intoxicated parson was trying to save the soul of "a bereaved widow." So he addressed her always as "my bereaved friend and widow."

The devil himself could not have quoted Scripture more fluently.

≪ It excited me so – I quickly took opium, and *that* I kept up. It enables me to retain every particle of mind or sense or brains I ever have and so quiets my nerves that I can calmly reason and take rational views of things otherwise maddening. . . . < and have refused to accept overtures for peace and forgiveness. After my stormy youth I did so hope for peace and tranquil domestic happiness. There is none for me in this world.> "The peace this world cannot give, which passeth all understanding." Today the papers say peace again. Yesterday the *Telegraph* and the *Herald* were warlike to a frightful degree. I have just read that Pugh is coming down south – another woman who loved me, and I treated her so badly at first. I have written to Kate[1] that I will go to her if she wants me – dear, dear sister. I wonder if other women shed as bitter tears as I. They scald my cheeks and blister my heart. Yet Edward Boykin wondered and marveled at my elasticity – was I always so bright and happy, did ever woman possess such a disposition, life was one continued festival, &c&c – and Bonham last winter shortly said it was a *bore* to see anyone always in a good humor. Much they know of me – or my power to hide trouble – much trouble.

≪ This [life?] is full of strange vicissitudes, and in nothing more remarkable than the way people are reconciled, ignore the past, and start afresh in life, here to incur more disagreements and set to bickering again – one of them. . . .

≪ I wonder if it be a sin to think slavery a curse to any land. Summer said not one word of this hated institution which is not true. Men and women are punished when their masters and mistresses are brutes and not when they do wrong – and then we live surrounded by prostitutes. An abandoned woman is sent out of any decent house elsewhere. Who thinks any worse of a negro or mulatto woman for being a thing we can't name? God forgive us, but ours is a *monstrous* system and wrong and iniquity. Perhaps the rest of the world is as bad – this *only* I see. Like the patriarchs of old our men live all in one house with their wives and their concubines, and the mulattoes one sees in every family exactly resemble the white children – and every lady tells you who is the father of all the mulatto children in everybody's household, but those in her own she seems to think drop from the clouds, or pretends so to think. Good women we have, *but* they talk of all *nastiness* – tho' they never do wrong, they talk day and night of [*erasures illegible save for the words* "all unconsciousness"] my disgust sometimes is boiling over – but they are, I believe, in conduct the purest women God ever made. Thank God for my countrywomen – alas for the men! No worse than men everywhere, but the lower their mistresses, the more degraded they must be.

≪ My mother-in-law told me when I was first married not to send my female servants in the street on errands. They were then tempted, led astray – and then she said placidly, so they told *me* when I came here, and I was very particular, *but you see with what result*.

≪ Mr. Harris said it was so patriarchal. So it is – flocks and herds and slaves – and wife Leah does not suffice. Rachel must be *added*, if not *married*.[2] And all the time they seem to think themselves patterns – models of husbands and fathers.

≪ Mrs. Davis told me everybody described my husband's father as an odd character – "a millionaire who did nothing for his son whatever, left him to struggle with poverty, &c." I replied – "Mr. Chesnut Senior thinks himself the best of fathers – and his son thinks likewise. I have nothing to say – but it is true. He has no money but what he makes as a lawyer." And again I say, my countrywomen are as pure as angels, tho' surrounded by another race who are the social evil!≫

Notes

1 M. B. C.'s younger sister, Catherine Boykin (Miller) Williams.
2 In Genesis 29–30, Jacob, unhappy with his wife Leah, also marries her sister Rachel. He has children by both women and by their handmaidens as well. M. B. C. apparently believed old Mr. Chesnut had children by a slave whom she calls "Rachel".... She confesses no such suspicions of her husband.

Plantation Mistresses' Attitudes toward Slavery in South Carolina

Marli F. Weiner

In *Mistresses and Slaves*, Marli Wiener explores the impact of race and gender ideologies on the daily life of plantation mistresses and their female slaves. She argues that, though race formed an insurmountable barrier, some white women perceived gender as overriding racial differences and even went as far as viewing slaves as individuals. In a few cases, mistresses' belief that they shared with their female slaves a common oppression based on gender

Marli F. Weiner, *Mistresses and Slaves: Plantation Women in South Carolina, 1830–1880* (Urbana and Chicago: University of Illinois Press, 1998), pp. 88–112.

discrimination led mistresses to be highly critical toward both patriarchy and slavery. Wiener shows that most elite women – such as Gertrude Thomas and Mary Chesnut – who expressed negative views about slavery complained in private mainly about its moral and sexual consequences. At the other end of the spectrum, intellectuals such as Caroline Gilman and Louisa McCord were outspoken pro-slavery advocates who justified both slaveholding and women's subordination as necessary not just for the survival but also for the advancement of southern society.

The ideology of domesticity as well as the daily challenges of interacting with slaves influenced the way white women thought about slavery. Their attitudes ranged from full acceptance to mild or moderate criticism to questioning to condemning its evil consequences. Well aware of the South's official position regarding its peculiar institution, plantation mistresses struggled to define their understanding of the consequences of slavery in the privacy of their journals and in correspondence with one another. They complained about the constant burdens of living with slaves and deplored the immoral consequences of slavery on family life. A few defended the institution publicly, particularly in a rash of novels refuting the portrait of the South and slavery in *Uncle Tom's Cabin.* Attitudes at the critical end of the spectrum may well have been common among women, but were never expressed publicly in South Carolina. . . . Plantation mistresses' beliefs about slavery were a complex mix of mostly unexamined assumptions about race, gender, and class.

The strongest defenders of slavery developed their ideas primarily in the suitably genteel form of the novel. Conventions of nineteenth-century southern society limited women's political expression, but the novel lent itself to domestic settings and values and was adopted by those eager to express themselves in the debates of the day. Most of the writers, like Mary Howard Schoolcraft and Mary Eastman, were quite self-conscious about their reasons for writing and their defense of slavery. Some agreed with the widespread southern belief that slavery was divinely ordained. Mary Herndon put her beliefs into the mouth of Mr. Manville: "'I believe that the white race are special favorites with our Heavenly Father; that he made the negro for their benefit, just as much as I believe that he made for our use the horse, the cow, or the sheep, only He favored us more in the mental structure of the negro, for He gave them power to think, to understand, what we desire them to do, and to converse with us in an intelligible manner.'" Herndon believed "African slavery will exist, as long as there is a white man on the earth," in part because "freedom, amongst negroes, is just as useless as razors amongst children."[1]

Pro-slavery women like Caroline Lee Hentz asserted that slaves were well treated. Hentz... claimed she had "never *witnessed* one scene of cruelty or oppression, never beheld a chain or a manacle, or the infliction of a punishment more severe than parental authority would be justified in applying to filial disobedience or transgression.... On the contrary, we have been touched and gratified by the exhibition of affectionate kindness and care on one side, and loyal and devoted attachment on the other." Like many of her contemporaries, Hentz believed that slaves were better cared for and happier than other laboring groups, particularly northern and English industrial workers and servants.[2] Martha Haines Butt was convinced "there is not a place on earth where servants are treated more kindly, or have better care taken of them." She offered an ultimatum to northerners: "If the Northern people have any sympathy to spare, let them give it to their poor white servants, for our slaves do not stand in any need of it at all."[3] Mary Eastman was particularly critical of northerners' racism: "I know 'lots' of good men there, but none good enough to befriend colored people. They seem to me to have an unconquerable antipathy to them."[4] By contrast, Eastman and others believed that slaveholders were kind and generous toward slaves.

As defenders of slavery white women were publicly united in their belief that, as Eastman put it, "most of our Southern slaves are happy, and kindly cared for; and for those who are not, there is hope for the better." Mary Howard Schoolcraft knew that society would take care of slaves in such a position: "Public opinion in South Carolina so scorns a master that is unjust or cruel to those that God has placed entirely in his power, that such a monster would not be tolerated for a moment. Indeed his neighbors would publicly prosecute him, if he overworked or was cruel to his slaves." One of Hentz's characters concurred: " 'I know of some bad masters, and, what is still worse, bad mistresses; but public opinion brands them with its curse. Their character is considered as unnatural and execrable as the cruel and tyrannical parent of the North.' " Herndon, however, was not so optimistic, recognizing that laws were necessary to hold men accountable for their treatment of slaves: "The laws of the country must force people to do their duty to their slaves, and punish them if they do not do it. It is the cruelty of a few, who have been permitted to escape the penalty of the law, that has disgraced the reputation of the many, who own slaves, and who treat them with humanity."[5]

According to most defenders of slavery, the majority of slaveholders were not only aware of their obligations to slaves; the best also sought " 'improvement in their modes of living – improvement in our systems of government – above all, [improvement] by earnest and persevering efforts to communicate to them sound moral and religious instruction.' "[6] . . . Novelists went to great lengths to demonstrate the benevolence of slavery: virtually every slave character in each of the novels is happy, devoted to the white family, and, by the end of the novel at least, reconciled to being a slave. In several of the novels, slaves offered freedom either reject it outright or come to regret having accepted it. The title character of *Aunt Phillis's Cabin* confessed on her deathbed that she thought for a time

> that God did not mean one of his creatures to be a slave . . . [and] would often be put out, and discontented. It was wicked, I know, but I could not help it for a while. When my children was born, I would think "what comfort is it to give birth to a child when I know it's a slave." I struggled hard though, with these feelings, sir, and God gave me grace to get the better of them, for I could not read my Bible without seeing there was nothing agin slavery there; and that God had told the master his duty, and the slave his duty.[7]

Aunt Phillis, of course, was a figment of a white person's imagination.

But even the most ardent defenders of slavery could not avoid some reservations. One of Eastman's white pro-slavery characters claimed he would " 'like to see every man and woman that God has made, free, could it be accomplished to their advantage. I see the evils of slavery, it is sometimes a curse on the master as well as the slave.' "[8] Several of the pro-slavery women writers criticized the domestic slave trade, particularly the separation of slave families. Slave traders who sought "the glory of earthly grandeur" were "an infringement upon the moral law," according to Herndon. . . . McIntosh proclaimed: "Yet it cannot be denied, . . . that no step was so unpopular at the South, when voluntary, or considered so indicative of utter ruin, when involuntary, as the sale of slaves."[9] Despite these doubts, the novelists made quite clear their defense of slavery as institution and as practice.

A somewhat different defense of slavery was proposed by an unidentified Georgia woman in an article in *DeBow's Review* about Stowe's *Key to Uncle Tom's Cabin*. This author argued that "slavery, even if it be an evil in the abstract, is not one in our case, because emancipation would lead to still greater evils." She credited God with creating slaves as " 'nothing but niggers' " and asserted that "emancipation never can whiten those black skins, or elevate those weak intellects." In fact, slavery was the best condition for slaves because under it they did not suffer from the effects of racism as did free blacks in the North: "If the slave is anywhere to look for friends to improve his condition, certainly they are to be found among enlightened and liberal Southerners, in whom this prejudice is, as might naturally be imagined, mitigated, from having played with them, been nursed by them, and surrounded by them from childhood."[10] At the same time, she was willing to consider the possibility of "endeavoring to correct the abuses of the system, to Christianize and humanize it." . . . However, humanizing slavery would be possible only if the abolitionists "cease the efforts which so stir up the masses, as to tie the hands of those who would act in this way."[11]

Few women elaborated such careful defenses of slavery in their letters, diaries, or other personal papers because they had little inclination or time for such sustained expression. Most simply jotted down their ideas, often in response to political events. . . .

The vast majority of plantation mistresses left no trace of their views before the institution was directly threatened by war; their silence most likely suggests acceptance of the prevailing assumptions of southern culture. Many, like Catherine Edmondston, found that the responsibilities and frustrations of daily interactions with slaves shaped their views of the institution itself. When the slave woman assigned to supervise the slave children complained "its powerful hard on me" because the older children were sent to work in the fields just when they were old enough to watch the younger ones, Edmondston countered in her diary: "So it goes Cuffy. Your aim & I suppose the aim of the whole world is to keep things from getting 'powerful on yourself'!" She fumed about blacks' awkwardness, inefficiency, laziness, and incompetence, and did "not think negroes possess natural feeling. I see so many instances of neglect & insensibility to each other amongst them that I seriously doubt it."[12] Unwilling to defend slavery or to criticize it, Edmondston and women like her simply accepted its presence in their lives and society and dealt with it as best they could.

Women who expressed doubts about slavery generally confided their thoughts only to their diaries or close friends. These private acts offered no direct challenge to slavery as an institution, in contrast to the deliberately political acts of publishing novels and essays. Yet even such private acts and beliefs affected southern society. Anne Firor Scott has argued that many white women saw slavery as evil. In addition to those former mistresses who, following the war, "recalled" their opposition to slavery although they had not articulated it, Scott categorizes mistresses' private complaints about slaves and the work they caused as opposition to slavery: "Most southern women who expressed themselves on the peculiar institution opposed slavery and were glad when it was ended."[13] Suzanne Lebsock reaches a similar conclusion, claiming that slaveholding women's complicity in slavery was "unsteady" because "there was in women's willingness to make the personal exception a quality of sabotage." She attributes women's "uneasiness with slavery" to their belief "that slavery was sinful because of what it did to the slave," to their self-interest, and to their religious and moral convictions.[14]

Many mistresses grounded their doubts about slavery on the threat it presented to the bonds of marriage and family among both blacks and whites. Regrets when separating slave families and complex reactions to miscegenation were for some a short step away from discomfort with the institution that caused these things. Charlotte Ann Allston let slip a degree of doubt about some of the harsher consequences of slavery while writing to her son about the division of her husband's estate: "The poor Negroes appear in dread I feel for them, but it is evident they all cannot belong to me." When Eliza Ann DeRosset confided in her sister Mary Curtis in 1838, she made more explicit the connection between her reluctance to separate black husbands and wives and the institution of slavery: "Poor Fanny is in trouble – her husband's master sent for him to Fayetteville about a fortnight ago and intends carrying him to the West.... It is really a sin to separate them they are so affectionate – is not it the most deplorable thing connected with slavery – I wish it were possible to prevent it."[15]

Doubts about slavery were not linked exclusively to convictions about the importance of family life. Amie Lumpkin reported that her mistress was favorably impressed by the attitude of a black man caught trying to stow away to Charleston in hopes of making his way to Massachusetts and from there to his home in Africa. According to Lumpkin the mistress said: " 'Put yourself in this slave's shoes, and what would you do? Just as he has.' " Lumpkin reported that this man considered himself freed by the Emancipation Proclamation, but told the mistress he would stay and work for her until the end of the war.[16] ... Eliza Ann DeRosset, Lumpkin's mistress, and other women like them throughout the South disliked at least some of the consequences of the institution of slavery, largely because they empathized with individual slaves. Kate Stone linked empathy for slaves and doubts about slavery a bit more precisely:

> As far as Mamma could, the Negroes on our place were protected from cruelty and were well cared for; they were generally given Saturday evening and had plenty to eat and comfortable clothes. Still there were abuses impossible to prevent. And constantly there were tales circulated of cruelties on neighboring plantations, tales that would make one's blood run cold. And yet we were powerless to help. Always I felt the moral guilt of it, felt how impossible it must be for an owner of slaves to win his way into Heaven. Born and raised as we were, what would be our measure of responsibility?[17]

While Stone's comments clearly bear the stamp of hindsight, sympathy for slaves and the impulse to aid them were genuinely felt contemporaneously with ruling over them. Slaveholding presented a responsibility and a moral dilemma these women could not ignore.

Other women also challenged the South's unqualified acceptance of slavery because of the obligations and personal commitment it demanded. At least one woman, Elizabeth Allston Pringle's paternal aunt Elizabeth Blythe, apparently felt the responsibility so strongly that she chose to marry for her slaves' benefit. According to her niece, Blythe inherited a plantation and many slaves, which she felt were "a great trust and responsibility and most difficult to manage, for it was almost impossible to get an overseer who would treat the Negroes with gentleness and justice." Since she could not claim the authority to care for them alone, she married. "She was then able to live on her plantation and see that her Negroes were kindly and properly managed and looked after." H. R. Warren also felt the burdens imposed by slaveholding but chose a different solution, perhaps because of her greater age or lack of suitors. In 1849 she asked her attorney to sell her slaves or give them to relatives, claiming these were better solutions than hiring them out or moving them....

Most of the women who sympathized with slaves and were sensitive to the practical and moral responsibilities they represented did not want to abandon the institution of slavery. Most kept their doubts to themselves or articulated them in vague terms to female correspondents; they did not develop a program to end slavery nor could they imagine a world without it. A few, however, turned their sense of sympathy with the plight of slaves and their discomfort with slaveholding into questions about the institution. They expressed doubts about slavery on theoretical humanitarian grounds as well as on their personal awareness of its consequences. However, none of the few South Carolina women who expressed doubts about slavery was willing to act on her beliefs, and all stopped far short of pushing their thinking to its limits. Though they might have been critical of slavery, they acknowledged its legitimacy and did not wish to end it. Shortly before the outbreak of war, Keziah Brevard wrote in her diary about her doubts about slavery, or at least about fighting to defend it: "I think we all have some, the fewest in number, who would not butcher us – but I am sure the most of them would aim at freedom – tis natural they should and they will try for it. O that God would take them out of bondage in a peaceable way. Let no blood flow. We are attached to our slaves."[18]

The few white women who dared to develop their doubts about slavery based them on its moral and sexual consequences. Gertrude Thomas argued that slavery degraded women of both races. Ella Gertrude Clanton Thomas was a Georgia woman who used her long-term journal to record her ideas and thoughts regarding her world. Unusually well educated and well read for a woman in her culture, she was a careful and informed observer of political activities affecting her section of the country. She based her doubts about slavery on its implications for southern morality and her sympathy for the plight of light-skinned black women, who were "subject to be bought by men, with natures but one degree removed from the brute creation and with no more control over their passions – subjected to such a lot are they not to be pitied. I know that this is a view of the subject that it is thought best for women to ignore but when we see so many cases of mulattoes commanding higher prices, advertised as 'Fancy girls,' oh is it not enough to make us shudder for the standard of morality in our Southern homes?" Miscegenation destroyed family life, claimed Thomas, but unable to reject slavery, she despaired of finding a solution. She believed that she, like other southern women, was powerless to solve a problem she did not create.[19] . . . Thomas criticized the sexual double standard prevalent in the South that condemned white women for transgressions that not only did not bring any criticism to white men but could elevate them in the eyes of other men. . . .

Thomas also objected to the treatment of pregnant black women, including those owned by family members. When two slave women were close to confinement, she wrote: "In that condition I think all women ought to be favored. I know that had I the sole management of a plantation, pregnant women should be highly favored. A woman myself, I can sympathize with my sex, wether white or black." . . . In spite of her professed sympathy for black women, Thomas's doubts did not lead her to contemplate a world without slavery. She was certainly unwilling to admit those of even partial African descent to positions of social equality. When the son of an acquaintance fled to the North with a mulatto slave and tried to marry her, Thomas was not surprised by the father's mortification and efforts to have the son declared insane: "I can well understand his horror of that kind of marriage."[20] . . .

Gertrude Thomas's objections to slavery and her inability to imagine a world without it were shared in large measure by Mary Chesnut, easily the most famous of southern women diarists. . . . Like . . . Thomas, . . . Chesnut had real doubts about the morality of slavery. Although she enjoyed both its material benefits and the social world it created, she deplored the effects it had on women of both races, arguing that it was a curse because it degraded morals and encouraged the brutality of white men. She combined what have been termed feminist and antislavery arguments in her understanding of southern life, although both her feminist and antislavery ideas were muted by her reluctance to admit the possibility of social equality and her racism. Her ideas are worth quoting at length:

> I wonder if it be a sin to think slavery a curse to any land.... Men and women are punished when their masters and mistresses are brutes and not when they do wrong – and then we live surrounded by prostitutes. An abandoned woman is sent out of any decent house elsewhere. Who thinks any worse of a Negro or mulatto woman for being a thing we can't name? God forgive us, but ours is a *monstrous* system and wrong and iniquity. Perhaps the rest of the world is as bad – this *only* I see. Like the patriarchs of old our men live all in one house with their wives and their concubines, and the mulattoes one sees in every family exactly resemble the white children – and every lady tells you who is the father of all the mulatto children in everybody's household, but those in her own she seems to think drop from the clouds, or pretends so to think. Good women we have, *but* they talk of all *nastiness* – tho' they never do wrong, they talk day and night of [erasures illegible] my disgust sometimes is boiling over – but they are, I believe, in conduct the purest women God ever made. Thank God for my countrywomen – alas for the men! No worse than men everywhere, but the lower their mistresses, the more degraded they must be.[21]

While sharing the racist assumptions of her class, Chesnut was nevertheless able to imagine herself in the situation of individual slaves, a leap not encouraged by white southern society. She sympathized with the matrimonial difficulties of her maid and refused to condemn black women who had children without being married.[22] When she saw a woman sold in Montgomery, Alabama, she reported feeling faint and tried hard to explain the situation to herself: "I sat down on a stool in a shop. I disciplined my wild thoughts. You know how women sell themselves and are sold in marriage, from queens downward, eh? You know what the Bible says about slavery – and marriage. Poor women. Poor slaves."[23] She blamed the horrors of slavery on white men and applauded the efforts of white women to improve the quality of slaves' lives....

Like a few other southern women, Mary Chesnut both hated slavery and yet could not imagine a world without it. She translated the teachings of nineteenth-century culture regarding women into a sophisticated understanding of her own position and into a critique of slavery, yet was unable to act on her beliefs. Gertrude Thomas bemoaned her own ineffectiveness: "The happiest of homes are destroyed but what is to be done.... This is a mystery I find I cannot solve."[24] Mary Chesnut implied that white women could do very little about slavery: "women were brought up not to judge their fathers or their husbands. They took them as the Lord provided – and were thankful." For Chesnut, in this helpless condition women were no better off than slaves. Late in the war, she recorded this conversation with the wife of General Johnston:

> Mrs. Johnston said she would never own slaves.
> "I might say the same thing. I never would. Mr. Chesnut does, but he hates all slavery, especially African slavery."
> "What do you mean by African?"
> "To distinguish that form from the inevitable slavery of the world. All married women, all children, and girls who live on in their father's houses are slaves."

Given their own difficulties, Chesnut could only try to reassure herself that women were not responsible for slavery: "As far as I can see, Southern women do all that missionaries could do to prevent and alleviate the evils."[25]

Unable to imagine a world without slavery in spite of their distaste for its consequences, Chesnut and other elite women in South Carolina who shared her views struggled with their own ineffectiveness but were essentially alone. Because South Carolina women whispered their distaste for the worst consequences of slavery only to their diaries or to one another they were forced to work individually to counteract it and could help only the black men and women on their own plantations. Influenced by the ideology of domesticity to behave sympathetically and benevolently, some mistresses worked hard to improve conditions for their slaves. But, taught to defer to men and unable to unite politically, they did not develop their dislike of slavery beyond the individual emotional level. Their complaints about slavery and their dismay at its consequences remained private and apolitical.

In the antebellum years, three South Carolina women defied the dictates of their culture to publish their ideas about gender, race, slavery, and other important topics of the day. As writers and intellectuals Caroline Howard Gilman, Louisa McCord, and Mary Howard Schoolcraft were exceptional for their time and place. These political women were simultaneously rigorous defenders and sharp critics of the separation of spheres, slavery, and race and gender relations. Like reformers elsewhere in the country, they believed that bringing the problems of their society to light would help to eliminate them. Yet for all three women, criticisms of southern society were tempered by genuine acceptance of its assumptions and institutions. An examination of their very different ideas offers the potential to develop the connection between ideology and behavior more closely, as well as to assess the complex attitudes and expectations defining the place of white women in slaveholding society.

Caroline Howard Gilman was born in 1794 in Boston; in 1819 she married a Harvard Divinity School graduate and moved to Charleston, where her husband was appointed minister of the Unitarian church.

Charleston remained her home for most of the rest of her life. . . . In 1832 she founded a magazine for children called the *Rose Bud, or Youth's Gazette*; she changed its name to the *Southern Rose* in 1835 because, she said, the buds had blossomed. The magazine ceased publication in 1839 but was followed by a series of annual gift books intended for women that were filled with advice, stories, and other material similar to that included in the magazine. Gilman also published two novels, *Recollections of a Housekeeper* (1834) and *Recollections of a Southern Matron* (1838), both of which had been serialized in the magazine. She claimed the novels were as true to life as possible and even solicited anecdotes from the readers of the magazine to weave into the stories if appropriate.[26]

In all of her writing, . . . Gilman defined and defended the ideology of domesticity, both as it applied in the North and in the form directed at plantation mistresses. She believed that white women had a special mission and that their domestic responsibilities were essential to the success of their families and the nation. She filled many pages of her magazine and annual registers with poems and stories . . . extolling the importance of women's activities, particularly as mothers and homemakers. . . . Mothers, she said, were to be always supportive of their sons: "Whilst his mother lives, he will have one friend on earth who will not listen when he is slandered, who will not desert him when he suffers, who will solace him in his sorrow, and speak to him of hope when he is ready to despair. Her affections know no ebbing tide. It flows on from a pure fountain, spreading happiness through all this vale of tears, and ceases only at the ocean of eternity." Gilman did not indicate that daughters should receive similar treatment.[27]

These nurturing activities were extremely important for Gilman, and she sometimes chided men . . . for their failure to appreciate women's significance. In the brief essay "The Wife" she celebrated women's ability to manage husbands, homes, children, and social obligations successfully and asked what would happen if a man were "only for one day, in their position? The servants would all be discharged, the children whipped and sent to bed, and himself, by nightfall, just fit for Bedlam."[28] . . . By celebrating the importance of women's activities and offering advice both general and specific on how to accomplish them more effectively, Gilman presented herself as a powerful public champion of the ideology of domesticity and of women.

Gilman had equally strong views about slavery and race relations. In spite of her northern upbringing, she considered herself a southerner after her marriage and remained loyal to the South during the war. She had few moral objections to the institution of slavery but advocated more considerate treatment of slaves. White women, she felt, had a particular responsibility to be considerate toward blacks and to teach their children to treat blacks with kindness. The narrator's grandmother in *Recollections of a Southern Matron* demonstrated Gilman's model of ideal behavior: "The influence of her manners was evident on the plantation, producing an air of courtesy even among the slaves. It was beautiful to witness the profound respect with which they regarded her." Gilman applauded the real contributions plantation mistresses made to the health and well-being of those in their care, in spite of the apparent indolence made possible by slavery:

> Many fair, and even aristocratic girls, if we may use this phrase in our republican country, who grace a ball room, or loll in a liveried carriage, may be seen with these steel talismans [keys], presiding over store houses, and measuring with the accuracy and conscientiousness of a shopsman, the daily allowance of the family; or cutting homespun suits, for days together, for the young and the old slaves under their charge; while matrons, who would ring a bell for their pocket handkerchief to be brought to them, will act the part of a surgeon or physician, with a promptitude and skill, which would excite astonishment in a stranger. Very frequently, slaves, like children, will only take medicine from their superiors, and in this case the planter's wife or daughter is admirably fitted to aid them.

Gilman assigned duties to men as well as women. The well-prepared slaveholder had to learn "personal discipline" and study medicine and mechanics. He had to be "aware that he controlled the happiness of a large family of his fellow creatures. He neither permitted himself to exercise oppression, nor tolerated it in others. . . . He felt how much a planter has to answer to man and to God in the patriarchal relation he holds, and he shrank not indolently from the arduous demand."[29] Under these circumstances, with both male and female slaveholders fulfilling their obligations to slaves, Gilman believed slavery was advantageous for everyone, including the slaves themselves. . . .

Gilman's acceptance of slavery was expedient: the institution was desirable because it allowed white women to fulfill their domestic responsibilities effectively. She never considered the perspective of African Americans except to assume they accepted their place and their owners without question. . . . For Gilman, slavery was a positive institution for both whites and slaves because each group recognized and fulfilled its responsibilities to the other. White women had particular obligations of care and protection, which were repaid with reliable service and personal devotion from black women and men. Many of Gilman's readers must have been inspired by these ideas because she sympathized with their difficulties and offered them a vision and a prescription for success in coping with lovable but irritating husbands, complex households, and slaves who never behaved as they were expected to. Gilman's success as a writer of southern domesticity was her ability to acknowledge both the ideal to which women should aspire and the reality that made that ideal difficult – but not impossible – to achieve.

Unlike Gilman, Mary Howard Schoolcraft developed a rigorous defense of slavery based not only on its advantages for the domestic life of whites but also on its presumed beneficial effects for blacks. Born in the Beaufort District of South Carolina to a long-established and well-connected family, she moved to Washington sometime before 1851; in 1860 she said she no longer owned slaves nor did she expect to again. Around this time she published an essay in the form of a novel called *The Black Gauntlet*. . . .

Schoolcraft considered blacks inferior to whites and was "so satisfied that slavery is the school God has established for the conversion of barbarous nations, that were I an absolute Queen of these United States, my first missionary enterprise would be to send to Africa, to bring its heathen as *slaves* to this Christian land, and keep them in bondage until *compulsory* labor had tamed their beastliness, and civilization and Christianity had prepared them to return as missionaries of progress to their benighted black brethren."[30] . . .

Schoolcraft did not absolve slaveholders from all responsibility. No one dared "assert that the degraded African heathen has not been benefitted, for time and eternity, by being brought even as a slave to this Christianized country." Although these supposed benefits were the result of the care whites provided for blacks, that care resulted from self-interest.[31] . . . "As long as negroes are *property*, no master, unless he was a lunatic, would ever hurt them. Shooting or beating a slave to death, would insure the prepetrators being sent to the asylum for the insane; for such an episode, in plantation policy, could not occur, unless the *reason*, and with it, the *self-love* of the master, was dethroned."[32]

Schoolcraft emphasized the parallels between slaveholders' self-interested protection of slaves and parents' care of children. She contrasted both with the poor conditions of free blacks in the North and Canada. There, a former slave "is alike despised and deserted, and left to famish, or exist in a place so small and filthy that our cows could not survive a winter in them. . . . Poor slave! you once had a master, whose interest and whose humanity protected you, and supplied your every want; who kept you from idleness and drunkenness, and from the indulgence of crime and fiendish passions."[33] . . .

Schoolcraft was so confident that slavery was beneficial for blacks because she was convinced that white women adequately provided for them. All slaveholders were motivated by self-interest, but a mistress had an even more direct responsibility: "She has not only every principle of self-interest to urge her to be up and doing at sunrise; but from her very nursery she is taught that the meanest creature on God's earth is a master or mistress who neglects those that Providence has made utterly dependent on them. Her conscience, educated to this self-denying nobility of action, would feel as wounded by the neglect of her helpless children as by disregard for her hard working slaves." Schoolcraft was contemptuous of northern women who condemned southern women for idleness: "Let a Yankee lady fancy herself surrounded by a family of two hundred persons (as is often the case with a Southern planter's wife), all dependent, more or less, on herself." A planter's wife was responsible for a wide variety of tasks; she was to be "a responsible, conscientious 'sister of charity' to her husband's numerous dependants."[34]

Indeed, Schoolcraft argued that white women suffered more than slaves: "I am certain that wives have suffered more intense, more hopeless anguish, from brutal, non-appreciative husbands, than any slave has ever experienced . . . for the slave being made, by the mercy of his Creator, property, secures a more undying interest, in a selfish master's heart, than a wife, who can be so easily replaced, particularly when her husband begins to get tired of her; which is so often the case." Schoolcraft believed self-interested masters showed they valued slaves more than their wives in very practical ways: "It is an undoubted fact, that a *bad* master will take more care of his slaves in sickness and in health, than he will of his wife; will sit up with him, administer every dose of medicine, and send for the doctor, and the parson, too, if the slave's mind is troubled so as to increase his fever; while his own poor wife may make her exodus to the other world as soon as she pleases, and her place can be easily, and perhaps profitably supplied, by his marrying a young heiress."[35] . . .

No matter how inferior men were, Schoolcraft maintained women were "still required to bow as *inferiors*" to them. . . . Although she condemned both men and women, the outcome was the same. Women who felt superior in "morals and practical sense" to "these boys in men's clothes that have been palmed on us, with few exceptions, for husbands, ever since Adam lost his godlike, manly dignity" nevertheless had to treat them with respect because of biblical command: "God orders the wife to be obedient to her own husband, to honor and love him." Women who thought they were "wiser than our Creator" and asserted their independence were the anomalous creatures of women's rights conventions: "Instead of ruling the men with our dimples, and our curls, and our smiles, and our moral loveliness, and refined dependence on them to vote for us, and work for us, and fight for us, and let us stay at home to enjoy the magnificent privilege of teaching the young idea how to shoot; instead of this sublime destiny for mothers and wives, we should have a race of coarse, ugly Amazons, scratching and biting all who oppose them." Women should not aspire to men's activities but should use their power over the human heart to create a more moral society.[36]... Schoolcraft believed the surest way for women to improve their situation was to defer to men, even when those men were not worthy of deference. No matter how inferior men were, they were still superior to women, who had little choice but obedient acceptance of their destiny. The key for Schoolcraft was for women to bow gracefully, without sacrificing virtue or responsibility....

Schoolcraft's vision of race and gender relations was complex and contradictory. Critical as she was of men and their actions, she was unwilling to consider any significant challenges to their authority; religion demanded submission even when men's behavior was unacceptable. Acceptance of male authority was the only path for white women to follow to a moral life, just as acceptance of white authority was the only possible path of improvement for slaves. Whether or not slaves and women liked their inferior condition was simply irrelevant because God had willed their subordination and their circumstances; she advised both groups not to challenge God's will.

Schoolcraft's arguments about race and gender were particularly appealing to female readers. She advocated a profoundly apolitical stance for women, sanctioned by God, suggesting that their only legitimate form of influence was in the domestic realm. While applauding their efforts to improve their society within the safety of socially accepted norms, she warned them of the dangers of violating those norms even in the name of improvement. But at the same time, by insisting on deference to men she offered an explanation for women's inability to be completely effective even there. She exhorted women about proper behavior but sympathized with the circumstances that prevented it from having the desired effect. Such reasoning reassured southern women... because it removed the necessity of taking action... and absolved them of direct responsibility for virtually everything. Schoolcraft offered her readers a way to simultaneously support and criticize their society, which no doubt comforted many struggling plantation mistresses.

If Mary Howard Schoolcraft's work would allow white women the illusion of power through submission to men and acceptance of God's will, Louisa Cheves McCord's writing offered a more active version of the same advice. The only South Carolina woman who regularly published her essays in the *Southern Quarterly Review, DeBow's Review,* and other periodicals not aimed specifically at women, McCord became a leading theoretician of the ideology of domesticity and of pro-slavery thought.[37] ...

In her essays and poetry... McCord defended the view of womanhood defined by the southern ideology of domesticity from the heresies against God and nature committed by northern women's rights advocates. Unlike Schoolcraft, who saw women as inferior to men, McCord recognized women's inferiority in "corporeal strength" but argued that "each [person] is strong in his own nature. They are neither inferior, nor superior, nor equal. They are different." She defined woman's mission as

> even nobler than man's, and she is, in the true fulfillment of that mission, certainly the higher being... Woman's duty, woman's nature, is to love, to sway by love; to govern by love, to teach by love, to civilize by love!... Pure and holy, self-devoted and suffering, woman's love is the breath of that God of love, who, loving and pitying, has bid *her* learn to love and to suffer, implanting in her bosom the one single comfort that she is the watching spirit, the guardian angel of those she loves.... Each can labour, each can strive, lovingly and earnestly, in her own sphere.

She warned women to reject the follies of those who wanted to vote: "Woman, *cherish thy mission.* Fling thyself not from the high pedestal whereon God has placed thee." She outlined women's mission in terms that would have been familiar to other advocates of domesticity: "The woman must *raise* the man, by helping, not by rivalling him.... She it is who softens; she it is who civilizes; and, although history acknowledges her not, she it is who, not in the meteoric brilliancy of warrior or monarch, but in the quiet, unwearied and unvarying path of duty, the home of the mother, the wife and the sister, teaching man his destiny, purifies, exalts, and guides him to his duty."[38]...

Louisa McCord also defended slavery in closely reasoned essays. She was convinced that human society was "improving, improvable, ceaselessly and boundlessly" and that slavery was inherent in human progress.[39] She argued that the institution was a Christian system, beneficial to both slaves and slaveholders: "The master gives protection; the slave looks for it." She claimed that slavery brought the greatest good to the greatest number, including blacks, who were "Nature's outcast" and "unfit for all progress."[40] Although slavery encompassed crime, sin, and abuse of power, abolition was not the solution because it disrupted what would otherwise be harmonious relationships: "Our system of slavery, left to itself, would rapidly develop its higher features, softening at once to servant and master." Abolition also was not best for slaves: "The Negro, left to himself, does not dream of liberty. He cannot indeed grasp a conception which belongs so naturally to the brain of the white man." The best solution was Christian slavery: "Make your laws to interfere with the God-established system of slavery, which our Southern states are beautifully developing to perfection, daily improving the condition of the slave, daily waking more and more the master to his high and responsible position; make your laws, we say, to pervert this God-directed course, and the world has yet to see the horrors which might ensue from it. The natural order of things perverted, ill must follow."[41]

By defending slavery as beneficial to blacks, McCord joined a long intellectual tradition in the South. However, she added another dimension to the argument when she wrote about women. In her review of *Uncle Tom's Cabin*, McCord criticized Stowe's portrait of the wife of a brutal slaveholder and in the process illustrated her own expectations of plantation mistresses: "This very sensible, moral and religious lady, when made acquainted with her husband's brutal conduct, is very naturally distressed at it. But what remedy does she find? Does she consult with him as a wife should consult? Does she advise as a woman can advise? Does she suggest means and remedies for avoiding such a crisis? Does she endeavor to show her husband the folly and madness, as well as the wickedness of his course?" Stowe's heroine clearly did not live up to McCord's ideal southern woman.[42] . . .

Slavery, then, was an institution both beneficial to African Americans and carrying great responsibility for white women. Female slaveholders' unique obligations encouraged them to curb the abuses of their husbands and treat slaves humanely. McCord raised these issues indirectly in an 1852 essay, in which she defined the differences between men and women:

> Her mission is one of love and charity to all. It is the very essence of her being to raise and to purify wherever she touches. Where man's harder nature crushes, her's exaults. Where he wounds, she heals. . . . God, man and nature alike call upon her to subdue her passions, to suffer, to bear, to be meek and lowly of heart; while man, summoned by nature, and often by duty, to the whirl of strife, blinded in the struggle, forgets too often where wrath should cease and mercy rule. What, then, more beautiful than woman's task to arrest the up-lifted arm, and, in the name of an all-pardoning Heaven, to whisper to his angry passions – "Peace, be still!"[43]

While McCord was not specifically referring to behavior toward slaves, she may well have had slaves in mind when she wrote. Women reading her essay would very likely interpret her words as a suggestion to curb the tempers of men toward them.

Louisa McCord combined ideas about gender and race into a vision of southern society that defined white women and all blacks as inferior, but not doomed to passivity and insignificance: "Inferiority is not a curse. Every creature is suited for its position, and fulfilling that position can certainly not be called cursed. . . . As He has made you to be women and not men – mothers and sisters, and not (according to the modern improvement system), soldiers and legislators, so has He fitted the negro for his position and suited him to be happy and useful in it."[44] Both women and blacks needed the protection of white men, and both must pay for that protection "by the abandonment of privileges which otherwise might seem to be [their] right."[45] McCord relied on both physical and moral inferiority and a divine plan to justify the subordination of women and blacks. To challenge was impossible, and those antislavery and women's rights advocates who did so deserved stinging rebukes. Only by acceptance of the laws of God and nature could human society be improved and harmony and prosperity achieved. McCord believed that duty was white women's highest virtue, and, rather than seeking to imitate men in any way, they should strive only to be more womanly. Similarly, McCord believed that all people of African descent were suited by God and nature for slavery and insisted that it was a beneficent institution when southern whites were allowed to practice it according to their own traditions.

For each of these three South Carolina writers, justifying the subordination of white women was a primary intellectual task. Each recognized that subordination and each accepted it as part of God's plan for humanity. Similarly, each accepted slavery as beneficial for blacks and a responsibility for whites. Each established a connection between gender and race that placed special obligations for the well-being of slaves on the shoulders of white women. The survival and advancement of society required white women and slaves to accept subordination.

In many respects, the theories of these South Carolina intellectuals were little more than carefully articulated and developed versions of the views that shaped the daily activities and interactions of many of the plantation mistresses of the state. Mistresses who sought to understand themselves, their slaves, and their society as they fulfilled their domestic responsibilities struggled to come to terms with the implications of assumptions about gender and race. Unable to imagine the South without slavery, mistresses and intellectuals made a variety of efforts to justify its existence and improve its consequences by appealing to what they considered the fundamental characteristics of blacks and of white women. Only a very few white women interpreted those characteristics in ways that challenged domesticity or slavery, and they remained isolated and largely silent.

Notes

1 Mary E. Herndon, *Louise Elton; Or Things Seen and Heard* (Philadelphia: Lippincott, 1852), pp. 237, 239, 240.
2 Caroline Lee Hentz, *The Planter's Northern Bride* (Philadelphia: T. B. Peterson, 1854), I, p. v.
3 Martha Haines Butt, *Antifanaticism: A Tale of the South* (Philadelphia: Lippincott, Grambo, 1853), pp. 267–8.
4 Mary H. Eastman (Mary Henderson), *Aunt Phillis's Cabin, or, Southern Life as it is* (New York: Negro Universities Press, 1968), p. 279; see also p. 96.
5 Ibid., p. 277; Mary Howard Schoolcraft, *The Black Gauntlet; a Tale of Plantation Life in South Carolina* (Philadelphia: J. B. Lippincott & Co., 1860), p. 49; Herndon, *Louise Elton*, pp. 247–8.
6 Maria J. McIntosh, *The Lofty and the Lowly, or, Good in All and None All-Good* (New York: D. Appleton, 1853), ii. 318.
7 Eastman, *Aunt Phillis's Cabin*, p. 258, see also pp. 102–3.
8 Ibid., p. 233.
9 Herndon, *Louise Elton*, pp. 245–6; McIntosh, *Lofty and Lowly*, i. 295.
10 "Southern Slavery and its Assailants: *The Key to Uncle Tom's Cabin*," *DeBow's Review*, 15 (Nov. 1853) pp. 488, 491, 492.
11 "Southern Slavery and its Assailants: *The Key to Uncle Tom's Cabin – Again*," *DeBow's Review*, 16 (Jan. 1854), p. 55.
12 Catherine Anne Devereaux Edmonston, *"Journal of a Secesh Lady": The Diary of Catherine Anne Deveraux Edmonston, 1860–1866*, ed. Beth G. Crabtree and James W. Patton (Raleigh: North Carolina Division of Archives and History, Department of Cultural Resources, 1979), pp. 45, 418, and *passim*.
13 Anne Firor Scott, *The Southern Lady: From Pedestal to Politics, 1830–1930* (Chicago: University of Chicago Press, 1970), pp. 48–50, quote from p. 48.
14 Suzanne Lebsock, *The Free Women of Petersburg: Status and Culture in a Southern Town, 1784–1860* (New York: Norton, 1984), pp. 141–5; idem, "Complicity and Contention: Women in the Plantation South," *Georgia Historical Quarterly*, 74 (Spring 1990), pp. 75–6.
15 J. H. Easterby, *The South Carolina Rice Plantation as Revealed in the Papers of Robert F. W. Allston*, ed. J. H. Easterby (Chicago: University of Chicago Press, 1945), p. 51; Eliza Ann DeRosset to Mary D. Curtis, Sept. 18, 1838, in Moses Ashley Curtis Family Papers, Southern Historical Collection, University of North Carolina, Chapel Hill.
16 Amie Lumpkin, *The American Slave: A Composite Biography*, ed. George P. Rawick, 19 vols. (Westport, Conn.: Greenwood Press, 1972), iii. 130–1.
17 Sarah Katherine Holmes, *Brokenburn; the Journal of Kate Stone, 1861–1907*, ed. John Q. Anderson (Baton Rouge: Louisiana State University Press, 1955), p. 8.
18 *A Plantation Mistress on the Eve of the Civil War: The Diary of Keziah Goodwyn Hopkins Brevard, 1860–1861*, ed. John Hammond Moore (Columbia: University of South Carolina Press, 1993), Jan. 8, 1961.

19 Ella [Gertrude Clanton] Thomas, *The Secret Eye: The Journal of Ella Gertrude Clanton Thomas, 1848–1889*, ed. Virginia Ingraham Burr (Chapel Hill: University of North Carolina Press, 1990), Jan. 2, 1859.
20 Ibid., Aug. 18, 1856; Jan. 2, 1859.
21 Mary Boykin Miller Chesnut, *Mary Chesnut's Civil War*, ed. C. Vann Woodward (New Haven: Yale University Press, 1981), pp. 29–31.
22 Ibid., pp. 53, 31, 54.
23 Ibid., p. 15, see also pp. 169, 729.
24 Thomas Journal, Jan. 2, 1859.
25 Chesnut, *Mary Chesnut's Civil War*, pp. 169, 729, 307.
26 Caroline Gilman, *Recollections of a Southern Matron*, (New York: Harper and Bros., 1838), p. vii; [Caroline Howard Gilman], "Recollections of a Housekeeper, Chap. III," *Southern Rose Bud* 2 (Feb. 1, 1834), p. 90.
27 [Gilman], *Housekeeper's Annual, 1844*, p. 88.
28 Gilman, "The Wife," p. 65.
29 [Caroline Howard Gilman], "Recollections of a Southern Matron, Chapter III," *Southern Rose Bud*, 3 (June 27, 1835), p. 170; [Caroline Howard Gilman], "Recollections of a Southern Matron, Chap. VI," p. 1; [Caroline Howard Gilman], "Recollections of a Southern Matron, Chap. XXVIII," *Southern Rose*, 5 (Nov. 26, 1836), p. 49.
30 Schoolcraft, *Black Gauntltet*, pp. v–vii.
31 Mary Schoolcraft, *Letters on the Condition of the African Race in the United States by a Southern Lady* (Philadelphia: T. K. and P. G. Collins, 1852), p. 10.
32 Schoolcraft, *Black Gauntlet*, p. 83.
33 Ibid., pp. 46–7.
34 Ibid., pp. 114–15.
35 Ibid., pp. viii, 84, 238.
36 Ibid., pp. 546–8.
37 Edward T. James, Janet Wilson James, and Paul S. Boyer (eds.), *Notable American Women: A Biographical Dictionary*, 3 vols. (Cambridge, Mass: Harvard University Press, 1971), vol.2, pp. 450–2.
38 Louisa S. McCord, "Enfranchisement of Women," in McCord, *Political and Social Essays*, ed. Richard C. Lounsbury (Charlottesville: University Press of Virginia, 1995), pp. 331, 325–7.
39 L[ouisa] S[usannah] M[cCord], "Justice and Fraternity," *Southern Quarterly Review* 15, (July 1849), p. 357.
40 L[ouisa] S[usannah] M[cCord], "*Uncle Tom's Cabin:* A Book Review," *Southern Quarterly Review*, n.s. 7 (Jan. 1853), pp. 111, 118.
41 Ibid., pp. 118–19, 109.
42 Ibid., pp. 94, 98.
43 McCord, "Woman and her Needs," in *Political and Social Essays*, pp. 285–6.

44 McCord, "British Philanthropy and American Slavery," in *Political and Social Essays*, p. 264.
45 McCord, "Carey on the Slave Trade," in *Political and Social Essays*, pp. 168–9.

8

Masters and Slaves: Paternalism and Exploitation

Introduction

The master–slave relationship was characterized by an unequal distribution of power which often manifested itself in a violent way. Violence was the main instrument whereby masters and overseers enforced discipline among the slaves. The threat of a whipping was a constant feature of slave life on the plantation. In those regions of the South where planters were especially concerned with realizing higher returns from the production and sale of staple crops, harsh discipline and frequent punishments made slave life far more unbearable than elsewhere. A recent study of the coastal swamps of South Carolina has argued that the rice planters of the low country ran their plantations as capitalist enterprises and literally worked slaves to death in the quest for increased rice production. Slaves responded in a variety of ways to physical and psychological abuse; they learned how to cope with day-to-day exploitation with acts of resistance that kept the masters from turning them into subjugated childlike "sambos." An increasing number of studies show that in many regions slaves were able to continue with their own lives even in conditions of extreme oppression.

Most historians argue that violence was only part of the master–slave relationship; masters strove to exercise control through a more subtle approach, one that was linked to the ideology of paternalism. For scholars influenced by neoclassical economics, such as Robert Fogel and Stanley Engerman, paternalism did not conflict with the capitalist character of the master class. For these historians, masters could think and act in paternalistic ways toward their slaves just as bosses behave paternalistically toward dependents in their business firms. In this case, paternalism was an attitude that masters held toward slaves in order to maximize production and keep work place conflict to a minimum. However, in Marxist historian Eugene Genovese's view, paternalism worked in a quite different way. For Genovese, paternalism implied a personal relationship between master and slave; it was strictly related to the non-capitalist character of the master class. Based on close personal relationships, paternalism helped produce a cultural hegemony of masters over slaves, one in which the slaves came to accept some of the premises on which slavery rested. At the same time, paternalism left some room for the agency of the slaves, who – though not questioning slavery – through a process of continuous bargaining with their masters, obtained the recognition of some basic rights.

One of the best-studied cases of paternalism and hegemony is certainly the one of James Henry Hammond. In 1831, Hammond acquired Silver Bluff, a cotton plantation with 147 slaves in the South Carolina up-country. Hammond had in mind a design for total control over his slaves. Ideally, he wanted to influence every aspect of their lives, but he never achieved this aim because of the slaves' opposition. He replaced the slaves' religious worship with a white church and made attendance compulsory. He tried to impose his own work rhythms upon slaves through frequent punishment; and he repeatedly attempted to manipulate the slaves' minds. At the same time, Hammond showed the softer side of paternalistic manipulation. Like his fellow South Carolinian Charles Manigault, he gave rewards to the most diligent field hands, and he distributed gifts at Christmas, together with special rations of sugar, coffee, and tobacco. Through these small acts Hammond strove to achieve psychological control over his slaves. However, his bondspeople resisted his attempts at achieving "hegemony" in a thousand different ways. When Hammond forbade independent black religion, the slaves continued their African practices in covert ways. When he attempted to impose the grueling gang labor system, they performed badly, feigned illness or broke tools, ultimately forcing a return to the task system. Moreover, between 1831 and 1835, 53 slaves resisted their master's search for "despotic sway" by running away from the plantation.

Further reading

Dusinberre, W., *Them Dark Days: Life in the American Rice Swamps* (New York: Oxford University Press, 1996).
Elkins, S., *Slavery: A Problem in American Institutional and Intellectual Life* (Chicago: University of Chicago Press, 1959).
Faust, D. G., *James Henry Hammond and the Old South: A Design for Mastery* (Baton Rouge: Louisiana State University Press, 1982).
Genovese, E. D., *Roll, Jordan, Roll: The World the Slaves Made* (New York: Pantheon Books, 1974).
Johnson, W., *Soul by Soul: Life Inside the Antebellum Slave Market* (Cambridge, Mass., and London: Harvard University Press, 1999).
Kolchin, P., *American Slavery, 1619–1877* (New York: Hill & Wang, 1993).
Stampp, K., *The Peculiar Institution* (New York: Vintage, 1955).
Tadman, M., *Speculators and Slaves: Masters, Traders, and Slaves in the Old South* (Madison: University of Wisconsin Press, 1989).
Young, J. R., *Domesticating Slavery: The Master Class in South Carolina and Georgia, 1670–1830* (Chapel Hill: University of North Carolina Press, 1999).

James Henry Hammond Battles Slave Illness (1841)

The diaries of James Henry Hammond – which he intended to remain secret – provide us with a remarkable and revealing portrait of the mind of a planter in the antebellum South. In Hammond's diaries, one can read a sincere – though biased – firsthand account of the struggles that characterized the master–slave relationship on a large cotton plantation. Hammond's attempts to impose his absolute rule at Silver Bluff collapsed because of the obstinate resistance of his slaves. An uninterrupted series of slave illnesses and deaths contributed greatly to the undermining of his authority. In these two 1841 diary entries, Hammond expresses genuine sorrow over the loss of his slaves. Yet, it is clear that his main disappointment lay in the keen awareness of his inability to look after his work force effectively – what he took as a "design of heaven" to prevent him from accumulating wealth from the labors of his human property.

Source: Carol Bleser (ed.), *Secret and Sacred: The Diaries of James Henry Hammond, a Southern Slaveholder* (Oxford and New York: Oxford University Press, 1988), pp. 72–3

. . . [Silver Bluff] Sept. 4 [1841]

Have had several days of anxiety and fatigue among my sick people. The Overseer and his family are down and several others very sick. To-day however has been the most painful of all. A valuable [slave] woman was taken in labour yesterday and last night it was ascertained that the presentation was wrong. Dr. Foreman was sent for who called in Dr. Bradford. There was also a spasmodic contraction of the womb. Three pounds of blood were taken without producing any relaxation. She was then steamed without effect and Lobelia given to nauseate. Finally she was put in a warm bath. Relaxation to syncope took place, the child was turned, but she never rallied sufficiently to bring it forth. The bloodletting had exhausted nature. The pain and the steam had its effect and I am not sure the Lobelia might not have increased or perhaps produced the spasm tho' the parts were perfectly rigid before. The bleeding I think mainly deprived her of the strength for re-action. In spite of every stimulant she died. She was a good creature as ever lived. Her child had been dead several days.

[Silver Bluff] Sept. 5 [1841]

Another death to-day. It happened up here. A child near 3 years old who for 8 months I have had up here. It died of dropsy in its sleep. The end of rickets. This the 4th instance since I came over and two deaths, stillborn children. It is the 9th this year exclusive of stillbirths which have been 3 in all. It is, exclusive of such births, the 78th death among my negroes in a little less than ten years. Which is more than half the number [of deaths] I had ten years ago and rather more. It is nearly half I have now. There have been only 72 births in that time. One would think from this statement that I was a monster of inhumanity. Yet this one subject has caused me more anxiety and suffering than any other of my life. I have adopted every possible measure to promote health and save life, but all in vain it seems. Every thing dies, not only people, but mules, horses, cattle, hogs – life seems here to be the mere sport of some capricious destiny. Whether it is a judgement on me or on the place I know not. No one has ever prospered here since old Galphin died. His son, Goodwyn and Ransey, McKinne, and Mr. Fitzsimons [Hammond's father-in-law] all failed or died [here]. Yet it may be my fortune. I am reputed fortunate, yet, except in one single event of my life, ill-luck has pursued me at every turn. And were it not that I might appear ungrateful for that one, I should esteem myself one of the most unfortunate of men. I sometimes think I see in these deaths the finger of God pointing to me to go elsewhere. Sometimes I think it means that

I should part with my plantations and keep around me as few things that have life as possible. Sometimes I think it marks the deliberate design of heaven to prevent me from accumulating wealth and to keep down that pride which might in such an event fill my heart. Yet I feel conscious that I am not one of those who are elated with prosperity, and, as far as human views can extend, I feel justified in saying that I have ever duly acknowledged in my inward and outward man all the goodness of God to me. If I have not, then my standard is erroneous. I have in this respect come up to what I *thought* right, and still think so, yet I may have fallen far short of the reality. God only knows. If these unheard of deaths occurred but once or twice I should think they were judgments, but would fate pursue one so for 10 years? Nor is the place sickly. It is as healthy as the neighborhood, more healthy I believe. This is a most painful theme. It dwells in my mind much and embitters my life. I must seek some change. *Must*. I should have done so long ago, but for a series of events which I can hardly recall. A mixture of political motives and personal bad health. Let my health revive and politics will not long keep me here. I wish I was only clear of my Columbia property. I do not feel like I ever wished to go there again.

Rules on the Rice Estate of Plowden C. Weston, South Carolina (1846)

One of the most popular topics of discussion among slaveholders in the antebellum South was the proper conduct of an overseer in the treatment of slaves. Articles appeared regularly in the specialized journals issued by agricultural societies, and prominent planters routinely published rules of conduct to guide overseers. A particularly successful example of these rules was the contract issued by South Carolinian planter Plowden C. Weston in 1846 and republished in *DeBow's Review* in 1857. The contract was a model of clarity and paternalistic ethics. It held the overseer responsible for the "care and well being of the negroes." At the same time, while it included detailed provisions restricting the liberty of the slaves, it recommended the enforcement of discipline through the use of the whip only in exceptional circumstances and never out of rage.

Source: *DeBow's Review*, 21 (Jan. 1857), pp. 38–44; reprinted in John R. Commons, Ulrich B. Phillips, Eugene A. Gilmore, Helen L. Sumner, and John B. Andrews (eds.), *A Documentary History of American Industrial Society*, vol. 1: *Plantation and Frontier* (Cleveland, Ohio: The Arthur H. Clark Company, 1910), pp. 116–22

The Proprietor, in the first place, wishes the Overseer most distinctly to understand that his first object is to be, under all circumstances, the care and well being of the negroes. The Proprietor is always ready to excuse such errors as may proceed from want of judgment; but he never can or will excuse any cruelty, severity, or want of care towards the negroes. For the well being, however, of the negroes, it is absolutely necessary to maintain obedience, order, and discipline; to see that the tasks are punctually and carefully performed, and to conduct the business steadily and firmly, without weakness on the one hand, or harshness on the other. For such ends the following regulations have been instituted. . . .

Allowance – Food. – Great care should be taken that the negroes should never have less than their regular allowance: in all cases of doubt, it should be given in favor of the largest quantity. The measures should not be *struck*, but rather heaped up over. None but provisions of the best quality should be used. If any is discovered to be damaged, the Proprietor, if at hand, is to be immediately informed; if absent, the damaged article is to be destroyed. The corn should be carefully winnowed before grinding. The small rice is apt to become sour: as soon as this is perceived it should be given out every meal until finished, or until it becomes too sour to use, when it should be destroyed.

Work, Holidays, &c. – No work of any sort or kind is to be permitted to be done by negroes on Good Friday, or Christmas day, or on any Sunday, except going for a Doctor, or nursing sick persons; any work of this kind done on any of these days is to be reported to the Proprietor, who will pay for it. The two days following Christmas day; the first Saturdays after finishing threshing, planting, hoeing, and harvest, are also to be holidays, on which the people may work for themselves. Only half task is to be done on every Saturday, except during planting and harvest, and those who have misbehaved or been lying up during the week. A task is as much work as the meanest full hand can do in nine hours, working industriously. The Driver is each morning to point out to each hand their task, and this task is never to be increased, and no work is to be done over task except under the most urgent necessity; which over-work is to be reported to the Proprietor, who will pay for it. No negro is to be put into a task which they cannot finish with tolerable ease. It is a bad plan to punish for not finishing task; it is subversive of discipline to leave tasks unfinished, and contrary to justice to punish for what cannot be done. In nothing does a good manager so much excel a bad, as in being able to discern what a hand is capable of doing, and in never attempting to make him do more.

No negro is to leave his task until the driver has examined and approved it, he is then to be permitted immediately to go home; and the hands are to be encouraged to finish their tasks as early as possible, so as to have time for working for themselves. Every negro, except the sickly ones and those with suckling children, (who are to be allowed half an hour,) are to be on board the flat by sunrise. One driver is to go down to the flat early, the other to remain behind and bring on all the people with him. He will be responsible for all coming down. The barn-yard bell will be rung by the watchman two hours, and half an hour, before sunrise.

Punishments. – It is desirable to allow 24 hours to elapse between the discovery of the offence, and the punishment. No punishment is to exceed 15 lashes: in cases where the Overseer supposes a severer punishment necessary, he must apply to the Proprietor, or to ——, Esq., in case of the Proprietor's absence from the neighborhood. Confinement (not in the stocks) is to be preferred to whipping: but the stoppage of Saturday's allowance, and doing whole task on Saturday, will suffice to prevent ordinary offences. Special care must be taken to prevent any indecency in punishing women. No Driver, or other negro, is to be allowed to punish any person in any way, except by order of the Overseer, and in his presence.

Charles Manigault Instructs his Overseer about "My Negroes" (1848)

The personal papers of South Carolina planter Charles Manigault (1795–1874) include hundreds of letters exchanged with his overseers at his Gowrie estate in Georgia. The letters are an illuminating example of the kind of issues that arose from the management of rice plantations. Between 1848 and 1850, while Manigault toured Europe, Jesse T. Cooper served as overseer at Gowrie. In his very first letter to Cooper, Manigault laid out his rules for proper slave management. Displaying a pronounced paternalistic attitude, Manigault recommended that Cooper give his slaves "the kindest treatment" and supply them with meat, rice, and clothes whenever he deemed necessary. Yet, Manigault really aimed to achieve the strictest possible supervision of the slaves' activities, since he knew that they were likely to run away or resist Cooper's directives, as they had already done several times with previous overseers.

Source: Charles Manigault to Mr. J. T. Cooper, Gowrie (Naples, 10th January 1848), in James M. Clifton (ed.), "The Antebellum Rice Planter as Revealed in the Letterbook of Charles Manigault, 1846–1848," *South Carolina Historical Magazine*, 74 (1973), pp. 307–9

To Mr. J. T. Cooper Gowrie

Dear Sir

Naples January 10, 1848

I received a Letter from "Mr. Habersham" informing me of his having engaged you to attend to my planting affairs & interests. Your residence being on Mr. Barclay's plantation (near mine) and I now write you a few lines to give you some of my *rules & regulations* in relation to my Concerns now under your Charge which have been always strictly attended to. My Negroes have the reputation of being *orderly & well disposed* – but like *all Negroes*, they are up to anything, if not watched & attended to. I expect the *kindest treatment of them* from you – for this has always been a principal *thing with me*. I never suffer them to work *off* the place – or to *exchange work* with any plantation. I never lend my flat, or anything from my plantation nor do I wish to borrow. I have suffered enough already from this *lending* to my neighbours.

Anything you think my Place is in want of, just send to Mr. Habersham, & he will furnish you with it for my account. It has always been my plan to give out allowance to the Negroes on Sunday in preference to any other day, because *this* has much influence in keeping them at home that day whereas, if they received allowance on *Saturday* for instance, Some of them would be off with it *that same evening* to the shops to trade & perhaps would not get back until Monday morning. I allow no strange Negro to take a wife on my place, & none of mine to keep *a boat* & should there be one belonging to me at the landing I request you to have it *locked*, & keep *the Key yourself.* Cut up, or lock up in the mill *any Negro Canoe* found anywhere on my place, & particularly *near the Mill* – whether it be on my land or on "Mr. Potter's" as that gentleman requested me, to do so, if I found any near my Mill on his land.

I allow no one to cut wood on my Island opposite "Mr. Legare's" place, & I request you to attend *to this* as far as lays in your power. You will get Cotton Oznaburgs in May, & give 5 1/2 yards to the women, & 6 to the men, & proportionally to the Children, with a Handkerchief to each female, who works. I wish you to engage as soon as possible 20,000 Staves, to be put away in the Coopers' Shop early in the summer, by which they will be *well seasoned* for making Barrels when you set the Coopers at work in midsummer. Put *nothing* under my dwelling House, you can help, & don't have a plank across the ditch anywhere near it. Make all pass thro the settlement, for I dislike a public way so near my dwelling & as there is *no white person* now residing *on the place*, I beg you to nail up *the necessary door* – it is not intended for Negroes.

The garden is very productive, & if you have anyone who has nothing else to do (such as "Old Ned") who would attend to it it would add much to their health & comfort, & I wish you to keep up *the fences* around the garden, the Barn Yard, & my house, and have everything of the kind looking *snug* & in good repair, just as if I was living on the place. "Mr. Barclay" gives more meat than I do but my people besides being the *best clothed in the Country* have other advantages – for instance, I keep all the small Rice *for them*, unless on one or two occasions when they have done anything wrong, when I have sold the whole of it. The *Dirty Rice* amounting usually to 10 or 12 Barrels, is always kept *for them at harvest* when *hard work* don't give them time to grind Corn. But you will give them *meat*, now & then, when you think proper.

The *House* in the High Land you will look to now & then, when convenient, & have it in repair for the little Children in May. You will sell the Rice Flour for me to the best advantage, or if you find it accumulating, & no demand for it, you will inform "Mr. Habersham," who will probably be able to sell it by the quantity to someone, who will send a boat for it. If you Keep it *to March*, or April, it will get heated, & turn sour. You take charge of *my interests* under high recommendations. I am therefore prepossessed *in your favor.*

"Mr. Bagshaw", a distinguished Rice Planter, while living on an adjoining place, managed all my affairs for 7 years. I began *with him* at a salery [sic] of $150 per an[num]. But I am quite satisfied to pay you what *Mr. H[abersham]* writes me, viz., $250 per an[num] *for your services*. If things go on well, it can be increased a little for another year. I request you to write me once a month. Just put my name on the letter. Mr. H[abersham] will add my address in Europe. I shall be home in October next.

Paternalism and Exploitation in the Antebellum Slave Market

Walter Johnson

Walter Johnson's *Soul by Soul* is a study of the master–slave relationship in the context of the antebellum slave market. Johnson pays particular attention to the way in which slaveholders "read the bodies" of slaves at auctions. He explores these readings and examines purchasers' expectations to unmask the contradictions of paternalistic ideology with regard to the commodification of the

Walter Johnson, *Soul by Soul: Life Inside the Antebellum Slave Market* (Cambridge, Mass., and London: Harvard University Press, 1999), pp. 19–30, 102–16.

slaves. In this excerpt, Johnson demonstrates how the idea of slave sale was inextricably linked to what a contemporary source called the "chattel principle" – the fact that slaves were taught from an early age to think of themselves as pieces of property, albeit "living property." Yet, even under these premises, pro-slavery advocates constructed an image of the master–slave relationship in which paternalistic masters bought slaves in order to rescue them from the market, therefore treating them as anything but simple pieces of property. As part of their general justification of slavery, slaveholders needed to provide an explanation for their use of an institution – the slave market – which was the embodiment of the contradictions at the heart of paternalistic ideology.

Long after he had escaped from slavery and settled in Canada, William Johnson's memory stuck on one thing his owner used to say: "Master," he recalled, "used to say that if we didn't suit him he would put us in his pocket quick – meaning that he would sell us."[1] That threat, with its imagery of outsized power and bodily dematerialization, suffused the daily life of the enslaved. Like other pieces of property, slaves spent most of their time outside the market, held to a standard of value but rarely priced. They lived as parents and children, as cotton pickers, card players, and preachers, as adversaries, friends, and lovers. But though they were seldom priced, slaves' values always hung over their heads. J. W. C. Pennington, another fugitive, called this the "chattel principle": any slave's identity might be disrupted as easily as a price could be set and a piece of paper passed from one hand to another.[2] Of the two thirds of a million interstate sales made by the traders in the decades before the Civil War, twenty-five percent involved the destruction of a first marriage and fifty percent destroyed a nuclear family – many of these separating children under the age of thirteen from their parents. Nearly all of them involved the dissolution of a previously existing community. And those are only the interstate sales.

As revealing as they are, these statistics mask complicated stories. Signing a bill of sale was easy enough; selling a slave was often more difficult. Many slaves used every resource they had to avoid being sold into the slave trade. Families and friends helped some slaves escape the slave trade entirely and gave others a chance to negotiate the terms of their sale into the trade. Whether they were sold for speculation, debt, or punishment, many slaves refused to go quietly. They disrupted their sales in both philosophy and practice. In philosophy by refusing to accept their owners' account of what was happening, by treating events that slaveholders described in the language of economic necessity or disciplinary exigency as human tragedy or personal betrayal. In practice

by running away or otherwise resisting their sale, forcing their owners to create public knowledge of the violent underpinnings of their power. However they resisted, hundreds of thousands ended up in the slave trade. These were the "many thousands gone" memorialized in the stories and songs out of which antebellum slaves built a systemic critique of the institution under which they lived. In these rituals of remembrance, the disparate experiences of two million human tragedies were built into the ideology of the "chattel principle."

Living property

From an early age slaves' bodies were shaped to their slavery. Their growth was tracked against their value; outside the market as well as inside it, they were taught to see themselves as commodities. When he was ten, Peter Bruner heard his master refuse an offer of eight hundred dollars (he remembered the amount years later), saying "that I was just growing into money, that I would soon be worth a thousand dollars." . . . [By] the time she was fourteen, Elizabeth Keckley had repeatedly been told that even though she had grown "strong and healthy," and "notwithstanding that I knit socks and attended to various kinds of work . . . that I would never be worth my salt." Years later the pungency of the memory of those words seemed to surprise Keckley herself. "It may seem strange that I should place such emphasis upon words thoughtlessly, idly spoken," she wrote in her autobiography.[3] Condensed in the memory of a phrase turned about her adolescent body, Elizabeth Keckley re-encountered the commodification of her childhood.

Through care and discipline, slaves' bodies were physically incorporated with their owners' standards of measure. Henry Clay Bruce nostalgically remembered his youth as an easy time when "slave children had nothing to do but eat, play, and grow, and physically speaking attain a good size and height." But, Bruce also remembered, the daily routine he enjoyed was charted along a different axis by an owner interested in his growth: "a tall, well-proportioned slave man or woman, in case of a sale, would always command the highest price paid." As John Brown remembered it, the daily incorporation of his youthful body with his enslavement was a matter of coercion as much as care. Brown's mistress "used to call us children up to the Big House every morning and give us a dose of garlic and rue to keep us 'wholesome,' as she said and make us 'grow likely for the market.'" Having staked a right to her slaves that stretched into the fibers of their form, she would turn them out to run laps around a tree in the yard, lashing them to make them "nimbler," forcibly animating their bodies with the spirit she imagined buyers would desire.[4]

Brown's memory makes another thing clear: the process by which a child was made into a slave was often quite brutal. As an adolescent, Henry was adjudged "right awkward" and beaten by his mistress, who thought his arms too long and hands too aimless for work in her dining room. . . . Thirteen-year-old Celestine was beaten until her back was marked and her clothes stained with blood because she could not find her way around the kitchen. Twelve-year-old Monday was whipped by his mistress because his lupus made his nose run on the dinner napkins.[5] Just as the bodies of slaveholding children were bent to the carefully choreographed performances of the master class – in their table manners, posture and carriage, gender-appropriate deportment, and so on – motion by disciplined motion, the bodies of slave children were forcibly shaped to their slavery.

. . . Whether by care or coercion (or by their peculiar combination in the nuzzling violence that characterized slaveholding "paternalism"), enslaved children were taught to experience their bodies twice at once, to move through the world as both child and slave, person and property.

Just as the chattel principle was worked into the bodies of enslaved people, it was also present in their families and communities. As Thomas Johnson remembered it, one after another his childhood friends were "missed from the company." Hearing that the man who took them away was a "Georgia trader," Johnson and his friends would run and hide whenever they saw "a white man looking over the fence as we were playing." The threat of sale, Johnson later remembered, infused his friendships with fear.[6] Thomas Jones remembered that the trade was present in his most intimate relations from the time he was very young: "my dear parents . . . talked about our coming misery, and they lifted up their voices and wept aloud as they spoke of us being torn from them and sold off to the dreaded slave trader."[7] . . . Under the chattel principle, every advance into enslaved society – every reliance on another, every child, friend, or lover, every social relation – held within it the threat of its own dissolution.

Slaveholders used that threat to govern their slaves. As slaveholder Thomas Maskell proudly put it to a man who had sold him some family slaves: "I govern them the same way your late brother did, without the whip by stating to them that I should sell them if they do not conduct themselves as I wish."[8] No matter how benign Maskell thought his own rule, it is hard to imagine that his slaves were not living in terror of making a mistake. Henry Clay Bruce remembered the nominally non-violent power of men like Maskell from the other side: "Slaves usually got scared when it became clear that Negro-Trader [John] White was in the community. The owners used White's name as a threat to scare the slaves when they had violated some rule."[9] . . . Like a disease that attacks the body through its own immune system, slaveholders used the enslaved families and communities that usually insulated slaves from racism and brutality as an instrument of coercion, to discipline their slaves. Among slaveholders, this peculiar mixture of ostensible moderation and outright threat was called paternalism.

As well as threatening social death – the permanent disappearance of a person as a playmate, parent, child, friend, or lover – the slave trade was understood by slaves as threatening literal death. After years of answering questions at antislavery meetings, Lewis Clarke explained slaves' fear of the slave trade to an imagined interlocutor: "Why do slaves dread so bad to go to the South – to Mississippi or Louisiana? Because they know slaves are driven very hard there, and worked to death in a few years." Or as Jacob Stroyer put it, "Louisiana was considered by the slaves a place of slaughter, so those who were going there did not expect to see their friends again."[10] . . .

"Perpetual dread," "always apprehensive," "the trader was all around," "the pens at hand" – the terms in which ex-slaves remembered the trade collapse the distinction between the immediate and the distant. Fear of Louisiana was a constant in Virginia, future sale was always a present threat. For slaves, especially those in the exporting states of the upper South, time and space were bent around the ever-present threat of sale to a slave trader. Hundreds of thousands of times in the history of the antebellum South was this sinuous description of the relation of time, space, and slavery ratified in experience. It is, however, only in contrast to the carefully delimited accounts of the trade offered by their owners that the ideological importance of the slaves' version of the chattel principle can be fully understood.

Slaveholders' stories

Among slaveholders, the slave market existed in a different place and time. Far from being ever-present in cities like New Orleans, the slave market was a quarantined space, legally bounded by high walls to "prevent them from being seen from the street" and banned from many neighborhoods throughout the antebellum period. . . . Like the business they conducted, slave traders were marginalized, through rhetoric more than regulation: "Southern Shylock," "Southern Yankee," and "Negro Jockey" they were called, the sorts of insults that marked them as figurative outcasts from slaveholding society. When Daniel Hundley sat down to write the description of slave traders that would be included in his proslavery account, *Social Relations in Our Southern States* (1860), he described the slave traders as a caste apart and assumed that they would be readily identifiable to even the most casual observer.[11] . . .

Hundley's description of the traders' business represents a summary statement of a half century of white southern efforts to riddle out the implications that this thriving trade in people had for their "domestic" institution. He began by noting that the slave trader "is not troubled evidently with conscience, for although he habitually separates parent from child, brother from sister, and husband from wife, he is yet one of the jolliest dogs alive." But, Hundley continued, the trader's "greatest wickedness" was not his "cruelty to the African." It was the dishonesty and the avarice with which he threatened to poison social relations among white people: "nearly nine tenths of the slaves he buys and sells are vicious ones sold for crimes or misdemeanors, or otherwise diseased ones sold because of their worthlessness as property. These he purchases for about one half what healthy and honest slaves would cost him; but he sells them as both honest and healthy." Slave traders, according to slaveholders like Hundley, were family separators in a land of organic social relations, sharp dealers in a society of "honorable men," merchants of disease and disorder in an otherwise healthy social body. In the figure of the slave trader were condensed the anxieties of slaveholding society in the age of capitalist transformation: paternalism overthrown by commodification, honor corrupted by interest, and dominance infected with disorder.[12]

By embodying the economy in people in the stigmatized figure of the trader, Hundley was doing what countless southern laws and slaveholding commonplaces attempted to do: maintain an artificial and ideological separation of "slavery" from "the market."... [F]or Hundley, the traders' contaminating presence served as a measure of general cleanliness, an easily isolated element of an otherwise sound system, acknowledged only to be explained away. Isolating the slave market as a place and limiting their definition of slave trading to a full-time profession allowed "ordinary" slaveholders... to insulate themselves from responsibility for the family separations, sharp dealing, and uncertainty that characterized their "domestic" institution. Scapegoating the traders was a good way to defend the rest of slavery.

But just as their money seeped through the southern economy and their prepackaged fantasies suffused the dreams of slave buyers, the traders' practice could not be contained by the bricks and mortar that bounded the pens. The entire economy of the antebellum South was constructed upon the idea that the bodies of enslaved people had a measurable monetary value, whether they were ever actually sold or not. Slaves were regularly used as collateral in credit transactions; indeed, rather than giving an IOU when they borrowed money, many slaveholders simply wrote out a bill of sale for a slave who would actually be transferred only if they failed to pay their debt. The value attached to unsold slaves was much more useful to antebellum businessmen than that attached to land, for slaves were portable and the slave traders promised ready cash. . . . Everyday all over the antebellum South, slaveholders' relations to one another – their promises, obligations, and settlements – were backed by the idea of a market in slaves, the idea that people had a value that could be abstracted from their bodies and cashed in when the occasion arose. . . .

The daily interchange between "slavery" and "the market" was so dense as to make the boundary between them indistinguishable; though bounded in place, in practice the slave market suffused the antebellum South. Slave traders held collateral on much of the economy and ideology of the slaveholding South: commercial instruments, daily business practice, common figures of speech, all of these depended on the slave market to make them make sense. References to the cash value of slaves signaled more than a simple awareness that any slave could be sold in the market: they were a central way of underwriting, understanding, and justifying antebellum social relations. . . .

What "ordinary" slaveholders like Hundley believed distinguished them from slave traders, however, was that they could usually come up with a noncommercial reason for selling a slave. That is not to say that they were not capricious or greedy, for they often were. It is rather to say that "ordinary" slaveholders generally supplied public reckonings of what they did, reasoned explanations – accidents, opportunities, practicalities, necessities – that made clear why at one moment they decided to sell a slave whom they would otherwise have wanted to keep. . . .

There were probably almost as many reasons given to justify the selling of slaves in the slaveholding South as there were slaves sold. Josiah Henson, like many others, was sold because his master died and the estate needed to be divided equally among the heirs. Two men known by Isaac Williams were sold because they had run away after receiving a brutal beating; likewise, one of the men with whom Christopher Nichols had run away was sold out of the jail where he was taken upon his capture. Hunter was sold because he did not work hard enough for his owner, and John Brown was sold because his master was building a new house and found himself in need of some ready cash to pay for the work. William was sold to pay for the support of his owner's three illegitimate children. Moses Grandy was sold because his master defaulted upon a mortgage that Grandy had not even known existed. . . . The list could go on and on: slaveholders always had some reason for selling a slave – an estate to divide, a debt to pay, a transgression to punish, a threat to abate. What they rarely had when they sold a slave, it seems from the accounts they gave of themselves, was any direct responsibility for their own actions. . . .

At the heart of the slave market, then, there was a contradiction and a contest. The contradiction was this: the abstract value that underwrote the southern economy could only be made material in human shape – frail, sentient, and resistant. And thus the contradiction was daily played out in a contest over meaning. Were slave sales, as so many slaveholders insisted, the unfortunate results of untimely deaths, unavoidable debts, unforeseeable circumstances, and understandable punishments, or were they, as so many slaves felt, the natural, inevitable, and predictable result of a system that treated people as property? Was a slave sale an untimely rupture of the generally benign character of the relation between master and slave or hard evidence of the hidden structure of that relation, a part of slavery that revealed the malign character of the whole? In the contest over defining what it was that was happening, slaveholders had every advantage their considerable resources could support – state power, a monopoly on violence, and a well-developed propaganda network that stretched from church pulpits to planter-class periodicals like *DeBow's Review* – to enforce their ideologically situated account as a transparent truth. And yet slaves were not without resources of their own: a developed underground that provided intelligence about coming sales and supported efforts to resist or escape the trade, knowledge of slaveholders' incentives and ideology that they could appropriate to subversive purposes, and, ultimately, an alternative account of what was going on – a systemic critique of slavery – which through their practical resistance they forced into the public record of the antebellum South. . . .

The Old South was made by slaves. The fields cleared from the forests and the crops with which they were planted, the fine dinner parties and leisured white women, the expanding black population and the living legacies through which slaveholders reproduced their society over time, all of the things that made the South the South were accomplished through the direct physical agency of slaves. Yet through the incredible generative power of slaveholding ideology, the slave-made landscape of the antebellum South was translated into a series of statements about slaveholders: about their manly independence, their able stewardship of a family legacy, their speculative savvy, or their managerial skill, about their planter-class leisure and their luminous good cheer, about their well-ordered households and well-serviced needs, about their wise and generous provision for their families and their futures. Slaveholders became visible as farmers, planters, patriarchs, ladies, and so on, by taking credit for the work they bought slaves to do for them. Sometimes, however, it was not in the slave-made world that the slaveholders sought to make their virtues visible to everyone else but in the slaves themselves

– in the fiber of their form, the feelings in their hearts, and the fear that the slaveholders could sometimes see in their eyes.

Usually, slaveholders bought slaves to do their work for them, but sometimes the slaves themselves were to be the slaveholders' work. John Brown, for example, remembered being traded to a doctor who had cured him of a mysterious illness. The doctor's intention was to use Brown for "a great number of experiments" concerning remedies for (forcibly induced) sunstroke, the effects of bleeding, and the depth of black skin (raised layer by layer by blistering). As Brown told it, the result for the doctor was quite a success: he made his reputation as a healer of sunstroke into a fortune by selling pills made of flour.[13] Dr. Robert Dawson was another man who thought he could buy a reputation for medical skill in the slave market. When Dawson first examined fourteen-year-old Martha in June 1858 he was being paid by the man who was trying to sell her. After Dawson had examined the girl – in the kitchen, out of the sight of the other men – he reported that she had syphilis. "He said it was very bad – a pretty bad case," the prospective buyer remembered. The buyer was still willing to pay a thousand dollars "country paper" for Martha if the seller would guarantee her health, thus taking upon himself the risk that her condition would deteriorate, but the seller refused: he had bought Martha without guarantee and would sell her that way. Later on, the prospective buyer thought that Dr. Dawson had tried to extract a bit of cash from the expertise his examination demonstrated: "I think Dr. Dawson proposed that if I bought the Negro he would cure her for $50. I am not sure of this but think he did."[14] His offer rebuffed, Dawson bought Martha himself and spent the next three months trying to cure her. Dawson was gambling – and quite publicly, since a number of people knew she was sick – on his ability to heal her. Martha's body became the site of Dawson's demonstration of his confidence, and, when she died, the site of his failure.

Of course, these experiments were also speculations: a doctor like Dawson stood to make some money if he could buy sick slaves on the cheap and sell them for a greater sum.... But they were also claims on one of the most precious commodities in the antebellum South: the language of honor. Many historians have argued that the white male culture of the antebellum South was suffused by the idea of honor, the idea that appearances and reputation mattered above all else, even truth. When contradicted or "given the lie," slaveholders sometimes backed their reputations and opinions with their own lives, issuing a challenge and fighting a duel. And in the slave market – as in the cock pit or the race track or the countless other sites where slaveholders contended with one another for precedence of reputation – slaveholding honor was daily measured out in cash as slaveholders put down their money to back their stated claims of expertise. Listen to a slave-market doctor named Johnston describing a disagreement with the slave dealer who had employed him to diagnose Critty and Creasy in Waterproof, Louisiana, in 1856: "Told Chadwick . . . that one or both of them were Consumptive. Chadwick would not believe it . . . Witness offered to bet in order to back his Judgment but Mr. Chadwick declined."[15] That, as much as any duel, was an affair of honor. . . . Slaveholders spent a great deal more time buying and selling slaves than they did choosing seconds and choreographing duels; "affairs of honor" were more likely to be played out in the slave market than on the dueling ground. . . .

If healing slaves' bodies was one way that slave buyers tried to extract reputation and honor from the people they bought, breaking their spirits was another. Solomon Northup wrote that Edwin Epps, to whom he was sold in 1843 after beating up his previous owner, John Tibeats, was known as a " 'breaker,' distinguished for his faculty of subduing the spirit of a slave, as a jockey boasts of his skill in managing a refractory horse."[16] By putting the word "breaker" in quotation marks, Northup highlighted the recognizably social character of Epps's role, and by making the comparison between the breaker's reputation and that of another man's "boasts," Northup pointed to the pride with which Epps inhabited that role. Being a breaker was less a profession than a pose – a way of treating slaves and of talking to and about them, a way of building a reputation for indomitability out of brutality.

How else can we understand Charles McDermott – who was told by the dealer who sold him Billy that the slave would "run and play off from his work," who had seen the scars on Billy's back inflicted by previous owners, who whipped Billy a dozen times for running away without thinking about returning him to the dealer – than as a man buying a reputation as a breaker?[17] How else can we understand Andrew Skillman – who "frequently" inquired about purchasing Henry, though the slave's character, "which was bad," was generally known, who said at the time of sale that he knew "the Boy had stolen goods and run off" but that he would not blame any Negro "for so doing when allowed the same liberty" as Henry had been allowed, who bought Henry though the slave was sold in chains from the jail, who asked Henry "if he would live with him" and removed the slave's chains "as soon as he bought him," who told Henry in the hearing of other white men "if he ran away from him once he would not run away again" – but as a man who sought honor among whites by publicly threatening his slave?[18] These men were demonstrating that they were not afraid of scars or chains or bad character, that the common caution of the slave market was expendable for men as forceful as themselves: they were buying the chance to match their will against that of a slave.

More than that: breakers were buying the chance to match their ability as masters against that of their neighbors. Skillman's comment that Henry's bad behavior had been due to his "liberty," his public removal of the chains applied by the previous owner, and his equally public threat to murder Henry if he ran away all drew rhetorical force from a slave-holders' commonplace: that the behavior of slaves reflected the ability of their owners.[19] Attributing Henry's bad behavior to his prior owner's lax management and proclaiming his ability to break Henry's spirit, Skillman was buying the chance to show that he was a better master – more discerning, more confident, more formidable, more *honorable* – than any other man around. At least he was so up to the point that Henry ran away, taking with him three of Skillman's other slaves. After that he was simply angry; and when he sued and the Louisiana Supreme Court ruled that he had got what he deserved, out of luck.

If healers tried to wring honor from their slaves' bodies, breakers tried to wring it from their souls. Moses Roper remembered that his eventual buyer tried to inscribe his authority in Roper's mind long before he ever beat him: "Previously to his purchasing me, he had frequently taunted me, by saying 'You have been a gentleman long enough, and, whatever may be the consequences I intend to buy you.' "[20] Peter Bruner was similarly threatened when, after having run away and been captured, he was addressed by his owner's sister: "She said she wanted to buy me for the sole purpose of whipping me; she said if she could whip me and break me in she could stop me from running off."[21] A final example comes from William Wells Brown, who remembered that Robert More purchased John after a carriage the slave was driving had splashed him with mud with the "express purpose . . . to '*tame him.*' " This he did by chaining and beating John until the slave's limbs hung limp at his side. At that point, John had no value left but as a symbol of More's power. These slaves were brought to be broken, to be turned from unruly subjects into perfect symbols of their owners' will. Indeed, they were bought to be the embodied registers of the indomitability of that will, for the slaves themselves were the ultimate audience for their buyers' brutal performances.[22]

These slaves, then, embodied a type of public recognition – a type of honor – that could be beaten out of their backs. In buying them, slaveholders boasted that their own mastery would inhabit their slaves' every action. Their slaves would be extensions of themselves, the actions of the enslaved indistinguishable from the will of the enslavers. Slave breaking was a technology of the soul. Buying slaves to break them represented a fantasy of mastery embodied in the public subjugation of another, of private omnipotence transmuted into public reputation. In that way, it was not so different from paternalism.

As slaveholders progressed through stages of social standing by buying ever more slaves, they were able to accomplish another remarkable rhetorical inversion, perhaps one of the most remarkable of all time: they began to say they were acting on behalf of the people whom they had bought to act for them. That claim, like those based upon brutal subordination, was a reputation wrung from the soul of a slave, but it had a much nicer sounding name than slave breaking: paternalism. Indeed, the slave-buyer-as-paternalist was a recognizable enough figure to become a trope of pro-slavery fiction: the slaveholder who bought slaves in order to reunite families that had been divided by the disembodied power of the marketplace (often debts to a northern merchant). Buying slaves in these novels was a form of charity, a benevolence extended to the purchased on the part of slaveholders so attached to their slaves that they were willing to enter the unfamiliar and potentially contaminating confines of the slave pen to redeem their loved ones and treasured friends.

An explicit balancing of the needs of master and slave, of commercial and paternal language, animated Richard T. Archer's slave buying as he described it to Joseph Copes. "I consider Negroes too high at this time," Archer began with a gesture of speculative savvy, "but there are some very much allied to mine both by blood and intermarriage that I may be induced from feeling to buy, and I have one vacant improved plantation, and could work more hands with advantage."[23] The vacant plantation was an objective necessity, but what was "feeling" worth? Archer was negotiating a complicated deal in which consideration for his slaves' needs, along with evaluation of the market and the need to work an open field, was tallied and entered into his relationship with Copes. By asking the question (and sharing it with Copes), Archer was figuring the slaves' needs alongside his own as he thought about buying them. Perhaps by sharing the dilemma with Copes he hoped to be better able to judge how another would balance the dictates of necessity and humanity; perhaps to be dissuaded from buying while still gaining credit for "feeling." Feeling, then, could be bought, but only at a price....

The pro-slavery construction of slave-market "paternalism" was highly unstable: it threatened to collapse at any moment beneath the weight of its own absurdity. One could go to the market and buy slaves to rescue them from the market, but it was patently obvious even to the most febrile reader of pro-slavery novels that the market in people was what had in the first place caused the problems that slave-buying paternalists claimed to resolve. Some slaveholders solved this problem the same way they solved other problems: through ever more elaborate fantasies about the slave market. Writing in his private diary, for instance, Matthew Williams described his purchase of "a Negro boy" as "a new responsibility." He continued: "I bought him from a Negro trader. I feel satisfied that however inadequately I may discharge my duty towards this boy that he is better off with me than with the man from whom I bought him."[24] Carried with him into the slave market, Williams's paternalism was redemptive: the slave market was a bad thing in itself; sale to anyone was therefore better than sale to no one; Williams was doing the slave a favor, saving him from the market by buying him. . . .

John Knight's search for paternalism threatened to lead him into an endless series of trips into the slave market. When he received Jane (one of the people out of whom he was building his household), Knight also received a message from his father-in-law that his new slave had come to him at the cost of her own unwilling separation from her sister. As well as passing on the news, Knight's father-in-law was perhaps passing on the responsibility, for Knight immediately took up the issue: "If she still desires to come to this country, and reside with us in the vicinity of Jane, I authorize you to purchase her for me . . . If she is a faithful servant I will guarantee her a good master."[25] And, a year later: "We find that we require another female house servant . . . If Jane's sister can yet be bought as you advised me sometime since I should be very glad to own her as I could employ her to much profit."[26] Knight moved freely back and forth between considerations of his household's "requirements" and advertisement of his own good will.

It is not clear whether the person Knight's father-in-law eventually sent was Jane's sister. Her name was Ann, and the letter Knight wrote upon her arrival suggests both the father-in-law's bad faith in raising the issue of family separation in the first place and John Knight's dogged intention to do (or at least say – and often) the right thing in the slave market. Noting that Ann had arrived and was "pleased" with Natchez, Knight sent yet another slave-market request: "I wish you could purchase her brother for me for $700."[27] Knight's paternalism was pushing him deeper and deeper into slave buying. It is not clear how Knight's father-in-law would have read this request: perhaps as a reprimand for breaking up the family; perhaps as another effort to establish a reputation for good will. But however it was intended and however it was read, Knight's request was tendered wholly in the language of charity: he did not want a waiter or a hosteler or a carriage driver, he wanted Ann's brother.

To suggest that John Knight was trying to buy a reputation for charity along with his slaves is not to suggest that he did not care for his slaves' feelings. Indeed, he seems to have cared a great deal: he wanted his slaves to be happy, and he thought their happiness said enough about him that it would prove something to his father-in-law. . . . Knight's feelings were heavily leveraged: he was extracting credit for good intentions out of incomplete purchases, out of transactions that might remain as imaginary as those in the novels. Knight was borrowing against feelings he had himself imagined for his future slaves – the happiness he was granting them – to prove the tenor of his offer. Through their own earnest incantations, practiced slave buyers like Knight portrayed themselves as charitable sojourners in the slave market, redeeming slaves rather than buying them.

Paternalism, then, was something slaveholders could buy in the slave market. Rather than being a prebourgeois social system or a set of rules by which slaveholders governed themselves, paternalism, like speculation, was a way of going about buying slaves, one answer among many that slaveholders gave to the question "What is slavery?" For every "capitalist" who wrapped the purchase of a slave in a detailed account of business cycle and material necessity, there could be a "paternalist" whose self-described motive in buying slaves was to treat them well or save them from the market. The point here is not to try to sort which of these representations were sincere and which were mendacious – slaveholders' real selves emerged only in real time and in confrontation with real slaves. The point, rather, is to emphasize the plasticity of slaveholding paternalism. Because it was a way of imagining, describing, and justifying slavery rather than a direct reflection of underlying social relations, because it was portable, paternalism was likely to turn up in the most unlikely places – in slaveholders' letters describing their own benign intentions as they went to the slave market....

Along with the social distinction, honor, and paternalism that could be wrung from the bodies and souls of the enslaved, slave traders were selling the buyers another fantasy: that other people existed to satisfy their desires. The word "fancy" has come down to us as an adjective modifying the word "girl," an adjective that refers to appearance perhaps, or manners or dress. But the word in its other meaning describes a desire: "he fancies ..." The slave-market usage embarked from this second meaning: "fancy" was a transitive verb made noun, a slaveholder's desire made material in the shape of a little girl "13 years old Girl, Bright Color, nearly a fancy for $1135."[28] That was how slave dealer Phillip Thomas described a child he had seen sold in Richmond: an age, a sex, a complexion that were her own; a fantasy and a price applied in the slave market.

Buying slaves for sex or companionship was no less public than any other kind of slave buying. The slave market was suffused with sexuality: the traders' light-skinned mistresses, the buyers' foul-mouthed banter, the curtained inspection rooms that surrounded the pens. But more than anything, there were the high prices. The "New Orleans Slave Sale

Sample" shows prices paid for women that occasionally reached three hundred percent of the median prices paid in a given year – prices above $1500 in the first decade of the century and ranging from $2000 to $5233 afterwards. Contemplating prices like that, William Wells Brown wrote in his novel *Clotel*, "We need not add that had those young girls been sold for mere house servants or field hands, they would not have brought half the sum they did."[29]

The scene Brown was describing, the imaginative site of the "fancy trade," was an auction. For, though "fancy" women were sold through private bargaining as well as public crying, the open competition of an auction – a contest between white men played out on the body of an enslaved woman – was the essence of the transaction.[30] The price paid, Solomon Northup remembered, was as much a measure of the buyer as of the bought: "there were men enough in New Orleans who would give five thousand dollars for such an extra fancy piece . . . rather than not get her."[31] The high prices were a measure not only of desire but of dominance. No other man could afford to pay so much; no other man's needs could be so substantially measured; no other man's desires would be so spectacularly fulfilled. And high prices were public knowledge, reported in newspapers and talked about by slaves and slaveholders alike. Lewis Clarke remembered that as a slave he had heard of "handsome girls being sold in New Orleans for from $2000 to $3000." And a Virginia slave dealer wrote to his partner in the 1850s: "There is here the highest field hand that has ever been sold in Richmond . . . he belongs to that man who bought that high priced Fancy at $1780."[32] "That man" had bought a reputation along with his slaves: he was known through the people he bought. His potency was gauged by his buying power.

Whether they were buying these high-priced women to be their companions or simply their toys, these slaveholders showed that they had the power to purchase what was forbidden and the audacity to show it off. To buy a "fancy" was to flirt publicly with the boundaries of acceptable sociability. John Powell, an editor of the New Orleans *Picayune*, for example, entertained his dinner guests at a house inhabited by his "Quadroon mistress" and the couple's child – their presence at the party showed Powell to be a man who was at once civilized and sensational. Theophilus Freeman, a New Orleans slave dealer, received visitors while lying in bed with Sarah Connor, a woman he had once owned. Through this carefully publicized intimacy with his own former slave, Freeman demonstrated his own freedom from convention – his liberation was made evident in her carefully displayed body.[33]

In the public transcript of the antebellum South, however, these performances of potency were often doubled back on themselves. When they stepped into the notary's office to register their stake in the high-priced women they had bought, slaveholders described them not as "mistresses" or "fancies" but as "cooks" or "domestics" or "seamstresses" or, most commonly, not at all. The double discourse of fancy was reflected in the public assessments of those in the know. Joseph A. Beard, a man who earned his money by auctioning slaves, spoke of the child of George Botts, a slave dealer, and Ann Maria Barclay, Botts's former slave, this way: "a young girl who was generally supposed to be Botts' child though called Maria's sister." Louis Exinois preserved the same doubleness when describing a doctor who visited the house of an enslaved woman: "[he] appeared to be her friend or cher amie."[34] "Generally supposed," "appeared to be": both Beard and Exinois drew attention to the fact that they were speaking doubly, to the fact that there was a polite way of describing such things and another way of seeing them.

As with other forms of Victorian politeness, the rudeness lay with people who described things the way they saw them. Asked in public about his relations with a family whom his uncle owned, Pierre Pouche of Pointe Coupée responded in a way that was at once defensive and accusatory: "I have had connexion with most of the females and am not ashamed to confess it, although I do not think the question pertinent, I would blush to steal but not to answer this question." Talk about such things, Pouche implied, was gossip; it reflected as badly upon the knower as the known. As Mary Chesnut put it, sex between slaveholding white men and their female slaves was "the thing we can't name." Thus was patriarchy defended by the silence of politeness, and by a kind of magical denial that allowed a white household to persist in its public performance, though its foundation had disappeared in practice: "Every lady tells you who is the father of all the mulatto children in everybody's household, but those in her own she seems to think dropped from the clouds or pretends so to think."[35] Slaveholders' "fancies" existed in a state of public erasure: they were unspeakable.

Behind the shroud of patriarchal prerogative, some slaveholders hid fantasies of domination that could be seen only by their slaves. Dr. James Norcom sneaked after his slave Harriet Jacobs, trapped her, and whispered his dirty fantasies into her ear. Robert Newsome bought Celia to replace his dead wife and raped her before they had returned from the slave market.[36] ... These secret slaveholders sought victims, not companions. In their most private moments, these men existed only in the slaves whose bodies provided the register for their secret desires and their evident power. By hiding their private desires from everyone but their slaves, they recapitulated the ultimate logic of the slave market: their phantasms of independent agency were built out of practical dependence upon people bought in the market – their selves were built out of slaves.

The slave market was everywhere in the antebellum South. It supplied slaveholders' farms and households; it suffused their fantasies and figures of speech; it was incorporated into their social relations and their selves. Exigency, want, need, desire, wish, fancy, fantasy: answers to every one of these could be found in the slave market. All of the values associated with the antebellum South – the poses and the posturing, the whiteness and independence, the calculation and mastery, the hospitality and gentility, the patriarchy and paternalism, the coming of age and staging of obligation, the honor, brutality, and fancy – were daily packaged and sold in the slave market. All were embodied in slaves and turned out for display in the fields, farms, streets, and parlors of southern slaveholders. More than that, those values and the slaves bought to embody them were knitted together in countless letters, conversations, and court cases which gave cultural meaning to the economy in people. Sometimes that meaning was public – narrated, remarked upon, advertised. Sometimes it was secret – hushed, investigated, hidden. But always it depended upon the slaves.

As slaveholders became ever wealthier and their slave buying ever more elaborate, they became adept at covering their dependency on their slaves with a variety of very durable cultural languages that emphasized their own agency. They bought slaves to make themselves frugal, independent, socially acceptable, or even fully white; they acted in accordance with the necessities of their business or the exigencies of their households; they covered the contingency of their own identities in the capacious promises of paternalism, buying on behalf of the bought; they obscured the dependency of their fantasies with the brutality of their mastery. Using the ideological imperatives of slaveholding culture – whiteness, independence, rationality, necessity, patriarchy, honor, paternalism, and fancy – they produced, in the classic formulation, freedom out of slavery.

In doing so, however, they brought the slave market into their lives, their plans, and their reputations, for their self-amplifying fantasies could be made material only in the domain of the traders and through the frail and resistant bodies of their slaves.

Notes

1 William Johnson interviewed in Benjamin Drew (ed.), *The Refugee: A North-side View of Slavery* (1846), reprinted in *Four Fugitive Slave Narratives* (Reading, Mass.: Addison-Wesley, 1969), p. 19. . . .

2 J. W. C. Pennington, *The Fugitive Blacksmith: Or Events in the Life of James W. C. Pennington* (London, 1849), pp. iv–vii.

3 Peter Bruner, *A Slave's Adventures toward Freedom* (Oxford, Ohio, n.d.), p. 13. . . . Elizabeth Keckley, *Behind the Scenes: or Thirty Years a Slave and Four Years in the White House*, in Henry Louis Gates, Jr. (ed.), *Six Women's Slave Narratives* (New York: Oxford University Press, 1988), p. 21. See, generally, Wilma King, *Stolen Childhood: Slave Youth in Nineteenth-Century America* (Bloomington: Indiana University Press, 1995).

4 Henry Clay Bruce, *The New Man: Twenty-nine Years a Slave and Twenty-nine Years a Free Man* (York, PA, 1875), p. 14. John Brown, *Slave Life in Georgia: A Narrative of the Life Suffering, and Escape of John Brown, a Fugitive Slave now in England*, ed. L. A. Chamerovzow (London, 1835; Savannah, GA: Beelive Press, 1991), p. 7.

5 Elizabeth Powell Conrad to Burr Powell, December 25, 1829 (?), quoted and analyzed in Brenda Stevenson, *Life in Black and White: Family and Community in the Slave South* (New York: Oxford University Press, 1996), p. 198; *Pilié v. Ferriere*, #1724, 7 Mart. (N.S.) 648 (La. 1829), testimony of Mary Ann Poyfarre and Celeste, UNO [University of New Orleans, Supreme Court of Louisiana Collection, Archives and Special Collections, Earl K. Long Library]; *Bloom v. Beebe*, #5921, 15 La. Ann. 65 (1860), testimony of Catherine Klopman and L. Klopman, UNO.

6 Thomas Johnson, *Twenty-Eight Years a Slave, or the Story of My Life in Three Continents* (Bournemouth, 1909), p. 2.

7 Thomas H. Jones, *The Experience of Thomas H. Jones Who Was a Slave for Forty-Three Years* (Worcester, 1857), p. 2.

8 Thomas Maskell to Dr. Samuel Plaisted, August 8, 1838, Samuel Plaisted Correspondence, LSU [Louisiana State University].

9 Bruce, *The New Man*, pp. 102–3. . . .

10 Lewis Clarke, *Narrative of the Sufferings of Lewis Clarke during a Captivity of More than Twenty-Five Years Amongst the Algerines of Kentucky* (Boston, 1845), p. 84; Jacob Stroyer, *My Life in the South* (Salem, 1890), p. 40.

11 Daniel Hundley, *Social Relations in Our Southern States* (New York, 1860; reprinted Baton Rouge, 1960), pp. 139–49.

12 Ibid., pp. 140–2.

13 Brown, *Slave Life in Georgia*, pp. 40–3.

14 *Virgin v. Dawson*, #854 (Monroe), 15 La. Ann. 532 (1860), testimony of John W. Hooler (direct, cross, and re-examination) and R. Burns, UNO.

15 *Dixon v. Chadwick*, #4388, II La. Ann 215 (1856), testimony of Dr. Johnston, UNO.

16 Solomon Northup, *Twelve Years a Slave: Narrative of Solomon Northup, Citizen of New York Kidnapped in Washington City in 1841 and Rescued in 1853 from a Cotton Plantation near the Red River in Louisiana* (Auburn, 1853), p. 138.

17 *McDermott v. Cannon*, #5706, 14 La. Ann. 313 (1859), testimony of J. W. Boazman and F. Withers, UNO.

18 *Dunbar v. Skillman*, #1575, 6 Mart (N.S.) 539 (La. 1828), testimony of Robert J. Nelson, Kendall Dunbar, and George Long, UNO.

19 Ariela Gross, "Pandora's Box: Slave Character on Trial in the Antebellum Deep South," *Yale Journal of Law and the Humanities*, 7 (1995), pp. 281–8.

20 Moses Roper, *A Narrative of the Adventures and Escape of Moses Roper from American Slavery*, originally published 1834 (New York: Negro Universities Press, 1970), p. 71.
21 Bruner, *A Slave's Adventures toward Freedom*, p. 33.
22 William Wells Brown, *Narrative of William Wells Brown: A Fugitive Slave, Written by Himself* (1847), in Gilbert Osofsky (ed.), *Puttin' on Ole Massa* (New York: Harper & Row, 1969), p. 186.
23 Richard T. Archer to Joseph Slemmons Copes, March 3, 1854, Joseph Slemmons Copes Papers, TU [Tulane University, Archives and Special Collections, Howard – Tilton Memorial Library, New Orleans].
24 Matthew Williams Diary, October 11, 1850, Matthew Williams Papers, DU [Duke University, Archives and Special Collections, Perkins Memorial Library Durham].
25 John Knight to William Beall, March 1, 1834, John Knight Papers, RASP [Records of Antebellum Southern Plantations on Microfilm, ed. K. M. Stampp].
26 John Knight to William Beall, February 16, 1835, John Knight Papers, RASP.
27 John Knight to William Beall, October 9, 1835, John Knight Papers, RASP.
28 Phillip Thomas to William Finney, July 26, 1859, William A. J. Finney Papers, RASP.
29 William Wells Brown, *Clotel: or, the President's Daughter: a Narrative of Slave Life in the United States* [1853] (New York, 1969), p. 208.
30 For "fancy" women sold in private sales see *White v. Slatter*, #943, 5 La. Ann. 27 (1849), and *Fisk v. Bergerot*, #6814, 21 La. Ann. 111 (1869), UNO.
31 Northup, *Twelve Years a Slave*, p. 58.
32 Frederic Bancroft, *Slave Trading in the Old South* (Baltimore, 1931), pp. 38, 50–1, 328–34; Clarke, *Narrative of the Sufferings of Lewis Clarke*, p. 85; Phillip Thomas to William Finney, December 24, 1859, William A. J. Finney Papers, RASP.
33 Anton Reiff, "Journal," 23, Anton Reiff Journal, LSU [Louisiana State University Lower Mississippi Valley Collection, Hill Memorial Library, Baton Range]; *Dunbar v. Connor*, unreported Louisiana Supreme Court case #1700 (1850 and 1851), testimony of Samuel Powers, UNO.
34 *Barclay v. Sewell*, #4622, 12 La. Ann. 262 (1857), testimony of Joseph A. Beard, UNO; *Dunbar v. Connor*, unreported Louisiana Supreme Court case #1700 (1850 and 1851), testimony of Louis Exinois, UNO.
35 *Eulalie and her Children v. Long and Mabry*, #3237, 9 La. Ann. 9 (1853), and #3479, 11 La. Ann. 463 (1853), testimony of Pierre Pouche, UNO; C. Vann Woodward (ed.), *Mary Chesnut's Civil War* (New Haven: Yale University Press, 1981), p. 29 (March 18, 1861).
36 Harriet A. Jacobs, *Incidents in the Life of a Slave Girl, Written by Herself*, ed. Jean Fagan Yellin (Cambridge, Mass.: Harvard University Press, 1987); Melton A. McLaurin, *Celia, a Slave* (Athens, GA: University of Georgia Press, 1991).

9
Life in the Slave Quarters

Introduction

Families provided slaves with the most important kind of shelter from the brutality of life in bondage. Although they had neither legal sanction nor institutional support, slave families managed to survive under extremely oppressive conditions. Slave families were large, with women giving birth to an average of seven children. Slave marriages could be long-lasting, provided that families were not broken up by sale and husbands and wives kept their commitment through the difficulties and harshness of slavery. Since they had no legal status, and little property was involved, slave wives were relatively free from the social pressures and legal subjection of white patriarchy. Moreover, slave husbands were much more likely to be hired out than wives, leaving women as the only authority dealing with children within the household. Most often, both parents were out in the fields, and children were left under minimal supervision. Slave children shared much of their plantation life with the masters' children, but quickly learned to respect the very real differences in status and power, especially if they were taken into the Big House as domestic servants, or if they saw their parents or relatives punished.

The biggest threat to slave families was always the sale of one or more members. Masters were contradictory in their attitude toward slave families. On the one hand, they encouraged them as part of the paternalistic attitude and as part of a very calculated concern for the well-being of their workers and the reproduction of their work force. On the other hand, they often threatened slaves with the prospect of selling them away from their families if they did not submit to their master's absolute authority. Families responded remarkably well to these threats, and in many cases managed to survive even the separation of husband and wife. Married slaves continued to keep in contact and see each other as often as they could, even if they lived far apart, striving to provide a sense of family and identity to their children. Moreover, by giving their children names whose pattern repeated from one generation to the next, slaves were able to keep track of their family history and maintain a sense of their own collective identity.

On a day-to-day basis slaves lived quite isolated from their masters in the slave quarters. This remove from the master's control and prying eyes helped them live their lives with a certain degree of autonomy. In their quarters, slaves could express themselves freely and enjoy leisure activities together. They sang, ate, courted, prayed, and talked. Over time, they managed to create autonomous cultural expressions which contributed to a collective resistance to their master's pretensions that they were merely pieces of properties. During this process, slaves planted the seeds of African American culture. Slaves whose origins were in Africa but were born in America absorbed parts of white culture and mixed them with the survivals of what remained of a very powerful African tradition. They thus created a culture that was distinctively American and southern, but at the same time significantly different from the American culture of the white South.

One of the clearest examples of this process is the emergence of African American religion. During the 1830s, the Second Great Awakening swept across the South. Much like the first, it stressed the importance of spontaneous religious experience and downplayed the importance of institutional churches. It was characterized by mass meetings, where the crowds reached a climax of religious enthusiasm by singing and praying until they were exhausted. Baptist and Methodist preachers traveled from plantation to plantation to convert and perform. The contact with white American religion in its evangelical and revivalist form was a momentous one for the slaves. These forms of Christian worship emphasized spontaneity, a personal relationship with God, and above all the importance of religious fervor. Slaves combined these characteristics with a stress upon those parts of Christian theology that fitted their condition. For instance, the stories of Moses' deliverance of the chosen people from Egypt and Jesus' death and resurrection were told over and over again in religious songs, which were then charged with a special meaning of resistance.

Within this syncretistic African American religion, Christian worship and theology comprised the core, around which slaves added what they remembered of their old African traditions of worship. During religious services, there was a particular pattern of song, whereby the preacher called, and his congregation responded in a rhythmic crescendo of fervor. When performing gospels and spirituals, slaves sang the biblical stories of Moses and Jesus according to this "call and response" pattern. Although there were many other distinctively African features in slave religion – including dance – the "call and response" pattern was the clearest indication of the syncretistic nature of African American worship. However, it was not restricted to performance in churches; it was implemented in virtually every song the slaves sang.

Further reading

Abrahams, R. D., *Singing the Master: The Emergence of African American Culture in the Plantation South* (New York: Pantheon Books, 1992).

Blassingame, J. W., *The Slave Community: Plantation Life in the Antebellum South* (New York and Oxford: Oxford University Press, 1979).

Campbell, E. D. and Rice, K. S. (eds.), *Before Freedom Came: African American Life in the Antebellum South* (Richmond: Museum of the Confederacy and University Press of Virginia, 1991).

Genovese, E. D., *Roll, Jordan, Roll: The World the Slaves Made* (New York: Pantheon Books, 1974).

Gilroy, P., *The Black Atlantic* (London: Verso, 1995).

Grey-White, D., *Ar'n't I a Woman? Female Slaves in the Plantation South* (New York: Norton, 1985).

Gutman, H. G., *The Black Family in Slavery and Freedom, 1750–1925* (New York: Pantheon Books, 1975).

Hudson, L. E., *To Have and to Hold: Slave Work and Family Life in Antebellum South Carolina* (Athens: University of Georgia Press, 1997).

Jones, Jacqueline, *Labor of Love, Labor of Sorrow: Black Women, Work, and the Family from Slavery to the Present* (New York: Vintage, 1985).

Joyner, C., *Down by the Riverside: Life in a South Carolina Slave Community* (Urbana: University of Illinois Press, 1984).

Levine, L., *Black Culture, Black Consciousness: Afro-American Folk Thought from Slavery to Freedom* (New York: Oxford University Press, 1977).

Malone, A. P., *Sweet Chariot: Slave Family and Household Structure in Nineteenth-Century Louisiana* (Chapel Hill: University of North Carolina Press, 1993).

Owens, L. H., *This Species of Property: Slave Life and Culture in the Old South* (New York: Oxford University Press, 1976).

Rabouteau, A. J., *Slave Religion: The Invisible Institution* (New York: Oxford University Press, 1979).

Stevenson, B., *Life in Black and White: Family and Community in the Slave South* (New York and Oxford: Oxford University Press, 1996).

Frederick Douglass Remembers his Childhood (1845)

Born a slave in Maryland, Frederick Douglass managed to escape, and in 1845 published his autobiography, *Narrative of the Life of Frederick Douglass*. The book was an instant popular success, and established his reputation as a black Abolitionist leader. Combining personal recollection with the vigorous style of the antislavery pamphlets, Douglass's autobiography was as much a document of slave life as a compelling example of Abolitionist propaganda. In this excerpt, in which he described his early years, Douglass told readers that, like many other slaves, he was not sure of his age, but knew that he was the son of a black female slave and a white man. As the story proceeded, readers learned about the young boy's separation from his mother when his master hired him out to work as a field hand on a nearby farm. In crafting this section of the *Narrative*, Douglass emphasized two common practices that tended to destroy slave families: miscegenation and slave sale.

I WAS born in Tuckahoe, near Hillsborough, and about twelve miles from Easton, in Talbot county, Maryland. I have no accurate knowledge of my age, never having seen any authentic record containing it. By far the larger part of the slaves know as little of their ages as horses know of theirs, and it is the wish of most masters within my knowledge to keep their slaves thus ignorant. I do not remember to have ever met a slave who could tell of his birthday. They seldom come nearer to it than planting-time, harvest-time, cherry-time, spring-time, or fall-time. A want of information concerning my own was a source of unhappiness to me even during childhood. The white children could tell their ages. I could not tell why I ought to be deprived of the same privilege. I was not allowed to make any inquiries of my master concerning it. He deemed all such inquiries on the part of a slave improper and impertinent, and evidence of a restless spirit. The nearest estimate I can give makes me now between twenty-

---

Source: Frederick Douglass, *Narrative of the Life of Frederick Douglass*, in Henry Louis Gates, Jr. (ed.), *The Classic Slave Narratives* (New York: Penguin Books, 1987), pp. 255–7

seven and twenty-eight years of age. I come to this, from hearing my master say, some time during 1835, I was about seventeen years old.

My mother was named Harriet Bailey. She was the daughter of Isaac and Betsey Bailey, both colored, and quite dark. My mother was of a darker complexion than either my grandmother or grandfather.

My father was a white man. He was admitted to be such by all I ever heard speak of my parentage. The opinion was also whispered that my master was my father; but of the correctness of this opinion, I know nothing; the means of knowing was withheld from me. My mother and I were separated when I was but an infant – before I knew her as my mother. It is a common custom, in the part of Maryland from which I ran away, to part children from their mothers at a very early age. Frequently, before the child has reached its twelfth month, its mother is taken from it, and hired out on some farm a considerable distance off, and the child is placed under the care of an old woman, too old for field labor. For what this separation is done, I do not know, unless it be to hinder the development of the child's affection toward its mother, and to blunt and destroy the natural affection of the mother for the child. This is the inevitable result.

I never saw my mother, to know her as such, more than four or five times in my life; and each of these times was very short in duration, and at night. She was hired by a Mr. Stewart, who lived about twelve miles from my home. She made her journeys to see me in the night, travelling the whole distance on foot, after the performance of her day's work. She was a field hand, and a whipping is the penalty of not being in the field at sunrise, unless a slave has special permission from his or her master to the contrary – a permission which they seldom get, and one that gives to him that gives it the proud name of being a kind master. I do not recollect of ever seeing my mother by the light of day. She was with me in the night. She would lie down with me, and get me to sleep, but long before I waked she was gone. Very little communication ever took place between us. Death soon ended what little we could have while she lived, and with it her hardships and suffering. She died when I was about seven years old, on one of my master's farms, near Lee's Mill. I was not allowed to be present during her illness, at her death, or burial. She was gone long before I knew any thing about it. Never having enjoyed, to any considerable extent, her soothing presence, her tender and watchful care, I received the tidings of her death with much the same emotions I should have probably felt at the death of a stranger.

Called thus suddenly away, she left me without the slightest intimation of who my father was. The whisper that my master was my father, may or may not be true; and, true or false, it is of but little consequence to my purpose whilst the fact remains, in all its glaring odiousness, that slaveholders have ordained, and by law established, that the children of slave women shall in all cases follow the condition of their mothers, and this is done too obviously to administer to their own lusts, and make a gratification of their wicked desires profitable as well as pleasurable; for by this cunning arrangement, the slaveholder, in cases not a few, sustains to his slaves the double relation of master and father.

I know of such cases; and it is worthy of remark that such slaves invariably suffer greater hardships, and have more to contend with, than others. They are, in the first place, a constant offence to their mistress. She is ever disposed to find fault with them; they can seldom do any thing to please her; she is never better pleased than when she sees them under the lash, especially when she suspects her husband of showing to his mulatto children favors which he withholds from his black slaves. The master is frequently compelled to sell this class of his slaves, out of deference to the feelings of his white wife; and, cruel as the deed may strike any one to be, for a man to sell his own children to human flesh-mongers, it is often the dictate of humanity for him to do so; for, unless he does this, he must not only whip them himself, but must stand by and see one white son tie up his brother, of but few shades darker complexion than himself, and ply the gory lash to his naked back; and if he lisp one word of disapproval, it is set down to his parental partiality, and only makes a bad matter worse, both for himself and the slave whom he would protect and defend.

Tempie Herndon Remembers her Wedding (ca. 1850)

A great deal of what we know about slave marriage and other features of slave life stems from a collection of more than 3,000 interviews with ex-slaves compiled by the Works Progress Administration in the 1930s and published as the multi-volume *The American Slave: A Composite Autobiography* by George Rawick in the 1970s. When discussing marriage, several of the interviewees mentioned the expression "jumping the broom"; this led scholars to believe

Source: George Rawick (ed.), *The American Slave: A Composite Autobiography* (Westport, Conn., 1972–8), vol. 5, pt 5, pp. 329–30; reprinted in John W. Blassingame, *The Slave Community: Plantation Life in the Antebellum South* (New York and Oxford: Oxford University Press, 1979), pp. 166–7

that the act was part of a marriage ritual. However, as John Blassingame has pointed out – and as this excerpt by ex-slave Tempie Herndon makes clear – the act of jumping the broom was actually part of the post-nuptial revelries. In Blassingame's words, "the partner jumping over first, highest, or without falling was recognized by the wedding party as the one who would 'wear the pants' or rule the family" (J. W. Blassingame, *The Slave Community: Plantation Life in the Antebellum South* (New York and Oxford: Oxford University Press, 1979), p. 166).

When I growed up I married Exter Durham.... We had a big weddin'. We was married on de front porch of de Big House. Marse George killed a shoat and Mis' Betsy had Georgianna, de cook, to bake a big weddin' cake all iced up white as snow with a bride and groom standin' in de middle holdin' hands... I had on a white dress, white shoes, and long white gloves dat come to my elbow, and Mis' Betsy done made me a weddin' veil out of a white net window curtain. When she played de weddin' march on de piano, me and Exter marched down de walk and up on de porch to de altar Mis' Betsy done fixed. Dat de prettiest altar I ever seed. Back 'gainst de rose vine dat was full of red roses, Mis' Betsy done put tables filled with flowers and white candles. She done spread down a bed sheet, a sure 'nough linen sheet, for us to stand on, and dey was a white pillow to kneel down on... Uncle Edmond Kirby married us. He was de nigger preacher dat preached at de plantation church. After Uncle Edmond said de last words over me and Exter, Marse George got to have his little fun. He say, "Come on, Exter, you and Tempie got to jump over de broom stick backwards. You got to do dat to see which one gwine be boss of your household." Everybody come stand round to watch. Marse George hold de broom about a foot high off de floor. De one dat jump over it backwards, and never touch handle, gwine boss de house. If both of dem jump over without touchin' it, dey won't gwine be no bossin', dey just gwine be congenial. I jumped first, and you ought to seed me. I sailed right over dat broom stick same as a cricket. But when Exter jump he done had a big dram and his feets was so big and clumsy dat dey got all tangled up in dat broom and he fell headlong. Marse George he laugh and laugh, and told Exter he gwine be bossed 'twell he scared to speak lessen I told him to speak.

William Cullen Bryant Recollects a Corn-Shucking Ceremony (1850)

Religious rituals and ceremonies are among the most interesting aspects of slave culture. The study of slave ceremonies is interdisciplinary and frequently involves collaboration between historians and cultural anthropologists or folklorists. This combined effort has often led to an improved understanding of slave culture and has shed light upon many little-known features of slave life. The study of the corn-shucking ceremony – pioneered by folklorist Roger Abrahams – is particularly valuable. During the antebellum period, the shucking of the corn was at the center of an elaborate ceremony performed by slave field hands with singing and dancing. Several travelers described the ritual in detail. In this excerpt, traveler William Cullen Bryant described the ceremony, mentioning the fact that slaves mimicked animals while performing; as he perhaps hinted at, the ceremony was as much a chance for slaves to express their African roots as an opportunity to comment on their condition and mock their masters.

But you must hear of the corn-shucking. The one at which I was present was given on purpose that I might witness the humors of the Carolina negroes. . . .

The light-wood fire was made, and the negroes dropped in from the neighboring plantations. The driver of the plantation, a colored man, brought out baskets of corn in the husk, and piled it in a heap; and the negroes began to strip the husks from the ears, singing with great glee as they worked, keeping time to the music, and now and then throwing in a joke in an extravagant burst of laughter. The songs were generally of a comic character; but one of them was set to a singularly wild and plaintive air. . . . These are the words:

Johnny come down de hollow.
Oh hollow!
Johnny come down de hollow.
Oh hollow!
De nigger-trader got me.
Oh hollow!

Source: William Cullen Bryant, *Letters of a Traveller* (New York: G. P. Putnam, 1850), pp. 84–7; reprinted in Roger D. Abrahams, *Singing the Master: The Emergence of African American Culture in the Plantation South* (New York: Pantheon Books, 1992), pp. 223–5

De speculator bought me.
Oh hollow!
I'm sold for silver dollars.
Oh hollow!
Boys, go catch de pony.
Oh hollow!
Bring him around the corner.
Oh hollow!
I'm goin' away to Georgia.
Oh hollow!
Boys, good-by forever!
Oh hollow!

The song of "Jenny gone away," was also given, and another, called the monkey-song, probably of African origin, in which the principal singer personated a monkey, with all sorts of odd gesticulations, and other negroes bore part in the chorus, "Dan, dan, who's de dandy." One of the songs, commonly sung on these occasions, represents the various animals of the woods as belonging to some profession or trade. For example –

De cooter is de boatman –

The cooter is the terrapin, and a very expert boatman he is.

De cooter is de boatman,
John, John Crow.
De red-bird de soger.
John, John Crow.
De mocking-bird de lawyer.
John, John Crow.
De alligator sawyer.
John, John Crow.

The alligator's back is furnished with a toothed ridge, like the edge of a saw, which explains the last line. When the work of the evening was over the negroes adjourned to a spacious kitchen. One of them took his place as musician, whistling, and beating time with two sticks on the floor. Several of the men came forward and executed various dances, capering, prancing, and drumming with heel and toe upon the floor, with astonishing agility and perseverance, though all of them had performed their daily tasks and had worked all the evening, and some had walked from four to seven miles to attend the corn-shucking. It became necessary for the commander to make a speech, and confessing his incapacity for public speaking, he called upon a huge black man named Toby to address the company in his stead. Toby, a man of powerful frame, six feet high, his face ornamented with a beard of fashionable cut, had hitherto stood leaning against the wall, looking upon the frolic with an air of superiority. He consented, came forward, demanded a piece of paper to hold in his hand, and harangued the soldiery. It was evident that Toby had listened to stump-speeches in his day. He spoke of "de majority of Sous Carolina," "de interests of de state," "de honor of ole Ba'nwell district," and these phrases he connected by various expletives, and sounds of which we could make nothing. A (sic) length he began to falter, when the captain with admirable presence of mind came to his relief, and interrupted and closed the harangue with an hurrah from the company....

[A] light-wood fire was made, and the negroes dropped in from the neighboring plantations, singing as they came...various dances, capering, prancing and drumming with "heel and toe upon the floor" that came after the feast.

Slave Marriage and Family Relations in Antebellum Virginia

Brenda E. Stevenson

In *Life in Black and White*, Brenda Stevenson analyzes the daily life of slaveholders and slaves in Loudun County, Virginia; her focus is on the constraints which slavery imposed upon elite women, yeomen households, and slave families. In her analysis, Stevenson treats black and white families as if they inhabited two separate worlds, whose only interaction was violent as a result of the abuses produced by the slavery system. In this excerpt, Stevenson rejects the view that slave families were nuclear and characterized by the presence of two parents. Slave sales and slave sexual abuse allowed little room for family life; even after two slaves were married, the master continued to have absolute authority over their private life. As a consequence, extended families and families headed by females or matrifocal were far more common than nuclear families. For the same reason, most slave families were also matrilocal, with few fortunate fathers being granted permission to visit their spouses and children on weekends and holidays.

Brenda E. Stevenson, *Life in Black and White: Family and Community in the Slave South* (New York and Oxford: Oxford University Press, 1996), pp. 226–57.

African American romance and marriage within the context of the institution of slavery could be the most challenging and devastating of slave experiences. From the initiation of a romance, black men and women had to confront and compromise with their masters about control of their intimate lives, aware that their owner typically had the final say about if and when they could marry, and even who. Even after a slave's marriage, his or her master still commonly decided when slave husbands and wives could see each other, if and when they could live or work together, the fate of their children, and sometimes even the number of children they had.

Slaves nonetheless had their own way of doing things, refusing to concede too much, sometimes refusing to concede at all. If the slave master's interference in the slave's personal life was interminable, so too was the slave's resistance to this kind of intervention. Like their owners, slave attitudes and decisions about courtship and marriage were shaped by gender convention and community concerns, but not necessarily the same conventions or concerns. The matrifocality of many slave families, for example, meant that the realities of slave manhood and womanhood differed substantially within the context of family life from those whose familial experiences were nuclear and patriarchal. Likewise, extended families and slave communities were important, not just because they monitored slave behavior and maintained slave values, thereby protecting the integrity of the community. Members of slave communities also actually played substantial physical, material, and emotional roles in the lives of slaves. To a large extent, they were the slave's family. The presence of meaningful kinship ties embodied in the extended family or community, therefore, allowed slaves to take on a variety of marital arrangements and familial structures. One's master might have had the final authority, but there also were other slaves and slave institutions that exerted influence, perhaps more influence than masters realized. Within the broad contours of slave life that masters insisted on designing, slaves found spaces of their own, choosing what lines to and not to cross as they constructed their own domestic terrain.

It was a terrain structured by diverse, yet nonetheless respected rules and standards. Those who wanted to marry, for example, had to consult their parents or other black authority figures first. . . . [M]ale slaves and owners controlled much of this process, but mothers and elderly women also held power in certain slave quarters, particularly in relation to younger slave women. They could control vital aspects of a woman's courtship and marriage, sometimes even to the exclusion of owners or slave men.

The predominance of matrifocality and the large percentages of slave women in smaller holdings, therefore, had significant impact on slaves' domestic lives, giving slave women great influence in their families and communities. It was an influence not recognized in the larger society's hierarchy, but nonetheless functional in the slave's world view. Elderly slave women who had lived in the quarters for years, particularly where adult females were in the majority, were accorded great respect. Their long lives and the wisdom assumed derived from it, their years of service to their families, and their knowledge of their community's history were the basis for their authority. Likewise, mothers who raised their children without paternal input commanded their children's obedience and deference.

Female power in slave families and communities was not power that they took lightly or used sparingly. . . . Caroline Johnson Harris explained of her courtship and marriage that "Ant Sue," and not her master, had to give permission to the slave couples in her quarters before they could marry. As an elder and a holy woman, "Ant Sue" especially compelled communal respect. Harris recalled that when she and her prospective husband approached the powerful woman for her blessing, "She tell us to think 'bout it hard fo' two days, 'cause marryin' was sacred in de eyes of Jesus." Having followed her directions carefully, Caroline and Mose (the would-be-fiancé), returned to "Ant Sue" and told her that, after much consideration, they still wanted to marry. The elderly woman then assembled the other members of the slave community and asked them to "pray fo' de union dat God was gonna make. Pray we stay together an' have lots of chillun an' none of 'em git sol' way from de parents." A broomstick ceremony followed her prayer, but not before "Ant Sue" queried the couple again about the certainty of their decision.[1]

"Ant Sue's" and the discriminating mother's control carried considerable weight in their slave communities. Masters who where unaware of or disinterested in slaves' distribution of social power within their world claimed that their authority as owner took priority. If the couple had the same master, there usually was no problem in gaining his or her permission. . . . If the couple had different owners, both masters had to give their permission and usually the husband and wife continued to live separately after their marriage. "My father was owned by John Butler and my [mother] was owned by Tommy Humphries," Loudoun slave George Jackson explained. "When my father wanted to cum he had to get a permit from his massa. He would only cum home on Saturday. He worked on the next plantation joinin' us." A few owners bought a favorite slave's spouse. William Gray of "Locust Hill" just outside of Leesburg, for example, purchased Emily, the wife of his male slave George, after their first child was born in 1839. The couple had five more children during the next eight years. Gray later sold the slave family to a local farmer in 1853, "all at their own request" for $3200.[2]

Emily and George, as most slaves, probably had a brief, "informal" wedding. Despite its brevity and seeming informality, however, slave weddings and the commitments they symbolized were extremely important events for black families and communities. William Grose, for example, was appalled when a new master insisted that he marry again simply because he had been sold far away from his first wife. He was equally distressed when the owner presented him with a new wife without any "ceremony."[3] Slave marriage rituals varied considerably. "Jumping the broom" was popular among some. Georgianna Gibbs remembered that when the slaves on her farm married they had to "jump over a broom three times" before they actually were considered married.[4]

The act of "jumping the broom" as part of slave marriage ritual is important to consider, not only because it was a popular practice, but also because of its cultural and sociopolitical implications. Although many contend that "jumping the broom" had African origins, evidence suggests otherwise. "Jumping the broom," in fact, was a popular practice in early Anglo-Saxon villages where a couple jumped together across a broom placed at their family's threshold in order to signify that they entered the residence as husband and wife. Jumping backward across the broom to the other side of the threshold meant the end to a marriage. Since "jumping the broom" was a pre-Christian ritual in much of western Europe, it probably passed down to later generations as an amusing, perhaps quaint, relic of their "pagan" past. By imposing this cultural albatross on slaves, southern whites suggested the lack of respect and honor that they held for their blacks' attempts to create meaningful marital relationships. The slave's acceptance of this practice, on the other hand, demonstrated the ability of slave culture to absorb, reconfigure, and legitimize new ritual forms, even those masters imposed out of jest or ridicule.[5]

Those slaves who did not "jump the broom" solemnized their marriages in other ways. Slave masters sometimes participated, reading a few words from the Bible or giving their own extemporaneous text....

... [I]nevitably some masters refused to respect the choices that their slaves made about their private lives. Despite family or community support, those slaves who defied their masters paid a high price. Still slaves willingly, and sometimes willfully, chose to marry in spite of their owner's wishes. Martha and David Bennett, for example, married without her master's permission. David belonged to Captain James Taylor and Martha was a slave of George Carter. Taylor seemed not to resent the union, but evidence suggests that Carter felt otherwise – Martha reported that Carter had had her stripped naked and "flogged" "after her marriage."[6]

Whether or not Carter rejected the marriage, however, is only part of this puzzle. What is perhaps more intriguing is why Martha married

David in the first place. Why would Martha, a member of a slaveholding that boasted a large and equal number of men and women, choose a man with whom she could not live and whose children she would have to raise without their father's daily input? Why would she commit to an abroad marriage and a functionally matrifocal family style when she did not have to do so? Why didn't she choose instead one of the men on Carter's plantation? Certainly for her to do so would have added some measure of security to her marriage and family. It also would have pleased her owner. Martha's marriage begs a number of important questions not only about the reasons why slaves married who they married, but also about the kinds of marriage and family styles they deemed acceptable.

Slaves so frequently married persons belonging to other masters that Martha's behavior does not seem odd. But Martha was not confronted with the kinds of conditions that usually are attributed to abroad marriage. Neither the demographic conditions nor residential patterns of Carter's plantation mandated that Martha marry abroad. Neither did the domestic slave trade nor slave rental business, for Carter did not routinely sell or rent out his slaves. Martha's marriage to George Bennett, therefore, suggests that there may have been other reasons why so many slaves had abroad marriages and matrifocal households.

While this question may never be completely answered, there are some partial explanations. Complex rules of exogamy, notions of slave manhood and womanhood, and a desire to extend one's social world beyond one's residential community were significant considerations. So too was the slave's psychological need to establish some "emotional distance" between oneself and one's loved ones, to say nothing of the slave's cultural heritage. All these factors contributed to what "choices" slaves made about their domestic lives within the context of the rigid constraints that masters imposed.

The slaves' great concern about marriage to a close blood relation, for example, could have influenced greatly the numbers of abroad marriages that existed even among quarters like those of George Washington, William Fitzhugh, or George Carter where there were many men and women from which to choose a spouse. In generations-old quarters such as these, long years of intermarriage and procreation created intricate and complex kinship ties, ties that may have been discernible only to slave community members. While older quarters housed particularly stable communities because of extended family networks, they also contained closely connected kin (first cousins, for example) whom slaves would consider ineligible as marriage partners. Unfortunately, this kind of avoidance is practically undetectable by scholars who have to rely on slave lists produced by owners or overseers who had different rules of exogamy. Even so, many masters seemed to have realized that their slaves were upholding stringent rules of exclusion....

Martha Bennett, therefore, may have looked for a husband outside of Carter's slaveholding because his quarters presented her with a preponderance of male kin. There also may have been other reasons why she agreed to marry abroad. Growing up in communities filled with matrifocal slave families, it is not surprising that slave women like Martha were socialized to function in such. Slave women may have foreseen other benefits as well. Having abroad husbands and matrifocal households, for example, allowed them a kind of management of their children and day-to-day domestic life that live-in husbands may not have. As such, matrifocality had the potential to define effectively slave womanhood in ways that were quite distinct from free womanhood. Likewise, abroad marriages could give women greater domestic power, ideally affording them the moral sanctity of marriage, but also lessening some of their responsibilities – physical and emotional – to their husbands.

Slave men like David Bennett would have had other motives for choosing an abroad wife, some linked to African American conventions of manhood and leisure. Nineteenth-century black men, as white, often viewed travel and "adventure" as a "natural" desire and activity of a "man." [...] Abroad marriage also had other implications for slave men. The slave husband's sense that his "manhood" in part hinged on his ability to protect his wife and children inspired some to marry abroad – at least he did not have to witness his family's daily abuse. When local slave Dan Lockhart's wife was sold to a man who lived eight miles away from him, he believed it was "too far" and he managed to get his owner to sell him to someone who lived closer. He stayed with his new master for more than three years before he decided to run away to avoid seeing his wife and children being whipped. He explained that he "could not stand this abuse of them, and so I made up my mind to leave."[7]...

Love and romance were as important reasons as any that slaves insisted on choosing their spouses even if it meant a long-distance marriage. The story of Loudoun slave William Grose and his free black wife is instructive. Grose's owner never approved of his abroad marriage to the free woman, for he feared that she would find some means to help William escape. Eventually he decided that the best way to protect his investment was to sell William to a long-distance trader. Sent to New Orleans, he was sold again, this time as a domestic to a creole widower. Grose's new owner, who seemed to have several slave wives himself, insisted that William marry another woman. "He sent for a woman, who came in, and said he to me, 'That is your wife,' " William explained. "I was scared half to death, for I had one wife whom I liked, and didn't want another.... There was no ceremony about it – he said Cynthia is your wife."[8]

It is not certain from Grose's autobiographical account whether or not he and Cynthia ever lived as husband and wife, but he continued to care deeply for the Loudoun free black woman he had married. Remarkably, the two managed to remain in contact. A year later, Grose's Virginia wife arrived in New Orleans and managed to get a position as a domestic in the same family in which he worked... and the two secretly carried on their marriage. Grose's master eventually found out about their relationship and she was forced to leave New Orleans. But this was not the end of their story. "After my wife was gone," William confessed, "I felt very uneasy. At length, I picked up spunk, and said I would start." William finally managed to escape to Canada where he, his Loudoun wife, and their children finally were reunited.[9]...

The large numbers of abroad marriages, the substantial incidence of serial marriages, even the rare examples of polygamy, therefore, can be linked both to the slave's lack of control over his or her domestic life and to his or her resilient assertion of control. Jo Ann Manfra and Robert Dykstra's survey of late antebellum slave couples who resided in the southside of Virginia indicates that serial marriages often resulted from the 10.1 percent of slave marriages that ended with mutual consent and another 10.8 percent that ended because of spousal desertion. John Blassingame's analysis of slave couple breakage in Mississippi, Tennessee, and Louisiana suggests similar conclusions. One of the most compelling examples of slave choice and its impact on slave marital structures and relations is that offered by ex-slave Israel Massie. Massie insisted that slave men and women not only "understood" polygynous marital relations, but some sought them out. His insistence helps to further establish the premise that slaves adopted a variety of marriage and family styles and that they were comfortable with that variety. According to Massie, slaves sometimes made a conscious choice to create certain marital arrangements and family structures which were not monogamous and nuclear.[10]

"Naw, slaves didn't have wives like dey do now," he began his explanation. "Ef I liked ya, I jes go an' tell marster I wanted ya an' he give his consent." "Ef I see another gal over dar on another plantation, I'd go an' say to de gal's marster, 'I want Jinny fer a wife.'... Hit may be still another gal I want an' I'll go an' git her. Allright now, dars three wives an' slaves had as many wives as dey wanted." Massie insisted that the multiple wives of one slave man "didn't think hard of each other" but "got 'long fine together." He illustrated antebellum slave polygyny with an example from his own farm. "When Tom died," he continued, "dar wuz Ginny, Sarah, Nancy, an' Patience." According to Massie, all of Tom's wives came to his funeral and publicly mourned for him. "Do ya kno' . . . dem women never fou't, fuss, an' quarrel over dem men folks? Dey seemed to understood each other."[11]

Polygyny, or something akin to it in which a slave man had long-standing, contiguous intimate relationships with more than one woman, probably was a much more popular alternative among slaves than heretofore has been realized. The unavailability of marriageable slave men in smaller holdings and the scarce number of men in those slave communities hit particularly hard by the domestic slave trade provided the physical conditions for polygamy, particularly when coupled with pressures (internal and external) on women to "breed." Moreover, at least scarce knowledge of ancestral domestic arrangements (in Islamic or many traditional African religious groups) and a continual tradition of matrifocality among slaves provided cultural sanction for polygamy. . . .

It is not unreasonable to assume, therefore, that even when demographic conditions theoretically could provide a high incidence of monogamy and nuclear families among the slaves of a particular holding, black men and women sometimes made other choices based on a complex combination of reasons; choices that, on occasion, resulted especially in abroad marriages and functionally matrifocal families, sometimes serial marriages, or even polygamy. Operative extended kin networks of various description undoubtedly allowed slaves some assurance that these kinds of decisions would not result in dysfunctional marriages or families.

Slave marriages, like those of any group, varied in terms of their internal dynamics, longevity, and the ways in which the couple acted out their roles as husband and wife. Given the variety of conditions under which slaves married and the numerous forms of marriage and family households they formed, it is difficult to discuss conclusively the various ideals which guided their domestic behavior. Yet one can begin to comprehend these roles if one has an understanding of operative adult sex roles among them.

The emphasis on gender-specific behavior became an important part of child socialization as slave youth grew older. Slave females, who were more likely than males to remain in their families of birth through adolescence, received most of their gendered socialization from their mothers, other female kin, or community women. Usually by the time slave girls reached their teens, these women already had prepared them to take on the most important commitments of their adult lives – motherhood and marriage. Slave women taught their girls that as adults it would be their responsibility to cook, clean, bear, and rear children for their families, all this despite the labor demands of masters. They were supposed to take pride in their "womanly" skills and service they rendered their families.

Clara Allen, for one, placed great esteem on the domestic arts that her mother taught her and her service to her family. Contrasting the skilled talent and familiar commitment of slave women with the carefree, unsolicitous attitudes of early twentieth-century black women, Allen openly disapproved of the abandonment of domestic skills that had been so important to Virginia slave women; that had, in fact, helped to define them as women. "Nowadays, do you think any dese girls w'd set still long enuf to WEAVE?" she asked rhetorically: "No sir, dey cyan't set still long 'nuff to thread a darnin' needle . . . dey cyan't weave, nor cook, nor do up a silk mull dress, nor flute de curtain ruffles, nor make pickle an' p'serbs, nor tend a baby liken it oughter be tended. Dey doan know nuttin'!" Allen added coolly, with a sense of female pride and purpose, "I could take the wool offen the sheep's back an' kerry it thru ter CLAWTH. Wash it, card it, spin it, weave it, sew it inter clothes – an' (with a laugh) wear it, when I gotter chance."[12] This sphere of domestic labor that Allen specified – taught, supervised, and performed almost exclusively by females – reinforced within slave girls and women a sense of their "femaleness" while helping them to maintain strong bonds across generational, cultural and occupational boundaries.

A woman's role as head of a matrifocal family mandated that she make some of her family's most vital decisions and suffer the consequences if her master or her abroad husband disagreed. It meant that she had to act protectively and aggressively for the sake of her dependents, often in open conflict with her owner. Slave mothers, for example, routinely rebelled against the poor material support owners provided, especially the amount and quality of their food. Few hesitated to steal, lie, and cheat in order to guarantee their physical survival or that of their children. Marrinda Jane Singleton, for example, remembered that as a single mother she stole food – vegetables and meat – in order to feed herself and her children. Speaking of one particular incident, she explained: "Dis pig was now divided equally and I went on to my cabin wid equal share. All de chillun was warned not to say nothin' 'bout dis. If dey did, I tole 'em I would skin 'em alive, 'cause dis pig was stole to fill their bellies as well as mine."[13] . . .

The challenges of slave matrifocality, therefore, inspired idealized behavioral traits of self-protection, self-reliance, and self-determination among many black women. It was these ideals, in turn, which contextualized their physical and psychological resistance to white authority and shaped their roles within their families.

Slave women across age, cultural, and occupational lines were forthright in their appreciation of self-reliant, determined black females who had the wherewithal to protect themselves and theirs, confrontationally if need be. Of course, most women were not able to act in any openly confrontational manner for fear of severe retaliation. But it is clear that slave women held great pride and esteem for those who did so. These were the women whom other slave females spoke most often about in "heroic" terms, attributing to them what seem like . . . fantastical deeds and attitudes. Thus, while white southern society believed that this kind of female conduct was unfeminine, if not outright masculine, slave women utilized aggressive, independent behavior to protect their most fundamental claims to womanhood; that is, their female sexuality and physicality, and their roles as mothers and wives.

True stories about slave female rape and physical abuse, for example, abound in the records produced by slaves. Most slave women found no way to fight back (and win). Those women who found some manner to resist emerged in the lore and mythology of slave women as both heroic and ideal. Slave mothers, in fact, often told stories of these women to their daughters as part of their socialization. Virginia Hayes Shepherd, for one, spoke in glowing terms of three heroic slave women she had known personally or through her mother's stories – one successfully avoided the sexual pursuit of her owner, while the other two refused to be treated in the fields like men, that is, to be worked beyond their physical endurance as childbearing women.[14] . . .

Fannie Berry told many accounts of female slave resistance to sexual abuse, including her own. But she was most proud of Sukie Abbott's daring rebuff of both her owner's sexual overtures and the slave trader's physical violation. Both Berry and Abbott rightfully linked the two as equally dehumanizing.

Sukie was the Abbott house slave who, according to Berry, had been the target of her master's unwarranted sexual advances. One day while Sukie was in the kitchen making soap, Mr. Abbott tried to force her to have sex with him. He pulled down her dress and tried to push her onto the floor. Then, according to Berry, "dat black gal got mad. She took an' punch ole Marsa an' made him break loose an' den she gave him a shove an' push his hindparts down in de hot pot o'soap. . . . He got up holdin' his hindparts an' ran from de kitchen, not darin' to yell, 'cause he didn't want Miss Sarah Ann [his wife] to know 'bout it." A few days later, Abbott took Sukie to the slave market to sell. The defiant woman again faced sexual abuse and physical invasion as potential buyers stared, poked, and pinched her. According to Fannie, Sukie got mad again. "She pult her dress up an' tole those ole nigger traders to look an' see if dey could fin' any teef down dere. . . . Marsa never did bother slave gals no mo," Berry concluded with relish.[15]

Many witnesses at the slave market that day no doubt thought Sukie vulgar and promiscuous, a perfect picture of black "womanhood." Fannie Berry concluded something altogether different. In Berry's estimation, Sukie had exacted a high price from the men who tried to abuse her. It was true that the slave woman had lost her community when Mr. Abbott sold her in retaliation for her resistance; but she still managed to deny her owner his supposed right to claim her "female principle." She also demanded that her new buyer see her for what she was, a woman, not an animal, by insisting that he acknowledge her female sexual organs. Perhaps most important, Sukie's response to Mr. Abbott's attempted rape deterred him from violently pursuing other slave women on his plantation. The moral of Berry's story of Sukie Abbott lies, therefore, not only in Sukie's ability to sacrifice her "privilege" as a domestic and her permanence in a nurturing community in order to protect her female body and her humanity, but also in the good that sacrifice did for others. Fannie Berry's rendition of the Sukie Abbott biography, whether true or embellished, is an important example of the kinds of stories of female heroism and humanity that slave women told and retold as a kind of inspirational socialization and legitimizing process.[16] . . .

Of course terms like sexual seduction, exploitation, and abuse are relative to one's time and place. Slave women probably would not have chosen contemporary language or their definitions to describe their sexual relationships with slave men, particularly their husbands. Slave wives, even abroad wives, were expected to submit to their husband's will, particularly those who had regular contact. A woman's submission to her man went hand in hand with her service to her family and community. . . .

. . . [W]hile many slave couples did not live together on a daily basis and many abroad wives believed they had to take on an aggressive, protective, somewhat independent stance with regard to family matters, many slave husbands still wanted to be their families' protectors and supporters. Thomas Harper, for example, was a local blacksmith who decided to escape to Canada because he "thought that it was hard to see . . . [his family] in want and abused when he was not at liberty to aid or protect them." Dan Lockhart also decided to escape because he could not stand to see his wife and children whipped without being able to do anything to prevent it. Numerous . . . black men, such as Samuel Anderson, Peter Warrick, Joseph Cartwright and Cupid Robinson, managed to secure the freedom of their wives and/or children in order to insure that they could protect them.[17] . . .

A wife's submission and service to her husband, therefore, was supposed to be rewarded by his efforts to aid and protect her and her children. Sex complicated this brokered balance because it virtually was impossible for some slave women to submit to their husband's desire for sexual exclusivity. Loudoun slave masters who believed that they held sexual rights to their female slave property continued to be an enormous problem for couples. Some masters actually reserved the most attractive slave women for themselves, regardless of the woman's marital status or even their age....

Miscegenation is a sterile, emotionless term that often shrouds acts of sexual submission characterized by violence and degradation. The women and their biracial children clearly were the true victims in these situations; but slave men also could faced grave consequences. Many often found themselves in the precarious, if not dangerous, position of competing with slaveholding men for the same slave women. Slave beaus and husbands could suffer brutal physical and emotional consequences if a slaveholding man wanted his woman. Undoubtedly when white men raped black women they did so not only to subject these females to a violent and dehumanizing experience, but also to emasculate husbands and male kin. The various reactions of male slaves, therefore, were equally responses to their own sense of powerlessness as they were a recognition of the physical and psychological pain that these females experienced. "Marsters an' overseers use to make slaves dat wuz wid deir husbands git up, [and] do as they say," one ex-slave man noted. "Send husbands out on de farm, milkin' cows or cuttin' wood. Den he gits in bed wid slave himself. Some women would fight an' tussel. Others would be [h]umble – feared of dat beatin'. What we saw, couldn't do nothing 'bout it. My blood is b[o]ilin' now [at the] thoughts of dem times. Ef dey told dey husbands he wuz powerless."[18]

When slave husbands did intervene, they suffered awful retaliatory actions – sometimes permanent separation from their families, severe beatings, or murder. Many probably felt as did Charles Grandy, who concluded of the fatal shooting of a male slave who tried to protect his wife from the advances of their overseer: "Nigger ain't got no chance." Some slave husbands targeted the female victims of rape rather than the powerful white males who attacked them. Regardless of whomever they struck out at, however, their responses usually had little effect on the abusive white men involved.[19]

But not all sexual relations between slave women and white men were physically coerced, just as not all sex between slave women and men was voluntary. Masters and slave men had many ways to gain control of and manipulate black women's sexuality. Some slave women responded to material incentives like food, clothing, and better housing that white men offered in exchange for sexual favors. Certainly they were much more able than slave suitors to "romance" slave women with gifts and promises of a better life. Others promised, and sometimes granted, emancipation. The unavailability of marriageable slave men, particularly for those women who lived in small holdings, also could have been something of a coercive factor. It is not inconceivable that some of these women established sexual/marital relations with available white men, just as these kinds of demographic conditions may have enjoined some to commit to polygynous relations with whatever black men were available.

One also cannot discount the impact on biracial sexual relations of a combination of factors endemic to life in a racialist constructed society, including internalized racism and a desire to identify with and be accepted by the "superior" race. Under these circumstances, some slave women may have agreed to become concubines to, or may have even desired, white men. Racially mixed slave women who were socialized to be more culturally akin to whites than blacks could be particularly vulnerable to the sexual overtures of white men. Ary, for example, was a quadroon slave woman raised, as the favored domestic, in the home of her father's brother. By the time she reached young womanhood, she had become the concubine of her young master, her paternal first cousin. Convinced that she was her father's favorite child, Ary often boasted of her elite white parentage and her young master's love for her. Remembering her lover's pronouncement that she was to have nothing to do with "colored men" because they "wern't good enough" for her, Ary was determined not to associate too closely with any blacks.[20]

Despite Ary's belief that white men were superior to black, men of both races lived by a double and privileged sexual standard. Tales of male sexual prowess were applauded in the slave community, while female promiscuity was frowned on. Masters followed the same sexual code in their white communities and, therefore, understood only too well the importance of sexual conquest to the male ego. Some undoubtedly used the masculine esteem derived from sexual triumph to help convince slave men to act as "breeders." West Turner was born in about 1842 and remembered well the tales of breeding men: "Joe was 'bout seven feet tall an' was de breedinges' nigger in Virginia," he began one story. "'Member once ole Marsa hired him out to a white man what lived down in Suffolk. Dey come an' got him on a Friday. Dey brung him back Monday mo'nin'. Dey say de next year dere was sebenteen little black babies bo'n at dat place in Suffolk, all on de same day."[21] . . .

Slave men traditionally applauded their sexual potency, celebrating it in song, dance, jokes, and heroic tales. Unlike slave women, men did not have to restrict their sexual activity to marital or procreative duties. A man could derive great status from having sexual relations with as many women as possible, or as many times as possible with one woman, without marriage or children being at issue. Even elderly men like Cornelius Garner still spoke proudly of their youthful sexual verve and refused to accept that the possibility of infertility diminished their record of sexual performance or their status as men. Speaking of his three wives, Garner boasted: "Pretty good ole man to wear out two wives, but de third one, ha, ha may wear me out." When asked if he had any children, Garner was quick to answer that he had never had any children, but that that was not his fault: "I did what God tole me. 'Wuk and multiply,' ha ha. I wuked but 'twon't no multiplying after de wuk."[22]

The emphasis that slave men placed on their sexual prowess had profound impact on slave courtship and marriage, particularly when they treated their women as sexual objects to pursue and dominate, often without a hint of marriage or longstanding commitment. The impact of slavery on the relationships that slave males had with their families, especially the women in their families, may have helped to exaggerate female sexual objectification.... It was typical for slave boys to be raised in matrifocal households. It also was typical for them to leave these households as they reached puberty. They did so, temporarily, as part of the redistribution of prime males to their owners' more labor-intensive units. They also endured more permanent leave as part of the domestic slave trade or slave rental process, or to take up residence in all-male households in the quarters. This abrupt withdrawal from a social and socializing world of women to one of men was a difficult transition. Unfortunately, this separation experience was only the first of what could be two or three more for slave men. This constant experience and fear of separation, along with the need to be able to adjust, physically and emotionally, to it, may have inhibited some slave men from allowing themselves to construct complex relationships with the women with whom they came in contact, resulting instead in their sexual objectification....

Casual sex in the quarters... rarely had casual consequences. When casual sex translated into adultery, stakes were very high. Slave men were jealous not only of the sexual attention that white men paid their wives, but also of the flirtations and seductions of other black men. Slave women were equally intolerant. Records from the era, however, indicate that both slave men and women would stray. As early as May 1774, for example, records of the local Broad Run Baptist Church documented that the church excommunicated the "Negro Dick" for "having lived in Adultery." Several years later, they excommunicated "Negro Grace belonging to Mr. Colbert for adultery." Over the next fifty years, the church ousted several other slave worshippers, the majority for adultery.[23]

Few Loudoun slave masters held great concern for the complex and diverse conventions of gendered behavior, beauty, marriage, or family that slaves respected and tried to maintain within their families and communities. Even if they had wanted to know, and do, more about these aspects of black life, slaves were quick to shelter the less obvious details of their personal lives and choices from their masters' control. . . . For the slave master the slave family had two important roles: it gave an owner the opportunity to manipulate for the owner's benefit a slave's concern for his or her family; and it was the center of slave procreation.

Some masters undoubtedly promoted long-term slave marriages if the couple proved to be amply fertile. . . . Sometimes slave owners promised female slaves material rewards such as larger food allowances, better clothing, or more spacious cabins if they would consent to have many children. Some undoubtedly accepted these incentives, while others resented their masters' attempts to control their bodies. A slave woman's sexuality and her reproductive organs were key to her identity as a woman and she claimed a right to have power over that identity. . . . Some female slaves in fact may have taken the matter of reproduction into their own hands, secretly using contraceptive methods in order to maintain control over their procreation. One slave woman, for example, indicated that she was able to regulate her childbearing when she explained that she used to have a child every Christmas, " 'but when I had six, I put a stop to it, and only had one every other year.' "[24]

Masters often suspected slave females of using contraceptives and inducing miscarriage, but rarely were able to prove it. . . . A few slave mothers went so far as to commit infanticide. The Loudoun *Democratic Mirror* reported on November 11, 1858, for example, that the court had found a slave woman named Marietta guilty of infanticide and ordered her deportation to the lower South.[25]

Sometimes what slaveholders might have construed as a slave woman's resistance to bearing children, however, was a result of temporary or permanent female infertility. Given their overall poor physical condition due to heavy work loads, regular harsh treatment, nutritionally deficient diets, and limited access to proper medical attention, it is not difficult to understand why many black women were unable to reproduce as quickly as some of their owners might have wanted. Even though slave women usually began having children earlier than white women, they eventually had fewer, and the space between their live births was lengthier and more erratic. . . .

The statistics which define natural slave increase document the impact of their harsh lifestyles on childbearing women and on the health of their children. While it is uncertain the number of times slave women conceived, had spontaneous abortions, ectopic pregnancies, or miscarried, it is known that the number of live slave births was much smaller than for white women. Moreover, the number of slave children who survived the first decade of their lives was fewer than those of white women. Demographer Richard Steckel, for example, calculates that, throughout the South, more than one-half of slave infants died before they were one year old, a mortality rate that was almost double that of whites. Although the survival rate for slave children improved after they reached the age of one, their mortality rate was still twice that of white children until they became fourteen years old. Among many slaveholdings, infant and small children had mortality rates of almost 50 percent.[26]

Not only did slave parents have to contend with a devastating number of child deaths, they also had the difficult task of socializing those who survived. The most important barrier they faced was a legal one. Put simply, slave kin were not the legal guardians of their children, slaveholders were.

Masters took seriously their ownership of slave youth and often preempted parental authority. Not only did slave masters sell and give away slave youngsters, but they also assigned them tasks when their parents felt that they were either too young, ill, or otherwise indisposed to perform them; punished them without parental knowledge or consent; and sometimes offered "favorites" protection from parental disciplinary measures. It was difficult for slave parents to wrestle control from their masters, particularly when owners believed that all slaves, young and old, were psychologically and cognitively like "children" and insisted on publicly treating adult slaves like they were....

Sometimes slave parents tried to challenge an owner's control of their children, but with little tangible success.... White owners balked at overt attempts by kin or any other potential authority figure to gain control of slave children without their permission. Slaveholders understood that such challenges to their rights as owners by black parents were potent signs of rebellion; that slaves were teaching their children, through example, to resist their oppression. Not surprisingly, most slave masters met this kind of resistance with extreme hostility and brutality, often punishing the would-be usurper and slave child.

Loudoun slave owners typically did not allow parents to reduce their labor quotas in order to care for their children. New mothers usually spent about two weeks with their infants before they had to return to their hectic work schedules. Given the work loads of slaves, one or two persons, even the child's parents, rarely were able to attend to all of the components of the childrearing task. Parents, therefore, had to share childcare and rearing with others. While they relied on other members of their families, nuclear and extended, for aid, owners assigned temporary caregivers of their own – usually infirm, elderly, or very young female slaves. Slaveholders, therefore, not only claimed a large role in the lives of slave children, but they also shared their authority with others who were not slave parents or kin. In addition to a slave child's kin, slaveholding women, white overseers, black drivers, and slave nurses especially were important authority figures at various stages of a slave youngster's development.

Within the auspices of the slave family and extended kin network, the importance of one's contribution to the rearing of slave children was determined by a number of conditions. Parents, grandparents, step parents, older siblings, aunts, uncles, and sometimes cousins and community associates contributed to the upbringing of slave children if circumstances of the slave family made it necessary to do so. The closeness of the consanguinous tie and one's gender generally implied differential responsibility. The size of the family and the slaveholding, as well as the birth order, also were determinants. So too were the ages and health of possible rearers; their availability and willingness to do so; and certainly the opinions of kin and owners. Clearly there were a number of operative variables. Yet slave masters generally made the final decision as to who took care of slave children and under what conditions....

Many slave families were not only matrifocal, but also matrilocal. Those fathers who lived locally had the privilege of seeing their families on weekends and holidays. George Jackson, who lived near Bloomfield in Loudoun, recalled that his father lived on the next plantation, but could visit only on Saturdays and Sundays. John Fallons allowed his slave Moses to visit his wife, who lived some twelve miles away, each Sunday. Fallons even supplied Moses with transportation. "Every Sunday Marster let Uncle Moses take a horse an' ride down to see his wife an' their two chillun, an' Sunday night he come riding back; sometimes early Monday morning just in time to start de slaves working in de field," the slave's nephew recalled.[27] ...

Most slave fathers who had an opportunity to do so served their families in a number of capacities. Ideally, they provided emotional support and affection, moral instruction, discipline, and physical protection. Some also were able to give material support, particularly food. Many taught their boys how to hunt, trap, and fish. Those with lucrative skills did likewise, passing down their knowledge of metal and wood working, carpentry, and blacksmithing along with a host of other traditional skills such as folk medicine. George White, for one, recalled: "Papa was a kinda doctor... an'... knowed all de roots. I know all de roots too.... My daddy... showed dem to me."[28] In their absence, other available male kin, such as uncles and grandfathers, assumed some of these duties....

The manner in which slave kin and owners perceived slave children in relation to themselves directly influenced the ways in which they treated these youngsters and tried to shape their development. Slave children were potentially important resources for family members and their masters. Slaves viewed their young as extensions of themselves and kinship lines, often naming them for favorite family members. Slave children also were providers of future security for their parents and kin, persons whom they could depend on for love, comfort, and service once they became old and infirm.

Slave masters, on the other hand, regarded slave children as a financial resource who were valuable only as obedient, submissive, efficient workers. Many also anticipated a kind of loyalty, respect, and affection from their slave property which did not differ greatly from the expectations of parents. These different perceptions were the source of great internal and external conflict. Slaves responded in a variety of ways, from overt resistance to passive acceptance of an owner's will.

Slave parents and kin, for example, clandestinely challenged brutal lessons of owners about obedience, docility, submission, and hard work with words and acts of kindness and care that reassured slave youth of their self-worth and humanity. They also taught slave youngsters through stories and example that it was possible to outmaneuver and manipulate white.... Obviously many others learned that it was possible to leave [an] oppressive environment through careful planning and with the assistance of family members and friends. Escape became the inevitable fantasy of the young and old.

Persistent pressure on marital relations and family life was a primary reason that many Loudoun slaves initiated escape plans. David Bennett and his wife Martha, who were both from Loudoun, readily admitted that they decided to escape with their two children, a little boy and a month-old infant, because of the cruelty of Martha's owner, George Carter. Although the Bennetts gave no details of how they managed to leave Loudoun without detection, there was a county Underground Railroad station run by local Quakers and free black ferryman....

Some of the most successful slave escapes ... were group affairs comprising family members and friends. On Christmas Eve, 1855, for example, six county slaves began their journey to Canada. The group included one married couple, Barnaby Grigby and his wife Elizabeth, Elizabeth's sister Emily, her fiancé Frank Wanzer, and two other male friends from neighboring Fauquier County. The slaves traveled both by carriage and horseback, "courtesy" of their unsuspecting masters. The owners, William Rogers and Townsend McVeigh of Middleburg, Lutheran Sullivan of Aldie, and Charles Simpson of Fauquier, did not initially believe that their missing slaves had run away. As was the custom, they had extended their slaves the right to travel short distances in order to visit friends and loved ones during the Christmas holidays. It was not until the next day, when the slaves were approximately forty miles from Loudoun, that whites discovered that these slaves, connected by blood, marriage, and friendship, were fugitives. . . .

Unfortunately, not everyone was able to escape with family members in tow. Even those who left with one or a few still faced the pain of leaving others behind. Women with small children, the elderly, those who were physically weak or lacked the psychological resolve to succeed were not allowed to go along. Considerations of group size, and the related issue of safety, also determined who was included. The larger the group, the greater chance of discovery and failure. Vincent Smith, for example, successfully escaped with his wife, but felt compelled to leave his mother and several siblings behind if he hoped to avoid detection. . . .

. . . [S]laves not only "ran away" from the pain, humiliation, and material deprivation that slave masters imposed, but also "ran to" family members. Many resisted the separations that slave owners engineered, clandestinely returning to their homes and families. The November 12, 1836, edition of the *Washingtonian*, for example, carried an advertisement by William Schaffer describing a "Dark Mulatto Woman, 25 years old" who had escaped from his custody. Schaffer presumed that the woman was on her way to visit some of her relatives who were the property of George Carter at "Oatlands." Carter recently had sold her to one of his cousins, Fitzhugh Carter of Fairfax. "I think it is likely she is in that settlement, or about Mr. George Carter's Oatlands, as she has connexions there," Schaffer explained in the notice. Relatives worked hard to maintain the safety of these fugitives, sometimes successfully shielding them from detection for months or even longer.[29] . . .

Of course, the large majority of slaves never escaped. . . . Many who remained . . . learned to take solace in their families and friends whom they were spared to live near. The development of a strong sense of identity and community ethos was one of the most important ways slaves coped with and resisted the stress on their domestic relations. Slave kin, for example, hoped to teach their children not only how to survive as individuals, but also the importance of the slave community and their responsibility to help others. They emphasized the value of demonstrating respect for other slaves and, in complete opposition to the lessons of owners, instructed their youngsters in a code of morality that paid homage to blacks rather than to whites. They preached against lying to and stealing from one another, the importance of keeping slave secrets, protecting fugitive slaves, and sharing work loads. Teachers working among contraband slaves in Virgina noted the affection that slaves held for one another and the many polite courtesies they extended among themselves. One ex-slave eloquently explained the basis for such relations. "The respect that the slaves had for their owners might have been from fear," she admitted, "but the real character of a slave was brought out by the respect that they had for each other." "Most of the time there was no force back of the respect the slaves had for each other. [T]hey were for the most part truthful, loving and respectful to one another."[30]

But slaves . . . were not always successful in their attempts to withstand long-term pressures on their domestic or social relations. As individuals with the same range of emotions and capable of the same moral triumphs and failures as free persons, many acted inappropriately toward their loved ones. Adultery was not the only internal problem which occasionally plagued . . . slave marriages and rocked slave families or communities. The slave quarter often was a place of smoldering emotions and anger. Disagreements and frustrations could erupt into violence, while verbal and physical abuse were sometimes responses to complicated issues of discord within slave marriages and families. Spousal abuse was not uncommon. . . . Child abuse and neglect also were well-documented phenomena.

Alcoholism seemed to have been a problem which often interfered with smooth slave marital and familial relations. Drinking was as popular a pastime for slaves as for free people. Those who habitually consumed large quantities typically were less responsive to their families' needs. Drinking also enhanced other disruptive behavior, sometimes triggering arguments and abuse. Divisive attitudes within slave families and communities, such as social status based on color or occupation, also proved to be problematic. So too were the cynicism and alienation of some who came to accept prevailing societal attitudes about the legitimacy of slavery and the "natural" degradation of slaves. The continual demands of the domestic slave trade, coupled with the other devastating conditions slave owners imposed, sometimes effectively eroded slave communities and family networks that had been functional for generations. Those who witnessed and were part of this destruction could not escape its physical or emotional impact.

Faced with overwhelming problems, as well as their own individual pressures and priorities, some slave couples responded in ways that further damaged rather than protected their marriages and families. More than a few voluntarily separated. . . . [O]f those slave marriages terminated before general emancipation, at least 20 percent did so because of the desire of at least one spouse.

The slave's family and community, therefore, often faced profound conflicts and problems which they responded to in a variety of ways, sometimes successfully, sometimes not. Slave masters and their representatives involved themselves in and tried to influence many vital aspects of their slave property's private lives. Slaveholders' economic and social priorities, in particular, often were in direct opposition to the needs of slaves trying to organize and function as family groups. Consequently, slave marital relationships, family structure, composition, and performance differed significantly from those who were not slaves, particularly whites.

Clearly many, if not most . . . slaves lived in family groups that were matrifocal and matrilocal. But there also was a diversity of structure, membership, and relations that cannot be denied. This diversity was due not only to the pressures of slave life, but also to the cultural and situational choices of the slaves themselves. The question as to whether slaves preferred a nuclear family structure still looms large and undoubtedly will shape future historiography. What is clear, however, is that throughout, extended family membership and flexibility were at the foundation of most functional slave families, not monogamous marital relationships. Indeed, the high volume of slaves exported as part of the domestic slave trade meant an ever-increasing number of husband or father-absent slave families.

Moreover, slave husbands were not patriarchs. To establish this reality of the role of the slave father and husband in the slave family does not characterize him as "inadequate," but rather testifies to the harshness of slave life. It also challenges traditional, western-centered, ideals of fathers and husbands. Much the same can be said for the slave mother whose labor for her owner had to come before her duty to her family.

Neither "fathering" nor "mothering," therefore, were embodied in one person in a slave family. But there were some similarities between slave and free "domesticity." Gender-differentiated expectations and behaviors at home, for example, were not so different. Females, for example, performed most of the tasks associated with the day-to-day care of children, their families' clothing, and food preparation. Yet by the last decade of the antebellum era, the group being hardest hit by this trade were not young men, but rather young women – many of whom were mothers. . . .

Despite all this, the . . . slave family survived and served many of its constituents well. It did not necessarily exist or function in the ways of other southerners. Slaves drew on rich African, European, and American cultural heritages, but also were forced by oppressive socioeconomic and political conditions and diverse domestic climates to construct domestic ideals and functional families that were different from the "norm." Given the difference that their status and cultures made in all other aspects of their lives, certainly it is not surprising that enslaved blacks in the American South also defined family life differently.

Notes

1 J. W. Blassingame (ed.), *Slave Testimony: Two Centuries of Letters, Speeches, Interviews, and Autobiographies* (Baton Rouge: Louisiana State University Press, 1977), pp. 561–2; *The Negro in Virginia*, compiled by the Virginia Federal Writers' Project of the Work Projects Administration in the State of Virginia (New York: Hastings, 1940), p. 81.
2 George P. Rawick (ed.), *The American Slave*, vol. 16: *Virginia* (Westport, Conn.: Greenwood Press, 1972), p. 45; Gray Family Bible; Gray Farm Book, Jan. 1 1853, Gray Family Papers, Virginia Historical Society, Richmond (hereafter referred to as VHS).
3 Benjamin Drew (ed.), *A North-Side View of Slavery, the Refugee; or the Narratives of Fugitive Slaves in Canada Related by Themselves with an Account of the History and Condition of the Colored Population of Upper Canada* (Boston: John Jewett, 1856), p. 31.
4 John W. Blassingame, *The Slave Community: Plantation Life in the Old South* (New York: Oxford University Press, 1972), pp. 165–77.
5 Randal D. Day and Daniel Hook, "A Short History of Divorce: Jumping the Broom And Back Again," *Journal of Divorce* 10, no. 3/4 (Spring/Summer 1987), pp. 57–8.
6 William Still (ed.), *The Underground Railroad: A Record of Facts, Authentic Narratives, Letters, etc.* (Philadelphia: Porter and Coates, 1872; New York: Arno Press, 1968), p. 260.
7 Drew (ed.), *North-Side View of Slavery*, p. 31.
8 Ibid., pp. 56–8.
9 Ibid., pp. 58–9.
10 JoAnn Manfra and Robert Dykstra, "Serial Marriage and the Origins of the Black Stepfamily: The Rowanty Evidence," *Journal of American History*, 72, no. 1 (June 1985), p. 32; Blassingame, *Slave Community*, tables 1 and 2, p. 90.
11 Charles L. Perdue, Thomas E. Barden, and Robert K. Phillips (eds.), *Weevils in the Wheat: Interviews with Virginia Ex-Slaves* (Charlottesville: University Press of Virginia, 1976), p. 209.
12 Perdue et al. (eds.), *Weevils*, p. 6.
13 Ibid., pp. 201–2, 244–5, 266–7.
14 Ibid., pp. 255–61.
15 Ibid., pp. 257–9.
16 Ibid., pp. 48–9.
17 Still (ed.), *Underground Railroad*, p. 41; Drew (ed.), *North-Side View of Slavery*, p. 31; Dorothy Sterling (ed.), *We Are Your Sisters: Black Women in the Nineteenth Century* (New York: W. W. Norton, 1984), pp. 45–6.
18 Perdue et al. (eds.), *Weevils*, pp. 117, 207.
19 Ibid.
20 Henry Swint (ed.), *Dear Ones at Home: Letters from Contraband Camps* (Nashville, Tenn.: Vanderbilt University Press, 1966), (ed.), pp. 39, 55–56, 73; Perdue et al. (eds.), *Weevils*, pp. 108, 293.

21 Perdue et al. (eds.), *Weevils*, p. 291.
22 Ibid., p. 101.
23 Broad Run Baptist Church Record, Broad Run Baptist Church Papers, Virginia Historical Society, Richmond, entries dated May 18, 1774; March 22, 1783, and *passim*.
24 Swint, ed., *Dear Ones at Home*, p. 61; Herbert Gutnan, *The Black Family in Slavery and Freedom, 1750–1925* (New York: Pantheon, 1976), pp. 76–7; 80–3n.; Deborah White, *Ar'n't I a Woman?: Female Slaves in the Plantation South* (New York: W. W. Norton, 1985), pp. 84–6, 98–103.
25 *Democratic Mirror*, Nov. 10, 1858.
26 Steckle's findings summarized in Michael Johnson, "Upward in Slavery," *New York Review of Books*, 36, no. 20 (Nov. 21, 1989), p. 53...
27 Rawick (ed.), *American Slave*, p. 45.
28 Perdue et al. (eds.), *Weevils*, p. 310.
29 *Washingtonian*, Nov. 12, 1836, VSL.
30 See for example, the lessons of slave parents and kin in Rawick (ed.), *American Slave*, 16, pp. 25, 29; Perdue et al. (eds.), *Weevils*, pp. 67, 85, 91, 128, 211, 235, 265, 317, 332 (quote from p. 235); Swint (ed.), *Dear Ones at Home*, pp. 36, 55–6, 123; Norman Yetman (ed.), *Voices from Slavery* (New York: Holt, Rinehart and Winston, 1970), p. 133.

10
Slave Resistance and Slave Rebellion

Introduction

It is important to remember that the main feature of plantation life was discipline. Slaves who failed to accomplish their tasks by the end of the day or who could not keep pace with the rest of the gang were punished. Slaves responded to this daily violence in different ways. They could wear a mask – what Bertram Wyatt-Brown has called the "mask of obedience" – and feign submissive behavior, pleasing their master and showing no signs of open resistance, as in the stereotype of the "sambo." Or they could resist by acts such as breaking tools, feigning illness, or collectively slowing the pace of work on a day-to day basis. In doing so, they both defined the boundaries within which the master could force acceptance of his will and, at the same time, compelled the master to recognize their own prerogatives and even rights. An extreme act of resistance was fighting against the overseer, the driver, or whoever was in charge of punishment, as Frederick Douglass did with Mr. Covey. Research has shown that this kind of resistance was surprisingly effective; slaves who did not submit easily to whipping were not whipped as often as others.

An extreme form of resistance was running away. Slaves ran away constantly from the plantations, hoping that they could find freedom. However, most of the time, they were chased, captured, and punished publicly, so that all the other slaves would see and remember. Recent research has shown that running away was far more widespread than once thought in the antebellum South. Running away was a form of resistance that fell short of collective revolt; it was an act of individual, non-organized rebellion against the oppression brought by slavery. Slaves ran away not just in response to particularly harsh treatment, but also when they thought they had the opportunity to escape slavery, either because of the sudden death of their master, the careless management of an overseer, or simply because – if they lived in border states – they had a greater chance of reaching the North. Once on the run, slaves usually had very little chance of reaching freedom if they were in the South; there were very few places where they could hide for a long time without being discovered. Most runaways managed to stay away from the plantation for only a few days or, at best, a few weeks; they either returned by themselves, after seeing the impossibility of surviving an escape without starving to death, or they were discovered by the slave-catchers hired by their masters or by the slave patrols.

To transform these acts of individual resistance into a collective rebellion, however, was an entirely different matter. Although there were 4 million slaves in the South in 1860, they were still a minority compared to the white population, which was double their number. More important, blacks were a minority in most of the states. Also, most slaves lived with a few others on small farms and plantations, where they were closely watched and supervised by overseers and masters; they had very little chance of becoming acquainted with other slaves, let alone organizing a revolt. The only successful rebellion was that led by Nat Turner in Southampton County, Virginia, in 1831. It occurred in an isolated and backward region with a small, sparse population of a few thousand. The landscape consisted of a forest with a few isolated farms, with most of the slave-owners holding from 10 to 20 slaves. The ratio of slaves to whites, however, was significant, since there were 6,573 whites and 7,756 slaves, plus 1,745 free blacks. Southampton County was an area with a black majority, with African Americans forming 60 percent of the total population. Nat Turner was by all measures an exceptional character. From childhood he had shown signs of extraordinary intelligence, and his mother was deeply convinced that he would become a prophet. Accordingly, he developed an austere life-style based on religious texts and principles; he gradually became convinced that he had been divinely chosen to fight slavery. From the 1820s onwards Nat Turner experienced a series of divine revelations – visions in which he saw a supernatural entity, which he called the Spirit, who urged him to leave earthly concerns and seek the Kingdom of Heaven. In time, the visions became increasingly focused on the fight against the Serpent

– a metaphor for slavery – and Turner believed and convinced his followers that he had been chosen to carry the burden of Christ and destroy the Serpent. Between August 21 and 22, 1831 – after a solar eclipse – Turner and 70 of his followers rose and killed 60 whites before the local militia could restore order. Turner himself was captured and hanged on November 5, 1831.

Further reading

Egerton, D., *Gabriel's Rebellion* (Chapel Hill: University of North Carolina Press, 1993).

Franklin, J. H. and Schweninger, L., *Runaway Slaves: Rebels on the Plantation* (New York and Oxford: Oxford University Press, 1999).

Genovese, E. D., *From Rebellion to Revolution: Afro-American Slave Revolts in the Making of the Modern World* (Baton Rouge: Louisiana State University Press, 1979).

Genovese, E. D., *Roll, Jordan, Roll: The World the Slaves Made* (New York: Pantheon Books, 1974).

Greenberg, K. (ed.), *The Confessions of Nat Turner and Related Documents* (Boston and New York: St. Martin's Press, 1995).

Harding, V., *There is a River* (San Diego: Harcourt, Brace, and Company, 1984).

Jones, N., *Born a Child of Freedom, Yet a Slave* (Hanover: University Press of New England, 1992).

Oates, J. B., *The Fires of Jubilee* (New York: Harper Collins, 1990).

Robertson, D., *Denmark Vesey* (New York: Vintage, 2000).

Sidbury, J., *Ploughshares into Swords: Race, Rebellion, and Identity in Gabriel's Virginia* (New York: Cambridge University Press, 1997).

The Confessions of Nat Turner (1831)

Though published in Baltimore as if it was the work of Nat Turner, the *Confessions* was actually written by Virginia planter and lawyer Thomas Grey. In the course of three days, Grey managed to interview the rebel while he was awaiting his execution. He subsequently edited and published the manuscript, which sold thousands of copies. In editing the interview, Grey left most of the original testimony intact in the early section, in which Turner spoke about his extraordinary childhood and his "call" to become a prophet; however, he heavily intervened in the later part of the *Confessions*, where Turner described the murders of white farmers and their families, adding numerous gruesome details. It is now clear that Grey wished to appeal to his white readership through a portrayal of Nat Turner as a fanatical, mentally disturbed black whose acts were the result of madness, rather than being caused by the oppression brought by slavery.

SIR, – You have asked me to give a history of the motives which induced me to undertake the late insurrection, as you call it – To do so I must go back to the days of my infancy, and even before I was born. I was thirty-one years of age the 2d of October last, and born the property of Benj. Turner, of this county. In my childhood a circumstance occurred which made an indelible impression on my mind, and laid the ground work of that enthusiasm, which has terminated so fatally to many, both white and black, and for which I am about to atone at the gallows. It is here necessary to relate this circumstance – trifling as it may seem, it was the commencement of that belief which has grown with time, and even now, sir, in this dungeon, helpless and forsaken as I am, I cannot divest myself of. Being at play with other children, when three or four years old, I was telling them something, which my mother overhearing, said it had happened before I was born – I stuck to my story, however, and related some things which went, in her opinion, to confirm it – others being called on were greatly astonished, knowing that these things had happened, and caused them to say in my hearing, I surely would be a prophet, as the Lord had shewn me things that had happened before my birth. And my father and mother strengthened me in this my first impression, saying in my presence, I was

---

Source: Kenneth Greenberg (ed.), *The Confessions of Nat Turner and Related Documents* (Boston and New York: St. Martin's Press, 1995), pp. 44–56

intended for some great purpose, which they had always thought from certain marks on my head and breast....

...As I was praying one day at my plough, the spirit spoke to me, saying "Seek ye the kingdom of Heaven and all things shall be added unto you.["] *Question* – what do you mean by the Spirit? *Ans.* The Spirit that spoke to the prophets in former days – and I was greatly astonished, and for two years prayed continually, whenever my duty would permit – and then again I had the same revelation, which fully confirmed me in the impression that I was ordained for some great purpose in the hands of the Almighty.... And about this time I had a vision – and I saw white spirits and black spirits engaged in battle, and the sun was darkened – the thunder rolled in the Heavens, and blood flowed in streams – and I heard a voice saying, "Such is your luck, such you are called to see, and let it come rough or smooth, you must surely bare it." I now withdrew myself as much as my situation would permit, from the intercourse of my fellow servants, for the avowed purpose of serving the Spirit more fully – and it appeared to me, and reminded me of the things it had already shown me, and that it would then reveal to me the knowledge of the elements, the revolution of the planets, the operation of tides, and changes of the seasons. After this revelation in the year 1825, and the knowledge of the elements being made known to me, I sought more than ever to obtain true holiness before the great day of judgment should appear, and then I began to receive the true knowledge of faith.... [A]nd the Spirit appeared to me again, and said, as the Saviour had been baptised so should we be also – and when the white people would not let us be baptised by the church, we went down into the water together, in the sight of many who reviled us, and were baptised by the Spirit – After this I rejoiced greatly, and gave thanks to God. And on the 12th of May, 1828, I heard a loud noise in the heavens, and the Spirit instantly appeared to me and said the Serpent was loosened, and Christ had laid down the yoke he had borne for the sins of men, and that I should take it on and fight against the Serpent, for the time was fast approaching when the first should be last and the last should be first....

...It was then observed that I must spill the first blood. On which, armed with a hatchet, and accompanied by Will, I entered my master's chamber, it being dark, I could not give a death blow, the hatchet glanced from his head, he sprang from the bed and called his wife, it was his last word, Will laid him dead, with a blow of his axe, and Mrs. Travis shared the same fate, as she lay in bed. The murder of this family, five in number, was the work of a moment, not one of them awoke; there was a little infant sleeping in a cradle, that was forgotten, until we had left the house and gone some distance, when Henry and Will returned and killed it; we got here, four guns that would shoot, and several old muskets, with a pound or two of powder. . . . Monday morning, I proceeded to Mr. Levi Waller's, two or three miles distant. I took my station in the rear, and as it 'twas my object to carry terror and devastation wherever we went, I placed fifteen or twenty of the best armed and most to be relied on, in front, who generally approached the house as fast as their horses could run; this was for two purposes, to prevent their escape and strike terror to the inhabitants – on this account I never got to the houses, after leaving Mrs. Whitehead's, until the murders were committed, except in one case. I sometimes got in sight in time to see the work of death completed, viewed the mangled bodies as they lay, in silent satisfaction, and immediately started in quest of other victims. . . . During the time I was pursued, I had many hair breadth escapes, which your time will not permit you to relate. I am here loaded with chains, and willing to suffer the fate that awaits me.

Frederick Douglass Remembers Resisting Mr. Covey (1845)

In January 1834 Frederick Douglass's master, Thomas Auld, hired him out to Edward Covey, a brutal and violent man who had a reputation as a slave-breaker. Predictably, Douglass's time at Covey's farm during the following six months, was characterized by frequent beatings. Tired of being continuously abused, Douglass resolved to run away and seek the help of his master; however, not only did Auld decline to aid him, he also ordered him to go back to Covey. When Covey tried to whip Douglass after his return, something extraordinary happened: the slave – who was only 16 – fought back and effectively prevented his master from punishing him. As Douglass explained in his autobiography, this was the turning point of his life, and the experience through which he became a man. He considered his act of resistance as an inspiring example for countless oppressed slaves, and he regularly mentioned it in the antislavery lectures he was invited to give in northern Abolitionist circles.

. . . Long before daylight, I was called to go and rub, curry, and feed, the horses. I obeyed, and was glad to obey. But whilst thus engaged, whilst in the act of throwing down some blades from the loft, Mr. Covey entered the

---

Source: Frederick Douglass, *Narrative of the Life of Frederick Douglass*, in Henry Louis Gates, Jr. (ed.), *The Classic Slave Narratives* (New York: Penguin Books, 1987), pp. 297–9.

stable with a long rope; and just as I was half out of the loft, he caught hold of my legs, and was about tying me. As soon as I found what he was up to, I gave a sudden spring, and as I did so, he holding to my legs, I was brought sprawling on the stable floor. Mr. Covey seemed now to think he had me, and could do what he pleased; but at this moment – from whence came the spirit I don't know – I resolved to fight; and, suiting my action to the resolution, I seized Covey hard by the throat; and as I did so, I rose. He held on to me, and I to him. My resistance was so entirely unexpected, that Covey seemed taken all aback. He trembled like a leaf. This gave me assurance, and I held him uneasy, causing the blood to run where I touched him with the ends of my fingers. Mr. Covey soon called out to Hughes for help. Hughes came, and, while Covey held me, attempted to tie my right hand. While he was in the act of doing so, I watched my chance, and gave him a heavy kick close under the ribs. This kick fairly sickened Hughes, so that he left me in the hands of Mr. Covey. This kick had the effect of not only weakening Hughes, but Covey also. When he saw Hughes bending over with pain, his courage quailed. He asked me if I meant to persist in my resistance. I told him I did, come what might; that he had used me like a brute for six months, and that I was determined to be used so no longer. With that, he strove to drag me to a stick that was lying just out of the stable door. He meant to knock me down. But just as he was leaning over to get the stick, I seized him with both hands by his collar, and brought him by a sudden snatch to the ground. By this time, Bill came. Covey called upon him for assistance. Bill wanted to know what he could do. Covey said, "Take hold of him, take hold of him!" Bill said his master hired him out to work, and not to help to whip me; so he left Covey and myself to fight our own battle out. We were at it for nearly two hours. Covey at length let me go, puffing and blowing at a great rate, saying that if I had not resisted, he would not have whipped me half so much. The truth was, that he had not whipped me at all. I considered him as getting entirely the worst end of the bargain; for he had drawn no blood from me, but I had from him. The whole six months afterwards, that I spent with Mr. Covey, he never laid the weight of his finger upon me in anger. He would occasionally say, he didn't want to get hold of me again. "No," thought I, "you need not; for you will come off worse than you did before."

This battle with Mr. Covey was the turning-point in my career as a slave. It rekindled the few expiring embers of freedom, and revived within me a sense of my own manhood. It recalled the departed self-confidence, and inspired me again with a determination to be free. The gratification afforded by the triumph was a full compensation for whatever else might follow, even death itself. He only can understand the deep satisfaction which I experienced, who has himself repelled by force the bloody arm of slavery. I felt as I never felt before. It was a glorious resurrection, from the tomb of slavery, to the heaven of freedom. My long-crushed spirit rose, cowardice departed, bold defiance took its place; and I now resolved that, however long I might remain a slave in form, the day had passed forever when I could be a slave in fact. I did not hesitate to let it be known of me, that the white man who expected to succeed in whipping, must also succeed in killing me.

From this time I was never again what might be called fairly whipped, though I remained a slave four years afterwards. I had several fights, but was never whipped.

Frederick Law Olmsted on Runaway Slaves in Virginia (1861)

During the antebellum period, runaway slaves became a chronic problem on southern plantations. The exhausting pace of labor and harsh discipline were among the primary reasons for running away; and even the threat of severe punishment was not always an effective deterrent. However, slaveholders believed that they treated their slaves well and that there was no reason why slaves should leave a master who fed them and did not overwork them. As a consequence, southern physicians who studied the problem – such as the one mentioned by Frederick Olmsted – argued that black slaves suffered from a particular kind of disease which caused them to feel dissatisfaction without reason and a craving for flight. Unsurprisingly, the doctors maintained that the only cure was a sound whipping. The idea of a disease-inspired running away shows how the planters' fiction of the paternalistic benefits of slavery became increasingly difficult to sustain at the end of the antebellum period.

The interruption and disarrangement of operations of labour, occasioned by slaves "running away," frequently causes great inconvenience and loss to those who employ them. It is said to often occur when no immediate motive can be guessed at for it – when the slave has been well treated, well fed, and not over-worked; and when he will be sure to suffer hardship from it, and be subject to severe punishment on his return, or if he is caught.

Source: Arthur M. Schlesinger (ed.), *The Cotton Kingdom: A Traveller's Observations on Cotton and Slavery in the American Slave States* by Frederick Law Olmsted (New York: Alfred A. Knopf, 1953), pp. 94–7

This is often mentioned to illustrate the ingratitude and especial depravity of the African race. I should suspect it to be, if it cannot be otherwise accounted for, the natural instinct of freedom in a man, working out capriciously, as the wild instincts of domesticated beasts and birds sometimes do.

But the learned Dr. [Samuel A.] Cartwright, of the University of Louisiana, believes that slaves are subject to a peculiar form of mental disease, termed by him *Drapetomania*, which, like a malady that cats are liable to, manifests itself by an irrestrainable propensity to *run away*; and in a work on the diseases of negroes [*Report on the Diseases and Physical Peculiarities of the Negro Race*, prepared for the Louisiana State Medical Society], highly esteemed at the South for its patriotism and erudition, he advises planters of the proper preventive and curative measures to be taken for it.

He asserts that, "with the advantage of proper medical advice, strictly followed, this troublesome practice of running away, that many negroes have, can be almost entirely prevented." Its symptoms and the usual empirical practice on the plantations are described: "Before negroes run away, unless they are frightened or panic-struck, they become sulky and dissatisfied. The cause of this sulkiness and dissatisfaction should be inquired into and removed, or they are apt to run away or fall into the negro consumption." When sulky or dissatisfied without cause, the experience of those having most practice with *drapetomania*, the Doctor thinks, has been in favour of "whipping them *out of it*." It is vulgarly called, "whipping the devil *out of them*," he afterwards informs us.

Another droll sort of "indisposition," thought to be peculiar to the slaves, and which must greatly affect their value, as compared with free labourers, is described by Dr. Cartwright, as follows: –

> DYSÆSTHESIA ÆTHIOPICA, or Hebetude of Mind and Obtuse Sensibility of Body.... From the careless movements of the individuals affected with this complaint, they are apt to do much mischief, which appears as if intentional, but is mostly owing to the stupidness of mind and insensibility of the nerves induced by the disease. Thus they break, waste, and destroy everything they handle – abuse horses and cattle – tear, burn, or rend their own clothing, and, paying no attention to the rights of property, steal others to replace what they have destroyed. They wander about at night, and keep in a half-nodding state by day. They slight their work – cut up corn, cane, cotton, and tobacco, when hoeing it, as if for pure mischief. They raise disturbances with their overseers, and among their fellow-servants, without cause or motive, and seem to be insensible to pain when subjected to punishment....

... There are many complaints described in Dr. Cartwright's treatise, to which the negroes, in slavery, seem to be peculiarly subject.

More fatal than any other is congestion of the lungs, *peripneumonia notha*, often called cold plague, etc....

The *Frambœsia*, Piam, or Yaws, is a *contagious* disease, communicable by contact among those who greatly neglect cleanliness. It is supposed to be communicable, in a modified form, to the white race, among whom it resembles pseudo syphilis, or some disease of the nose, throat, or larynx....

Negro-consumption, a disease almost unknown to medical men of the Northern States and of Europe, is also sometimes fearfully prevalent among the slaves. "It is of importance," says the Doctor, "to know the pathognomic signs in its early stages, not only in regard to its treatment, but to detect impositions, as negroes afflicted with this complaint are often for sale; the acceleration of the pulse, on exercise, incapacitates them for labour, as they quickly give out, and have to leave their work. This induces their owners to sell them, although they may not know the cause of their inability to labour. Many of the negroes brought South, for sale, are in the incipient stages of this disease; they are found to be inefficient labourers, and are sold in consequence thereof. The effect of superstition – a firm belief that he is poisoned or conjured – upon the patient's mind, already in a morbid state (dysæsthesia), and his health affected from hard usage, over-tasking or exposure, want of wholesome food, good clothing, warm, comfortable lodging, with the distressing idea (sometimes) that he is an object of hatred or dislike, both to his master or fellow-servants, and has no one to befriend him, tends directly to generate that erythism of mind which is the essential cause of negro-consumption."... "Remedies should be assisted by removing the *original cause* of the dissatisfaction or trouble of mind, and by using every means to make the patient comfortable, satisfied, and happy."

Longing for home generates a distinct malady, known to physicians as *Nostalgia*, and there is a suggestive analogy between the treatment commonly employed to cure it and that recommended in this last advice of Dr. Cartwright.

The Impact of Runaway Slaves on the Slave System

John Hope Franklin and Loren Schweninger

In *Runaway Slaves*, John Hope Franklin and Loren Schweninger analyze in detail the most common form of slave rebellion, and argue that running away was a

John Hope Franklin and Loren Schweninger, *Runaway Slaves: Rebels on the Plantation* (New York and Oxford: Oxford University Press, 1999), pp. 263–94.

much more widespread and significant act of resistance than previously thought. Franklin and Schweninger also show how running away became such a chronic problem that slaveholders tried to prevent it – without success – both by an increasingly strict control of slave movement and by the threat of particularly cruel punishment. In this excerpt, Franklin and Schweninger argue that slaveholders proved incapable of coping with the problem of runaway slaves, since they never made any serious effort to understand the reasons behind it. They also correct previous statistics on the number of runaway slaves, and argue that their total figure per year during the antebellum period was actually higher than 50,000.

"DICKERSON CALLED ON ME to Know what Kind of a negro she was," explained William Butler, the son of a man who wanted to sell a female slave to Henry Dickerson of Barren County, Kentucky. They were sitting at the son's kitchen table in January 1819, waiting for the father to return with the slave. She was twenty-eight years old, strong and healthy, Butler said, and could be used as a field hand or house servant. "[H]e asked me how often she had runaway," the son recalled; two or three times he replied. When the father arrived with the woman, Dickerson scrutinized her closely. Discovering she had lost several toes on one foot from frostbite, he instructed her to take off her stocking and to walk across the floor. When she did so without a limp, he said he would take her home and try her out for a few days and if he liked her he would buy her. The next morning, Dickerson returned, said he would take her and promised to pay $600 in two installments for the slave woman Rody.[1]

Within a short time, Rody ran away, was captured, and ran away again. Indeed, it soon became apparent that "she was in the habit of running away & staying out . . . for weeks & months at a time." She absconded so often and stayed out so long each time that Dickerson thought she was mentally unbalanced and doubted whether she was "capable of proper reflection & judgment." If this were not enough, he now recalled what he had been told at the time of the purchase: Butler assured him that he "had never whiped said negro that she was no eye servant but was industrious & attentive to business & require no looking after." In truth, as he discovered in an interview with one of Butler's neighbors, she had been whipped repeatedly, and after each whipping, she had run away. Discovering this, he refused to pay the balance on his note. When he went to Adair County, where Butler lived, to confront Butler, he discovered that Butler himself had departed for Tennessee. There was now nothing left for him to do except send the slave to the New Orleans market. It took him a year before he sold her, and when he did, she brought only 40 percent of the original purchase price.[2] Even with his refusal to make full payment and with money from the sale, Dickerson had lost a substantial amount, paying for her capture, transportation, food and clothing, as well as the auctioneer's fees and other expenses in New Orleans.

Dishonor among masters

William Butler and his father's duplicity in dealing with a potential buyer was by no means unique in the slave South. Many other owners were equally deceptive. Putting slaves up for auction or approaching individual buyers, they rarely admitted, much less advertised, their slaves as habitual runaways. To do so would make a potential sale difficult, and even if it could be consummated, the price would certainly fall below market value. Slaves known as "runners" lost a significant percentage of their market value and were often difficult to sell. If word got out that a slave was rebellious or had attacked whites, it might be impossible to consummate a sale. . . .

The domestic slave trade was fed in part by masters seeking to rid themselves of unmanageable and unruly slaves by selling them to distant markets. Even in local markets, however, owners disguised the fact that they were selling runaways. As a number of lawsuits suggest, masters frequently sold runaways to unsuspecting buyers. . . . In their discussions concerning "a negro Fellow named Will," owner William Harris told the prospective buyer that the slave was "a faithful industrious and honest fellow and might be depended on as an excellent Plantation Negro." Henry Peeples, a planter in Greene County, Georgia, accepted the owner's word and purchased Will in September 1802 for $600. It did not take him long to realize that he had been duped. The black man was "lazy rougueish & unfaithful in every respect & one whom it was impossible to keep at his work he ever being disposed to Elope." In his equity court suit, Harris noted that Will had "repeatedly runaway" and by his "profligate conduct in this and many other respects" had become entirely "useless."[3]

The same scenario was repeated in West Baton Rouge Parish, Louisiana, in 1820, when Sebastian Hiriart, a planter, crossed the Mississippi River to purchase "a certain negro fellow," about twenty-two years of age. Hiriart promised to pay $1,020 in two equal installments a year apart. The "negro fellow" was represented as a "prime specimen," and Hiriart paid nearly twice the going rate. He soon discovered, however, that he had been swindled. Not only was the slave a habitual runaway, but when brought to Hiriart's plantation, he refused to respond to any command. Indeed, the new owner thought he was deaf. The slave was "of no use or service." In Maryland, Charles Digges of Prince George's County bought the unexpired term of the twenty-three-year-old slave Enoch in 1848 for $300. In making payments of $40 a year until the term of servitude ended in 1856, there was a good possibility that the owner would make a profit. A strong, young male slave would bring three times that amount in annual hire. But he, too, quickly discovered he had been defrauded. Enoch was a habitual runaway, and Digges lost a substantial amount trying to hire him out.[4] In these and other cases, angry and hostile slave owners told of misrepresentation, deceit, and fraud. When sold, slaves were described as hardworking, trustworthy, and submissive. The new owners soon discovered just the opposite was true. . . .

Some owners went to great lengths to conceal their slaves' behavior patterns. The conversation between the agent of a Missouri planter and a commission merchant and auctioneer in New Orleans revealed how far some owners were willing to go to rid themselves of chronic runaways. "I was about to sell said Slave Lewis to a respectable man, a friend of mine," the auctioneer reported, and he asked the owner's agent "to be candid in his representations of said slave Lewis." He wished to know his character, as the law of the state differed from the common law. He wanted a guarantee that the slave was "free of vices and maladies according to the law of Louisiana." This meant the slave had to be certified against insanity, leprosy, consumption, ill-health, and running away. The agent told the auctioneer that the slave in question had "no faults and no vices" and was "a good plantation negro."[5] The auctioneer's friend, Henry Crane, purchased Lewis in early 1851 with a full warranty.

Within days, Lewis absconded. It was an especially cold January, and by the time he was captured, after being out for some time, Lewis had developed a deep and persistent cough. Taken to the slave pen, he got dysentery. Crane was so outraged that he booked passage for the slave and himself on an upriver steamer, to return Lewis to his owner in Ste. Genevieve, Missouri. Within a short time, however, the slave died. A postmortem examination revealed that Lewis was "weak and greatly emaciated," his right lung was "absorbed and wasted in great part" with "numerous abscesses" and filled with "tuberculous matter." Though he had died of consumption, the physician said, Lewis had an enlarged liver and several ounces of a reddish fluid in the "penicardicum." In a civil litigation . . . Crane charged that he been duped: he was sold a seriously ill slave who was "addicted to the habit of running away."[6]

The sale and resale of runaways reached such dimensions in Louisiana that lawmakers listed running away, along with ill-health and disease, as a "redhibitory" vice. Even if a purchaser could not prove that a slave had previously run away, the presumption of guilt on the part of the seller was assumed if the slave absconded within a few months after the sale. . . .

To allay the fears of slave owners in the Lower Mississippi River Valley, slave traders in the upper states obtained sworn affidavits that the slaves they offered were not habitual runaways. "We, John Porter and James Porter freeholders in the County of Shelby and State aforesaid [Kentucky], do certify that a certain negro Man slave for life, aged about twenty-six years named John about five feet 7 or 8 inches high, dark complected, and is a good field hand," one such affidavit on a printed form stated in 1829, "that he has not, within their knowledge, been guilty or convicted of any crime – but that he has, on the contrary, a good moral character – and that he is not in the habit of running away." Virginia traders, too, printed up affidavits during the 1820s stating that slaves were not habitual runaways. Such documents, signed by prominent "freeholders," justices of the peace, clerks of court, and magistrates, accompanied bills of sale to Mississippi and Louisiana.[7]

Even with such safeguards, the buying and selling of runaways continued apace. Those who transported slaves from one state to another could be miles away when it was discovered that the slave sold as a "prime" and "likely" field hand was, in fact, a habitual absconder. Even when buyers were able to bring their cases to court, it was nearly impossible to recoup their losses. . . . Nor were judgments easy to collect even when the seller lived in the same jurisdiction. A West Baton Rouge Parish man said he had been put to "great expense in paying charges & pursuing him the sd Slave when he has been runaway." Even with a favorable court order for repayment, he was unable to force the seller to repay what he had lost. . . . In other instances, there were suits, countersuits, trials, retrials, appeals, temporary injunctions, confiscations of property, and years of bitter litigation.[8] . . .

Not only did owners misrepresent their slaves, a few owner-traders dealt largely in buying and selling runaways. This was risky and highly speculative, but the profits from purchasing obstreperous slaves in one area and selling them as "prime" and "likely" hands in another could be substantial, especially during the 1840s and 1850s as demand in the west drove prices spiraling upward. . . . Other masters who were in the process of buying and selling slaves kept a sharp eye out for the profits that they might gain by purchasing runaways in one section of the South and selling them in distant markets at inflated prices. . . .

To mislead potential buyers, false papers, improper titles, and fraudulent references could be obtained. At times, traders bought slaves without papers or abducted them for resale. It was not usually masters who became involved in such unseemly conduct, but occasionally slave owners themselves stole other owners' slaves. John Peters of Florence, Alabama, wrote Governor A. P. Bagby in 1839 about a Kentucky owner who stole several of his mother's slaves. Peters instituted a suit in Kentucky to reclaim his mother's property. "I was influenced by those considerations wch address the feeling interest and patriotism of every Southerner upon any invasion of this species of our property," Peters wrote as he sought assistance from the governor. Slaveholders must be protected in their possession of slave property "as guaranteed to us by Solemn Compact and the fundamental laws of this Govt."[9]

But slave stealing and kidnapping occurred frequently in various parts of the South. Isaac Briggs, a planter in both Maryland and Georgia, explained that there were many "avaricious and unprincipled" whites who abducted blacks – "some free, some manumitted to be free in a limited time, and some slaves." They transported them to different parts of the South, then secretly took them before a magistrate and, for a price, secured false titles and other legal documents saying that they were the owners of the slaves. . . . Kidnappers carried on a brisk traffic in people of color, Briggs asserted. It was so brisk that in some sections even legitimate owners were put on the defensive. When the runaway Alabama slave Ben was sold out of the Pikeville jail in 1836, Jeremiah Pritchett, Ben's owner, not only failed to prove ownership but was accused of perfidy. "Is Pritchett held among his acquaintances as an honest, honorable man?" the court asked. "Is he a man of Known truth? Is he or not to be fully credited on his word or his oath?" Pritchett described Ben, produced a bill of sale, and brought witnesses to back up his story. "You put me to the trouble to prove my character," he wrote the judge of the Marengo Country Court, assuring him that he would never lie about such a matter "for what wd it proffit me to gain the whole world and lose my own soul."[10]

Others were less concerned with quoting Scripture than profiting from the sale of runaways. In 1808, Dr. John Newnan, a physician in Johnson City, Tennessee, sold farmer Thomas Stewart a slave woman without informing him that she was in a Salisbury, North Carolina, jail under arrest as a runaway. The doctor also sold to the same farmer the woman's daughter, who had been left behind. The woman was returned to Tennessee and delivered to Stewart. When he learned he had bought a fugitive, he refused to pay, but neither would he return the slaves. Newnan hired an agent to retrieve his property. When the agent appeared, Stewart "got into a passion" and took him into the kitchen "& taking hold of said Negros by the hand Viz Rachel & Patt he said 'here I deliver these negros to you as the property of Dr. Newnan.'" But before the agent could take them away, the farmer's son, Montgomery Stewart, appeared and refused to turn over mother and daughter. It was sometime later that Dr. Newnan himself, in the middle of the night, crept onto the Stewart farm, "kidnapped" Rachel and her daughter, and took them to Nashville for auction.[11]

That a prominent physician would sneak onto another man's farm in the middle of the night to retrieve his slave property and then set out under cover of darkness to a city halfway across the state to auction Rachel and her daughter to the highest bidder reveals the impact runaways had on the slaveholding class. The selling of runaways and the deception involved in this case were by no means unique. Indeed, one could argue that men and women who owned other human beings often found themselves in a position where even the most honorable among them were forced into acts of dishonor and deception. In the sale of runaways, such was often the case.

The conspiracy theory

Slave owners seemed to find it difficult to understand why so many slaves ran away. It was one thing for a few vicious, unruly, and unmanageable slaves to leave the plantation, but most, they argued, were gentle, obedient, and happy. How was it that such a contended group, sometimes even the most skilled and privileged among them, took their leave without uttering a word? Masters admitted that some slaves wanted to be with loved ones, take a holiday, and avoid hard work. They also admitted that some slaves found it difficult to make proper decisions, had some "defect" in their personalities, or suffered from depression or other mental problems. Little Charles stole away from his Louisiana plantation and broke into a meathouse on a neighboring farm. When he was caught and whipped by three white men and still ran away again, his master said he suffered from "mental alienation" and "fits of insanity."[12]

The "mental alienation" theory was given scientific authority by Dr. Samuel Cartwright, a prominent New Orleans physician. In an article in *De Bow's Review* in 1851, Cartwright explained that many slaves suffered from "drapetomania, or the disease causing negroes to run away."... Absconding from service was "as much a disease of the mind as any other species of mental alienation," Cartwright wrote.... To cure the disease, Cartwright proposed that owners provide slaves with adequate food, housing, and fuel. If the disease persisted, however, owners should whip them until they fell "into that submissive state which it was intended for them to occupy in all aftertime."[13]

Whatever the reason, slave owners believed it was not because most blacks disliked slavery or their masters and mistresses. When a Virginia runaway burned down the jail to effect his escape, his owner insisted that he did not do so out of any "malice." Some owners felt their runaways had simply made a childish mistake and would return if given an opportunity. "Should Nancy return of her own accord," a South Carolina owner explained in an advertisement, "she will be forgiven and likewise furnished with a ticket to find another owner if required." Almost exactly the same words were used by other slave owners seeking a return of their property: "If he returns of his own accord, he will be forgiven," "If Prince will return to me in two weeks, there shall be no questions asked." ... Such "compassion" stemmed from the belief that these slaves were not unhappy with their lot but were irresponsible or unstable.[14]

Even after many months, sometimes years, owners continued to hold out hope that their runaways would come to their senses and return of their own accord. They continued to reject the notion that their slaves actually wanted to be free. Charleston owner William H. Smith tried everything to prevent his slave Tenah from running away, but nothing seemed to work. She had absconded on several occasions, each time remaining away for several months. When she left during a trip to Barnwell District in 1830, Smith offered a $100 reward. Six months later, he still could not believe she wished to be permanently free. "[I]f she comes in of her own accord, within one month from this time, no punishment will be inflicted, and she shall have a ticket to select an owner in the city." If not, however, he would have her "transported beyond the limits of the State."[15]

If it were not slave owners, then who was at fault? Masters often pointed to slaves from outside the United States, intruders from the North, free blacks, or a few lawless whites. These groups did not understand the master–slave relationship or that most slaves were contented. Rather, they sought to stir up discontent. In 1793, slave owners in South Carolina observed that slaves were becoming increasingly insolent and aggressive. The militia was put on standby. It was widely believed that "the St. Domingo negroes" – those imported from the Caribbean – were sowing the "seeds of revolt." They were doubtless influenced by black revolutionary Toussaint L'Ouverture. During the 1790s, some southern states restricted the entry of black people from the West Indies. In the early nineteenth century, slave owners pointed to "French Negroes," those from French possessions in the Caribbean, as continuing to foment unrest among the slaves in the southern states. They observed that slave revolts were often organized and planned by runaways.[16]

To others, it was not French-speaking Caribbean blacks who were inciting slaves to run away. Instead, it was whites from the North. In 1804, a group of fifty-four residents of Richmond, Virginia, accused northern ship captains of corrupting the morals of their slaves. Trading vessels from New York and the New England states frequently moved up the James, York, Rappahannock, and Potomac rivers; the captains of these ships, the group of Richmonders asserted, tried to inculcate in the "weak minds" of slaves a spirit of "discontent, tending to insurrection," and in many instances enticed them to abscond. [...] The same arguments appeared in later years, during tranquil and tumultuous times, in the Upper and Lower South, along the seaboard and in the interior.[17] ...

The theory of meddlesome intruders corrupting the morals of slaves could be seen in the attitudes of individual slave owners. Virtually all misbehavior by slaves against their masters – violence, insurrection plots, running away – was ascribed by Rachel O'Connor, the mistress of Evergreen Plantation in Louisiana, to evil and diabolic nonslaveholding whites. When slaves absconded in the Feliciana parishes in 1835, she observed that "mean white men" were the "sole cause of all." When a slave woman assaulted her mistress on a nearby plantation, O'Connor wrote: "I have no doubt, of some mean white man being the cause of the trouble." And when a group of slaves along Thompson's Creek conspired to revolt, she had little doubt that the plot was instigated by two white men who "made their escape."[18]

In their runaway notices, some masters also revealed their belief that their slaves would never run off on their own. "I have no doubt but they are conducted by some villain," Jesse Williams said in 1813 of the two field hands he had recently purchased for his plantation in Logan County, Kentucky. They were both "keen and sensible." Why would they want to run away? ... Others said they had last observed their slaves with whites, had noticed white men "lurking about the plantation" shortly before a slave absconded, had a feeling their slaves were being "persuaded away" by whites, or learned that their slaves had been promised passage "out of the state" by whites.[19] ...

If slaves eluded capture, or made difficult escapes, masters said they must have done so with the aid of outsiders. Late one night, George, who managed his master's financial affairs, led his wife, three children, a grandchild, and a ten-year-old black girl away from the master's plantation in Jefferson County, Florida. His owner immediately said that George must have been "backed by some white man, who will try to carry the negroes out of the country."[20]

Rumors, innuendos, accusations, and false reports flourished following the departure of runaways who were thought to have been enticed away or hidden by "some designing white men." In some sections, even being accused of such activity could be disastrous. ... [T]he mere hint of collusion with runaway slaves could ruin a man's reputation, whether guilty or innocent. ... [T]he conspiracy theory was articulated so often that southerners came to believe that many of their runaways were indeed lured away. ...

Another strand of the conspiracy theory involved free persons of color. Many owners believed that free blacks were loyal to their slave brethren and would do anything to assist them in betraying their masters. During the 1840s and 1850s, these fears surfaced often, especially in Virginia, with its large slave population so close to the North. A group of slave owners recommended that the time period slaves be allowed to remain in the state after emancipation be reduced from twelve months to one month. That would not allow the emancipated sufficient time to become acquainted with the roads through the mountains, and they could not "purloin off our slaves and reach a free state." ... White Virginians should also be watchful for free people of color arriving from northern cities, another group warned, for the black intruders sowed seeds of "discord and disaffection" among the slaves.[21]

It is not difficult to understand how slave owners became so attached to the conspiracy theory. It fitted neatly into their political struggle with the North; it absolved them of blame for slave discontent; and it offered a simple explanation for a complex human problem. Thus, despite the profusion of runaways in their midst, they could deny that blacks were resisting slavery.

Estimating frequencies and owners' costs

Among the first things J. D. B. DeBow did after arriving in Washington, DC, in 1853 as superintendent of the United States Census was to oversee the publication of *A Compendium of the Seventh Census*. Coming from New Orleans, where he had spent seven years as founder and editor of *DeBow's Review*, a journal strong in the defense of slavery, DeBow was now in a position to strengthen his defense. One of the questions census marshals asked slave owners in 1850 was how many bondsmen and bondswomen had run away during the previous year and had remained at large? In DeBow's opinion, the statistics compiled from the question offered further evidence of the benign nature of southern slavery: in Alabama, the number of successful fugitives stood at 29, in Arkansas 21, Florida 18, South Carolina 16, and there were fewer than a hundred each in Kentucky, Louisiana, and Georgia. Maryland led all states with 279, and the South's total stood at only 1,011. A decade later, census takers counted even fewer fugitives. During the year ending 1 June 1860, among 3,949,577 slaves, the census said, there were only 803 escaped slaves who remained at large, about one in every 5,000 blacks, or one-fiftieth of one percent.

Marshals asked slaveholders to list their runaways. The replies not only produced flawed results, but the narrowly constructed question about those still at large failed even to hint at the magnitude of the problem. From various primary and secondary sources, several generalizations can be made about the size of the runaway population. First, while the number of newspaper notices for fugitives increased with the expansion of the slave population between 1790 and 1860, only a small fraction of runaways was advertised. Second, the journals, diaries, correspondence, and records of slaveholders indicate that it was a rare master who could boast that none of his slaves had absconded. In fact, the vast majority admitted just the opposite. Third, some farmers and planters owned "habitual" runaways, slaves that set out on numerous occasions and were usually sold or severely punished or both. Such slaves ran off two, three, four, or more times each year. Thus, while runaways constituted a small minority of the slave population, they were of enormous significance in the plantation universe.

It will never be known how many slaves ran away at any given time, but the following examples from a group of small slaveholders, from an industrial master, and from one large plantation were unexceptional. When Maryland farmer William Biggs died and left his estate to his widow, Catherine, under the supervision of his son-in-law, one of the first things the son-in-law did was to seek to "recover some slaves who had runaway some time ago." Similarly, in the reports of guardians for children who owned slaves there is commentary on runaways. . . . Among the eleven slaves in the estate of Isaac B. Nelson, a Giles County, Tennessee, farmer who died in 1854, was Isaac, who ran away five times in a single year, lying out weeks at a time during all seasons. For farmers and small planters, the record book of Basil Kiger during a two-year period reveals what many others experienced. He made the following payments, as they appeared in his record book:[22]

Sept 11th	[1849]	To cash pd. jail fees for Ezekiel	14[.]25
	[1849]	To cash pd [jail fees] Archy	17[.]17 . . .
[Oct.] 26	[1849]	To Cash paid Mrs Collins Boy For runaway	5[.]00
Augst 16	[1850]	To Cash paid. Runaway Negroes	18[.]00 . . .
[May] 1st.	[1851]	To Cash Paid for catching Isham	5[.]00 . . .
Oct 12	[1851]	To Cash Paid Expenses for Runaway	13[.]00

. . . An inventory of slaves on Homestead Plantation in St. James Parish, Louisiana, in December 1860, illustrates the problem of runaways on a large plantation. The slaves were owned by Reine Welham, the widow of William P. Welham, and as was the case on other sugar plantations, men outnumbered women. But among a total of 125 slaves, there were twenty-two family units. Only three women had husbands living elsewhere, and there were only five orphaned youngsters. The adults worked as cooks, gardeners, washerwomen, house servants, carpenters, nurse, cooper, hostler, driver, sugar maker, plant foreman, water carrier, and field hands. The ages of the slaves reveal a remarkably stable slave community: Old Sandy, a gardener, was eighty-five, there was one slave in her seventies, several in their sixties, eighteen in their fifties, and the same in their forties. Most labor in the cane fields was performed by the fifty slaves in their teens, twenties, and thirties.

Homestead was a typical large plantation during the late antebellum period. If anything, with 60 percent of the slaves either too young (ages one to twelve) or too old (over forty) to perform exhaustive labor in the fields, it was more benign than most, and the widow Welham more caring than a majority of her fellow planters. Among the 64 male slaves at least thirteen years of age, 4 were listed as "Runaway": twenty-three-year-old Henry Smith; Washington Jr., the same age; John Miles Jr.; and his father, forty-one-year-old John Miles Sr. . . . Among the 32 women in the same age group, none was cited as a runaway. Thus, about 4 percent of slaves age thirteen and older had absconded.[23]

While it is not possible to use percentages or proportions over two generations for the South as a whole, . . . if anything, Welham's experience with runaways would represent the conservative side of the compendium. This was certainly the case in several Mississippi counties during the 1850s, when sheriffs and magistrates used printed forms to process the volume of runaway slaves committed to jail in their jurisdictions.

Touring the South during the 1850s, Frederick Law Olmsted asserted that on every large or moderate plantation he visited masters complained about runaways. Even in sections of the Deep South where blacks had "no prospect of finding shelter within hundreds of miles, or of long avoiding recapture and severe punishment, many slaves had a habit of frequently making efforts to escape temporarily from their ordinary condition of subjection." . . . It should be kept in mind that "throughout the South," Olmsted concluded, "slaves are accustomed to 'run away.' "[24]

Olmsted was essentially correct. A close examination of planters' records, runaway advertisements, county court petitions, and other primary sources reveals that it was an unusual planter (generally defined as one with twenty or more slaves) who could boast that none of his or her slaves had ever run off. Indeed, many confronted the problem at least once or twice a year, and a few struggled to control a plague of runaways. Nor was it uncommon for blacks to flee from slaveholders who owned fewer than twenty slaves. These owners too often faced severe problems with runaways.

In 1860, there were about 385,000 slave owners in the South, among whom about 46,000 were planters. Even if only half of all planters experienced a single runaway in a year, and if only 10 or 15 percent of other slaveholders faced the same problem (both extremely conservative estimates) the number of runaways annually would exceed 50,000. Add to this the number of slaves who, like Sam King on Morville Plantation, continually ran away, and it becomes clear that Olmsted's impressionistic observation was far more accurate than the "scientific" data provided in the United States Census.

Just as the exact number of runaways will never be known, neither can we know for certain the financial losses suffered by slaveholders. But here, too, several generalizations can be made from circumstantial evidence. First, most runaways remained out only a few weeks or months and so the loss to planters was primarily a loss of labor. Second, comparatively few runaways were successful in their bid for freedom, and thus the capital losses remained minimal. Third, while running away could not be eliminated, it could be controlled with relatively modest financial outlays. Fourth, the average reward offered for advertised slaves (fifteen dollars in the early period and twenty-five dollars in the later period, including those who offered no reward) represented a tiny fraction (less than 5 percent) of the value of the slaves....

...[O]ther costs were less readily evident. Slaveowners struggled to maintain an efficient workforce, but the time and energy they spent coping with the runaway problem caused inefficiency. This could be seen not only in the loss of labor, which for small planters could be substantial, but in the turmoil runaways created when they abandoned the plantation. In addition, owners were beset by a constant loss of their property – their own stolen slaves, items pilfered from their plantations, and runaways. Indeed, the clandestine slave economy in some sections was maintained and sustained by outlying slaves. Nor is it easy to measure the cost of living in the midst of violence, hostility, and subversive activity.

The impact of runaways on the peculiar institution

The determination of masters to rid themselves of persistent runaways, the formulation of a conspiracy theory, and costs associated with runaways reveal only part of the impact this group had on the institution of slavery. Masters were forced to explain how "contented" and "well cared for" servants abandoned them in such large numbers. Not a few owners concluded that slaves who ran away on numerous occasions or who failed to change their behavior after severe punishments were insane, imbalanced, or suffered mental "afflictions." That so many slaves apparently suffered from the same affliction was difficult to explain. Also difficult to understand was the flight of so many apparently loyal and obsequious slaves. Bequeathed from father to son, the thirty-two-year-old Maryland slave Annetta Irvine had lived with the same family most of her life. A few years before her term of servitude was to end, as stipulated in the father's will, she ran away to Pennsylvania. The family expressed dismay that she would demonstrate such ingratitude after they had treated her so well. She was soon caught and returned, however, and her term of servitude extended ten years.[25]

As suggested by the response of this Maryland family, the impact of fugitives on the attitudes of the master class was profound. At the heart of the slave system was the need to control laborers and produce profits. Both seemed to be jeopardized by the behavior of runaways. Substantial energy and time were devoted to the question of how to control the movement of slaves. Planters prohibited them from leaving their plantations without written permission, instructed overseers and managers to watch the slave quarters at night, and joined militia and patrols to keep the peace and capture runaways. They supported city ordinances and state laws designed to regulate and control the movement of slaves. They warned ship captains and steamboat owners about the penalties of harboring escaped slaves. Authorities in Richmond, Charleston, Savannah, New Orleans, and other cities made concerted efforts to prevent slaves from sneaking aboard ocean-going vessels. They watched harbors and estuaries at night for possible hideaways. They created a system whereby slaves who ran away and were jailed could be returned to their owners at a relatively small cost. They supported a group of professional slave hunters willing to travel substantial distances and go to great lengths to recover the owner's property.

Despite these and other attempts at control, the escapes continued. So prevalent were runaways in some sections that whites became anxious, even fearful. . . . They were especially apprehensive following revolts and conspiracies in the nineteenth century, such as the Gabriel plot in 1800, the revolt in Louisiana in 1811, the Denmark Vesey conspiracy in 1822, and the Nat Turner revolt in 1831. They were also anxious when groups of runaways committed various "depredations" in their neighborhoods. Despite their insistence that their own servants would never become involved in such activity, slave owners spoke of the possibility of "conspiracy" and "insurrection," of slaves who were "pround & malignant, with great impudence," of the "plotting and conspiring" to murder whites.[26] . . .

What weighed most heavily on the minds of slave owners and, indeed, contributed to their increasing defense of southern civilization, was the knowledge that so many slaves were neither docile nor submissive. Runaways symbolized the very aspect of bondage that they could not reconcile with their belief that slavery was beneficial for both master and slave. Few owners were unaware of the dissatisfaction or hostility among some of their slaves. Yet they could not publicly, or even privately, admit that such widespread unrest existed. To do so would undermine the very foundations of their arguments about slaves and slavery.

The influence that runaways exerted on their fellow slaves is difficult to assess. The harsh reprisals meted out to slaves who ran away and were caught and brought back were designed in part to dissuade others from following in their footsteps. There was also fear and at times resentment among those who remained behind because they were punished for the actions of absconders. Yet, most slaves had genuine sympathy, compassion, and hidden admiration for those who defied the system in such a manner. It was painful to watch the beatings and whipping of runaways, especially if they were kin or close friends, but those who remained on the plantation secretly cheered their brethren who remained at large for weeks and months or never returned.

Even slaves who were captured and punished on a regular basis could count on support from their fellow slaves. Such was the case on James Henry Hammond's Silver Bluff Plantation on the Savannah River in South Carolina. Between 1831 and 1855, there was an average of two escapes per year (a total of fifty-three). The runaways did not fit precisely into the profile described earlier, being slightly older (average age thirty-three compared with twenty-seven), slightly more male (84 percent compared with 81 percent) and probably remaining out longer (an average of forty-nine days). Yet, they were typical in most respects, especially for the Lower South: not a single runaway gained permanent freedom, one-third of them came in of their own accord, and they received sustenance, support, and encouragement from slaves on the plantation. This happened despite the fact that Hammond was well aware that those who deserted were "lurking" about in a nearby swamp. He waged a continuous but unsuccessful battle to stop the flow of food and provisions to outlying blacks, including punishing the other slaves with more work – plantation management was "like a war without the glory" he ruefully commented – but the blacks remained loyal to their brethren and continued to supply them....

Ironically, running away in this respect brought slaves together. There were few slaves who could not picture themselves in the same position as those who were striking out for freedom. At times this commiseration and empathy, as on Silver Bluff... plantations, translated into practical support. Plantation slaves harbored runaways from other plantations, protected, clothed, and fed them, and offered information about routes of travel. Some fugitives hid out for many weeks, even months, on neighboring plantations. Considering the possible reprisals for engaging in such activity, the support given in this manner was remarkable. The bonds forged were strong ones, born in crisis and hardened by the fear of retribution.

Perhaps the greatest impact runaways had on the peculiar institution – among whites and blacks alike – was in their defiance of the system. Masters and slaves knew that there were blacks who were willing to do almost anything to extricate themselves from bondage. They ran away again and again, and in some cases were willing to sacrifice their lives. Being transported from Jefferson Parish, Louisiana, back to New Orleans by a local sheriff, George leaped into the swift-flowing Mississippi River in 1852, swam a short distance, and went under. Others also "unexpectedly jumped overboard" and were lost when it was apparent they would be returned to their former master or sold away from a husband or wife. A few committed suicide rather than remain enslaved. Such was the case for Bush, an Arkansas slave who hid out on a mail boat going up the Ohio River from Louisville to Cincinnati but was discovered as the boat came into port. Taken into custody, he was placed in a yawl; as they rowed toward shore, Bush jumped overboard and immediately sank. "Strange story," wrote the wife of the Arkansas planter whose brother owned the runaway, "Bush such a capital swimmer, and drowned in 5 feet of water!"[27]

In their escape attempts, most slaves neither died nor committed suicide, but the number who made it as far as Bush – from the Deep South to the Ohio shoreline and beyond – remained very small. Among those who did, perhaps none expressed himself more clearly and forcefully about the meaning of freedom than Frederick County, Virginia, runaway Joseph Taper, who wrote a letter to a white acquaintance in 1840 tracing his escape, near capture, stay in Pennsylvania, and arrival in Canada . . . Forced to flee "in consequence of bad usage," Taper ran off to the North in 1837, taking his wife and children. During a two-week stay in Somerset County, Pennsylvania, he read his own runaway notice in a local newspaper. When he was in Pittsburgh, he learned of the presence of George Cremer, a slave-catcher hunting "runaway servants." In August 1839, he took his family to St. Catherines, Ontario, rented a farm, and raised a crop of potatoes, corn, buckwheat, and oats, acquiring seventeen hogs and seventy chickens.

St Catherines W C, Nov 11th 1840

Dear Sir,

I now take this opportunity to inform you that I am in a land of liberty, in good health. After I left Winchester I staid in Pensylvania two years, & there met some of your neighbors who lived in the house opposite you, & they were very glad to see me; from there I moved to this place where I arrived in the month of August 1839.

I worked in Erie Penn where I met many of our neighbors from New Town. I there received 26 dollars a month

Since I have been in the Queens dominions I have been well contented, Yes well contented for Sure, man is as God intended he should be. That is, all are born free & equal. This is a wholesome law, not like the Southern laws which puts man made in the image of God, on level with brutes. O, what will become of the people, & where will they stand in the day of Judgment. Would that the 5th verse of the 3d chapter of Malachi were written as with the bar of iron, & the point of a diamond upon every oppressers heart that they might repent of this evil, & let the oppressed go free. I wish you might tell Addison John, & Elias to begin to serve the Lord in their youth, & be prepared for death, which they cannot escape, & if they are prepared all will be well, if not they must according to scripture be lost forever, & if we do not meet in this world I hope we shall meet in a better world when parting shall be no more....

We have good schools, & all the colored population supplied with schools. My boy Edward who will be six years next January, is now reading, & I intend keeping him at school until he becomes a good scholar.

I have enjoyed more pleasure with one month here than in all my life in the land of bondage....

My wife and self are sitting by a good comfortable fire happy, knowing that there are none to molest [us] or make [us] afraid. God save Queen Victoria, The Lord bless her in this life, & crown her with glory in the world to come is my prayer,

Yours With much respect
most obt, Joseph Taper[28]

Notes

1 Testimony of William Butler, ca. 1821, in Records of the Circuit Court, Barren County, Kentucky, Equity Judgments, *Henry Dickerson vs. John Butler*, July 9, 1821, Case # 192, reel #209,794, KDLA [Kentucky Department for Library and Archives, Frankfort, Ky.].

2 Petition of Henry Dickerson to the Circuit Court, in Records of the Circuit Court, Barren County, Kentucky, Equity Judgments, *Henry Dickerson vs. John Butler*, July 9, 1821, Case #192, reel #209,794, KDLA.

3 Records of the Superior Court, Greene County, Georgia, *Henry Peeples vs. William Harris*, August 1803, in Record Book 1803–1806, pp. 498–502, and Proceedings 1803–1806, pp. 389–94, County Court House, Greensboro, Georgia.

4 Records of the Parish Court, West Baton Rouge, Louisiana, Fourth District Court, *Pailhes vs. Hiriart*, June 5, 1820, #80, Parish Court House, Port Allen, Louisiana....

5 Prince George's County Court (Court Papers, Blacks), Petition of Thomas Baldwin to the County Court, July 8, 1850, reel M-11,024, SC, MSA [Maryland State Archives, Annapolis, Md.]; Baltimore City Register of Wills (Petitions), *Michael Moan vs. William Jones*, Negro Boy, Orphans

Court of Baltimore City, April 25, 1855, reel M-11,026, SC, MSA; Records of the Parish Court, West Feliciana Parish, Louisiana, Third District Court, *Collins Blackman vs. Matthias Wicker*, August 4, 1826, #358, Parish Court House, Francisville, Louisiana; *Matthias Wicker vs. Mary Rice*, August 17, 1826, #361, in ibid.; Copy of Petition of Cezar Jackson, free man of color, to the Circuit Court of Wilkinson County, Mississippi, January 6, 1826, with the *Wicker vs. Rice* suit; Records of the Circuit Court, Ste. Genevieve County, Missouri, *Henry Crane vs. Toussaint Lahay and Eloy LeCompte*, May 3, 1851, County Court House, Ste. Genevieve, Missouri. Information about Lewis in Records of the Circuit Court, Ste. Genevieve County, Missouri; Testimony of John P. Phillips, March 25, 1852, in *Henry Crane vs. Toussaint Lahay and Eloy LeCompte*, May 3, 1851, County Court House, Ste. Genevieve, Missouri.

6 Records of the Circuit Court, Ste. Genevieve County, Missouri, *Henry Crane vs. Toussaint Lahay and Eloy LeCompte*, May 3, 1851, County Court House, Ste. Genevieve, Missouri; Records of the Circuit Court, Ste. Genevieve County Missouri, Amended Petition of Henry Crane to the Ste. Genevieve Circuit Court, December 1, 1851, County Court House, Ste. Genevieve, Missouri. . . .

7 Affidavit of John and James Porter, December 12, 1828, Sworn Before Clerk of Court, Shelby County, Kentucky, Natchez Trace Slaves and Slavery Collection, Center for American History, University of Texas at Austin.

8 Prince George's County Court (Court Papers, Blacks), *Charles Digges vs. Negro Enoch*, November 13, 1848, reel M-11,024, SC, MSA; Bill of Sale, June 27, 1848, with ibid. . . .

9 John Peters to A. P. Bagby, January 3, 1839, A. P. Bagby Papers, Correspondence ADAH [Alabama Department of Archives and History].

10 . . . .Quotes on stealing in Isaac Briggs to Dudley Chase, February 5, 1817, Isaac Briggs Papers, Manuscripts Division, LC. John Dabney Terrell to Thomas Ringgold, November 12, 1836, John Dabney Terrell Papers, Correspondence, ADAH; Jeremiah Pritchett to Court of Marengo County, June 21, 1837, John Dabney Terrell Papers, Correspondence, ADAH.

11 Records of the Circuit Court, Washington County, Tennessee, *John Newnan vs. Montgomery Stewart*, October 4, 1815, in Civil and Criminal Cases, Accession #18, Box 74, folder 10, Archives of Appalachia, East Tennessee State University, Johnson City, Tennessee. . . .

12 G. Morgan, filed 13 January 1841 in *Philip Hicky vs Isham P. Fox*, # 2258, East Baton Rouge Parish Archives, Baton Rouge.

13 Samuel Cartwright, "Diseases and Peculiarities of the Negro Race," *DeBow's Southern and Western Review*, 11 (September 1851), pp. 331–3.

14 Legislative Petitions, Petition of the Citizens of James City, York, and surrounding counties to the Virginia General Assembly, January 11, 1858, Middlesex County, VSA [Virginia State Archives, Richmond, Va.]; Certificate of A. H. Perkins, November 8, 1856, written on signature page of above petition. *Charleston Mercury and Morning Advertiser*, November 14, 1822; *Charleston Mercury*, April 10, 1826.

15 *Charleston Mercury*, August 17, 1829.

16 Winthrop D. Jordan, *White Over Black: American Attitudes Toward the Negro, 1550–1812* (Chapel Hill: University of North Carolina Press, 1968), pp. 381–2, 383 n. 14.

17 Legislative Petitions, Petition of Sundry Inhabitants of the City of Richmond to the Virginia General Assembly, December 20, 1804, Richmond City, VSA . . .

18 Rachel O'Connor to A. T. Conrad, May 26, 1836, Weeks (David and Family) Papers, Special collections, Hill Memorial Library, LSU; Rachel O'Connor to Aldred Conrad, August 3, 1835, in Allie Bayne Windham Webb (ed.), *Mistress of Evergreen Plantation: Rachel O'Connor's Legacy of Letters, 1823–1845* (Albany: State University of New York Press, 1983), p. 173; Rachel O'Connor to Mary Weeks, January 11, 1830, and December 26, 1834, Weeks (David and Family) Papers, Special Collections, Hill Memorial Library, LSU.

19 *Nashville Whig*, April 14, 21, 28, 1813; *New Orleans Bee*, March 19, 1835; *New Orleans Picayune*, July 17, 1840; Records of the District Court, Travis County, Texas, *Benjamin and Isabella Grumbles vs. John and Benjamin P. Grumbles*, December 29, 1852, Case #222, reel #9, County Court House, Austin, Texas.

20 *New Orleans Picayune*, June 19, 1839.

21 Legislative Petitions, Petition of David M. Erwin, Thomas C. Burwell, William B. Woods, et al. to the Virginia General Assembly, ca. 1850, Greenbrier County, VSA.

22 Carroll County Court (Equity Papers) 47, *Catherine Biggs vs. Daniel Poole*, September 2, 1839, reel M-11,020, SC, MSA. . . . Plantation Record Book, 1848–1851, Kiger Family Papers, Natchez Trace Slaves and Slavery Collection, 2E636, Center for American History, University of Texas at Austin.

23 Reine Welham Plantation Record Book, December 1860. Special Collections, Hill Memorial Library, LSU [Louisiana State University].

24 Frederick Law Olmsted, *A Journey in the BackCountry* (New York: Mason Brothers, 1860), p. 476.

25 Baltimore County Register of Wills (Petitions and Orders), Estate of William E. Grimes, October 2, 1855, reel M-11,020, SC, MSA; St. Mary's County Court Register of Wills (Petitions), Petition of Henry Hammett, January 9, 1859, reel M-11,026, ibid.

26 Legislative Petitions, Petition of John Royall to the General Assembly, December 21, 1802, Nottoway County, VSA; Deposition of Richard Dennis, December 9, 1802, and Deposition of Ransom Hudgings, December 3, 1802, with ibid.; Records of the General Assembly, Petition of Thomas Key to the South Carolina Senate, November 27, 1811, #142, SCDAH [South Carolina Department of Archives and History]; Legislative Records, Petition of the Town Council of Georgetown to the South Carolina Senate, November 16, 1829, #98, SCDAH; Petition of John Wilson, William B. Pringle, et al. to the South Carolina Senate, 1829, #131, in ibid.; Records of

the Parish Court, West Baton Rouge Parish, Louisiana, *Smith vs. Blanchard*, July 5, 1846, #299, Parish Court House, Port Allen, Louisiana.

27 Affidavit of Gary Dunn, Justice of the Peace, Jefferson Parish, Louisiana, April 27, 1852, in Felix Limongi Papers, LC [Library of Congress]; Hilliard (Mrs. Isaac H.) June, LSU.

28 Joseph Taper to Joseph Long, November 11, 1840, Joseph Long Papers, Special Collections Library, Duke University, Durham, North Carolina. . . .

11
The Abolitionist Impulse

Introduction

The origins of Abolitionism are rooted in the spread of evangelical reform during the Second Great Awakening of the 1830s and 1840s. The idea of reform within religious denominations soon extended to all aspects of society, and produced reform movements in several different fields, including the struggle against slavery. The central tenet behind this wave of social reform was the belief that the individual, if stimulated in the right way, could improve both himself and society as a whole. Reformers were convinced that if people were persuaded to stop doing wrong, they would have automatically achieved the aim of creating a better society. This was also the central idea of the early Abolitionists, who engaged in a battle to convince their fellow Americans that it was morally wrong to keep other humans in bondage. In order to realize a better and more righteous republic, they believed, the institution of slavery had to be rejected. Related to this central idea was the idea of the "immediate" abolition of slavery, in contrast with the idea of gradual emancipation supported in most antislavery circles. Those who supported "immediatism" came to be called Abolitionists, a name which distinguished them from the more general antislavery advocates.

The official date of the birth of the Abolitionist movement is January 1831, when William Lloyd Garrison commenced publication of an antislavery newspaper called *The Liberator*, in which he wrote in support of antislavery activities in a new harsh and direct style and with a content that aimed to show the majority of the Americans the scandal and the ugliness of slavery upon their own supposed "sweet land of liberty." Garrison was a deeply convinced Reformed Protestant who believed that slavery was above all a sin in the eyes of God; consequently his battle against slavery was articulated as a moral and religious crusade against evil.

Garrison stood at the center of the original Abolitionist group in Boston; however, other groups of Abolitionists organized in different areas of the North. Garrison came almost immediately into contact with other prominent figures who agreed with his radical doctrine – among them Arthur and Lewis Tappan from New York and Theodore Weld from Ohio, who created their own circles of supporters pursuing Abolitionist objectives. The Tappan brothers and Weld were particularly instrumental in raising funds for the several programs related to the spread of Abolitionist publications and for the foundation of a national Abolitionist organization, the American Anti-Slavery Society, in 1833. The original Anti-Slavery Society's "Declaration of Sentiment" was written by Garrison; it maintained that slavery was a sin before God, and called for the immediate rejection of slavery and the extension of equal rights to blacks and whites. From the very beginning of the American Anti-Slavery Society, it was clear that Garrison and his supporters were very keen to collaborate with virtually every reform movement of the time, since they conceived the fight against slavery as part of a great war on the corrupt soul of America. On the other hand, many of Garrison's opponents within the movement wanted to focus exclusively on the battle against slavery, since they thought it was the most pressing problem in American society. After many years of conflict, the Abolitionist movement split in 1840: the Anti-Garrisonian New Yorkers broke away and founded the American and Foreign Anti-Slavery Society, while the Garrisonians remained in control of the original American Anti-Slavery Society, which was now diminished in terms of membership.

Most Abolitionists had a degree of racial prejudice, which showed in the way they tended to patronize African American Abolitionist leaders, expecting them to follow their guidance. But some African Americans took a leading role from the beginning and were not easily manipulated. The most outstanding were ex-slaves who could rely on their firsthand experience of slavery and could convince white Abolitionists of the importance of having them speak for themselves. The most famous of all was Frederick Douglass, an ex-slave who had fled from Maryland and had an uncommon gift of oratorical eloquence. Douglass published his autobiography, which sold thousands of copies and which became one of the most important pieces of Abolitionist literature. He also published his own newspaper, *The North Star*, based in Rochester, New York. Some of the most powerful figures in black Abolitionism were women. A few of them – such as Harriet Jacobs – published their own best-selling accounts of their life under slavery. Others – like Sojourner Truth – traveled across America preaching against the sin of slavery and in favor of both Abolitionism and Women's Rights.

Further reading

Aptheker, H., *Abolitionism: A Revolutionary Movement* (New York: Twayne, 1989).

Blackett, R. J. M., *Building an Antislavery Wall: Black Americans in the Atlantic Antislavery Movement* (Baton Rouge: Louisiana State University Press, 1983).

Cain, W. E. (ed.), *William Lloyd Garrison and the Fight against Slavery: Selections from* The Liberator (Boston and New York: St. Martin's Press, 1995).

Davis, D. B., *Slavery and Human Progress* (New York: Oxford University Press, 1984).

Dillon, M., *The Abolitionists: The Growth of a Dissenting Minority* (New York: Norton, 1976).

Goodman, P., *Of One Blood: Abolitionism and the Origins of Racial Equality* (Berkeley: University of California Press, 1998).

Lowance, M. (ed.), *Against Slavery: An Abolitionist Reader* (Harmondsworth: Penguin, 2000).

Mayer, H., *All on Fire: William Lloyd Garrison and the Abolition of Slavery* (New York: Macmillan, 1998).

McFeely, W., *Frederick Douglass* (New York: Norton, 1994).

Painter, N., *Sojourner Truth: A Life, A Symbol* (New York: Norton, 1996).

Pease, J. H. and Pease, W. H., *They Who Would Be Free: Blacks' Search for Freedom, 1830–1861* (Urbana: University of Illinois Press, 1974).

Stewart, J. B., *Holy Warriors: The Abolitionists and American Slavery* (New York: Hill & Wang, 1996).

Walters, R., *The Anti-Slavery Appeal: American Abolitionism after 1830* (New York: Norton, 1976).

Yellin, J. F., *Women and Sisters: The Antislavery Feminists in American Culture* (New Haven: Yale University Press, 1989).

William Lloyd Garrison, "I Will Be Heard" (1831)

On January 1, 1831, William Lloyd Garrison began publication of his Abolitionist newspaper *The Liberator.* At a time when Abolitionism implied for the majority of Americans the support of gradual, compensated emancipation, Garrison asked for the immediate and uncompensated abolition of slavery in the South. The effect of the argument was reinforced by Garrison's powerful eloquence and by the direct style which characterized his first address to the public. The piece included some of Garrison's central concepts, such as the fact that slavery violated the "self-evident truths" of the Declaration of Independence, according to which all men are created equal and entitled to life, liberty, and the pursuit of happiness. Garrison knew that little else could have appealed to his readers as effectively as the reference to Thomas Jefferson's words, and he used them to persuade his fellow Americans of the necessity of eliminating slavery in order to be consistent with the nation's founding principles.

In the month of August, I issued proposals for publishing "THE LIBERATOR" in Washington city; but the enterprise, though hailed in different sections of the country, was palsied by public indifference. Since that time, the removal of the Genius of Universal Emancipation[1] to the Seat of Government has rendered less imperious the establishment of a similar periodical in that quarter.

During my recent tour for the purpose of exciting the minds of the people by a series of discourses on the subject of slavery, every place that I visited gave fresh evidence of the fact, that a greater revolution in public sentiment was to be effected in the free states – *and particularly in New-England* – than at the south. I found contempt more bitter, opposition more active, detraction more relentless, prejudice more stubborn, and apathy more frozen, than among slave owners themselves. Of course, there were individual exceptions to the contrary. This state of things afflicted, but did not dishearten me. I determined, at every hazard, to lift up the standard of emancipation in the eyes of the nation, *within sight of Bunker Hill and in the birth place of liberty.* That standard is now unfurled;

Source: William Lloyd Garrison, "To the Public," *The Liberator*, Jan. 1, 1831; reprinted in William E. Cain (ed.), *William Lloyd Garrison and the Fight Against Slavery: Selections from* The Liberator (Boston and New York: St. Martin's Press, 1995), pp. 70–2

and long may it float, unhurt by the spoliations of time or the missiles of a desperate foe – yea, till every chain be broken, and every bondman set free! Let southern oppressors tremble – let their secret abettors tremble – let their northern apologists tremble – let all the enemies of the persecuted blacks tremble.

I deem the publication of my original Prospectus unnecessary, as it has obtained a wide circulation. The principles therein inculcated will be steadily pursued in this paper, excepting that I shall not array myself as the political partisan of any man. In defending the great cause of human rights, I wish to derive the assistance of all religions and of all parties.

Assenting to the "self-evident truth" maintained in the American Declaration of Independence, "that all men are created equal, and endowed by their Creator with certain inalienable rights – among which are life, liberty and the pursuit of happiness," I shall strenuously contend for the immediate enfranchisement of our slave population. In Park-street Church, on the Fourth of July, 1829, in an address on slavery, I unreflectingly assented to the popular but pernicious doctrine of *gradual* abolition. I seize this opportunity to make a full and unequivocal recantation, and thus publicly to ask pardon of my God, of my country, and of my brethren the poor slaves, for having uttered a sentiment so full of timidity, injustice and absurdity. A similar recantation, from my pen, was published in the Genius of Universal Emancipation at Baltimore, in September, 1829. My conscience is now satisfied.

I am aware, that many object to the severity of my language; but is there not cause for severity? I *will be* as harsh as truth, and as uncompromising as justice. On this subject, I do not wish to think, or speak, or write, with moderation. No! no! Tell a man whose house is on fire, to give a moderate alarm; tell him to moderately rescue his wife from the hands of the ravisher; tell the mother to gradually extricate her babe from the fire into which it has fallen; – but urge me not to use moderation in a cause like the present. I am in earnest – I will not equivocate – I will not excuse – I will not retreat a single inch – AND I WILL BE HEARD. The apathy of the people is enough to make every statue leap from its pedestal, and to hasten the resurrection of the dead.

It is pretended, that I am retarding the cause of emancipation by the coarseness of my invective, and the precipitancy of my measures. *The charge is not true*. On this question my influence, – humble as it is, – is felt at this moment to a considerable extent, and shall be felt in coming years – not perniciously, but beneficially – not as a curse, but as a blessing; and posterity will bear testimony that I was right. I desire to thank God, that he enables me to disregard "the fear of man which bringeth a snare," and to speak his truth in its simplicity and power. And here I close with this fresh dedication:

Oppression! I have seen thee, face to face,
And met thy cruel eye and cloudy brow;
But thy soul-withering glance I fear not now –
For dread to prouder feelings doth give place
Of deep abhorrence! Scorning the disgrace
Of slavish knees that at thy footstool bow,
I also kneel – but with far other vow
Do hail thee and thy hord of hirelings base: –
I swear, while life-blood warms my throbbing veins,
Still to oppose and thwart, with heart and hand,
Thy brutalising sway – till Afric's chains
Are burst, and Freedom rules the rescued land, –
Trampling Oppression and his iron rod:
Such is the vow I take – SO HELP ME GOD!

William Lloyd Garrison

Boston, January 1, 1831

Note

1 Benjamin Lundy's paper, *The Genius of Universal Emancipation*, with which Garrison had been associated and which had been based in Baltimore.

The American Anti-Slavery Society's Declaration of Sentiments (1833)

Less than three years after he started publishing *The Liberator*, William Lloyd Garrison became the leader of an Abolitionist organization which spread over several northern states and whose name was the American Anti-Slavery Society. In a national convention held in Philadelphia in December 1833, the society set out its principles and published a "Declaration of Sentiments." Authored mainly by Garrison, the document confirmed the call for immediate, uncompensated emancipation and rearticulated the idea that slavery violated the principles of the Declaration of Independence. Yet Garrison went even further, calling for the enjoyment of equal privileges by both whites and blacks and for the repeal of those articles of the Constitution which supported slavery. Moreover, Garrison made clear that the society intended

Source: W. E. Cain (ed.), *William Lloyd Garrison and the Fight against Slavery: Selections from* The Liberator (Boston and New York: St. Martin's Press, 1995), pp. 90–3

to engage in a great battle for "moral suasion" and for the influence of public opinion through the collaboration of church ministers and the diffusion of antislavery pamphlets.

The Convention, assembled in the City of Philadelphia to organize a National Anti-Slavery Society, promptly seize the opportunity to promulgate the following DECLARATION OF SENTIMENTS, as cherished by them in relation to the enslavement of one-sixth portion of the American people.

More than fifty-seven years have elapsed since a band of patriots convened in this place, to devise measures for the deliverance of this country from a foreign yoke. The corner-stone upon which they founded the TEMPLE OF FREEDOM was broadly this – "that all men are created equal; that they are endowed by their Creator with certain inalienable rights; that among these are life, LIBERTY, and the pursuit of happiness." At the sound of their trumpet-call, three millions of people rose up as from the sleep of death, and rushed to the strife of blood; deeming it more glorious to die instantly as freemen, than desirable to live one hour as slaves. – They were few in number – poor in resources; but the honest conviction that TRUTH, JUSTICE, and RIGHT were on their side, made them invincible.

We have met together for the achievement of an enterprise, without which, that of our fathers is incomplete, and which, for its magnitude, solemnity, and probable results upon the destiny of the world, as far transcends theirs, as moral truth does physical force.

In purity of motive, in earnestness of zeal, in decision of purpose, in intrepidity of action, in steadfastness of faith, in sincerity of spirit, we would not be inferior to them. . . .

Hence we maintain –

That in view of the civil and religious privileges of this nation, the guilt of its oppression is unequalled by any other on the face of the earth; – and, therefore,

That it is bound to repent instantly, to undo the heavy burden, to break every yoke, and to let the oppressed go free.

We further maintain –

That no man has a right to enslave or imbrute his brother – to hold or acknowledge him, for one moment, as a piece of merchandise – to keep back his hire by fraud – or to brutalize his mind by denying him the means of intellectual, social and moral improvement.

The right to enjoy liberty is inalienable. To invade it, is to usurp the prerogative of Jehovah. Every man has a right to his own body – to the products of his own labor – to the protection of law – and to the common advantages of society. It is piracy to buy or steal a native African, and subject him to servitude. Surely the sin is as great to enslave an AMERICAN as an AFRICAN.

Therefore we believe and affirm –

That there is no difference, *in principle*, between the African slave trade and American slavery;

That every American citizen, who retains a human being in involuntary bondage, is [according to Scripture] a MAN-STEALER;

That the slaves ought instantly to be set free, and brought under the protection of law; . . .

That all persons of color who possess the qualifications which are demanded of others, ought to be admitted forthwith to the enjoyment of the same privileges, and the exercise of the same prerogatives, as others; and that the paths of preferment, of wealth, and of intelligence, should be opened as widely to them as to persons of a white complexion.

We maintain that no compensation should be given to the planters emancipating their slaves –

Because it would be a surrender of the great fundamental principle that man cannot hold property in man;

Because SLAVERY IS A CRIME, AND THEREFORE IT IS NOT AN ARTICLE TO BE SOLD;

Because the holders of slaves are not the just proprietors of what they claim; – freeing the slaves is not depriving them of property, but restoring it to the right owner; – it is not wronging the master, but righting the slave – restoring him to himself;

Because immediate and general emancipation would only destroy nominal, not real property: it would not amputate a limb or break a bone of the slaves, but by infusing motives into their breasts, would make them doubly valuable to the masters as free laborers; and

Because if compensation is to be given at all, it should be given to the outraged and guiltless slaves, and not to those who have plundered and abused them.

We regard, as delusive, cruel and dangerous, any scheme of expatriation which pretends to aid, either directly or indirectly, in the emancipation of the slaves, or to be a substitute for the immediate and total abolition of slavery. . . .

These are our views and principles – these, our designs and measures. With entire confidence in the overruling justice of God, we plant ourselves upon the Declaration of our Independence, and upon the truths of Divine Revelation, as upon the EVERLASTING ROCK.

We shall organize Anti-Slavery Societies, if possible, in every city, town and village of our land.

We shall send forth Agents to lift up the voice of remonstrance, of warning, of entreaty and rebuke.

We shall circulate, unsparingly and extensively, anti-slavery tracts and periodicals.

We shall enlist the PULPIT and the PRESS in the cause of the suffering and the dumb.

Frederick Douglass Discusses the Fourth of July (1852)

In 1852 Frederick Douglass was invited to give the Fourth of July Oration by the Rochester Ladies' Antislavery Society. He accepted on condition that the speech would be moved to the following day, since he did not want to participate in a celebration of Independence when millions of slaves were in chains. The oration that he eventually delivered – his Fifth of July speech – was a powerfully argued and masterfully crafted indictment of the majority of Americans who allowed their black brothers to suffer in bondage. Douglass invited his audience to reflect upon the fact that to him and to most blacks the celebration of the Fourth of July was a hypocritical "hollow mockery." For this reason, the subject of his speech could not be American independence; it had to be American slavery, the sin that made the American nation guilty of injustice and cruelty at the very time it celebrated its own freedom.

Fellow Citizens: Pardon me, and allow me to ask, why am I called upon to speak here today? What have I or those I represent to do with your national independence? Are the great principles of political freedom and of natural justice, embodied in that Declaration of Independence, extended to us? And am I, therefore, called upon to bring our humble offering to the national altar, and to confess the benefits, and express devout gratitude for the blessings resulting from your independence to us?

Would to God, both for your sakes and ours, that an affirmative answer could be truthfully returned to these questions. Then would my task be light, and my burden easy and delightful. For who is there so cold that a nation's sympathy could not warm him? Who so obdurate

---

Source: Herbert Aptheker (ed.), *A Documentary History of the Negro People of the United States* (New York: Citadel, 1964), pp. 330–4

and dead to the claims of gratitude, that would not thankfully acknowledge such priceless benefits? Who so stolid and selfish that would not give his voice to swell the halleluiahs of a nation's jubilee, when the chains of servitude had been torn from his limbs? I am not that man. In a case like that, the dumb might eloquently speak, and the "lame man leap like a hare."

But such is not the state of the case. I say it with a sad sense of disparity between us. I am not included within the pale of this glorious anniversary! Your high independence only reveals the immeasurable distance between us. The blessings in which you this day rejoice are not enjoyed in common. The rich inheritance of justice, liberty, prosperity, and independence bequeathed by your fathers is shared by you, not by me. The sunlight that brought life and healing to you has brought stripes and death to me. This Fourth of July is *yours*, not *mine. You* may rejoice, *I* must mourn. To drag a man in fetters into the grand illuminated temple of liberty, and call upon him to join you in joyous anthems, were inhuman mockery and sacrilegious irony. Do you mean, citizens, to mock me, by asking me to speak today? If so, there is a parallel to your conduct. And let me warn you, that it is dangerous to copy the example of a nation whose crimes, towering up to heaven, were thrown down by the breath of the Almighty, burying that nation in irrecoverable ruin. I can today take up the lament of a peeled and woe-smitten people.

"By the rivers of Babylon, there we sat down. Yes! We wept when we remembered Zion. We hanged our harps upon the willows in the midst thereof. For there they that carried us away captive, required of us a song; and they who wasted us, required of us mirth, saying, Sing us one of the songs of Zion. How can we sing the Lord's song in a strange land? If I forget there, O Jerusalem, let my right hand forget her cunning. If I do not remember thee, let my tongue cleave to the roof of my mouth."

Fellow citizens, above your national, tumultuous joy, I hear the mournful wail of millions, whose chains, heavy and grievous yesterday, are today rendered more intolerable by the jubilant shouts that reach them. If I do forget, if I do not remember those bleeding children of sorrow this day, "may my right hand forget her cunning, and may my tongue cleave to the roof of my mouth!" To forget them, to pass lightly over their wrongs, and to chime in with the popular theme, would be treason most scandalous and shocking, and would make me a reproach before God and the world. My subject, then, fellow citizens, is "American Slavery." I shall see this day and its popular characteristics from the slave's point of view. Standing here, identified with the American bondman, making his wrongs mine, I do not hesitate to declare, with all my soul, that the character and conduct of this nation never looked blacker to me than on this Fourth of July. Whether we turn to the declarations of the past, or to the professions of the present, the conduct of the nation seems equally hideous and revolting. America is false to the past, false to the present, and solemnly binds herself to be false to the future. Standing with God and the crushed and bleeding slave on this occasion, I will, in the name of humanity, which is outraged, in the name of liberty, which is fettered, in the name of the Constitution and the Bible, which are disregarded and trampled upon, dare to call in question and to denounce, with all the emphasis I can command, everything that serves to perpetuate slavery – the great sin and shame of America! "I will not equivocate; I will not excuse"; I will use the severest language I can command, and yet not one word shall escape me that any man, whose judgment is not blinded by prejudice, or who is not at heart a slaveholder, shall not confess to be right and just. . . .

What to the American slave is your Fourth of July? I answer, a day that reveals to him more than all other days of the year, the gross injustice and cruelty to which he is the constant victim. To him your celebration is a sham; your boasted liberty an unholy license; your national greatness, swelling vanity; your sounds of rejoicing are empty and heartless; your denunciation of tyrants, brass-fronted impudence; your shouts of liberty and equality, hollow mockery; your prayers and hymns, your sermons and thanksgivings, with all your religious parade and solemnity, are to him mere bombast, fraud, deception, impiety, and hypocrisy – a thin veil to cover up crimes which would disgrace a nation of savages. There is not a nation of the earth guilty of practices more shocking and bloody than are the people of these United States at this very hour. . . .

Abolitionists and the Origins of Racial Equality

Paul Goodman

Paul Goodman's *Of One Blood* is an analysis of the origins and constituency of the Abolitionist movement; the focus is on the ideology of racial equality which characterized both leaders and rank-and-file Abolitionist activists. Through his study, Goodman demonstrates the importance of the support of both working men and women to the success of the movement. In this excerpt, Goodman explains that the Abolitionists' commitment to racial

Paul Goodman, *Of One Blood: Abolitionism and the Origins of Racial Equality* (Berkeley: University of California Press, 1998), pp. 246–60.

equality stemmed from both their Christian beliefs and their republican ideas; these influences were at the origin of their effort to promote interracial relations and overcome widespread racial prejudice. In order to achieve this aim, Abolitionists encouraged contacts between whites and blacks not only within the confines of antislavery organizations, but also in schools and churches. By 1840 – at the peak of its popularity – the Abolitionist movement had made significant progress towards its goal of changing perceptions of race relations in the northern states, by constantly advancing the principle that "God had created mankind of one blood."

The white abolitionist commitment to racial equality flowed from the rejection of colonization and from the effect of black opinion and example on the consciousnesses of the immediatist pioneers.... Colonizationists assumed that color prejudice was irremediable and that emancipation would flood the country with an immense outcast population whom whites would never accept as fellow citizens. "Perhaps nothing shows more clearly the leprous deadly effects of slavery," observed an abolitionist, "than the common remark, 'I am opposed to slavery but what will you do with them?' "[1]

...[I]mmediatists assumed that "this deadly negro hatred" was vulnerable to religious and secular argument and to the example of improvement among free blacks.[2] As serious Christians, they grounded their belief in human equality in faith. Scripture taught that God had created the nations of one blood, that He was no respecter of persons, and that He required Christians to do unto others as they would have others do unto them. As serious republicans, abolitionists also took the promise of equality in the Declaration of Independence as another absolute command. These beliefs and obligations, they believed, formed the foundation of a distinctive American national identity. And since most Americans professed to be Christians and republicans, abolitionists insisted that they could be persuaded to abandon racial prejudice.

Yet disdain for black people persisted on aesthetic, intellectual, and moral grounds, whatever their legal status, free or slave. As one African American leader explained: "The truth is, that the real ground of prejudice is not the *color of skin*, but the *condition*. We have so long associated *color* with *condition, that we have forgotten the fact, and have charged the offence to the wrong account*."[3] Abolitionists understood that the condition of free blacks in the Northern states gave empirical support to racial prejudice. Few whites there acknowledged that their own behavior toward the emancipated was largely responsible for the lowly state of black people. Treated like pariahs in the churches, denied access to jobs as skilled labor, kept out of schools or segregated in all-black schools, barred from voting in some states, and treated with contempt in almost every facet of everyday life, African Americans seemed fated to remain at the bottom of the social order. Relentlessly grinding down free blacks, whites nonetheless held them to exemplary standards of behavior, oblivious to how prejudice contributed to the lowly condition of those they scorned.

From this gloomy picture, white and black abolitionists plucked hope. By improving their condition, they believed, the free blacks of the North could contradict the assumptions upon which prejudice rested. That would not be easy. It would require an abandonment of prejudice among a vanguard of whites. And it would require heroic efforts by African Americans, aided by white abolitionists, to better their character and condition despite white prejudice. It would require white abolitionists and free blacks to show the prejudiced by concrete acts that all were in fact "of one blood."

There were grounds for optimism. Blacks already had made remarkable progress since the end of slavery in the North, building their own churches, cultural and benevolent institutions, and producing a small cadre of property-owning and literate leaders. Most whites professed ignorance of that progress, but the abolitionist movement would seek to replace ignorance with knowledge. By the 1830s, blacks were more eager than ever to speed the tempo of racial progress, and now as never before there were growing numbers of whites ready to aid them.

The Antislavery Women's Convention in 1837 put the case clearly: "The abandonment of prejudice is required of us as a proof of our sincerity and consistency. How can we ask our Southern brethren to make sacrifices if we are not even willing to enter inconvenience? First cast the beam from thine own eye, then will thou see clearly to cast it from his eye." And the appeal concluded with these lines from Philadelphia black abolitionist Sarah Forten:

> "We are thy sisters. God has truly said
> That of one blood the nation he has maid."[4]

By working together with free blacks, abolitionists not only conquered their own prejudices . . . but began to reintroduce black Americans to white Americans. Just as they had been converted to the antislavery cause by their encounters with free African Americans, they believed that other white Americans would have their prejudices shattered by the example of interracial cooperation on a larger scale. . . . In the logic of the antislavery cause, with its progression from colonization to emancipation, from gradualism to immediatism, from prejudice to respect, there thus was one more step: from segregation to an integrated society. . . .

Integration had to begin first among abolitionists, white and black. When the Massachusetts General Colored Association joined the New England Antislavery Society, it was a first step toward creation of a biracial, integrated movement. From time to time blacks presided at meetings of antislavery organizations, and thirteen served as officers of the American Antislavery Society in the 1830s, not an impressive number, but a beginning. The older antislavery societies had not admitted blacks. There were only a small number of black antislavery societies affiliated with the American Antislavery Society, six by 1838, either because blacks joined integrated societies, thought it too dangerous to join such societies at all, or preferred to invest their energies in the various self-improvement enterprises that proliferated in the 1830s.

Oberlin and Oneida led the way, opening their doors to blacks seeking advanced training and to a new level of biracial interaction. "It is important to make the two races feel kindness and respect for each other," explained Rev. Theodore Wright, referring to Oneida's racial integration, "even if but few do, so it will have an effect on others. Get two men to love each other, though of two nations, and it will make them love the whole class."[5] "This prejudice was never reasoned up and will never be reasoned down," Wendell Phillips said. "It must be lived down."[6]

There was no substitute for interracial relations in overcoming racial prejudice. This was recorded in a small way in the *Emancipator* in an account of a visit by a white woman abolitionist and her biased great aunt to Miss Paul's School for blacks in Boston, run by the black schoolteacher Susan Paul... Miss Paul boasted that there were as many good heads among her class as among comparable numbers of whites.... But the real proof lay in performance. The children promptly answered questions in their various lessons; whites hardly could do better. And when they sang sweetly, the visitor and her great aunt were deeply moved, exulting at the victory, even if only temporarily, "over aunt's prejudices." In the afternoon, the pair visited an African American church, where "the sight was truly gratifying." She rejoiced to be an "abolitionist, for it has given me an opportunity to see a portion of the human family to which I have too long been a stranger." For the first time in her life, she found herself in a black congregation, where she observed "that distinction which mind, cultivated mind, always gives, whether to white or black."[7] ...

In 1835 the schoolteacher in this interracial encounter, Susan Paul, authored *The Memoir of James Jackson, The Attentive and Obedient Scholar*.... James Jackson was a model of Christian piety, industry, obedience, a figure not unlike Little Eva in Harriet Beecher Stowe's epic nearly twenty years later, a being filled with Christian love who was too good to live long in a world of Christian sinners. "In this life," Paul explained to African American readers, "you shall see your children growing up to be respected in society, and in the world to come, they shall be acknowledged by our Lord as heirs to life eternal." . . .

In October 1833, he became ill and died a Christian death, singing hymns, longing for God, and forgetting his physical suffering. Paul appended to her heroic story a black mother's answer to a child's query, why do "people slight me so?":

> Tis this my child; your Maker gave
> To you a darker skin;
> And people seem to think that such
> Can have no mind within.
> Am I to blame? It cannot be:
> What God has done is right;
> And he must be displeased with those
> Who little black boys slight.[8]

Such appeals to original goodness were part of a strategy of combating prejudice. Susan Paul's focus on children was not unique. "It is in our childhood that this prejudice is imbibed, of which we are so tenacious in after-life," observed an abolitionist.[9] . . . White children were especially vulnerable to viewing blacks either positively or negatively, since none was born with prejudice and all were entirely dependent on upbringing. Prejudiced mothers transmitted fear and loathing of African Americans when they treated or regarded them as outcasts, attitudes that children readily absorbed. White parents used black folk as bogeymen to frighten their children if they misbehaved. . . .

In order to help prevent children from being infected with the prejudice of their elders, the American Antislavery Society appointed Henry C. Wright as a traveling agent to organize youth. By 1838, the American Antislavery Society claimed thirty-three juvenile societies in twenty-eight cities and towns, nineteen of which had female societies, suggesting that antislavery women played an important role in their formation. Abolitionists pointed out that mothers had a vital role to play in this process as well, and that they could do so without stepping beyond the most conventional notions of women's proper sphere. Mothers could crush such prejudice in the bud by teaching children that blacks are children of God, their skin color no reason to treat them any differently than whites.

White abolitionists also paid a great deal of attention to black education, helping blacks to found or improve schools by providing funds and teachers. Traveling antislavery agents visited black schools, praised children, and uplifted the hearts of parents and youth. These biracial relations affirmed the importance of working hard to improve the condition of blacks, and they made a dent in breaching the isolation of black communities. Now, for the first time, the races came together on more than a token basis. Now, for the first time, there was a nationwide movement that cared for the welfare of America's lowliest citizens. Abolitionists believed that few who observed the performance of African American children could remain prejudiced. . . . And none were more open to conversion than white children. In September 1836, the children of Miss Paul's school received greetings from the Union Evangelical Sunday School in Amesbury and Salisbury: "Wicked men tell us that black children have no souls. But we know that you have souls – and we are glad to hear that your souls are growing and filling up with wisdom and goodness under the instruction of a kind teacher." The white children sent three dollars, the candy money they received from their parents every Fourth of July: "We do this to show our respect for you and your teacher, and the interest we feel in your welfare. We hope that you will grow up to be very wise and good people, and so put to shame those wicked men who say that colored people have no souls."

The black students thanked their benefactors for the money and the confidence placed in them: "We know of some little children who do not love us because we are colored; but we pity them and pray for them." The letter was "the first one we ever received," they said, and the money went "for children in school who were most destitute." They invited the Amesbury and Salisbury students to visit them, "for we love you very much, although we never saw you," and they promised to sing songs about the enslaved, about Sunday school, and about the evils of intemperance.[10]

Exhibiting black talent before white audiences could have a telling effect. In July 1835, Garrison brought four young men ranging in age from sixteen to twenty-one from Boston to Plymouth, New Hampshire. They impressed whites with the simplicity and power of their oratory, besting earlier itinerant temperance speakers. The young men also attended a white church, where "the pew doors of our yeomanry, too respectable to be sneered down by all the dandyism and pomposity of the land, were opened to them, and they enjoyed the pleasure of associating with their brethren and countrymen and fellow sinners, on a proper and Christian footing." Here was an example of "Abolition in the *concrete*," Garrison wrote. Opposition to prejudice was the real test and required a willingness by whites to "walk the streets in friendly association with this object of public aversion and contempt – to ride in the chaise with him – to sit in the pew with him in the house of God – at your own table, in your social circle in the exercise towards him of the rites of hospitality."[11] . . .

Nowhere did white abolitionists work as hard on behalf of black education than in Ohio, a state that had attempted to drive out its free people of color in 1829 and that taxed them, but barred them from public schools. In 1835 and again in 1837, the Ohio Antislavery Society made social surveys of the state's black population in order to gauge its numbers, conditions, and resources. The 1835 survey counted seventy-five hundred, one-third in Cincinnati, a majority having been born in slavery, with many purchasing their freedom and that of their loved ones. As was the case everywhere, the Ohio abolitionists found "among this people, a latent intellect, not a whit behind that of white citizens."[12]

Since so many lived in Cincinnati, educational work centered there. Lane students concluded their great debate by devoting themselves to Sunday and grammar schools for blacks. As children and adults crowded the first school, abolitionists established three more to accommodate demand. The teachers found their work gratifying, as students, old and young, acquired the ability to read and write, some with startling rapidity. A nine-year veteran teacher in the city's public schools testified "that the colored people are not only equal to white people in natural capacity to be taught, but that they exceed them – they do not receive instruction, they seize it as a person who had been long famishing for food, seizes the smallest crumb."[13] . . .

In countless ways and places, blacks and whites mixed together repeatedly, and not just in schools. In Utica, a biracial group celebrated the Fourth of July with a procession, music, church services, and then dinner in a display that aimed "to beat down the prejudice which has long existed in regard to the moral elevation of the colored people" by proving that "there is a dignity in the character of the colored population."[14] In New York City and elsewhere, integrated Phoenix Societies, organized and mainly run by blacks, encouraged the formation of new free black societies devoted to uplift. Here, free blacks could hear a white minister recall the glory of Africa when barbarian, uncivilized people inhabited much of Europe and the Greeks and Romans sent their sons to Africa for education.[15] In 1834, the American Antislavery Society praised the anniversary meeting of the New York City Phoenix Society: "the audience was composed of the most opposite complexions" and "the speakers were about equally divided." This model meeting operated "on many minds like an admission to the general assembly of the universe," teaching whites to abandon "any conscious superiority on the ground of color, or any lingering doubts as to the native ability of the colored race."[16] . . .

Churches offered another important platform for integrating the races. Driven by humiliating treatment in the white churches, blacks formed their own, either within existing white denominations or by creating new black denominations. More important was the founding of "free churches." In free churches, attenders or members did not have to purchase or rent pews. Instead, worshippers were expected to donate funds according to their means. Some also repudiated common practices of racial segregation in seating.... [B]ut racial integration remained a very contentious issue.... Abolitionist efforts to integrate Christian worship hardly made a dent, especially since African Americans were developing their own distinctive worship styles and preachers, which they preferred. But they added one more arena, along with schools and Phoenix Societies, in which the two races could come together.

Modern readers should not dismiss these efforts as flawed by tokenism or white paternalism. For both races, the social and cultural gulf was immense. One gains a more realistic appreciation of these pioneering biracial encounters when one considers how much the races today remain strangers in everyday life, in interpersonal relations. To gauge the reaction of blacks to these new relations with whites, one has to remember how isolated African Americans were from the dominant race, except as menial employees. That is why the creation of the schools by white abolitionists... had such a dramatic effect.

At first, blacks were suspicious of these white do-gooders. By living in black homes, taking meals together, and worshipping together in black churches, the white teachers... quickly made clear that they were different from most white folks. Female abolitionists in Ohio intending to work for the betterment of local blacks received warnings that white prejudice toward blacks had fostered black prejudice toward whites. That required whites to be patient in seeking black confidence. Working with blacks briefly on a token basis never would pass muster. Only long-term commitments by whites could be productive.

Such commitments, once made, such confidence, once gained, paid off. Soon blacks responded in kind. A pious mother in Cincinnati "was delirious with joy for more than a week, at the bright prospect for her children." She revealed that "many times I have lain awake all night, and prayed for just such things, but when they came, I couldn't stand it." A black woman recently arrived from Virginia was equally astonished: "If we should go back and tell... how we have the white people to teach us, and how they treat us like brothers, – they couldn't believe us.... It is just like changing out of one world into another."... For whites, too, these were transforming experiences: "The gratitude which at time flows out from their *full*, warm *hearts*, is rich in blessing, and lightens all our labors."[17]...

Antislavery agent Henry C. Wright recalled lecturing on a steamboat from New York to Providence, Rhode Island, on behalf of racial equality. While seven or eight black waiters stood by, a white Southerner seized a black passenger, pushed him forward, and demanded to know if Wright regarded him as a brother and would walk, eat, and sleep with him.

Wright stood by his views, only to be cursed as an amalgamationist. The contrast with the reaction of blacks was telling. Wright declared that "the looks given me by the colored men I never can forget. It amply made up for the scowling contempt of the insolent white. The colored man's heart is a deep fountain of gratitude."[18]

As whites visited and mingled with them, blacks "became guarded and circumspect in all their demeanor" and "as they become intelligent, they lose their relish for gaudy tinsel and display." They become "convinced that character is based on mental and moral worth." Yet there was much pain in the process. After living with blacks for a year "on terms of perfect friendship and equality," whites reported that blacks displayed "an increased sense of moral and intellectual distance" as they now for the first time fully appreciated how much hard work lay ahead. "I feel as though I did not know anything, and never had done anything," one black man sadly confessed. Responses to prejudice varied as blacks gained a new sense of self-worth. A majority felt "pained and depressed" by white prejudice, but others tried to ignore it or looked down upon it "with utter contempt."[19] Most important, the new opportunities for biracial communication and cooperation enhanced black self-esteem, which strengthened the will and incentives for self-improvement....

The deepest harm slavery and prejudice inflicted on African Americans was to brainwash them and rob them of confidence in themselves. "Many among us have tacitly consented to admit that we were an inferior race," acknowledged an African American delegate to the American Antislavery Society convention in 1837. In the process of recovering a sense of self-worth, the respect of some white people was indispensable.[20] ...

Two years after the first encouraging reports from Cincinnati came troubling accounts of difficulty. The novelty of amiable relations between the races eventually wore off and no longer dazzled the eyes of the blacks as at first. "To break up old habits and form new ones ... to root out growing jealousy and cold-hearted neglect, and to cherish brotherly love, kindness, meekness, benevolence and humility" proved difficult.... To be sure, slavery and Northern prejudice were the ultimate sources of their failings, but that did not make any easier overcoming the harmful attitudes and behavior oppression had generated.[21] As much as students, young and adult, hungered for knowledge, when work beckoned as steamers pulled up to the piers at the riverside, they took off from school, to the teachers' frustration....

Abolitionists seriously underestimated the difficulties of helping the grossly disadvantaged and of converting the prejudiced, including those in their own ranks. As the movement rapidly expanded, many who joined proved far more committed to ending slavery than to racial equality. Abolitionists had to argue continually that one was not possible without the other. And the gulf between the races did not suddenly vanish.... In 1836, Lewis Tappan reported to Weld differences even within the Executive Committee of the American Antislavery Society, which refused to invite black leaders to speak at the forthcoming meetings of the society. Some may have been afraid of offending new converts to the cause, others of arousing more intense opposition from outside the movement, especially from mobs fearful of amalgamation. Even Tappan himself came under attack from fellow abolitionists as an amalgamationist for his personal relations with African Americans....

Outside their ranks, abolitionists had almost no success persuading master mechanics to train blacks and give them jobs in the skilled trades. Even a sympathetic master mechanic could not ignore the refusal of whites to work with black mechanics. Most white churches did not welcome black worshippers. In 1838, Pennsylvania took away the right of blacks to vote, and the campaign to restore it in New York in the later 1830s was just the beginning of a long, frustrating struggle. Most advanced schools – academies and colleges – remained for whites only, while public education for blacks either was not available or the schools were scandalously poor. In the 1830s, the gospel of self-help yielded meager rewards and tangible penalties. Nothing so inflamed the big-city mobs as the efforts by blacks to raise themselves and claim their rightful place in "respectable society."

Yet the resort to force by the mobs was also a sign of weakness. In the long run, violence could not entirely obscure improvements in the conditions of blacks or prevent the emergence of talented, impressive representatives of the race. The first statewide referendum in New York to give propertyless blacks the right to vote in 1846 lost, but found wide support in upstate New York, in communities where abolitionism and the Liberty Party were relatively strong. This suggests the substantial inroads against prejudice that had been made among a sizable minority.

Though the antislavery press and lecturers endlessly trumpeted the advances of African Americans, their voices had to compete with thousands of newspapers, magazines, ministers, and politicians who sang another song. Abolitionists had enormous faith in the example of African American schools to overcome prejudice, but there were severe barriers to spreading such experience beyond antislavery ranks. For two decades, the American Colonization Society and its influential supporters relentlessly had affirmed that blacks never could improve in the United States and required expatriation. Abolitionists credited the ACS with steeping the country in prejudice. William Goodell remembered that a black had attended school with him in Connecticut a generation earlier. Now, thanks to the work of the colonizationists, that experience was less common. In 1837, Henry Clay reasserted the colonizationist doctrine on racial difference in order to refurbish his campaign for the presidency. The black-faced minstrel show, which became increasingly popular by the 1840s, was potent entertainment that refuted abolitionist claims of the real progress made by African Americans.... [P]urveyors of racist humor made comedy out of malapropisms and mispronunciations of black English that assured whites of the blacks' ignorance and fecklessness, while depictions of efforts by blacks to imitate whites depicted blacks futilely pressing the limits of their color-bound inferiority.

By 1840 – only ten years after it became committed to racial equality – the abolition movement could claim much progress, yet the record of its achievement was mixed. Tens of thousands within the movement had embraced the principle that God had created mankind "of one blood" and had worked, often heroically, to advance that principle. Outside the movement, their example inspired numerous fellow travelers. Blacks received an electric shock from white efforts at integration, especially by white schoolteachers in black schools. These efforts breached the isolation of a pariah people, raised their self-esteem, encouraged the formation of reform societies that fought gambling and licentiousness, and advanced the educational and cultural level of African Americans.

The truly perplexing problem, however, was white inconsistency. As long as white people practiced racial prejudice in all its cruel, debilitating forms, they made it extraordinarily difficult, except for an especially talented or lucky few, to climb the mobility ladder that beckoned whites. Whites still attributed black poverty, crime, and lack of cultivation to the inherent inferiority of colored people, and they did so without any real willingness to put that theory to the test....

In spite of limited gains, white abolitionists took pride in their work. "As we have claimed more for the colored man than any class of abolitionists have in our country heretofore, we have created a deference to colored persons which never existed before," the pioneers Simeon Jocelyn and Beriah Green announced to a convention of the faithful.[22] Black leaders agreed. The abolitionists were not just against slavery. They actively worked to make freedom and equality a reality.

Notes

1 *Philanthropist*, March 3, 1837.
2 Ibid.
3 C. Peter Ripley (ed.), *The Black Abolitionist Papers*, 5 vols. (Chapel Hill, 1985–92), vol. 4, p. 227....

4 William C. Nell, *The Colored Patriots of the American Revolution* (1855; reprint, New York, 1968), pp. 350–1.
5 Ibid., p. 352.
6 Ibid., pp. 7–8.
7 *Emancipator,* July 2, 1836.
8 Susan Paul, *The Memoir of James Jackson, the Attentive and Obedient Scholar, Who Died in Boston, October 31, 1833, Aged Six Years and Eleven Months* (Boston, 1835), p. 87.
9 *New Hampshire Observer,* March 7, 1835.
10 *Emancipator,* September 15, 1836.
11 *Herald of Freedom,* July 25, 1835.
12 *Report of the Second Anniversary of the Ohio State Anti-Slavery Society* (Cincinnati, 1837), pp. 58–62.
13 "Report of the Condition of the People of Color in the State of Ohio," in *Proceedings of the Ohio Anti-Slavery Convention, Held at Putnam on the 22nd, 23d, and 24th of April, 1835* (n.p., n.d.), p. 4n.
14 *Emancipator,* August 12, 1833.
15 Ibid., April 15, 1834.
16 *First Annual Report of the American Anti-Slavery Society* (New York, 1834), p. 46.
17 "Report of the Condition of the People of Color in the State of Ohio," p. 7.
18 *Emancipator,* April 13, 1837.
19 "Report of the Condition of the People of Color in the State of Ohio," p. 11.
20 *Fourth Annual Report of the American Anti-Slavery Society* (New York, 1837), p. 13.
21 *Report of the Second Anniversary of the Ohio State Anti-Slavery Society* (1837), pp. 57–8.
22 *Emancipator,* November 10, 1836.

12
The Politics of Slavery

Introduction

The first episode in which sectional conflict over slavery came close to provoking secession and civil war was the Nullification Crisis. Between 1828 and 1832, the federal government passed two tariffs intended to protect northern industry. These tariffs led to a confrontation between South Carolina and the federal government when the South Carolina legislature, believing that the legislation threatened the already weakened cotton economy of the state, declared the laws null and void. In a standoff with President Andrew Jackson, South Carolina based its actions on the Nullification theory of John C. Calhoun. According to Calhoun, the federal tariff was a usurpation of local power and could be, in effect, vetoed by an individual state, since it violated the spirit of the Constitution. In 1832, the South Carolina legislature, following Calhoun's theories, voted unanimously for nullification, defending the rights of the southern states against the national government. By then, President Jackson was ready to send troops into Charleston, but a compromise reached at the last moment avoided escalation into armed conflict.

In 1845, the state of Texas – in the slaveholding southwest – was annexed, and the following year, the United States went to war with Mexico. The war lasted until 1848, and gave America 500,000 square miles of new territory in the West. An antislavery coalition took shape in 1848 with the goal of keeping slavery out of the new territories, and soon gave rise to a new political party: the Free-Soil Party. Far from being Abolitionist in outlook, the party sought simply to contain slavery within the territories where it already existed. In 1849, California applied for statehood as a free state, precipitating a move towards resolution of the slavery issue by prompting national debate and, eventually, Congressional compromise. Democratic Senator Stephen Douglas helped shape the formal settlement, which included five different measures: (1) California was to enter the Union as a free state; (2) New Mexico was to be made a territory, and Texas was to remain within the present borders, with a refund of $10 million; (3) Utah was to be made another territory, with no specific provision excluding or allowing slavery within its borders; (4) a new Fugitive Slave Act was to be placed under federal jurisdiction; (5) the slave trade was to be abolished in the District of Columbia. These five provisions became the compromise of 1850, which was accepted by both North and South.

Four years later Douglas was again at the center of sectional adjustment over the issue of slavery. He proposed a bill which provided for the organization of the territory of Nebraska – in the northern Midwest – in order to bring the area under civil control and eventual statehood. His bill, which became the Kansas–Nebraska Act, specified that all questions pertaining to slavery in the territories would be decided on the basis of popular sovereignty. It thus bypassed the provisions established by the Missouri Compromise of 1820, according to which slavery was confined south of the 36° 30′ line in the territory acquired with the 1803 Louisiana Purchase. The reactions to the Kansas–Nebraska Act led to the birth of a new antislavery political coalition, which called itself "Republican." The Republican Party was the first major party to take a stand against slavery, branding it in the 1856 presidential campaign a "relic of barbarism"; its ideology stemmed primarily from the political opposition to slavery that had grown and matured over the previous two decades. Within the Republican Party the idea that slavery should be prevented from taking root in the West – a position known as "Free Soil" – was joined to a belief in the economic and social superiority of the free labor system of the North.

In 1856, Abraham Lincoln, an Illinois lawyer and former one-term Congressman, joined the Republican Party, attracted by its position on slavery in the western territories. Two years later, he ran against Stephen Douglas for one of the two Illinois seats in the Senate. During the campaign, the two candidates debated in seven different locations around the state. In his "House Divided" speech delivered at Springfield, on June 16, 1858, Lincoln summarized his point of view regarding the presence of slavery in the Union. He compared the United States to a house which was internally divided, since half of the country was slave, half was free. He stressed the fact that the country, like a house, could not stand permanently divided without running the risk of collapse. Lincoln averred that before too long, the country would have to become either all slave or all free. By saying this, he revealed for the first time what later became the central tenet of his politics: the fact that the Union was to be preserved at all costs. Although the Democratic majority in the Illinois legislature returned the incumbent Douglas to the Senate for another term, the campaign was a public relations success for Lincoln, who rose to prominence as a leader of national stature within the Republican Party.

By the second half of the 1850s, a current of radical Abolitionism was committed to the project of provoking a general slave insurrection. On October 16, 1859, radical Abolitionist John Brown crossed the Potomac with 20 men and reached Harper's Ferry, Virginia, where the band planned to seize control of the federal arsenal and arm the slaves in the surrounding countryside. Brown managed to capture the arsenal, but he was soon forced to surrender, and later tried for treason and hanged. His death provoked an enormous outpouring of empathy in the North and the Midwest; he became a martyr for the antislavery cause, hailed as a saint by Ralph Waldo Emerson, and as a brave hero by William Lloyd Garrison. In the South, rumors of conspiracy increased dramatically and exacerbated the tensions between the sections, as every northerner was seen as a possible radical Abolitionist.

Further reading

Ashworth, J., *Slavery, Capitalism, and Politics in the Antebellum Republic* (New York: Cambridge University Press, 1995).

Boritt, G. (ed.), *Why the Civil War Came* (New York: Oxford University Press, 1995).

Donald, D. H., *Lincoln* (New York: Touchstone Books, 1995).

Fehrenbacher, D., *The Slaveholding Republic: An Account of the United States Government's Relations to Slavery* (New York and Oxford: Oxford University Press, 2001).

Foner, E., *Free Soil, Free Labor, Free Men: The Ideology of the Republican Party before the Civil War* (New York: Oxford University Press, 1970).

Freehling, W., *The Reintegration of American History: Slavery and the Civil War* (New York: Oxford University Press, 1994).

Freehling, W., *The Road to Disunion: Secessionist at Bay, 1776–1854* (New York: Oxford University Press, 1990).

Holt, F., *The Political Crisis of the 1850s* (New York: Norton, 1978).

Levine, B., *Half Slave & Half Free: The Roots of the Civil War* (New York: Hill & Wang, 1992).
Potter, D. M., *The Impending Crisis, 1848–1861* (New York: Harper & Row, 1976).
Ransom, R., *Conflict and Compromise* (New York: Cambridge University Press, 1990).
Sewell, R., *Ballots for Freedom* (New York: Norton, 1978).
Stampp, K., *America in 1857: A Nation on the Brink* (New York: Oxford University Press, 1990).

John C. Calhoun on States' Rights and Nullification (1828)

Many southerners regarded South Carolinian John C. Calhoun (1782–1850) as the father of southern nationalism. His Nullification theory – which he laid out in *South Carolina Exposition and Protest* (1828) – was a sophisticated, convincing argument in defense of the rights of the southern states and against interference from the federal government. As Calhoun put it, the crux of the matter was the unconstitutionality of the "Tariff System" and the fact that its burden lay heavily on southern agricultural economy. He argued that the government's economic measures were designed primarily to protect northern industrial products; therefore, the high duties hit particularly hard the profits of southern planters and farmers, and discouraged foreign manufacturers from purchasing southern crops, such as cotton and tobacco. In Calhoun's view, the federal government had disrupted the economic balance among the states of the Union by privileging northern over southern interests; it had acted well beyond the limits to its power set by the Constitution.

The Committee do not propose to enter into an elaborate, or refined argument on the question of the Constitutionality of the Tariff System. The Gen[era]l Government is one of specifick powers, and it can rightfully exercise only the powers expressly granted, and those that may be necessary and proper to carry them into effect, all others being reserved expressly to the States, or the people. It results necessarily, that those who claim to exercise power under the Constitution, are bound to show,

Source: Sean Wilentz (ed.), *Major Problems in the Early Republic, 1787–1848* (Lexington, Mass.: D. C. Heath, 1992), pp. 345–8

that it is expressly granted, or that it is necessary and proper as a means to some of the granted powers. The advocates of the Tariff have offered no such proof.

In the absence of argument drawn from the Constitution itself the advocates of the power have attempted to call in the aid of precedent. The Committee will not waste their time in examining the instances quoted. If they were strictly in point, they would be entitled to little weight. Ours is not a government of precedents, nor can they be admitted except to a very limited extent and with great caution in the interpretation of the Constitution, without changing in time the entire character of the instrument. . . .

So partial are the effects of the system, that its burdens are exclusively on one side, and the benefits on the other. It imposes on the agricultural interest of the south, including the South west, with that portion of our commerce and navigation engaged in foreign trade, the burden not only of sustaining the system itself, but that also of the Government. . . .

That the manufacturing States, even in their own opinion, bear no share of the burden of the Tariff in reality, we may infer with the greatest certainty from their conduct. The fact that they urgently demand an increase, and consider any addition as a blessing, and a failure to obtain one, a curse, is the strongest confession, that whatever burden it imposes in reality, falls, not on them but on others. Men ask not for burdens, but benefits. The tax paid by the duties on impost [*sic*] by which, with the exception of the receipts in the sale of publick land and a few incidental items, the Government is wholly supported, and which in its gross amount annually equals about $23,000,000 is then in truth no tax on them. Whatever portion of it they advance, as consumers of the articles on which it is imposed, returns to them . . . with usurious interest through an artfully contrived system. That such are the facts, the Committee will proceed to demonstrate by other arguments, besides the confession of the party interested through their acts, as conclusive as that ought to be considered.

If the duties were imposed on the exports, instead of the imports, no one would doubt their partial operation, and that the duties in that case would fall on those engaged in ["rearing products" *canceled and* "producing articles" *interlined*] for the foreign market; and as rice, tobacco and cotton constitute the great mass of our exports, such duties would of necessity mainly fall on the Southern States, where they are exclusively cultivated. . . .

We are told by those who pretend to understand our interest better than we do, that the excess of production, and not the Tariff, is the evil which afflicts us, and that our true remedy is a reduction of the quantity of cotton, rice and tobacco which we raise, and not a repeal of the Tariff.

They assert that low prices are the necessary consequence of excess of supply, and that the only proper correction is in diminishing the quantity. We would feel more disposed to respect the spirit in which the advice is offered, if those from whom it comes, accompanied it with the ["benefit" *canceled and* "weight" *interlined*] of their example. They also occasionally complain of low prices, but instead of diminishing the supply as a remedy for the evil, demand an enlargement of the market, by the exclusion of all competition. Our market is the world, and as we cannot imitate their example by enlarging it for our products through the exclusion of others, we must decline to their advice, which instead of alleviating would increase our embarrassment. We have no monopoly in the supply of our products. One half of the globe may produce them. Should we reduce our production, others stand ready by increasing theirs to take our place, and instead of raising prices, we would only diminish our share of the supply. We are thus compelled to produce on the penalty of loosing our hold on the general market. Once lost it may be lost forever; and lose it we must, if we continue to be compelled as we now are, on the one hand by general competition of the world to sell low, and on the other by the Tariff to buy high. We cannot withstand this double action. Our ruin must follow. In fact our only permanent and safe remedy is not the rise in the price of what we sell in which we can receive but little aid from our Government, but a reduction in that which we buy which is prevented by the interference of the Government. Give us a free and open competition in our own market, and we fear not to encounter like competition in the general market of the world. If under all of our discouragement by the acts of our Government, we are still able to contend there against the world, can it be doubted, if this impediment were removed, we would force out all competitors; and thus also enlarge our market, not by the oppression of our fellow citizens of other States, but by our industry, enterprizc [*sic*] and natural advantages....

Free-Soil Democrat Walt Whitman's View on Slavery and the Mexican War (1847)

New York journalist and poet Walt Whitman (1819–92) was one of the most controversial literary talents in antebellum America. In 1842, he started editing the *New York Aurora*, and four years later he assumed direction of the *Brooklyn Eagle*. His editorials in both newspapers were characterized by a radical tone and sharp criticism of political hypocrisy. A committed antislavery advocate, Whitman joined the Free-Soil Party in the wake of the Mexican War and used his editorials to argue for the necessity of keeping the western territories free from the influence of slaveholders. In this excerpt, he compares the aristocratic system of the South, dominated by planters, with the democratic system of the North, where the majority of the people were workingmen, and argued that the latter ran the risk of being outrun by the former in the race to settle the territories acquired in the Mexican War.

American Workingmen, versus Slavery

September 1, 1847

THE question whether or no there shall be slavery in the new territories which it seems conceded on all hands we are largely to get through this Mexican war, is a question between *the grand body of white workingmen, the millions of mechanics, farmers, and operatives of our country*, with their interests on the one side – and the interests of the few thousand rich, "polished," and aristocratic owners of slaves at the South, on the other side. Experience has proved, (and the evidence is to be seen now by any one who will look at it) that a stalwart mass of respectable workingmen, cannot exist, much less flourish, in a thorough slave State. Let any one think for a moment what a different appearance New York, Pennsylvania, or Ohio, would present – how much less sturdy independence and family happiness there would be – were slaves the workmen there, instead of each man as a general thing being his own workman. We wish not at all to sneer at the South; but leaving out of view the educated and refined gentry, and coming to the "common people" of the whites, everybody knows what a miserable, ignorant, and shiftless set of beings they are. Slavery is a good thing enough, (viewed partially,) to the rich –

Source: Sean Wilentz (ed.), *Major Problems in the Early Republic, 1787–1848* (Lexington, Mass.: D. C. Heath, 1992), pp. 540–2

the one out of thousands; but it is destructive to the dignity and independence of all who work, and to labor itself. An honest poor mechanic, in a slave State, is put on a par with the negro slave mechanic – there being many of the latter, who are hired out by their owners. It is of no use to reason abstractly on this fact – farther than to say that the pride of a Northern American freeman, poor though he be, will not comfortably stand such degradation.

The influence of the slavery institution is to bring the dignity of labor down to the level of slavery, which, God knows! is low enough. And this it is which must induce *the workingmen of the North, East, and West, to come up, to a man, in defence of their rights, their honor, and that heritage of getting bread by the sweat of the brow, which we must leave to our children.* . . . We call upon every mechanic of the North, East, and West – upon the carpenter, in his rolled up sleeves, the mason with his trowel, the stonecutter with his brawny chest, the blacksmith with his sooty face, the brown fisted shipbuilder, whose clinking strokes rattle so merrily in our dock yards – upon shoemakers, and cartmen, and drivers, and paviers, and porters, and millwrights, and furriers, and ropemakers, and butchers, and machinists, and tinmen, and tailors, and hatters, and coach and cabinet makers – upon the honest sawyer and mortarmixer too, whose sinews are their own – and every hard-working man – to speak in a voice whose great reverberations shall tell to all quarters that the *workingmen* of the free United States, and their business, are not willing to be put on the level of negro slaves, in territory which, if got at all, must be got by taxes sifted eventually through upon them, and by their hard work and blood. But most of all we call upon *the farmers*, the workers of the land – that prolific brood of brown faced fathers and sons who swarm over the free States, and form the bulwark of our Republic, mightier than walls or armies – upon them we call to say whether *they* too will exist "free and independent" not only in name but also by those social customs and laws which are greater than constitutions – or only so by statute, while in reality they are put down to an equality with slaves!

There can be no half way work in the matter of slavery in new territory: we must either have it there, or have it not. Now if either the slaves themselves, or their owners, had fought or paid for or gained this new territory, there would be some reason in the pro-slavery claims. But every body knows that the cost and work come, forty-nine fiftieths of it, upon the free men, the middling classes and workingmen, who do their own work and own no slaves. Shall *these* give up all to the aristocratic owners of the South? Will even the poor white freemen of the South be willing to do this? It is monstrous to ask such a thing!

. . . [A]ll practice and theory – the real interest of the planters themselves – and the potential weight of the opinions of all our great statesmen, Southern as well as Northern, from Washington to Silas Wright – are strongly arrayed in favor of limiting slavery to where it already exists. For this the clear eye of Washington looked longingly; for this the great voice of Jefferson plead, and his sacred fingers wrote; for this were uttered the prayers of Franklin and Madison and Monroe. But now, in the South, stands a little band, strong in chivalry, refinement and genius – headed by a sort of intellectual Saladin – assuming to speak in behalf of sovereign States, while in reality they utter their own idle theories; and disdainfully crying out against the rest of the Republic, for whom their contempt is but illy concealed.... Already the roar of the waters is heard; and if a few short-sighted ones seek to withstand it, the surge, terrible in its fury, will sweep them too in the ruin.

Abraham Lincoln's "House Divided" Speech (1858)

Abraham Lincoln's 1858 speech accepting the Republican nomination for Illinois' Senate seat was the first instance in which the future president clarified his views on slavery. Up until that point, Lincoln had been extremely cautious in his approach to the slavery issue, though he had made perfectly clear that he opposed the slave system on moral grounds. In the "House Divided" speech, for the first time he went beyond a general moral opposition to slavery and argued against its further spread in the western territories. With the Kansas–Nebraska Act and the Supreme Court's decision on the Dredd Scott case still fresh in his mind, Lincoln denounced the legal machinations which allowed the slave power to extend its influence using the false doctrine of popular sovereignty. Even though he spoke about the Union as though it had an equal chance of becoming either all free or all slave, with this speech Lincoln took a clear, powerful stand against the latter possibility.

If we could first know *where* we are, and *whither* we are tending, we could better judge *what* to do, and *how* to do it.

We are now far into the *fifth* year, since a policy was initiated, with the *avowed* object, and *confident* promise, of putting an end to slavery agitation.

Source: Roy P. Basler (ed.), *Abraham Lincoln: His Speeches and Writings* (Cleveland, Oh.: World Publishing Company, 1946), pp. 372–81

Under the operation of that policy, that agitation has not only, *not ceased*, but has *constantly augmented.*

In my opinion, it *will* not cease, until a *crisis* shall have been reached, and passed –

"A house divided against itself cannot stand."

I believe this government cannot endure, permanently half *slave* and half *free*.

I do not expect the Union to be *dissolved* – I do not expect the house to *fall* – but I *do* expect it will cease to be divided.

It will become *all* one thing, or *all* the other.

Either the *opponents* of slavery, will arrest the further spread of it, and place it where the public mind shall rest in the belief that it is in course of ultimate extinction; or its *advocates* will push it forward, till it shall become alike lawful in *all* the States, *old* as well as *new* – *North* as well as *South*.

Have we no *tendency* to the latter condition?

Let any one who doubts, carefully contemplate that now almost complete legal combination – piece of *machinery* so to speak – compounded of the Nebraska doctrine, and the Dred Scott decision. . . .

The *working* points of that machinery are:

First, that no negro slave, imported as such from Africa, and no descendant of such slave can ever be a *citizen* of any State, in the sense of that term as used in the Constitution of the United States.

This point is made in order to deprive the negro, in every possible event, of the benefit of that provision of the United States Constitution, which declares that –

"the citizens of each State shall be entitled to all privileges and immunities of citizens in the several States."

Secondly, that "subject to the Constitution of the United States," neither *Congress* nor a *Territorial Legislature* can exclude slavery from any United States Territory.

This point is made in order that individual men may *fill up* the territories with slaves, without danger of losing them as property, and thus enhance the chances of *permanency* to the institution through all the future.

Thirdly, that whether the holding a negro in actual slavery in a free State, makes him free, as against the holder, the United States courts will not decide, but will leave to be decided by the courts of any slave State the negro may be forced into by the master.

This point is made, not to be pressed *immediately*; but, if acquiesced in for a while, and apparently *indorsed* by the people at an election, *then* to sustain the logical conclusion that what Dred Scott's master might lawfully do with Dred Scott, in the free State of Illinois, every other master may lawfully do with any other *one* or one *thousand* slaves, in Illinois, or in any other free State.

Auxiliary to all this, and working hand in hand with it, the Nebraska doctrine, or what is left of it, is to *educate* and *mould* public opinion, at least *Northern* public opinion, to not *care* whether slavery is voted *down* or voted *up*.

This shows exactly where we now *are*; and *partially* also, whither we are tending.

It will throw additional light on the latter, to go back, and run the mind over the string of historical facts already stated. Several things will *now* appear less *dark* and *mysterious* than they did *when* they were transpiring. The people were to be left "perfectly free" "subject only to the Constitution." What the *Constitution* had to do with it, outsiders could not *then* see. Plainly enough *now*, it was an exactly fitted *nitch* for the Dred Scott decision to afterward come in, and declare that *perfect freedom* of the people, to be just no freedom at all. . . .

Slavery and Territorial Expansion

Don E. Fehrenbacher

In *The Slaveholding Republic*, Don Fehrenbacher traces the evolution of the American government's relationship with slavery and analyzes its implications. Fehrenbacher's focus is as much on constitutional developments as on political issues and sectional conflicts. He argues that whilst the Constitution bore a neutral attitude toward slavery, the federal government's attitude toward territorial expansion was decidedly in favor of the institution. In this excerpt, Fehrenbacher follows the development of United States policy from the Mexican War to the Dredd Scott case, and demonstrates that, in the ten years between 1848 and 1857, both the executive and the legislative branches had a sympathetic attitude toward slavery. Fehrenbacher also argues that the Republicans were the first politicians to desire "to end what they regarded as the unnatural hold of the slaveholding interest upon the government of the United States." For this reason, many Americans who lived in both North and South considered them revolutionaries.

Don E. Fehrenbacher, *The Slaveholding Republic: An Account of the United States Government's Relations to Slavery* (New York and Oxford: Oxford University Press, 2001), pp. 266–92.

The redevelopment of a two-party system in the decades that followed the Missouri crisis served to calm political passions on the slavery issue, at least temporarily. By heightening conflict over issues having nothing to do with slavery directly... the emergence of the Whig and Democratic parties effectively redirected the course of American politics. The Democratic party's two-thirds rule, adopted in 1832, that nominees for president and vice president have an extraordinary majority support, subtly restricted any new outburst of antislavery agitation, as aspiring northern Democratic leaders knew that they needed southern backing to win the ultimate prize. Party restraints also worked upon southern leaders. For example, President Andrew Jackson reluctantly delayed slaveholding Texas, which had declared its independence from Mexico in 1836, from immediately entering the Union, as he could not risk disrupting his intersectional party in a presidential election year. The new Whig party exercised similar restraining influences, at least up until John Tyler became the first vice president to assume the presidency upon the death of a sitting president.... A pro-slavery extremist, Tyler actively sought the annexation of Texas irrespective of the consequences. After two decades of relative intersectional calm, the issue of slavery's expansion into the West reawakened.

Stretching from California to Russian Alaska, the Oregon Country concurrently captured the imaginations of northern free-soil expansionists. Exploiting Oregon's potential to balance Texas, James K. Polk won the Democratic nomination for the presidency in 1844 upon a dual promise to add both areas to the United States. Seizing upon Polk's narrow victory over an anti-expansionist Henry Clay, annexationists declared a public mandate to admit Texas immediately, which was done by a joint resolution of Congress. Supposedly, clear title to the Oregon half of Polk's platform could follow in due course.

Texas, Oregon, and California were all linked in the westward-looking agenda of the Democratic party. As Mexicans viewed Texas as legitimately part of their nation, American annexation of Texas necessarily meant war, or at the very least very serious negotiations with Mexico in order to prevent hostilities. Whether by war or negotiations, Polk was intent upon acquiring at least part of Alta California. He went to the brink with Great Britain over Oregon as well, despite the fact that this European power could not be bullied as a weak Mexico might. In the contest with Great Britain, California was also key, given both the latter's proximity to Oregon and its extremely vulnerable condition....

In order to avoid the possibility of a two-front war, Polk divided the Oregon Country with Great Britain in 1846, at the same time, he went to war with Mexico over Texas to defend an extreme pro-slavery boundary claim. In retaliation for the president's compromise of free soil, northern congressmen, led by Pennsylvania Democrat David Wilmot, vowed to bar slavery from any territory taken from Mexico. For the first time in American history, a serious attempt was made to use the Constitution's territories clause to ban slavery from the West without any conciliatory gesture toward southern interests. Wilmot's proposal, made in the form of an amendment to a military appropriations bill, . . . repeatedly passed the House only to fail in a pro-southern Senate. There, John C. Calhoun countered by proclaiming that slavery followed the flag into any and all acquired provinces. . . .

The inability of the Wilmot Proviso to pass the senate possibly motivated Supreme Court Justice John McLean to suggest that the proviso's principle was inherent in the Constitution itself. A rare antislavery presence on a pro-slavery Court, McLean argued that under the Constitution, freedom was national, while slavery was only local, which logically suggested that territory acquired by the nation itself was automatically free soil. Other antislavery activists suggested that the Fifth Amendment's guarantee of individual liberty supported McLean's case. By contrast, slavery's defenders claimed that the Fifth Amendment protected slaveholders' property rights from any federal meddling, such as the Wilmot Proviso. In an environment that was rapidly reducing all political questions to matters of constitutional imperative, President Polk himself tentatively favored a more political approach, that of extending the Missouri Compromise line of 36° 30′ into any lands taken from Mexico. Yet none of these positions succeeded in winning sufficient congressional backing. Inexorably, the nation moved toward a new sectional crisis over slavery.

Lewis Cass, who was nominated by the Democrats to succeed Polk, held that the Constitution's territories clause, properly interpreted, did not empower Congress to pass either the Wilmot Proviso or extend the line of 36° 30′ into the Far West, as that language provided only the authority to make rules and regulations regarding the disposition of public lands. By his lights, allowing the people of each federal territory to decide the issue of slavery for themselves was in the tradition of the nation's founders, who fought Great Britain supposedly to establish the principle of local self-government. According to this logic, nonintervention, as made operational in 1787 south of the Ohio River, was in the tradition of local self-government, whereas Congress's imposed Northwest Ordinance of that same year was not. Stephen A. Douglas, who soon became the leading spokesman for "popular sovereignty," stopped short of claiming that the Constitution gave Congress no authority over the issue. Rather, he urged that Congress *should* be guided by "the great principle" of local self-government.[1]

One practical problem with popular sovereignty concerned exactly when the principle of local self-government should become operational during the territorial process. Historically, nonintervention, or noninterference by the federal government, had led to the effective establishment of slavery. Slavery, with other vices, could only be kept out of a territory by means of governmental proscription, which Cass hinted was still possible under his plan. In advocating local self-determination, Cass's rhetoric seemed to allow that territorial governments themselves might outlaw slavery well before applying for statehood. Indeed, before northern groups he suggested this option. Yet, when speaking before southern audiences, Cass tightly defined popular sovereignty as operating only at the moment when a territory petitioned Congress for entry into the Union as a sovereign state. Up until that time, laissez faire would allow slavery to become firmly established. Of course, by that late date, the issue would have already been determined by drift. For southern voters, popular sovereignty meant something else altogether. With this clever stratagem, Cass succeeded in shaping the national discourse, despite the fact of losing the presidential election to his Whig opponent, Zachary Taylor, hero of the Mexican War.

Although nonintervention and drift had heretofore aided slavery's extension, the Mexican Cession provided unique circumstances that possibly favored freedom, as Mexico had banned slavery by positive enactment prior to American acquisition. Until superceded by new congressional statutes, this Mexican law officially continued into the new American era. If federal officials on the scene had an intent to maintain the legal status quo, Congress's failure to resolve the dispute regarding slavery's extension in this instance clearly favored antislavery. However, the California gold rush prevented this scenario. As soldiers in the American occupying force deserted to the gold fields, California rapidly moved toward anarchy. In the wake of this historical event, drift became intolerable. Upon assuming the presidency in March 1849, Zachary Taylor was forced to act.

In April, Taylor dispatched a special agent to California to work with the American military governor in encouraging the burgeoning new population there to petition Congress for immediate statehood. Without knowledge of this presidential intention, California's military authorities had already begun to move in this direction. Three weeks before Taylor's inauguration, citizens met in San Francisco and called for the creation of a provisional civilian government. Well before Taylor's plan was known, the military governor decided to lead this popular groundswell rather than oppose it. . . .

President Taylor saw the entire Mexican Cession as unsuited to slavery. Indeed, had the gold rush not roughly intervened, a slaveholding southern president, intent upon carrying out an antislavery policy in the West through a quiet enforcement of Mexican law by American military administrators in territory left unorganized by Congress, might have effectively calmed the volatile sectional confrontation initiated by the Wilmot Proviso. But, of course, this is not what occurred. Rather, in attempting to resolve the issue of California anarchy, a politically inexperienced Taylor succeeded only in generating a strident opposition from his native South. Surrounded by northern antislavery advisors, Taylor naively convinced himself that by jumping over the normal territorial process and instead pushing for new states in both California and New Mexico he could avoid the issue of slavery in the territories.

North Carolina's Thomas L. Clingman expressed rising southern sentiment by noting that under Taylor's leadership California, Oregon, New Mexico, Deseret (Utah), and Minnesota all seemed likely to join the Union as free states, giving the North practical control of the Senate as well as the House. Once thus empowered, Clingman predicted, the North would soon move to destroy slavery in the southern states themselves.... He and others threatened that before the South would bow before this specter of northern domination, the Union itself would be torn asunder. The rage, present in the earlier Missouri crisis, emerged fully resurrected by the end of 1849. Constitutionalization of the issue of slavery in the West, and an emotional hardening of positions that accompanied this process, made an easy resolution virtually impossible.

The [California] Convention finished its work on October 13, 1849, adopting a constitution prohibiting slavery. The voters...ratified it on November 13. These actions, culminating on December 4 in President Taylor's recommendation that the new state be quickly admitted, precipitated the nation's greatest crisis over slavery in a generation. Refusing to follow Taylor's presidential leadership, Henry Clay offered his own plan for a sweeping compromise, only one part of which involved California's admission as a free state. The facts that Taylor (the titular head of the Whig party) had no political experience and that Clay (the historic leader of the Whig party) had failed five times to win the prize so easily acquired by Taylor, heightened the drama of this personal confrontation.

By encouraging both California and later New Mexico to become free states by their own initiative, Taylor created the appearance of validating the Wilmot Proviso without having Congress actually enact the measure. By contrast, Clay's plan called for California to become a free state but also divided the remainder of the Mexican Cession into two territories – New Mexico and Utah (the northern half of Taylor's "New Mexico") – "without the adoption of any restriction or condition on the subject of slavery." If and when the House passed Clay's plan, it would thereby formally reject the Wilmot Proviso, thus appeasing southern sensibilities. Clay was enough of a politician to know that symbolic acts are often as significant as material concessions....

...President Taylor, deeply offended by Clay's refusal to follow his lead, stood ready to kill his rival's plan. In the early summer of 1850, both the South and those antislavery Whigs supporting Taylor's plan blocked Clay's progress.

Then, Taylor died on July 9, following a very brief illness. Millard Fillmore, the new president, quickly swore allegiance to Clay as party leader. Yet, even with the elimination of presidential opposition, Clay's proposal stalled. Years of identifying the issue of slavery in the territories with constitutional imperatives seemingly prevented any resolution. Thereupon, an exhausted, aged Clay transferred the congressional management of his compromise plan to Stephen A. Douglas, a younger, more energetic man from the other major party. Concluding that true compromisers were in a minority, Douglas adopted a new strategy, alternatively coupling extreme factions with an unwavering procompromise minority to get each facet of the settlement through Congress in a piecemeal manner. In the months of August and September, Douglas trained the Senate and the House to do his bidding. Voting on each specific measure was largely along sectional lines. In the end, President Fillmore signed all parts of the so-called Compromise of 1850. Because of the extraordinary way in which each part of it was maneuvered through Congress, historian David M. Potter aptly termed the Compromise of 1850 as "a truce perhaps, an armistice, certainly a settlement, but not a true compromise."[2]

California thus became a free state. New Mexico and Utah's situation was more ambiguous. The enigma of Cass's popular sovereignty – which confusingly translated into either Calhoun's constitutional position effectively protecting slavery in the territories up until statehood *or* a possible instrument to kill slavery during the territorial stage well before any application for statehood – was built into the very structure of the settlement. Revealing just how far the issue of slavery in the territories had become constitutionalized, the law provided for any decisions made effecting slavery in either Utah or New Mexico during their territorial stages to be appealed to the United States Supreme Court....

Some parts of the Compromise of 1850 had nothing to do directly with the issue of slavery in the territories. Of these, the Fugitive Slave Act of 1850 is the principal example....However, the significance of the package rested primarily in the fact that the issue of slavery in the territories, which had first threatened the Union with the entry of Missouri and later with California, had seemingly been permanently laid to rest. Both Douglas and President Fillmore emphasized this point. However, the matter was far from dead. Four years later, Douglas himself reopened it by devising the Kansas–Nebraska Act, a measure that invited American settlement into the undeveloped part of the Louisiana Purchase above 36° 30′. In the process, the Missouri Compromise line barring slavery's northward advance was repealed. Born in northern reaction to Douglas's symbolic reawakening of an old issue, the Republican party thus came into being, devoted to halting the spread of slavery into new territories. In hindsight, Douglas's behavior seems almost inconceivable, given his earlier central role in supposedly settling the problem for all time.

To explain this course of events, the historian must recreate concerns and expectations of the times. First, one must consider the ambitions of Stephen A. Douglas himself. As a Democrat, he knew that he needed strong southern support if he ever hoped to become president of the United States. The role that he played in shaping the Kansas–Nebraska Act clearly enhanced his reputation in the South, where restriction of slavery north of the line of 36° 30′ rankled as a continuing symbol of congressional interference with that section's most significant domestic institution. But Douglas's southward-looking political motivations did not primarily determine his course. More important was his desire to develop economic opportunities for his Illinois constituents.

The nation was then experiencing dynamic technological growth. Railroads especially captured the public imagination. Every town, certainly every city, dreamed of becoming a commercial emporium. The westward migration of the American people continued unabated. Railroad construction promised to direct the course of empire. Yet, prior to the Kansas–Nebraska Act, a swath of wilderness ranging northward from 36° 30′ to the Canadian border remained closed to American settlement. Over the years, the federal government had made various treaties with Indian tribes promising them permanent guarantees against future encroachment if they would relocate far from areas of white settlement, beyond the western borders of Arkansas, Missouri, and Iowa. . . . This situation had become the practical negative result of the Missouri Compromise of over a generation before, as southerners stood ready to block any attempt to organize the region above 36° 30′ into free territories. Every year that the South succeeded in maintaining the status quo, the potential growth of Chicago and St. Louis remained unrealized, leaving commercial interests in both northern and southern Illinois frustrated. The dynamism of the age augured against any such permanent obstruction. . . .

Typical of American politicians of all seasons, Douglas explained his purposes in idealistic, democratic rhetoric. Jacksonian Democrats, of whom Douglas was a prime example, saw westward expansion as essential for the perpetuation of both individual freedom and republican government. . . . Democrats then typically believed that economic opportunity for the masses could only be kept alive by means of a continuously expanding agricultural frontier. The replanting of democratic institutions, characterized by local self-government, became Douglas's "great principle" underlying popular sovereignty. In his own mind, the Kansas–Nebraska Act was synonymous with American freedom, economic opportunity, and local self-determination, upon which the American democratic experiment rested. Most importantly, he believed in his own powers of political persuasion to communicate this vision to the American people.

Douglas's original bill had proposed to organize the entire area north of 36° 30′ as "Nebraska Territory." Dividing it subsequently into both Kansas and Nebraska made it more attractive to southerners, who could see in Kansas a possible future slave state, immediately to the west of slaveholding Missouri. Given the fact that Douglas himself had no strong personal moral revulsion concerning slavery, the change was seen by him as one that merely helped move western development forward. . . . Surrendering the moral sense of national prohibition that the Missouri Compromise line of 36° 30′ had come to represent was of no different order. For him, such moral condemnation was only abolitionist posturing over an abstraction, lacking in practical definition and deserving little serious consideration.

Douglas saw the Compromise of 1850 as having made the Missouri Compromise's earlier line of prohibition politically irrelevant. He portrayed the modern method of resolving the issue of slavery in the territories as present in the rules organizing Utah and New Mexico territories. Southerners could readily agree with Douglas, as the Illinois senator did not overemphasize the probable outcome of any meaningful popular sovereignty in Kansas Territory. Most westward-moving Americans were northerners, loyal to northern institutions and northern culture, and likely to restrict the introduction of slave agriculture. As a realist, Douglas knew what popular sovereignty, exercised during the territorial stage, was likely to produce in Kansas. But, as he prided himself a realist, it is interesting that he did not foresee the southern rage that inevitably resulted when these facts ultimately materialized. Focusing upon the immediate challenge of getting his bill enacted over vociferous antislavery opposition, Douglas chose to let the future take care of itself. . . .

Seventy percent of northern Democratic congressmen and senators who voted for the Kansas–Nebraska Act lost their seats in the midterm elections of 1854. Despite their harsh rejection at the polls, northern Democrats generally continued to opt for a harmonious relationship with southern Democrats. As for Douglas himself, he realized that the midterm election results virtually killed his own presidential ambitions for 1856. . . . While the Kansas–Nebraska Act hurt the Democrats, the party at least remained afloat as a national political organization.

Whig losses in the midterm elections were more serious. The deaths of Clay and Webster several years before contributed to the party's unraveling. With its traditional leadership disappearing, the party entered a steep descent. More fundamental problems further encouraged the Whig decline. Whigs had never shown the cleverness in managing the constitutionalization of the issue of slavery in the territories, which had characterized the party of Cass and Douglas. During and after the crisis of 1850, many northern Whigs had revealed themselves as essentially antislavery people, while southern Whigs at times occupied more strident pro-slavery positions than even southern Democrats. By 1852, the national Whig party appeared to have a sectionalized split personality so far as the slavery issue was concerned.

[Daniel] Webster had provided a model of a sectional Whig leader moderating his message to meet the needs of his national party, but few northern Whigs followed his example. . . . Accordingly, southerners fell away from the Whig party in droves following the Compromise of 1850. . . . Rather than hold onto an increasingly marginalized national Whig party, northern Whigs also exited their party in 1854, further relegating the party of Clay and Webster to a political grave. Two new parties – the national American (or Know-Nothing) party and a sectional, northern Republican party – quickly emerged.

It is important not to overemphasize the role that the slavery issue played in the death of the Whig party. Economic and personal issues had called the party into being in the 1830s, yet they were passé by the early 1850s. Clay's themes of protective tariffs, federally sponsored internal improvements, and the Bank of the United States no longer effectively divided the parties. With the passing of Andrew Jackson in 1845, continuing animosity toward "King Andrew" no longer had any relevance. A growing degree of interparty consensus on economic issues heightened intraparty sensitivities over slavery, especially within the Whig party.

Those northern Whigs gravitating toward the Know-Nothings did not jettison their antislavery views; rather they preferred, temporarily at least, to accentuate a presumably greater concern with cultural issues surrounding the changing demographics of European immigration. German Catholics came to the United States during this time, but it was particularly the increasing numbers of impoverished Irish Roman Catholic immigrants that sparked a nativist reaction among northern Know-Nothings. . . . [A] number of southern Whigs chose to experiment with this new national coalition, framed around a shared, intersectional

Protestant distrust of Roman Catholicism. Interestingly, while northern Know-Nothings tried to persuade voters that Irish Catholic newcomers tended to support slavery, southern Know-Nothings argued that immigrants in the North were the natural enemies of slavery and that their demographic growth was the greatest long-term threat that the South faced.

Some northern members of this new nativist party worked to mute their antislavery differences with their southern evangelical brethren, but such efforts were generally unsuccessful. These differences gradually undermined a *national* organization devoted to preserving Protestant practices and cultural understandings in American life and government. Republicans, made up mostly of former northern Whigs but containing antislavery Democrats as well, were not similarly restrained, given the lack of any southern branch in their party. This fact gave them a long-term advantage over the Know-Nothing party in the North. Republicans proudly resurrected the Wilmot Proviso, broadening it to apply to all federal territories, not just the Mexican Cession. Free-soil parties had existed in the past, but they had never represented more than a small minority of the American electorate. The Republican party posed a different threat to the South, for as a contender for major-party status in the most populous section of the Union, it had the ability to win the presidency without garnering a single southern vote.

The Republican party represented many shades of antislavery opinion. Some members were motivated by their hatred of the slave-system's injustices done to African Americans, whereas others were motivated by a racist contempt for blacks themselves and wished the nation to be rid of both slavery and blacks altogether. Republicans also trumpeted negative stereotypes of the arrogant and barbarous slaveholder. In general, Republicans were characterized by their cultural distance from both southern slavery and black people, rather than outright compassion for the slave or hatred for either slaveholders or African Americans. They spoke for many northerners who were tired of perpetually genuflecting before southern sensibilities, as they commonly saw all things southern as corrupting republican virtue and holding back national economic progress. By restricting the spread of slavery, they wanted the West to become culturally northern and entrepreneurial in spirit. . . . Republicans typically did not call for the destruction of slavery in the states where it already existed. Rather, they wished to restrict and slowly undermine slavery, without destroying the nation in the pursuit of immediate abolition.

Republicans wanted to end what they regarded as the unnatural hold of the slaveholding interest upon the government of the United States. They recalled the Declaration of Independence as having founded the nation upon an ideology unfriendly to the very concept of slavery. ... The Republican party wanted a nation guided by one cultural standard rather than remain a "house divided against itself." The focus of this orientation initially was the Republican resolve to put slavery on the course of national extinction. Cultural homogeneity was the watchword of the Know-Nothing party as well. While Republicans generally shunned Know-Nothingism as too extreme, northern nativists sensed that (unlike the Democratic party) Republicans would never be actively antinativist as an organization. ... Typically, Republicans were of Protestant backgrounds, distrusted Roman Catholicism, and were prone toward moralistic crusading, a trait most evident in their evangelical antislavery campaign. When the Know-Nothing party finally died after only several years of operation, most northern Know-Nothings found a welcome home in the Republican party.

Republicans and northern Know-Nothings joined in the fight against slavery in the territories, realizing that in Kansas the national destiny was unfolding. Specifically, the struggle over Kansas challenged whether popular sovereignty could ever serve as a practical solution to the issue of slavery in the territories. At first, fraudulent voting on the part of Missourians masquerading as Kansas settlers carried elections for proslavery. Antislavery forces then erected their own illegal territorial legislature to countermand a legal legislature elected by fraud. Springing up at the grassroots of this western struggle, eventual guerrilla warfare in Kansas sent shock waves across the nation. As small-scale violence in Kansas reached a crescendo in 1856, Republicans and Know-Nothings tested their relative strength in the political arena. The year before, the Know-Nothing party carried many state contests, and it then looked as if it would emerge as the premier rival of the Democrats. But this early assessment was premature, for in the presidential contest of 1856 the Know-Nothings effectively disintegrated over a national-convention plank regarding slavery in the territories. In that election, the Republicans emerged as the only real challenger to continuing Democratic control. Pennsylvania's James Buchanan, the Democratic nominee, went on to win that contest, but he and the rest of his party found the outcome uncomfortably close. The loss of several northern states from Buchanan's column – Pennsylvania and Illinois or Indiana, to be specific – would have given the victory to John C. Frémont, the Republican party's first presidential nominee.

For years, there had been talk of the Supreme Court providing a definitive statement on the issue of slavery in the territories. ... John C. Calhoun had thoroughly developed the constitutional reasoning that was ultimately employed in the Dred Scott decision. This logic held that the Constitution prevented congressional meddling with southern property rights in the commonly held federal territories. By fully exploiting the concept of state police powers in defining slave property, the Court transformed a state sovereignty protected by the Tenth Amendment into a doctrine of national pro-slavery power to determine the future course of the western territories.

Effectively, the Court told the rapidly rising Republican party that it should disband, that it could not carry out its principal *raison d'être*. In this case, the weakest branch of the federal government informed Congress, the strongest branch, that it lacked the power to accomplish the will of an emerging sectionalized national majority. The Court instructed the nation that the Constitution was indeed a pro-slavery compact. The result was a political explosion in the North. The Dred Scott decision, only the second instance in U.S. history of the Court invalidating a federal statute, was built upon both a weak legal argument and a misrepresentation of history. Republican refusal to accept the judgment followed, as party propagandists spread the notion of a conspiratorial "slave-power" that corrupted not only the government of the United States (including the Court), but even the Constitution itself. Republicans were not undone by the decision but instead were handed a new weapon – that being the well-grounded speculation that Chief Justice Roger Taney's court intended eventually to nationalize slavery by legalizing it within the northern states themselves....

As northerners absorbed the meaning of the Court decision, more threatening news arrived. The pro-slavery territorial legislature of Kansas chose to press the issue of immediate statehood. With each passing month, the real but officially unrecognized antislavery majority in the territory grew larger, which convinced the legislature to act while there was still a slim chance for victory. In an act of nonviolent resistance, antislavery settlers boycotted the election for a state constitutional convention, many of them fearing that their participation would only be overcome by pro-slavery fraud in any case. Robert J. Walker, Buchanan's handpicked territorial governor, valiantly tried to persuade antislavery voters that he was intent upon conducting a fair election, but his efforts were unsuccessful in getting them to vote. As a result, a pro-slavery constitutional convention was elected. Convening at Lecompton in the fall of 1857, the convention quickly drafted a pro-slavery state constitution.

In referring the document back to the people of Kansas for ratification, the convention refused to allow a simple "yes" or "no" vote. Instead it came up with a scheme that made a mockery of popular sovereignty itself. Kansas's voters were given a choice of the Lecompton constitution with slavery unrestricted or with slavery restricted to the current slaves then residing in the territory. If the latter option passed, roughly two hundred slaves already in Kansas would remain slaves for life, as would their descendents. Governor Walker renounced this method of referral as a sham and eventually resigned over the issue. Under extreme pressure from the pro-slavery wing of the Democratic party, Buchanan himself came out in favor of the unseemly process. . . .

Stephen Douglas, the principal politician then associated with popular sovereignty, refused to support Buchanan, thus triggering the disruption of the Democratic party. Unlike Buchanan, Douglas had little real choice in determining his course. His senate seat was up for election in 1858. If he . . . [backed] Buchanan, he knew that his career as an elected official would be over, such was the popular animus in Illinois against the Lecompton fraud. Douglas was forced to come out against this sham if he had any hope of appearing as a man of integrity. Given that he knew that Republican opposition against him would be intense in the senatorial race, Douglas chose not only to oppose the Lecompton constitution but fight it with a dramatic flair that would both confuse his opponents and rally his supporters for the coming campaign. . . .

Over the next several months, he forged a temporary practical alliance with Republicans in Congress. Buchanan, armed with the power of federal patronage to reward and punish, opposed them. In the end, neither side achieved outright victory. Instead, Congress passed the so-called English Compromise, which sent the Lecompton constitution back to the voters of Kansas to be voted up or down as a complete package. By the terms of this "compromise," if the voters voted against Lecompton and slavery, they would be forced to wait several years until the territorial population reached something more than 90,000, the number then used to justify one member of the House of Representatives. On August 2, 1858, with antislavery voters participating in the election, the Kansas electorate killed the Lecompton constitution by a majority of 11,300 to 1788.

Horace Greeley, the widely read Republican editor of the *New York Tribune*, praised Douglas's gallant fight against the Lecompton constitution and urged the Illinois branch of the Republican party not to contest his seat in the November election – advice that was firmly rejected. Illinois Republican leader Abraham Lincoln realized that Douglas was planning a trap even before the Little Giant's formal break with Buchanan. He wrote former Democrat Lyman Trumbull, who had become Illinois' first Republican senator in the previous election, that Douglas was scheming "to draw off some Republicans" in the upcoming campaign. He warned Trumbull that true Republicans should not encourage this trend.[3] When Greeley began to praise Douglas publicly, Lincoln privately exploded, accusing the New York editor of "sacraficing [*sic*] us here in Illinois."[4] Six months later, and a week before his own nomination to run against Douglas, Lincoln calmed down and wrote calculatingly that he would have to be "patient" regarding the unfortunate "inclination of some Republicans to favor Douglas."[5]

Lincoln knew his challenge in this unique historical context. First, he had to demonstrate to the voters that Douglas was not the quasi-Republican that he often appeared to be during the Lecompton fight. Likewise, he had to portray Douglas as intellectually and emotionally incapable of effectively protecting northern interests. Given that Douglas had effectively stolen the political center with his anti-Lecompton heroics, Lincoln knew that uncharacteristically he himself would have to take advanced antislavery positions to create any significant difference for the voters. Lincoln, who had never come close to achieving his unrelenting political ambitions, knew this as his defining moment. Douglas was a national political force. A contender who could match him blow for blow might become a national leader himself. Such was the test facing this prior one-term Whig congressman (1845–47).

Lincoln successfully pressured Douglas to a series of joint debates, to occur between August 21 and October 15, during which he intended to demonstrate that Douglas was still an integral part of the slave-power conspiracy, as much as when he led Congress to pass the Kansas–Nebraska Act. He meant to portray Douglas's role as that of a political salesman to the North, peddling the concept that popular sovereignty was the only rational solution to the problem of slavery in the territories. Once northerners accepted that position, Lincoln's conspiratorial theory concluded, they would be well along toward moral indifference, which was a necessary precondition to nationalizing slavery.

Lincoln's purpose was to expose the difference between true Republican ideology and Douglas's values – a difference that the Little Giant had temporarily successfully blurred during the Lecompton fight. In achieving this, Lincoln had to stray considerably from his party's preferred focus on the practical issue of slavery in the territories and instead emphasize abstract moral values. Nonetheless, this was a modification of tactics only. The basic strategy of convincing the public that slavery should be placed on the course of ultimate extinction through its elimination in the federal territories remained constant. Lincoln knew that Douglas did not share this Republican goal, despite appearances in the anti-Lecompton fight.

Lincoln summarized his campaign focus in this way: "The real issue in this controversy – the one pressing upon every mind – is the sentiment on the part of one class that looks upon the institution of slavery as a wrong, and of another class that does not look upon it as a wrong."[6] Throughout the debates, Lincoln repeated this moral theme. He emphasized that the best thinking of the Founding Fathers supported the current Republican position. He insisted that African Americans had to be included in the meaning of "all men" if the Declaration of Independence was to make any sense. He also claimed that the Constitution itself had been framed so as not to allow slavery any privileged constitutional position. The founders, he said, realized that the nation at the outset did not live up to the ideals of the Declaration. In stating that all persons have human rights, they had not intended to describe human relationships as they existed then or at any time in the recorded past. All that they intended, he emphasized, was to point the new nation in a progressive direction: "They meant to set up a standard maxim for a free society which should be familiar to all: constantly looked to, constantly labored for, and though never perfectly attained, constantly approximated and thereby deepening its influence and augmenting the happiness and value of life to all people of all colors, everywhere."[7] The framers, he asserted, had meant to put slavery on the course of ultimate extinction. But instead, during the interim, the federal government itself had become a tool of the slaveholding interest.[8]

Douglas disagreed that the founders had intended to include black people in the phrase "all men are created equal." Here he sided with Chief Justice Taney's opinion in the Dred Scott decision. The framers, Douglas emphasized, did not intend to proscribe slavery in any way; neither had they intended to promote the institution. . . . Subtly, Douglas contrasted his political party's tolerance of diversity with Republican preference for moral uniformity and cultural homogeneity. Douglas prided himself as being a practical man of the world in contrast to rigid idealists such as Lincoln, and so he readily let Lincoln define him as a person not guided by moral considerations. That which Lincoln intended as a criticism, Douglas accepted as an unintended compliment.

Lincoln warned that if the voting public validated Douglas's amoral stance by returning him to the Senate, the pro-slavery plan to divert the nation from its original purpose would be furthered. In both his "House Divided" speech at the outset of the campaign and also in the debate held at Ottawa, Illinois, Lincoln fantasized about a possible second Dred Scott case in which Taney would rule that even supposedly free states could not keep slavery outside their borders. He tied this nightmarish projection to Douglas's flexible morality and implied that if the voters wanted slavery in the free states themselves, they should vote for Douglas. . . .

Before racist crowds, especially in southern Illinois, Douglas emphasized that Lincoln's egalitarian logic led straight toward unthinkable racial amalgamation. Lincoln replied that he did not favor integrating African Americans into American life as social and political equals. In fact, he wished that American blacks could be returned to Africa. He advocated no change in northern society, where free blacks were oppressed at every turn. Lincoln had earlier proclaimed that a house divided against itself could not stand. Yet he saw no inconsistency in continuing the northern methods of maintaining a racially divided national community. While this political position was opportune if Republicans hoped to achieve majority status, here was an obvious ideological weak spot that eventually would stall their party's progressive advance.

In the Freeport debate, Douglas offered that which would come to be called the "Freeport Doctrine." Lincoln had first challenged him by asking how the senator could continue to support both popular sovereignty and Chief Justice Taney's opinion in the Dred Scott decision, as the two were in seeming contradiction. Douglas offered an answer that was not new. He had stated it before.... But in the context of this particular campaign, the answer took on an ominous character for southerners. Practically, Douglas said, slavery could not exist in the territories unless supported by slave codes that could be provided only by territorial legislatures. Hence, in order to keep slavery effectively out of a territory, that territory's legislature did not have to outlaw slavery directly, which in the Dred Scott decision Taney had suggested that it could not do anyway. All that it had to do was not pass any slave codes, the multifaceted, tyrannical police regulations that every slave society needed to keep its human property well behaved and orderly. By inactivity or indefinite procrastination, a territorial legislature could effectively outlaw slavery without ever conducting a frontal assault. Unlike Lincoln, Douglas saw no need to oppose Taney's opinion....

Eventually, Douglas had to deal with the aftermath of his Freeport Doctrine, but more immediately his challenge was to defeat Lincoln. Little was spared by either side in a campaign that at times was waged on a low level, in stark contrast to the classic character of the debates themselves.... Following the election, state legislators that were pledged to Douglas reelected their champion in the manner then prescribed by the Constitution. Writing to a friend that he would "now sink out of view, and... be forgotten," Lincoln added, "I believe I have made some marks which will tell for the cause of civil liberty long after I am gone." He was clearly disappointed at the result and thought that his political career might be at an end.[9] In reality, it had only barely begun. His keen mind and ability to reduce abstract principles to easily remembered fundamental maxims impressed newspaper readers of the debates across the North.... By comparison, both Douglas and Chief Justice Taney publicly exhibited a poor understanding of the Declaration's political philosophy. Indeed, a convenient forgetfulness regarding the nation's original ideals had facilitated the federal government's gradual seduction by the slaveholding interest. Lincoln's forceful protest demonstrated that the best way to end this pattern of drift was to recall and clearly reexpress first principles. . . .

By not allowing Douglas to rest upon his anti-Lecompton accomplishments during the campaign, Lincoln pushed the Republican party to a more advanced position than that advocated by those eastern Republicans who had wanted to allow Douglas to run uncontested in 1858. By his hounding of Douglas during the debates, Lincoln also insured that the clever Illinois senator could never repair his relations with the South. At Jonesboro, he asked Douglas if he would vote for a congressional slave code, if such an opportunity arose. Douglas's quick and negative response, fully in harmony with the principle of popular sovereignty, served notice to southerners that he would always be their enemy. Indeed, it was this very issue of a federal slave code for the territories that drove the generations-long sectional conflict toward its ultimate conclusion.

The Dred Scott decision had proclaimed abstract property rights for slaveholders in the territories, but these were empty promises unless supported by local police regulations, commonly known as slave codes. Southerners keenly felt that such regulations were their due, for without them the practical effect of the Dred Scott decision was undone. The Lecompton constitution's failure demonstrated how the earlier southern hope of the Kansas–Nebraska Act to produce one more slave state had been misplaced. Without a federal slave code for the territories, the Dred Scott decision also was worthless. In the midst of all of these dashed southern expectations was the figure of Stephen A. Douglas. On December 9, 1858, the Democratic senatorial caucus, controlled by the pro-slavery element in the party, announced that Douglas had been removed from his chairmanship of the committee on territories, a position that he had held for eleven years. The following year, President Buchanan called for Congress to protect slaveholders' property in the territories. On February 2, 1860, Jefferson Davis introduced a set of resolutions calling for a federal slave code for the territories. Knowing that his resolutions lacked the votes to be enacted, Davis focused upon getting the Democratic caucus to approve them as a litmus test of doctrinal acceptability. Meanwhile, Douglas tried vainly to explain the multiple nuances of his popular sovereignty doctrine to a national audience in an article in *Harper's Magazine* that appeared in September 1859. The ironic consensus of both Republicans and southern Democrats that congressional action was needed to resolve the issue of slavery in the territories once and for all revealed the weak position of Douglas entering into a presidential campaign.

On the eve of the Civil War, the South demanded national power to settle the issue of slavery in the territories. In 1859, the pro-slavery U.S. Supreme Court also promoted a nationalist interpretation of the Constitution in the case of *Ableman v. Booth*, which denied a Wisconsin constitutional challenge to the Fugitive Slave Act of 1850. Ironically, the slaveholding interest, which had long kept a potentially dangerous federal government in check by means of a strict states-rights interpretation of the Constitution, came to rely on a nationalist understanding in its hour of greatest challenge. Over the decades, the federal government had effectively become a pro-slavery instrument by means of multiple little decisions and unconscious drift. But with a northern majoritarian impulse threatening to overwhelm past practices, the South demanded that the federal government enforce what it had come to regard as binding constitutional guarantees. Of course, this declaration of national supremacy was not without an all-important caveat: If the federal government failed to fulfill its constitutional duty, as southerners perceived it, the dismemberment of the Union itself would necessarily follow.

In April 1860, the Democratic National Convention met at Charleston, South Carolina. The meeting lasted for only ten days, breaking up over Douglas's refusal to support a federal slave code for the territories. On June 18, Democrats met again at Baltimore, with the same result. This time, the convention disintegrated after only six days. Following this second debacle, sectional branches of the party met separately in that city. In this way, two separate Democratic platforms and sets of nominees for the presidency and vice presidency were finalized. Going into the presidential election of 1860, Democrats could find no common ground, thereby virtually assuring the election of Abraham Lincoln, who was nominated as the Republican presidential candidate in May. Lincoln's subsequent election set up the secession crisis and the bloody war that followed. . . .

Notes

1 *CG*, 31 Cong., 1 sess., pp. 343, 398, 454, 528; ibid., App., pp. 72–3, 151–2; Stephen A. Douglas, "The Dividing Line Between Federal and Local Authority. Popular Sovereignty in the Territories," *Harper's Magazine*, 19 (1859), pp. 519–37.

2 D. M. Potter, *The Impending Crisis, 1848–1861*, completed and edited by D. E. Fehrenbacher (New York: Harper & Row, 1976), p. 113.

3 Abraham Lincoln to Lyman Trumbull, November 30, 1857, HM Manuscripts, Huntington Library, San Marino, Calif.

4 Abraham Lincoln to Lyman Trumbull, December 28, 1857, HM Manuscripts.
5 Abraham Lincoln to Ward Hill Lamon, June 11, 1858, Lamon Collection, Huntington Library.
6 *Complete Works of Abraham Lincoln*, ed. Roy P. Basler (New Brunswick, NJ: Rutgers University Press, 1953–5), (*CWAL*), vol. 3, p. 312.
7 Ibid., p. 301.
8 Ibid., vol. 2, p. 491, 494, 514–15; vol. 3, pp. 306–8.
9 Abraham Lincoln to Anson G. Henry, November 19, 1858, in *Abraham Lincoln: A Portrait through his Speeches and Writings*, ed. with an introduction by Don E. Fehrenbacher (New York: New American Library, 1964), p. 831; Donald, *Lincoln* (New York: Simon & Schuster, 1995), p. 228.

13
Secession and Civil War

Introduction

In the presidential election of 1860, Abraham Lincoln ran on a Republican platform of resistance to the expansion of slavery, and was elected with a narrow margin in the popular vote. Soon after, on December 20, 1860, the South Carolina legislature gathered in a special convention which unanimously approved the Ordinance of Secession, dissolving that state's ties to the Union. In the *Declaration of the Immediate Causes of Secession*, the South Carolina activists wrote that a sectional party (the Republicans) had elected as president a man "whose opinions and purposes were hostile to slavery." Less than two months later, following South Carolina's example, Mississippi, Florida, Alabama, Georgia, Louisiana, and Texas ("the Deep South") seceded from the Union. Later that spring, the opening shots of the Civil War were fired at Fort Sumter, facing Charleston: on April 12, southern soldiers attacked the federal garrison, and two days later the fort surrendered. After the fall of Fort Sumter, Virginia, North Carolina, Tennessee, and Arkansas joined the secession movement. In Virginia, the Unionists in the western part of the state remained loyal, eventually forming the state of West Virginia; in the upper

South, the border states of Maryland and Delaware and Missouri and Kentucky remained under control of the Union.

At the beginning of the secession crisis, delegates of the seven seceding states met at Montgomery, Alabama, where they drafted a Constitution and adopted the title of the Confederate States of America (CSA). Soon after, they elected Jefferson Davis as president of the Confederacy and Alexander Stephens as vice-president. The Confederate Constitution closely resembled the United States Constitution; however, one section of the document prohibited the issue of protective tariffs such as the one that had sparked the Nullification Crisis. Likewise, states' rights received particular emphasis in the preamble, which declared that the Confederacy derived its power from "each State acting in its sovereign and independent character." The main difference from the US Constitution lay in the Confederate Constitution's protection of slavery. In Article I, which stated that "no bill of attainder, *ex post facto* law denying or impairing the right of property in negro slaves shall be passed," black slavery was specifically recognized and given explicit constitutional sanction and protection. The Confederate Constitution also affirmed the legitimacy of slavery in any territory which the new nation might acquire. Vice-President Alexander Stephens described slavery as "the cornerstone of the Confederacy."

In spite of the Confederate Army's string of initial victories, the war had a catastrophic impact on the finances of the Confederacy, mainly because its agriculture-based economy was ill equipped to face the consequences of a war of this scale. Already in 1861, the Confederacy levied duties on imports and exports and enacted a tax on most forms of property. By 1863, the Confederate government was in such a desperate situation that it enforced a 10 percent tax on all agricultural products, with the predictable result of aggravating both small farmers and planters; meanwhile, rampant inflation and food shortages generated a significant degree of civilian hostility toward the war effort. In April 1862, the Confederate Congress introduced conscription. Another law, passed in November 1862, exempted white men owning 20 or more slaves – the very individuals who had led the South into war – from service in the army. In 1863, the Confederacy introduced impressment, which allowed the army to confiscate food, animals, or other property from farmers, paying for these goods at prices fixed well below market value. By taking farm products destined for the market and rerouting them to the military, impressment intensified food shortages in the cities, and raised the specter of starvation. On April 2, 1863, a group of ironworkers' wives marched on the governor's mansion in Richmond, demanding food and causing a major riot. The violence ceased only when Jefferson Davis threatened to open fire on the women. Similar disturbances occurred in all the major cities of the Confederacy, as the motto "Bread or Blood" made itself heard.

The most momentous consequences of the war were felt in the countryside, where plantations and farms suffered an acute crisis, due to the disruption of the economic system. As war progressed, slaveholders great and small were forced to leave for the front and place their estates in the hands of relatives, overseers, or agents. On some estates, the master's absence and the slaves' familiarity with plantation routine allowed slaves greater control over their daily lives. Elsewhere, supervision by an overseer meant hard discipline and arbitary punishment without the recourse of an appeal to the master. But as overseers and younger sons followed masters into the army, leaving women and old men in charge, the balance of power gradually shifted, undermining slavery on farms and plantations far from the line of battle. Recent research on plantation mistresses during the Civil War has shed light on how they coped with the masters' absence and how they succeeded in imposing their own authority over the slaves. The new and difficult responsibilities that mistresses confronted were multiple: they had to manage the business related to the growing and selling of crops; they had to supervise increasingly sullen and hostile slaves; and they had to take care of their families and children. Historian Drew Faust has argued that the southern women's struggle to "do a man's business" on the plantation resulted in a reconsideration of their identities and their social roles as women. Toward the end of the war, many Confederate women came to question societal standards of feminine behavior, and expressed frustration and disillusionment with the Confederate project.

Further reading

Channing, S. A., *A Crisis of Fear: Secession in South Carolina* (New York: Norton, 1974).

Clinton, C., *Tara Revisited* (New York: Abbeville Press, 1996).

Faust, D. G., *The Creation of Confederate Nationalism* (Baton Rouge: Louisiana State University Press, 1988).

Faust, D. G., *Mothers of Invention: Women of the Slaveholding South in the American Civil War* (Chapel Hill and London: University of North Carolina Press, 1996).

Gallagher, G., *The Confederate War* (Cambridge, Mass.: Harvard University Press, 1997).

Grimsley, M., *The Hard Hand of War* (New York: Cambridge University Press, 1995).

Johnson, M. P., *Toward a Patriarchal Republic: Secession in Alabama* (Baton Rouge: Louisiana State University Press, 1977).

McPherson, J. M., *Battle Cry of Freedom: The Civil War Era* (New York: Oxford University Press, 1988).

McPherson, J. M., *For Cause and Comrades: Why Men Fought the Civil War* (New York: Oxford University Press, 1997).
McPherson, J. M. and Cooper, W. (eds.), *Writing the Civil War: The Quest to Understand* (Columbia: University of South Carolina Press, 1998).
Rable, G. C., *The Confederate Republic: A Revolution against Politics* (Chapel Hill: University of North Carolina Press, 1994).
Sinha, M., *The Counterrevolution of Slavery* (Chapel Hill: University of North Carolina Press, 2000).
Thomas, E., *The Confederate Nation* (New York: Harper Collins, 1979).

South Carolina's *Declaration of the Immediate Causes of Secession* (1860)

The *Declaration of the Immediate Causes of Secession* was a document that accompanied South Carolina's 1860 Ordinance of Secession. The document explained in detail the reasons why the state of South Carolina considered its obligations and ties to the Union dissolved. The core of the argument was that "the rights of property [meaning the right to own slaves] established in fifteen states and recognized by the Constitution" had been violated by the non-slaveholding states' support of antislavery activities and by the election of a president who was hostile to slavery. At the same time, the document also referred to the Declaration of Independence, according to which the original thirteen colonies had declared themselves free, sovereign, and independent states. It argued that this precedent justified South Carolina's decision to secede.

The people of the State of South Carolina, in Convention assembled, on the 26th day of April, A.D., 1852, declared that the frequent violations of the *Constitution of the United States*, by the Federal Government, and its encroachments upon the reserved rights of the States, fully justified this State in then withdrawing from the Federal Union; but in deference to the opinions and wishes of the other slaveholding States, she forbore at that time to exercise this right. Since that time, these encroachments have continued to increase, and further forbearance ceases to be a virtue.

Source: The Avalon Project at the Yale Law School: Confederate States of America; The Lilliam Goldman Law Library in Memory of Sol Goldman (http: www.yale.edu/lawweb/avalon/csa/csapage.htm)

And now the State of South Carolina having resumed her separate and equal place among nations, deems it due to herself, to the remaining United States of America, and to the nations of the world, that she should declare the immediate causes which have led to this act.

In the year 1765, that portion of the British Empire embracing Great Britain, undertook to make laws for the government of that portion composed of the thirteen American Colonies. A struggle for the right of self-government ensued, which resulted, on the *4th of July, 1776, in a Declaration*, by the Colonies, "that they are, and of right ought to be, FREE AND INDEPENDENT STATES; and that, as free and independent States, they have full power to levy war, conclude peace, contract alliances, establish commerce, and to do all other acts and things which independent States may of right do." [. . .]

We hold that the Government thus established is subject to the two great principles asserted in the *Declaration of Independence*; and we hold further, that the mode of its formation subjects it to a third fundamental principle, namely: the law of compact. We maintain that in every compact between two or more parties, the obligation is mutual; that the failure of one of the contracting parties to perform a material part of the agreement, entirely releases the obligation of the other; and that where no arbiter is provided, each party is remitted to his own judgment to determine the fact of failure, with all its consequences. . . .

The ends for which the *Constitution* was framed are declared by itself to be "to form a more perfect union, establish justice, insure domestic tranquility, provide for the common defence, promote the general welfare, and secure the blessings of liberty to ourselves and our posterity."

These ends it endeavored to accomplish by a Federal Government, in which each State was recognized as an equal, and had separate control over its own institutions. The right of property in slaves was recognized by giving to free persons distinct political rights, by giving them the right to represent, and burthening them with direct taxes for three-fifths of their slaves; by authorizing the importation of slaves for twenty years; and by stipulating for the rendition of fugitives from labor.

We affirm that these ends for which this Government was instituted have been defeated, and the Government itself has been made destructive of them by the action of the non-slaveholding States. Those States have assumed the right of deciding upon the propriety of our domestic institutions; and have denied the rights of property established in fifteen of the States and recognized by the *Constitution*; they have denounced as sinful the institution of slavery; they have permitted open establishment among them of societies, whose avowed object is to disturb the peace and to eloign the property of the citizens of other States. They have encouraged and assisted thousands of our slaves to leave their homes; and those who remain, have been incited by emissaries, books and pictures to servile insurrection.

For twenty-five years this agitation has been steadily increasing, until it has now secured to its aid the power of the common Government. Observing the *forms* of the *Constitution*, a sectional party has found within that *Article* establishing the Executive Department, the means of subverting the Constitution itself. A geographical line has been drawn across the Union, and all the States north of that line have united in the election of a man to the high office of President of the United States, whose opinions and purposes are hostile to slavery. He is to be entrusted with the administration of the common Government, because he has declared that that "Government cannot endure permanently half slave, half free," and that the public mind must rest in the belief that slavery is in the course of ultimate extinction. . . .

Mary Chesnut Recalls the Beginning of the Civil War (1861)

On April 11, 1861, General P. G. T. Beauregard issued an ultimatum to the Union garrison at Fort Sumter, which – even though without supplies – had held on to its precarious position since the preceding January. The following day, Beauregard attacked the fort, which, on April 14, fell into Confederate hands. Mary Chesnut's recollections describe the mixture of surprise, confusion, and euphoria that characterized the reaction of most South Carolinians to the event. The excitement that followed the news that the fort was aflame and that the garrison had surrendered soon gave way to more practical considerations, such as "Virginia and North Carolina are coming to our rescue – for now USA will swoop on us." Incidentally, the same day that Mary Chesnut wrote the following entry, Abraham Lincoln issued his first call for 75,000 volunteers to join the Union Army. A few days later, he received the news that ten times more men than he had requested had turned up prepared to fight.

Source: C. Van Woodward (ed.), *Mary Chesnut's Civil War* (New Haven and London: Yale University Press, 1981), pp. 49–51

April 15, 1861

I did not know that one could live such days of excitement. They called, "Come out – there is a crowd coming."

A mob indeed, but it was headed by Colonels Chesnut and Manning.

The crowd was shouting and showing these two as messengers of good news. They were escorted to Beauregard's headquarters. Fort Sumter had surrendered.

Those up on the housetop shouted to us, "The fort is on fire." That had been the story once or twice before.

When we had calmed down, Colonel Chesnut, who had taken it all quietly enough – if anything, more unruffled than usual in his serenity – told us how the surrender came about.

Wigfall was with them on Morris Island when he saw the fire in the fort, jumped in a little boat and, with his handkerchief as a white flag, rowed over to Fort Sumter. Wigfall went in through a porthole.

When Colonel Chesnut arrived shortly after and was received by the regular entrance, Colonel Anderson told him he had need to pick his way warily, for it was all mined.

As far as I can make out, the fort surrendered to Wigfall.

But it is all confusion. Our flag is flying there. Fire engines have been sent to put out the fire.

Everybody tells you half of something and then rushes off to tell something else or to hear the last news. ≪Manning, Wigfall, John Preston, &c, men without limit, beset us at night.≫

In the afternoon, Mrs. Preston, Mrs. Joe Heyward, and I drove round the Battery. We were in an open carriage. What a changed scene. The very liveliest crowd I think I ever saw. Everybody talking at once. All glasses still turned on the grim old fort.

≪Saw William Gilmore Simms,[1] and did not recognize him in his white beard. Trescot is here with his glasses on top of the house.≫

Russell, the English reporter for the *Times*, was there. They took him everywhere. One man got up Thackeray, to converse with him on equal terms. Poor Russell was awfully bored, they say. He only wanted to see the forts, &c&c, and news that was suitable to make an interesting article. Thackeray was stale news over the water.

Mrs. Frank Hampton and I went to see the camp of the Richland troops. South Carolina had volunteered to a boy. Professor Venable (The Mathematical) intends to raise a company from among them for the war, a permanent company. This is a grand frolic. No more. For the students, at least.

Even the staid and severe-of-aspect Clingman is here. He says Virginia and North Carolina are arming to come to our rescue – for now USA will swoop down on us. Of that we may be sure.

We have burned our ships – we are obliged to go on now. He calls us a poor little hot-blooded, headlong, rash, and troublesome sister state.

General McQueen is in a rage because we are to send troops to Virginia.

There is a frightful yellow flag story. A distinguished potentate and militia power looked out upon the bloody field of battle, happening to stand always under the waving of the hospital flag. To his numerous other titles they now add Y.F.

Preston Hampton in all the flush of his youth and beauty, his six feet in stature – and after all, only in his teens – appeared in lemon-colored kid gloves to grace the scene. The camp, in a fit of horseplay, seized him and rubbed them in the mud. He fought manfully but took it all naturally as a good joke.

Mrs. Frank Hampton knows already what civil war means. Her brother was in the New York Seventh Regiment, so roughly recived in Baltimore. Frank will be in the opposite camp.

Note

1 South Carolina novelist, biographer, historian, essayist, and orator.

Sarah Morgan Defends Slavery against Lincoln's Plan for Emancipation (1862)

In January 1862, when she started her Civil War diary, Sarah Morgan was just 19. Her father was a successful judge with influential contacts among the Louisiana planter elite; her family was moderately wealthy and owned eight slaves, all of whom worked as servants in the Morgan family house in Baton Rouge. The year before she began recording her thoughts, Sarah had seen her brothers leave to join the rebel army and Union soldiers occupy her hometown amidst the carnage of battle. Like most elite women, although she occasionally

Source: Charles East (ed.), *The Civil War Diary of Sarah Morgan* (Athens and London: University of Georgia Press, 1991), pp. 330–1

expressed reservations about gender discrimination, she never questioned the righteousness of either slavery or the war the South fought to preserve it. As is clear from the entry below, Sarah looked down on Abraham Lincoln's plans for the emancipation of southern slaves; she considered the president little more than a prejudiced Abolitionist. As far as she knew, slaves were treated well and had reason to be content; only ignorance had led Lincoln to believe the opposite.

Sunday Nov. 9th.

How the time flies! one would suppose the calendar was composed of Sundays. Our exile passes gaily here. In Clinton I should grow mad. But who could be unhappy at Linwood? Does not the dear General treat us like his own children? Are they not all as devoted and kind as brothers and sisters? Added to their dear loving hearts, who could be unhappy where there is space and fresh air? And fun and frolic too? Does not the General pass me all the ducks and fowls to carve, just as my... own dear father did, and does he not praise my skill, as father did too? And does he not like me to read the papers to him occasionally? That must be because I take such interest in the news, invariably sitting down to read the papers just as he and Gibbes do. And who does he call to help him on with his over coat, when he goes out in the fields? Who but me? Bless the General! He is too good.

I hardly know how these last days have passed. I have an indistinct recollection of rides in cain wagons to the most distant field, coming back perched on the top of the cane singing "Dye my petticoats" to the great amusement of the General who followed on horseback. Anna and Miriam comfortably reposing in corners were too busy to join in, as their whole time and attention was entirely devoted to the consumption of cane. It was only by singing rough impromptues on Mr Harold and Capt. Bradford that I roused them from their task long enough to join in the chorus of "Forty thousand Chinese." I would not have changed my perch, four mules, and black driver, for queen Victoria's coach and six. And to think old Abe wants to deprive us of all that fun! No more cotton, sugar cane, or rice! No more old black aunties or uncles! No more rides in mule teams, no more songs in the cain field, no more steaming kettles, no more black faces and shining teeth around the furnace fires!

If Lincoln could spend the grinding season on a plantation, he would recall his proclamation.[1] As it is, he has only proved himself a fool, without injuring us. Why last evening I took old Wilson's place at the baggasse shoot, and kept the rollers free from cane until I had thrown down enough to fill several carts, and had my hands as black as his. What cruelty to slaves! And black Frank thinks me cruel too, when he meets me with a patronising grin, and shows me the nicest vats of candy, and peels cane for me! Oh! very cruel! And so does Jules, when he wipes the handle of his paddle on his apron, to give "Mamselle" a chance to skim the kettles and learn how to work! Yes! and so do all the rest who meet us with a courtesy [*sic*] and "Howd'y young missus!"

Last night we girls sat on the wood just in front of the furnace – rather Miriam and Anna did while I sat in their laps – and with some twenty of all ages crowded around, we sang away to their great amusement. Poor oppressed devils! why did you not chunk us with the burning logs instead of looking happy, and laughing like fools? Really, some good old Abolitionist is needed here, to tell them how miserable they are. Cant mass Abe spare a few to enlighten his brethren?

I must not forget that this is Brother's birthday. One year ago yesterday that father was taken with that dreadful attack of asthma that killed him. In what agony we spent this day last year, when they told us he must die in half an hour! O dear father! as the days wear on, it grows harder and harder to realize your death. If it were not for the hope that every Christian has, of meeting those we love here after, I could never have borne it so. But why should I murmur when God takes, and calls me to follow? Father! Harry! I'll meet you again, pleas[e] God, where I shall never be called on to cry over another parting! This one is so short; why should I grow impatient?

Note

1 The Emancipation Proclamation was not issued until January 1, 1863, but on September 22, 1862, Lincoln made public a preliminary draft, and this is the proclamation Sarah is referring to. The document freed slaves in territory under Confederate control.

Confederate Women in the Crisis of the Slaveholding South

Drew Gilpin Faust

In *Mothers of Invention*, Drew Faust explores how the Civil War affected the lives of Confederate women in the South. Her study focuses on the changing

Drew Gilpin Faust, *Mothers of Invention: Women of the Slaveholding South in the American Civil War* (Chapel Hill and London: University of North Carolina Press, 1996), pp. 53–79.

attitudes of slaveholding women toward accepted conventions regarding female roles in the plantation household and in society at large. As mistresses took charge of the plantations and grappled with the task of managing increasingly unruly slaves, they became critical of the southern ideal of female submissiveness and ladylike weakness. As Faust shows in this excerpt, the experience of wartime plantation management gave southern women both an unprecedented degree of power and a host of unfamiliar problems. When they tried to resort to violence to discipline restive slaves, mistresses were forced to confront the full implications of the contradictions inherent in patriarchy, since "gender prescriptions specifically forbade elite women from exercising physical dominance" even over their slaves.

When slaveholding men departed for battle, white women on farms and plantations across the South assumed direction of the region's "peculiar institution." In the antebellum years white men had borne overwhelming responsibility for slavery's daily management and perpetuation. But as war changed the shape of southern households, it necessarily transformed the structures of domestic authority, requiring white women to exercise unaccustomed – and unsought – power in defense of public as well as private order. Slavery was, as Confederate vice-president Alexander Stephens proclaimed, the "cornerstone" of the region's society, economy, and politics. Yet slavery's survival depended less on sweeping dictates of state policy than on tens of thousands of individual acts of personal domination exercised by particular masters over particular slaves. As wartime opportunity encouraged slaves openly to assert their desire for freedom, the daily struggle over coercion and control on hundreds of plantations and farms became just as crucial to defense of the southern way of life as any military encounter. Women called to manage increasingly restive and even rebellious slaves were in a significant sense garrisoning a second front in the South's war against Yankee domination.

Nineteenth-century southerners often called slavery "the domestic institution." Such a designation is curious, however, for the term seems to imply a contrast with the public or the political. The very domesticity of slavery in the Old South, its embeddedness in the social relations of the master's household, made those households central to the most public aspects of regional life. The direct exercise of control over slaves was the most fundamental and essential political act in the Old South. With the departure of white men, this transcendent public duty fell to Confederate women.

Although white southerners – both male and female – might insist that politics was not, even in the changed circumstances of wartime, an appropriate part of woman's sphere, the female slave manager necessarily served as a pillar of the South's political order. White women's actions as slave mistresses were crucial to Confederate destinies, for the viability of the southern agricultural economy and the stability of the social order as well as the continuing loyalty of the civilian population all depended on successful slave control.

Public discourse and government policy in the Confederacy explicitly recognized the gendered foundation of the Old South's system of mastery. Indeed the very meaning of mastery itself was rooted in the concepts of masculinity and male power. From the outset, Confederate leaders were uneasy about the transfer of such responsibility to women. After the passage of the first conscription act in April 1862, critics challenged the wisdom of drafting overseers and other white male supervisors, especially from areas with heavily concentrated black populations. In part this concern was economic, for agricultural productivity and efficiency seemed to depend on effective management. . . . The prospect of even fewer men at home generated profound fears of slave revolt, which combined with a sense of the particular vulnerability of white women. These issues went beyond questions of gender; they represented deep-seated worries about sex.

As support grew in the fall of 1862 for some official draft exemption for slave managers, the *Macon Daily Telegraph* demanded, "Is it possible that Congress thinks . . . our women can control the slaves and oversee the farms? Do they suppose that our patriotic mothers, sisters and daughters can assume and discharge the active duties and drudgery of an overseer? Certainly not. They know better." In October Congress demonstrated that it did indeed know better, passing a law exempting from service one white man on each plantation of twenty or more slaves. But the soon infamous "Twenty-Nigger Law" triggered enormous popular resentment, both from nonslaveholders who regarded it as valuing the lives of the elite over their own and from smaller slaveholders who were not included in its scope.[1]

In an effort to silence this threatening outburst of class hostility and at the same time meet the South's ever increasing manpower needs, the Confederate Congress repeatedly amended conscription policy, both broadening the age of eligibility and limiting exemptions. . . . This erosion of the statutory foundation for overseer exemptions greatly increased the difficulty of finding men not subject to military duty who could, as the original bill had phrased it, "secure the proper police of the country." Women across the Confederacy would find themselves unable to obtain the assistance of white men on their plantations and farms.

Conscription policy reveals fundamental Confederate assumptions, for it represents significant choices made by the Confederate leadership, choices that in important ways defined issues of class as more central to Confederate survival than those of gender. The initial acknowledgment by Congress that a white woman could not effectively "discharge the active duties" of an overseer was all but forgotten amidst the storm of protest over the exemption law. In order to promote at least an appearance of equitability in the draft, the Confederacy retreated from its concern about women left alone to manage slaves. White women in slaveowning households found their needs relegated to a position of secondary importance in comparison with the demands of nonslaveholding men. These men could vote, and the Confederacy required their service on the battlefield; retaining their loyalty was a priority. Minimizing class divisions within the Confederacy was imperative – even if ultimately unsuccessful. Addressing emerging gender divisions seemed less critical, because women – even the "privileged" ladies of the slaveowning elite – neither voted nor wrote editorials nor bore arms.

With ever escalating military manpower demands, however, white women came to assume responsibility for directing the slave system that was so central a cause and purpose of the war. Yet they could not forget the promises of male protection and obligation that they believed their due. Women's troubling experiences as slave managers generated a growing fear and resentment of the burdens imposed by the disintegrating institution. Ultimately these tensions did much to undermine women's active support for both slavery and the Confederate cause. And throughout the South eroding slave control and diminishing plantation efficiency directly contributed to failures of morale and productivity on the homefront.

Unprotected and afraid

Women agreed with the Georgia newspaper that had proclaimed them unfit masters. "Where there are so many negroes upon places as upon ours," wrote an Alabama woman to the governor, "it is quite necessary that there should be men who can and will controle them, especially at this time." Faced with the prospect of being left with sixty slaves, a Mississippi planter's wife expressed similar sentiments. "Do you think," she demanded of Governor John Pettus, "that this woman's hand can keep them in check?" Women compelled to assume responsibility over slaves tended to regard their new role more as a duty than an opportunity. Like many southern soldiers, they were conscripts rather than volunteers. As Lizzie Neblett explained to her husband, Will, when he enlisted in the 20th Texas Infantry, her impending service as agricultural and slave manager was "a coercive one."[2]

Women's reluctance derived in no small part from a profound sense of their own incapacities. One Mississippi woman complained that she lacked sufficient "moral courage" to govern slaves; another believed "managing negroes . . . beyond my power." "Master's eye and voice," Catherine Edmondston remarked, "are much more potent than mistress'." . . . Even in anticipation the responsibility seemed daunting, and actual experience often bore out these anxieties. Slaves themselves frequently seemed to share their mistresses' views of their own incapacities. Ellen Moore of Virginia complained that her laborers "all think I am a kind of usurper & have no authority over them." As war and the promise of freedom encouraged increasing black assertiveness, white women discovered themselves in charge of an institution quite different from the one their husbands, brothers, fathers, and sons had managed before military conflict commenced.[3]

Female apprehensions about slave mastery arose from fears of this very rebelliousness and from a sense of the special threat slave violence might pose to white women. Keziah Brevard, a fifty-eight-year-old South Carolina widow, lived in almost constant fear of her sizable slave force. "It is dreadful to dwell on insurrections," she acknowledged. Yet "many an hour have I laid awake in my life thinking of our danger." Long accustomed to being alone with her slaves, Brevard grew more fearful as sectional conflict turned to Civil War. In the spring of 1861 she worried that "we know not what moment we may be hacked to death in the most cruel manner by our slaves." When her coffee tasted salty and her dinner rancid, she could not decide if her servants were attempting to poison her or just lodging a protest against their continued subjection.[4] . . .

Rumors of slave insurrections abounded, and stories of individual outrages seized women's attention. On July 11, 1861, Sarah Espy of Alabama recorded news of "a most atrocious murder – that of an old lady . . . by her negro woman – the negro to be hung tomorrow." Just two days later she noted the report of "an insurrectionary movement among the negroes of Wills Valley, which was suppressed, however." At the Glenn Anna Female Seminary in North Carolina, the girls were in the weeks after secession "dreadfully frightened" by stories about "negroes rising and killing," especially "as there were no men at the Seminary." Even though it was all but impossible to separate rumor from reality, a slave conspiracy near Natchez in the spring of 1861 was particularly terrifying. The captured insurgents seemed to confirm women's profoundest fears, indicating, at least as white men recorded their rather elegantly phrased testimony, an intention to "ravish" "Miss Mary . . . Miss Sarah . . . and Miss Anna," wives and daughters of prominent slaveholders. Although secession and the outbreak of military conflict greatly aggravated both fears and rumors of such uprisings, reports of insurrections continued throughout the war, increasing in number when Lincoln issued his Emancipation Proclamation, when Union troops made significant advances, and ultimately when Confederate power was obviously disintegrating in late 1864 and 1865.[5] . . .

By the middle years of the war, women had begun publicly to voice their fears, writing hundreds of letters to state and Confederate officials imploring that men be detailed from military service to control the slaves. Hattie Motley of Alabama begged the secretary of war for the discharge of her husband, supporting her request with a description of how the previous week only a few miles away "in the night, a monster in the shape of a negro man" entered the house and then the bedroom of a young girl. "Such occurrences," Motley declared, "make woman's blood run cold, when they think of being left defenseless." . . . A group of women living near New Bern petitioned North Carolina Governor Zebulon Vance for exemptions for the few men who still remained at home. "We pray your Excellency to consider that in the absence of all protection the female portion of this community may be subjected to a system of outrage that may be justly denomenated the harrow of harrows more terrable to the contemplation of the virtuous maiden and matron than death."[6] . . .

These women chose different euphemisms to express their anxieties – insult, outrage, "harrow of harrows," dishonor, stain, and molestation – but the theme was undeniably sexual. The Old South had justified white woman's subordination in terms of her biological difference, emphasizing an essential female weakness that rested ultimately in sexual vulnerability. In a society based on the oppression of a potentially hostile population of 4 million black slaves, such vulnerability assumed special significancc. On this foundation of race, the white South erected its particular – and particularly compelling – logic of female dependence. Only the white man's strength could provide adequate and necessary protection. The very word *protection* was invoked again and again by Confederate women petitioning for what they believed the fundamental right guaranteed them by the paternalistic social order of the South. . . . Denied such assurances of safety, many women would be impelled to question – even if implicitly – the logic of their willing acceptance of their own inferiority. In seeking . . . to protect themselves, Confederate women profoundly undermined the legitimacy of their subordination, demonstrating that they did not – indeed could not – depend on the supposed superior strength of white men.

Significantly, the "demonic" invaders these Mississippi women most feared were not Yankees but rebellious slaves. In their terror of an insurgent black population, white southern women advanced their own definition of wartime priorities, one seemingly not shared by the Confederate leadership and government. "I fear the blacks more than I do the Yankees," confessed Mrs. A. Ingraham of besieged Vicksburg. In Virginia, Betty Maury agreed. "I am afraid of the lawless Yankee soldiers, but that is nothing to my fear of the negroes if they should rise against us." . . . Living with slavery in wartime was, one Virginia woman observed, living with "enemies in our own households."[7]

The arrival of black soldiers in parts of the South represented the conjunction and culmination of these fears. Mary Lee of Winchester, Virginia, came "near fainting" when the troops appeared; she felt "more unnerved than by any sight I have seen since the war [began]." These soldiers were at once men, blacks, and national enemies – her gender, racial, and political opposites, the quintessential powerful and hostile Other. Their occupying presence in Winchester reminded her so forcefully of her weakness and vulnerability that she responded with a swoon, an unwanted and unwonted display of the feminine impotence and delicacy she had struggled to overcome during long years of her own as well as Confederate independence.[8]

Yet women often denied or repressed these profound fears of racial violence, confronting them only in the darkest hours of anxious, sleepless nights. Constance Cary Harrison remembered that in the daytime, apprehensions about slave violence seemed "preposterous," but at night, "there was the fear . . . dark, boding, oppressive and altogether hateful . . . the ghost that refused to be laid." Women sometimes questioned why they did not constantly feel overwhelmed by a terror that seemed all too appropriate and rational. . . . Catherine Edmondston marveled that with "eighty eight negroes immediately around me" and "not a white soul within five miles," she felt "not a sensation of fear."[9]

Some women in fact regarded their slaves as protectors, hoping for the loyalty that the many tales of "faithful servants" would enshrine in Confederate popular culture and, later, within the myth of the Lost Cause. Elizabeth Saxon, in a typically rose-colored remembrance of slavery during the war, recalled in 1905 that "not an outrage was perpetrated, no house was burned. . . . [O]n lonely farms women with little children slept at peace, guarded by a sable crowd, whom they perfectly trusted. . . . [I]n no land was ever a people so tender and helpful." The discrepancy between this portrait and the anxieties of everyday life on Confederate plantations underscores how white southerners, both during the war and afterward, struggled to retain a view of slavery as a benevolent institution, appreciated by blacks as well as whites. During the war such "faithful servant" stories served to calm white fears. But examples of persisting white trust and confidence in slaves cannot be discounted entirely, nor can the stories themselves be uniformly dismissed as white inventions. There were in fact slaves who buried the master's silver to hide it from the enemy; there were slaves... who drew knives to defend mistresses against Yankee troops. Such incidents reinforced white southerners' desire not to believe that men and women they thought they had known intimately – sometimes all their lives – had suddenly become murderers and revolutionaries.[10]

Much of the complexity of wartime relationships between white women and slaves arose because women increasingly relied on slaves' labor, competence, and even companionship at a time when slaves saw diminishing motivation for work or obedience. White women's dependence on their slaves grew simultaneously with slaves' independence of their owners, creating a troubling situation of confusion and ambivalence for mistresses compelled constantly to reassess, to interrogate, and to revise their assumptions as they struggled to reconcile need with fear. Although many agreed with Catherine Broun, who declared she was by 1863 "beginning to lose confidence *in the whole race*," other white women turned hopefully to their slaves as the only remaining allies in a dangerous wartime world.[11] ...

Kate McClure of South Carolina preferred her slave Jeff to the white men her husband had deputized to help manage plantation affairs during his military service. McClure believed Jeff to be more trustworthy and more knowledgeable, as well as more likely to accept her viewpoint and direction, than the two male neighbors. Maria Hawkins keenly felt the absence of her slave protector Moses and wrote to Governor Vance with a variation of the hundreds of letters to southern officials seeking discharge of husbands and sons. Hawkins requested Moses' release from impressment as a laborer on coastal fortifications. "He slept in the house, every night while at home, & protected everything in the house & yard & at these perilous times when deserters are committing depredations, on plantations every day...." In Hawkins's particular configuration of gender and racial anxieties, a black male protector was far preferable to no male at all.[12]

The fruits of the war

Within the context of everyday life in the Confederacy, most women slaveholders confronted neither murderous revolutionaries nor the unfailingly loyal retainers of "moonlight and magnolias" tradition. Instead they faced complex human beings whose desires for freedom expressed themselves in ways that varied with changing means and opportunities as slavery weakened steadily under unrelenting northern military pressure.

Often opportunity was greatest in areas close to Union lines, and slaveowners in these locations confronted the greatest challenges of discipline.... Ada Bacot, widowed South Carolina plantation owner, believed her "orders disregarded more & more every day. I can do nothing so must submit, which is anything but pleasant." When she left Carolina for a nursing post at the Monticello Hospital in Charlottesville, however, she soon discovered "Virginia Negroes are not near so servile as those of S.C." Even the chambermaid she had brought from home became insubordinate under the influence of her new environment. Slave intractability made Bacot's housekeeping duties "anything but pleasant."... Unlike many Confederate slave managers, though, Bacot did not live in a world comprised exclusively of women. She turned for aid to the white male doctors who were also residents of the household, and they whipped both irate mother and insolent child.[13]

For many white women this physical dimension of slave control proved most troubling. In the prewar South the threat – and often the reality – of physical force had combined with the coercive manipulations of planter paternalism to serve as fundamental instruments of oppression and thus of race control. The white South had justified its "peculiar institution" as a beneficent system of reciprocal obligations between master and slave, defining slave labor as a legitimate return for masters' protection and support. But in the very notion of mutual duties, the ideology of paternalism conceded the essential humanity of the bondspeople, who turned paternalism to their own uses, manipulating it as an empowering doctrine of intrinsic rights.

Desiring to see themselves as decent Christian men, most southern slaveholders of the prewar years preferred the negotiated power of reciprocity to the almost unchecked exercise of force that was in fact permitted them by law. The paternalistic ideal regarded whipping as a last, not a first, resort, and as a breakdown in control that was more properly exerted over minds than bodies. Yet violence was implicit in the system, and both planters' records and slaves' reminiscences demonstrate how often it was explicit as well.

Just as "paternalism" and "mastery" were rooted in concepts of masculinity, so violence was similarly gendered as male within the ideology of the Old South. Recourse to physical force in support of male honor and white supremacy was regarded as the right, even the responsibility, of each white man – within his household, on his plantation, in his community, and with the outbreak of war, for his nation. Women slave managers inherited a social order that depended on the threat and often the use of violence. Throughout the history of the peculiar institution, slave mistresses had in fact slapped, hit, and even brutally whipped their slaves – particularly slave women or children. But their relationship to this exercise of physical power was significantly different from that of their men. No gendered code of honor celebrated women's physical power or dominance. A contrasting yet parallel ideology extolled female sensitivity, weakness, and vulnerability. In the prewar years, exercise of the violence fundamental to slavery was overwhelmingly the responsibility and prerogative of white men. A white woman disciplined and punished as the master's subordinate and surrogate. Rationalized, systematic, autonomous, and instrumental use of violence belonged to men.

...[I]t was in...moments of rage that many Confederate women embraced physical force. But for the kind of rationalized punishment intended to function as the mainstay of slave discipline, [they] turned to men. Women alone customarily sought overseers, male relatives, or neighbors to undertake physical coercion of slaves, especially slave men. As white men disappeared to war, however, finding such help became increasingly difficult. Sarah Espy had depended on her neighbor Finley to carry out necessary whippings, but when he departed to Carolina, she was without recourse. Yet Espy would have agreed with the woman who declared that "the idea of a lady doing such a thing" was "repugnant."[14]

In the exigency of war, however, many mistresses did inflict violence with their own hands, but more often than not rage had to override deep-seated feelings of conflict and ambivalence to make such actions possible. Susan Scott of Texas seemed close to the limits of sanity when she stood in the midst of a poorly cultivated cornfield shouting tearful curses at her slaves in language "equal to any man." Then she "whipped one...awfully, and said she would be damned if she dident have every d— negro on the place whipped about the stand of corn." Emily Perkins of Tennessee was so infuriated at a slave woman who had announced she would never be whipped again that she hit her over the head with what she thought was a shovel. When it turned out to be just a broom, which broke instead of knocking the woman over, Perkins sent for a male slave to tie her down. Then Perkins "laid it on." Instead of an effective effort to exert dominance, white women's recourse to violence often represented a loss of control – over both themselves and their slaves.[15]

As slaves grew more assertive in anticipation of their freedom, their female managers regarded physical coercion as at once more essential and more impossible. Some white women began to bargain with violence, trying to make slavery seem benign in hopes of retaining their slaves' service, if not their loyalty. Avoiding physical punishment even in the face of insolence or poor work, they endeavored to keep their slaves from departing altogether....The Old South's social hierarchies had created a spectrum of legitimate access to violence, so that social empowerment was inextricably bound up with the right to employ physical force. Violence was all but required of white men of all classes, a cultural principle rendered explicit by the coming of war and conscription. Black slaves, by contrast, were forbidden the use of violence entirely, except within their own communities, where the dominant society chose to regard it as essentially invisible. White women stood upon an ill-defined middle ground, where behavior and ideology often diverged.

The Civil War exacerbated this very tension, compelling women in slaveowning households to become the reluctant agents of a power they could not embrace as rightfully their own. The centrality of violence in the Old South had reflected and reinforced white women's inferior status in that society. With Civil War, military conflict made organized violence the South's defining purpose and instrument of survival, marginalizing women once again. But even away from "the tented field," even on the homefront, women felt inadequate; their understanding of their gender undermined their effectiveness. Just as their inability to bear arms left Confederate women feeling "useless," so their inhibitions about violence made many females regard themselves as failures at slave management. As Lizzie Neblett wrote of her frustration in the effort to control eleven recalcitrant slaves, "I am so sick of trying to do a man's business when I am nothing but, a poor contemptible piece of multiplying human flesh tied to the house by a crying young one, looked upon as belonging to a race of inferior beings." The language she chose to describe her self-loathing is significant, for she borrowed it from the vocabulary of race as well as gender. Invoking the objective constraints of biology – "multiplying flesh" – as well as the socially constructed limitations of status – "looked upon as belonging to a race of inferior beings" – she identified herself not with the white elite, not with those in whose interest the war was being fought, but with the South's oppressed and disadvantaged. Increasingly, even though self-indulgently, she came to regard herself as the victim rather than the beneficiary of her region's slave society. Lizzie Neblett's uniquely documented experience with violence and slavery deserves exploration in some detail, for it illustrates not simply the contradictions inherent in female management, but the profound personal crisis of identity generated by her new and unaccustomed role.[16]

Troubled in mind

When her husband departed for war in the spring of 1863, Lizzie had set about the task of management committed to "doing my best" but was apprehensive both about her ignorance of agriculture and about the behavior she might expect from her eleven slaves. Their initial response to her direction, however, seemed promising. "The negros," she wrote

Will in late April, "seem to be mightily stirred up about making a good crop."[17]

By harvest, however, the situation had already changed. "The negros are doing nothing," Lizzie wrote Will at the height of first cotton picking in mid-August. "But ours are not doing that job alone[.] [N]early all the negroes around here are at it, some of them are getting so high in anticipation of their glorious freedom by the Yankees I suppose, that they resist a whipping." Lizzie harbored few illusions about the long-term loyalty of her own black family. "I dont think we have one who will stay with us."[18]

After a harvest that fell well below the previous year's achievement, Lizzie saw the need for new managerial arrangements. Will had provided for a male neighbor to keep a general supervisory eye over the Neblett slave force, but Lizzie wrote Will in the fall of 1863 that she had contracted to pay a Mr. Meyers to spend three half-days a week with her slaves. "He will be right tight on the negroes I think, but they need it. Meyers will lay down the law and enforce it." But Lizzie emphasized that she would not permit cruelty or abuse.[19]

Controlling Meyers would prove in some ways more difficult than controlling the slaves. His second day on the plantation Meyers whipped three young male slaves for idleness, and on his next visit, as Lizzie put it, "he undertook old Sam." Gossip had spread among slaves in the neighborhood – and from them to their masters – that Sam intended to take a whipping from no man.[20] Will Neblett had, in fact, not been a harsh disciplinarian, tending more to threatening and grumbling than whipping. But Meyers regared Sam's challenge as quite "enough." When Sam refused to come to Meyers to receive a whipping he felt he did not deserve, Meyers cornered and threatened to shoot him. Enraged, Meyers beat Sam so severely that Lizzie feared he might die....

Lizzie was torn over how to respond – to Meyers or to Sam. "Tho I pity the poor wretch," she confided to Will, "I don't want him to know it." To the other slaves she insisted that "Meyers would not have whipped him if he had not deserved it," and to Will she defensively maintained, "somebody must take them in hand[.] they grow worse all the time[.] I could not begin to write you...how little they mind me." She saw Meyers's actions as part of a plan to establish control at the outset: "he lets them know what he is...& then has no more trouble." But Lizzie's very insistence and defensiveness suggest that this was not, even in her mind, slave management in its ideal form.[21]

Over the next few days, Lizzie's doubts about Meyers and his course of action grew. Instead of eliminating trouble at the outset, as he had intended, the incident seemed to have created an uproar. Sarah, a cook and house slave, reported to Lizzie that Sam suspected the whipping had been his mistress's idea, and that, when well enough, he would run away until Will came home.[22]

To resolve the volatile situation and to salvage her reputation as slave mistress, Lizzie now enlisted another white man, Coleman, to talk reasonably with Sam. Coleman had been her dead father's overseer and continued to manage her mother's property. In the absence of Will and Lizzie's brothers at the front, he was an obvious family deputy, and he had undoubtedly known Sam before Lizzie had inherited him from her father's estate. Coleman agreed to "try to show Sam the error he had been guilty of." At last Sam spoke the words Coleman sought, admitting he had done wrong and promising no further insubordination.[23]

Two weeks after the incident, Lizzie and Sam finally had a direct and, in Lizzie's view at least, comforting exchange. Meyers had ordered Sam back to work, but Lizzie had interceded in response to Sam's complaints of persisting weakness. Taking his cue from Lizzie's conciliatory gesture and acting as well in accordance with Coleman's advice, Sam apologized for disappointing Lizzie's expectations, acknowledging that as the oldest slave he had special responsibilities in Will's absence. Henceforth, he promised Lizzie, he was "going to do his work faithfully & be of as much service to me as he could. I could not help," Lizzie confessed to Will, "feeling sorry for the old fellow[.] . . . he talked so humbly & seemed so hurt that I should have had him whipped so."[24]

Sam's adroit transformation from rebel into Sambo helped resolve Lizzie's uncertainties about the appropriate course of slave management. Abandoning her defense of Meyers's severity, even interceding on Sam's behalf against her own manager, Lizzie assured Sam she had not been responsible for his punishment, had indeed been "astonished" by it. Meyers, she reported to Will with newfound assurance, "did wrong" and "knows nothing" about the management of slaves. He "don't," she noted revealingly, "treat them as moral beings but manages by brute force." Henceforth, Lizzie concluded, she would not feel impelled by her sense of helplessness to countenance extreme severity. Instead, she promised Sam, if he remained "humble and submissive," she would ensure "he would not get another lick."[25]

The incident of Sam's whipping served as the occasion for an extended negotiation between Lizzie and her slaves about the terms of her power. In calling upon Meyers and Coleman, she demonstrated that, despite appearances, she was not in fact a woman alone, dependent entirely on her own resources. Although the ultimate responsibility might be hers, slave management was a community concern. Pushed toward sanctioning Meyers's cruelty by fear of her own impotence, Lizzie then stepped back from the extreme position in which Meyers had placed her. But at the same time she dissociated herself from Meyers's action, she also reaped its benefit: Sam's abandonment of a posture of overt defiance for one of apparent submission. Sam and Lizzie were ultimately able to join forces in an agreement that Meyers must be at once deplored and tolerated as a necessary evil whom both mistress and slave would strive ceaselessly to manipulate. Abandoning their brief tryouts as Simon Legree and Nat Turner, Lizzie and Sam returned to the more accustomed and comfortable roles of concerned paternalist and loyal slave. Each recognized at last that his or her own performance depended in large measure on a complementary performance by the other.

Lizzie's behavior throughout the crisis demonstrated the essential part gender identities and assumptions played in master–slave relations. As a female manager, Lizzie exploited her apparently close ties to Sarah, a house slave, in order to secure information about the remainder of her force. "Sarah is worth a team of negro's with her tongue," Lizzie reported to Will. Yet Lizzie's gender more often represented a constraint than an opportunity. Just before the confrontation between Meyers and Sam, Lizzie had written revealingly to Will about the physical coercion of slaves. Acknowledging Will's reluctance to whip, she confessed to feeling the aversion even more forcefully than he. "It has got to be such a disagreeable matter with me to whip, that I haven't even dressed Kate but once since you left, & then only a few cuts – I am too troubled in mind to get stirred up enough to whip. I made Thornton whip Tom once."[26]

Accustomed to occasional strikes against female slaves, Lizzie called on a male slave to whip the adolescent Tom, then, later, she enlisted a male neighbor to dominate the venerable Sam. Yet even this structured hierarchy of violence was becoming increasingly "disagreeable" to her as she acted out her new wartime role as "chief of affairs." In part, Lizzie knew she was objectively physically weaker than both black and white men around her. But she confessed as well to a "troubled . . . mind," to uncertainties about her appropriate relationship to the ultimate exertion of force upon which slavery rested. As wartime pressures weakened the foundations for the "moral" management that Lizzie preferred, what she referred to as "brute force" became simultaneously more attractive and more dangerous as an instrument of coercion.

Forbidden the physical severity that served as the fundamental prop of his system of slave management, Meyers requested to be released from his contract with Lizzie at the end of the crop year. Early in the agreement, Meyers had told Lizzie that he could "conquer" her slaves, "but may have to kill some one of them." It remained with Lizzie, he explained, to make the decision. In her moments of greatest exasperation, Lizzie was willing to consent to such extreme measures. "I say do it." But with calm reflection, tempered by Will's measured advice, considerations of humanity reasserted their claim. Repeatedly she interceded between Meyers and the slaves, protecting them from whippings or condemning Meyers when he disobeyed her orders and punished them severely. Yet despite her difficulties in managing Meyers and despite her belief that he was "deficient in judgment," Lizzie recognized her dependence on him and on the threat of force he represented. She was determined to "hold him on as long as I can." If he quit and the slaves found that no one was coming to replace him, she wrote revealingly, "the jig will be up." The game, the trick, the sham of her slave management would be over. Without a man – or a man part time for three half-days a week – without the recourse to violence that Meyers embodied, slavery was unworkable. The velvet glove of paternalism required its iron hand.[27]

Violence was the ultimate foundation of power in the slave South, but gender prescriptions carefully barred white women – especially those elite women most likely to find themselves responsible for controlling slaves – from purposeful exercise of physical dominance. Even when circumstances had shifted to make female authority socially desirable, it remained for many plantation mistresses personally unachievable. Lizzie's struggle with her attraction to violence and her simultaneous abhorrence of it embodied the contradictions that the necessary wartime paradox of female slave management imposed.... White women had reaped slavery's benefits throughout its existence in the colonial and antebellum South. But they could not be its everyday managers without in some measure failing to be what they understood as female. The authority of their class and race could not overcome the dependence they had learned to identify as the essence of their womanhood.

More expense than profit

Many women who feared experiences like Lizzie's hired out or sold their slaves rather than attempting to manage the troublesome property themselves. As food and clothing became scarcer in the ever more desperate South, simply finding someone else to assume responsibility for feeding slaves was often almost as important as securing cash income for their sale or rent....

For some white families, these changes... represented an opportunity too great to ignore, for war's disruptions had made slave ownership possible for the first time. Women acting as heads of such households often welcomed new slaveholding duties as a warborn chance for upward mobility. Mary Bell of Franklin, North Carolina, took full advantage of the new fluidity of the South's labor force to acquire in 1864 a family of three slaves moved from the Carolina coast to her mountain community.

After the departure of her husband, Alfred, for war in 1861, Mary had depended on two hired slaves nominally supervised by a white tenant to work her land. Tom and Liza were a constant aggravation, however, and by 1862 Tom had been discovered stealing meat as well as poisoning her brother-in-law's dog. Liza disappeared for days at a time, and Mary chafed with frustration at her inability to control her workers. Mary believed the situation resulted in part from the failure of the white men on whom she depended – her tenant and her father- and brother-in-law – to offer adequate assistance. "Your Pa does not control Tom as he ought to," she wrote Alf in May 1862. "He lets him have his own way too much. I wish I could be man and woman both until this war ends." As the white men upon whom she depended failed her, Mary wished for what she knew was impossible: the ability to exercise male power and male control herself.[28] . . .

But Mary identified the source of her discontent as a slave manager as not so much her gender – though she saw that as part of the problem – or the wartime disruptions of master–slave relations, but the legal tenuousness of her hold on her workers. She was not their owner; her connection with them was defined as temporary rather than permanent. Perhaps in full ownership, she thought, lay the resolution of her difficulties.

With the assistance and advice of a brother-in-law, Mary therefore executed her "nigger trade" in March 1864, acquiring Trim, his wife, Patsy, and their daughter, Rosa. At first she was ebullient about her new property and pronounced herself "so well pleased with my darkies." But her enthusiasm soon waned. In November she wrote Alf that when he came home from the army and saw how bad everything was, he would want to return to camp. Patsy had proven to be in poor health, plagued by fits that would make her "a burden on our hands as long as she lives." Moreover, it turned out that Mary had been deceived in the sale and that Patsy was in fact a free woman. This meant that Mary had actually purchased one slave, not three, for Rosa's status would follow that of her mother.[29] . . .

Mary began thinking of exchanging these slaves for others, but her expectations of what slavery might bring her had been scaled down considerably from her earlier hopes of upward mobility and increasing wealth. Burdened with a new baby of her own, Mary Bell, like Lizzie Neblett, came to regard slavery's greatest benefit as residing in the availability of someone to relieve her of household labor. Mary Bell's overwhelming desire by late 1864 was simply for a "woman that can get up and get breakfast. I am getting tired of having to rise these cold mornings."[30]

. . . Beginning her duties as slave manager with optimism and enthusiasm, Mary Bell came ultimately to share with Lizzie Neblett a profound sense of failure and personal inadequacy. As she repeatedly told Alf, "unless you could be at home," "unless you were at home," the system would not work. "You say," Mary Bell wrote her husband in December 1864, "you think I am a good farmer if I only had confidence in myself. I confess I have very little confidence in my own judgment and management. wish I had more. perhaps if I had I would not get so out of heart. Sometimes I am almost ready to give up and think that surely my lot is harder than anyone else."[31]

A growing disillusionment with slavery among many elite white women arose from this very desire to "give up" – to be freed from burdens of management and fear of black reprisal that often outweighed any tangible benefits from the labor of increasingly recalcitrant slaves. Few slaveowning women had seriously questioned the moral or political legitimacy of the system, although many admitted to the profound evils associated with the institution....

Southern slave mistresses began to convince themselves, however, that an institution that they were certain worked in the interest of blacks did not necessarily advance their own. Confederate women could afford little contemplation of slavery's merits "in the abstract," as its prewar defenders had urged. Slavery's meaning did not rest in the detached and intellectualized realms of politics or moral philosophy. The growing emotional and physical cost of the system to slaveholding women made its own forceful appeal, and many slave mistresses began to persuade themselves that the institution had become a greater inconvenience than benefit.

In 1863, still anticipating Confederate victory, Lila Chunn urged her husband to consider a line of work after the war that did not involve slaves. "I sometimes think that the fewer a person owns the better off he is." Sarah Kennedy of Tennessee decided in 1863 that she "would rather do all the work than be worried with a house full of servants that do what, how and when they please... [I]f we could be compensated for their value [we] are better off without them."... In 1862 Mrs. W. W. Boyce wrote her husband, a South Carolina congressman, "I tell you all this attention to farming is uphill work with me. I can give orders first-rate, but when I am not obeyed, I can't keep my temper.... I am ever ready to give you a helping hand, but I must say I am heartily tired of trying to manage *free* negroes." Gertrude Thomas noted in 1864 that she had "become convinced that the Negro as a race is better off with us... than if he were made free, but I am by no means so sure that we would not gain by having his freedom given him.... [I]f we had the same invested in something else as a means of support I would willingly, nay gladly, have the responsibility of them taken off my shoulders."[32]

Like Lizzie Neblett, many white women focused on slavery's trials and yearned for the peculiar institution – and all the troublesome blacks constrained within its bonds – magically to disappear. "I wish," wrote Keziah Brevard, "the Abolitionists & the negroes had a country to themselves & we who are desirous to practice *truth & love to God were to ourselves* – yes Lord Jesus – seperate us in the world to come, let us not be together." But like Neblett, many women who entertained such fantasies at the same time longed for just "one good negro to wait upon me." For white women, this would be emancipation's greatest cost.[33]

An entire rupture of our domestic relations

In the summer of 1862 a Confederate woman overheard two small girls "playing ladies." "Good morning, ma'am," said little Sallie to her friend. "How are you today?" "I don't feel very well this morning," four-year-old Nannie Belle replied. "*All my niggers have run away and left me.*"[34]

From the first months of the war, white women confronted yet another change in their households, one that a Virginia woman described as "an entire disruption of our domestic relations": the departure of their slaves. Sometimes, especially when Yankee troops swept through an area, the loss was total and immediate. Sarah Hughes of Alabama stood as a roadside spectator at the triumphant procession of hundreds of her slaves toward freedom. Her niece, Eliza Walker, en route to visit her aunt, described the scene that greeted her as she approached the Hughes plantation.

> Down the road [the Bluecoats] . . . came, and with them all the slaves . . . , journeying, as they thought, to the promised land. I saw them as they trudged the main road, many of the women with babes in their arms . . . old and young, men, women and children. Some of them fared better than the others. A negro woman, Laura, my aunt's fancy seamstress, rode Mrs. Hughes' beautiful white pony, sitting [on] the red plush saddle of her mistress. The Hughes' family carriage, driven by Taliaferro, the old coachman, and filled with blue coated soldiers and negroes, passed in state, and this was followed by other vehicles.

With the trusted domestics leading the way, Sarah Hughes's slaves had turned her world upside down.[35]

Usually the departure of slaves was less dramatic and more secretive, as blacks simply stole away one by one or in groups of two or three when they heard of opportunities to reach Union armies and freedom. In Middleburg, Virginia, Catherine Cochran reported, "Scarcely a morning dawned that some stampede was not announced – sometimes persons would awake to find every servant gone & we never went to bed without anticipating such an occurrence." In nearby Winchester, Mary Lee presided over a more extended dissolution of her slave force. Her male slaves were the first to leave in the spring of 1862. Emily and Betty threatened to follow, and Lee considered sending them off to a more secure location away from Federal lines in order to keep from losing them altogether. Having regular help in the house seemed imperative, though, even if it was risky. "I despise menial work," Lee confessed. But she had no confidence she would retain her property. "It is an uncomfortable thought, in waking in the morning, to be uncertain as to whether you will have any servants to bring in water and prepare breakfast.... I dread our house servants going and having to do their work."[36] ...

By the time of her exile from Winchester in February 1865, Mary Lee was surprised that her household still enjoyed the services of a mother and daughter, Sarah and Emily, who, despite repeated threats and stormy confrontations, had not yet fled to freedom. Mary Lee entertained few illusions about the continuing loyalty of her slaves. Early in the war, she made it clear that "I have never had the least confidence in the fidelity of any negro." Her grief at their gradual disappearance was highly pragmatic; she mourned their lost labor but did not seem to cherish an ideal of master–slave harmony to be shaken by the slaves' choice of freedom over loyalty.[37] ...

Pressed by the exigencies of the war and by the unrelenting demands of household labor, most white women soon focused, like Mary Lee, on the practical rather than the ideological significance of the departure of their slaves. When Catherine Broun lost a servant of nineteen years in December 1861, she complained that her husband did not understand her distress. "He does not know how much a woman's happiness depends on having good servants." In truth, it was more than simply a woman's happiness. The elite southerner's fundamental sense of identity depended on having others to perform life's menial tasks. South Carolina aristocrat Charlotte Ravenel had been compelled to do her own cooking for almost ten days when she located a slave to assume the work. "Newport has taken the cooking," she wrote tellingly in March 1865, "and we are all ladies again."[38] ...

In their reactions to slaves' departures, women revealed – to themselves as well as to posterity – the extent of their dependence on their servants. In our day of automated housework and prepared foods, it is easy to forget how much skill nineteenth-century housekeeping required. Many slave mistresses lacked this basic competence, having left to their slaves responsibility for execution of a wide range of essential domestic tasks. A generation ago historian Anne Firor Scott revolutionized prevailing wisdom about the southern lady. She was not, Scott insisted, the idle and pampered belle of myth and romance. Rather, Scott asserted, she was a worker, whose many contributions were essential to plantation efficiency and order. White women's reactions to the loss of their slaves offer a striking perspective on this argument. If plantation mistresses were indeed working hard, many of them, especially on larger farms and plantations, must have been devoting themselves overwhelmingly to organizational or managerial tasks – ordering food and clothing or planning and assigning work within the house – for war and emancipation revealed that many white women felt themselves entirely ignorant about how to perform basic functions of everyday life.[39]

A Louisiana lady who had "never even so much as washed out a pocket handkerchief with my own hands" suddenly had to learn to do laundry for her entire family. Kate Foster found that when her house servants left and she took on the washing, she "came near ruining myself for life as I was too delicately raised for such hard work." Mississippi planter Thomas Dabney was so horrified at the idea of ladies doing laundry that when his slaves departed, he insisted to his daughters that he himself would take on the washing. . . . Amanda Worthington reported her difficulties in learning to boil water and concluded she "never was cut out to be a cook."[40] . . .

The forte of the southern lady did not seem to lie in slave management either. These women were beginning to feel they could live neither with slaves nor without them. "To be without them is a misery & to have them is just as bad," confessed Amelia Barr of Galveston. Women already frustrated "trying to do a man's business" and direct slaves now discovered that they often felt equally incompetent executing the tasks that had belonged to their supposed racial inferiors.[41] . . .

The concept of female dependence and weakness was not simply a prop of southern gender ideology; in the context of war, white ladies were finding it to be all too painful a reality. Socialized to believe in their own weakness and sheltered from the necessity of performing even life's basic tasks, many white women felt almost crippled by their unpreparedness for the new lives war had brought. Yet as they struggled to cope with change, their dedication to the old order faltered as well. Slavery, the "cornerstone" of the civilization for which their nation fought, increasingly seemed a burden rather than a benefit. White women regarded it as a threat as well. In failing to guarantee what white women believed to be their most fundamental right, in failing to protect women or to exert control over insolent and even rebellious slaves, Confederate men undermined not only the foundations of the South's peculiar institution but the legitimacy of their power as white males, as masters of families of white women and black slaves.

Notes

1 *Macon Daily Telegraph*, September 1, 1862.
2 Mrs. B. A. Smith to Governor Shorter, July 18, 1862, Governor's Files, ADAH [Alabama Department of Archives and History]; Planter's Wife to Governor John J. Pettus, May 1, 1862, John J. Pettus Papers, MDAH [Mississippi Department of Archives and History, Jackson]; see also Letitia Andrews to Governor John J. Pettus, March 28, 1863, Pettus Papers, and Lizzie Neblett to Will Neblett, April 26, 1863, Lizzie Neblett Papers, UTA [Centre for American History, University of Texas, Austin].
3 Lucy A. Sharp to Hon. John C. Randolph, October 1, 1862, LRCSW [Letters Received, Confederate Secretary of War] S1000, RG 109, reel 72, M437, NA [National Archives]; Sarah Whitesides to Hon. James Seddon, February 13, 1863, LRCSW, RG 109, reel 115, W136, NA; Catherine Edmondston, *Journal of a Secesh Lady: The Diary of Catherine Ann Devereux Edmondston, 1860–1866*, ed. Beth G. Crabtree and James W. Patton (Raleigh: North Carolina Department of Archives and History, 1979), p. 240;... Amanda Walker to Secretary of War, October 31, 1862, LRCSW, RG 109, reel 79, W1106, NA.
4 Keziah Brevard Diary, November 28, 1860, April 4, 1861, December 29, 1860, SCL [South Carolina Library, University of South Carolina, Columbia].
5 Sarah Espy Diary, July 11, 13, 1861; see also June 3, 1861, ADAH; Reminiscences of Mrs. Ferrie Pegram, Lowry Shuford Collection, NCDAH [North Carolina Department of Archives and History]; Winthrop D. Jordan, *Tumult and Silence at Second Creek: An Inquiry into a Civil War Slave Conspiracy* (Baton Rouge: Louisiana State University Press, 1992), pp. 271, 288.
6 Hattie Motley to James Seddon, May 25, 1863, LRCSW, RG 109, reel 103, M437, M430, NA;... Nancy Hall et al. to Governor Zebulon Vance, August 11, 1863, Zebulon Vance Papers, NCDAH.
7 W. Maury Darst, "The Vicksburg Diary of Mrs. Alfred Ingraham," May 27, 1863, *Journal of Mississippi History* 44 (May 1982), p. 171;... Catherine Broun Diary, May 11, 1862, Broun Family Papers, RU [Woodson Research Center, Fondren Library, Rice University].
8 Mary Greenhow Lee Diary, April 3, 1864, HL [Winchester-Frederick Country Historical Society, Handley Library, Winchester, Va.]
9 Constance Cary Harrison, "A Virginia Girl in the First Year of the War," *Century*, 30 (August 1885), p. 606;... Edmondston, *Journal of a Secesh Lady*, p. 301.
10 Elizabeth Saxon, *A Southern Woman's War Time Reminiscences* (Memphis: Pilcher, 1905), p. 33; Eugene D. Genovese, *Roll, Jordan, Roll: The World the Slaves Made* (New York: Pantheon, 1974), p. 99.
11 Broun Diary, May 1, 1864, RU.
12 Joan Cashin, "'Since the War Broke Out': The Marriage of Kate and William McLure," in C. Clinton and N. Silber (eds.), *Divided Houses:*

Gender and the Civil War (New York: Oxford University Press, 1992), pp. 200–12.

13 Bacot Diary, May 3, December 25, 1861, March 17, September 8, 1862, SCL.

14 Espy Diary, March 12, 1862, ADAH....

15 Lizzie Neblett to Will Neblett, March 12, 1864, Neblett Papers, UTA; Emily Dashiell Perkins to Belle Edmondson, February 22, 1864, in *A Lost Heroine of the Confederacy: The Diaries and Letters of Belle Edmondson*, ed. William Galbraith and Loretta Galbraith (Jackson: University Press of Mississippi, 1990), pp. 192–3.

16 Lizzie Neblett to Will Neblett, August 28, 1863, Neblett Papers, UTA....

17 Ibid., April 26, 1863.

18 Ibid., August 18, 1863.

19 Ibid., November 17, 1863.

20 Ibid., November 23, 17, 1863.

21 Ibid., November 23, 1863.

22 Ibid., November 29, 1863.

23 Ibid.

24 Ibid., December 6, 1863.

25 Ibid.

26 Ibid., April 26, 1863....

27 Ibid., February 12, July 3, June 5, 1864.

28 Mary Bell to Alfred Bell, January 30, September 21, May 22, 29, 1862, Bell Papers, DU [Manuscript Department, Perkins Library, Duke University, Durham, NC].

29 Ibid., March 11, 19, November 17, December 8, 1864.

30 Ibid., November 24, 1864.

31 Ibid., December 16, 1864.

32 Lila Chunn to Willie Chunn, March 18, 1863, Chunn Papers, EU [Special Collections Department, Woodnuff Library, Emony University, Atlanta]; Sarah Kennedy Diary, August 19, 1863, TSL [Tennessee State Library and Archives, Nashville];... Mrs. W. W. Boyce to W. W. Boyce, April 12, 1862, quoted in *Letters of Warren Akin, Confederate Congressman*, ed. Bell I. Wiley (Athens: University of Georgia Press, 1959), pp. 4–5.

33 Brevard Diary, January 21, 1861, SCL; Lizzie Neblett to Will Neblett, undated letter fragment [1864], Neblett Papers, UTA.

34 Betty Herndon Maury, *The Confederate Diary of Betty Herndon Maury, 1861–1863*, ed. Alice Maury Parmalee (Washington, DC: privately printed, 1938), p. 89.

35 J. H. Beale, *The Journal of Jane Howison Beale of Fredericksburg, Virginia, 1850–1862* (Fredericksburg: Historic Fredericksburg Foundation, 1979), June 1, 1862, 47; Eliza Kendrick Walker Reminiscences, pp. 117–18, ADAH.

36 Catherine Cochran Reminiscences, March 1862, vol. 1, VHS [Virginia Historical Society]; Mary Greenhow Lee Diary, June 29, July 15, 1862, HL.

37 Mary Greehow Lee Diary, March 22, 1862, HL.

38 Broun Diary, Christmas 1861, RU; Charlotte Ravenel, March 1, 11, 1865, in *Two Diaries from Middle St. John's, Berkeley, South Carolina, February–May 1865: Journals Kept by Susan R. Jervey and Miss Charlotte St. J. Ravenel* (Pinopolis, SC: St. John's Hunting Club, 1921), p. 37.

39 Anne Firor Scott, *The Southern Lady: From Pedestal to Politics, 1830–1930* (Chicago: University of Chicago Press, 1970), pp. 28–32....

40 Kate Foster Diary, November 15, 1863, DU; Susan Dabney Smedes, *Memorials of a Southern Planter*, ed. Fletcher Green (New York: Knopf, 1965), p. 223;... Worthington Diary, August 13, 1865, MDAH.

41 Amelia Barr to My Dear Jenny, March 3, [1866?], Amelia Barr Papers, UTA.

14
Emancipation and the Destruction of Slavery

Introduction

Slaves had started fleeing from their masters and turning up in Union camps since the very start of the war. These runaways from plantations and farms posed a serious problem for federal policy toward slavery. Lincoln had made clear that his aim was simply the restoration of the Union. Fugitive slaves, however, forced him to reconsider this limited objective when it became clear that the legal status of slaves in occupied territory required clarification. In the absence of a consistent Union policy, it was up to individual commanding officers to decide the status of runaway slaves. In 1861, in the conquered portion of Virginia, General Benjamin F. Butler declared vagabond, captured, and runaway slaves "contrabands of war" and assigned them to work on fortifications. In Union-occupied areas of the West, John C. Fremont went even further, liberating the slaves of all masters who actively assisted the rebel cause. In the same year, 1861, Congress issued the first Confiscation Act, which stipulated that those slaves used by rebel military services were free. In Congress, the Republican majority wanted to take more definitive steps against slavery, but Lincoln was concerned about the effect of emancipation on the border states, which were slave states loyal to the Union. However, he started leaning toward the idea of striking directly at slavery in the Confederacy, and in April 1862, signed into law an act which abolished slavery in the District of Columbia and proposed federal compensation for voluntary emancipation.

In May 1862, General David Hunter issued a proclamation that freed the slaves in South Carolina, Florida, and Georgia. Lincoln promptly revoked this order amidst the hostility of the radical Republicans, who, even though a minority in Congress, were pushing the Republican Party in the direction of general slave emancipation. That summer, Congress issued a second Confiscation Act according to which the slaves of all persons aiding the Confederacy were declared free; the act also provided for the seizure and eventual confiscation of secessionists' property. In Congress, radical Republicans and their allies wanted to take additional steps toward emancipation; other, more moderate Republicans worried about the political consequences, while Democrats supported the war only as long as it was a war of reunion with no implications for slavery. Lincoln continued to search for a middle ground, and remained concerned about the impact that a declaration of emancipation might have upon the wavering border states. Still, on July 22, he drafted an Emancipation Proclamation, according to which all slaves in areas under Confederate control would be proclaimed free on January 1, 1863. He justified the act as a war measure necessary to secure reunion. On September 22, Lincoln issued the Preliminary Emancipation Proclamation. It was a revolutionary document cloaked in conservative terms. It reiterated reunion as the primary aim of the conflict, and spoke about gradual, compensated emancipation, followed by the colonization of blacks. However, it also warned that all slaves in areas still under Confederate control on January 1 would be declared free, and that the armed forces of the United States would be employed to "recognize and maintain the freedom of such persons." Thus the proclamation concerned only the areas which were not under Union control; ironically, slaves in Union-controlled territories remained in bondage. On January 1, 1863, Lincoln signed the Emancipation Proclamation, making good on his promise of the previous September; in doing so, he permanently changed the nature and scope of the Civil War.

In July 1862, Congress had provided for the enlistment of blacks with the Militia Act. However, it was only after the release of the Emancipation Proclamation that Lincoln publicly embraced the idea of having African Americans enrolled in the armed services. Soon, several all-black units led by white officers were formed. The revolutionary impact of the enlistment of blacks was seen clearly by Frederick Douglass, who remarked that fighting the same war side by side with blacks would force whites to reconsider their racial prejudices and stereotypes. One of the first all-black regiments – and one which would achieve everlasting fame – was the 54th Massachusetts, composed of free blacks and former slaves under the command of Robert Gould Shaw, a Harvard graduate and son of a prominent Abolitionist. Shaw knew that the only way to silence critics of emancipation was to show the world that African Americans would indeed fight for their freedom. On July 18, 1863, he led his regiment in a suicidal assault on Fort Wagner in South Carolina, where he died and was buried together with half of his men in a mass grave. The episode – which inspired the popular film *Glory* (1989) – did much to diminish racial prejudice among the Union ranks, and spurred the formation of additional black regiments. By 1865, 180,000 blacks were enlisted in the Union Army; they made a decisive contribution to the North's victory over the South in the Civil War.

Further reading

Berlin, I., Fields, B. J., Miller, S. F., Reidy, J. P., and Rowland, L. *Freedom's Soldiers: The Black Military Experience in the Civil War* (New York: Cambridge University Press, 1998).

Berlin, I., Fields, B. J., Miller, S. F., Reidy, J. P., and Rowland, L., *Slaves no More: Three Essays on Emancipation and the Civil War* (New York and Cambridge: Cambridge University Press, 1992).

Cox, L., *Lincoln and Black Freedom* (Columbia: University of South Carolina Press, 1981).

Foner, E., *Nothing But Freedom: Emancipation and Its Legacy* (Baton Rouge: Louisiana State University Press, 1983).

Franklin, J. H., *The Emancipation Proclamation* (Arlington Heights, Ill.: Harlan Davidson 1963).

Litwack, L., *Been in the Storm So Long: The Aftermath of Slavery* (New York: Vintage, 1979).

McPherson, J., *Drawn with the Sword* (New York: Oxford University Press, 1994).

McPherson, J., *The Negro's Civil War: How American Negroes Felt and Acted During the War for the Union* (Urbana: University of Illinois Press, 1965).

Mohr, C., *On the Threshold of Freedom: Masters and Slaves in Civil War Georgia* (Athens: University of Georgia Press, 1986).

Perman, M., *Emancipation and Reconstruction, 1862–1879* (Arlington Heights, Ill.: Harlan Davidson, 1987).

Quarles, B., *The Negro in the Civil War* (Boston: Little, Brown, and Company, 1953).

Ransom, R., and Sutch, R., *One Kind of Freedom; (New York: Cambridge University Press, 2001).*

Roark, J. L., *Masters without Slaves: Southern Planters in the Civil War and Reconstruction* (New York: Norton, 1977).

Abraham Lincoln's Emancipation Proclamation (1863)

The Emancipation Proclamation was, as Lincoln himself admitted, first and foremost a war measure. Its effects were valid only within the territory controlled by the Confederacy; both loyalist border states and loyalist enclaves in the South under Union control were exempted. However, in other respects the proclamation was a revolutionary document. Unlike the Preliminary Proclamation, it set as its objective the uncompensated emancipation of slaves in the Confederacy, and issued specific orders for their use in the Union Army "to garrison forts, positions, stations and other places, and to man vessels." The effects of these provisions were felt almost immediately after the release of the proclamation, when thousands of blacks enlisted in state regiments from Massachusetts to Ohio.

Whereas, on the twentysecond day of September, in the year of our Lord one thousand eight hundred and sixty two a proclamation was issued by the President of the United States, containing, among other things, the following, to wit:

"That on the first day of January, in the year of our Lord one thousand eight hundred and sixty-three, all persons held as slaves within any state, or designated part of a state, the people whereof shall then be in rebellion against the United States, shall be then, thenceforward and forever free; and the Executive Government of the United States, including the military and naval authority thereof, will recognize and maintain the freedom of such persons, and will do no act or acts to repress such persons, or any of them, in any efforts they may make for their actual freedom.

"That the executive will, on the first day of January aforesaid, by proclamation, designate the states and parts of states, if any, in which the people thereof, respectively, shall then be in rebellion against the United States, and the fact that any state, or the people thereof, shall on that day be in good faith represented in the Congress of the United States by members chosen thereto, at elections wherein a majority of the qualified voters of such state shall have participated, shall, in the absence of strong countervailing testimony, be deemed conclusive evidence that

Source: Roy P. Basler (ed.), *Abraham Lincoln: His Speeches and Writings* (Cleveland, Oh.: World Publishing Company, 1946), pp. 689–91

such state, and the people thereof, are not then in rebellion against the United States."

Now, therefore I, Abraham Lincoln President of the United States, by virtue of the power in me vested as Commander-in-Chief, of the Army and Navy of the United States in time of actual armed rebellion against authority and government of the United States, and as a fit and necessary war measure for suppressing said rebellion, do on this first day of January, in the year of our Lord one thousand eight hundred and sixty three, and in accordance with my purpose so to do publicly proclaimed for the full period of one hundred days, from the day first above mentioned, order and designate as the States and parts of States wherein the people thereof respectively, are this day in rebellion against the United States, the following, to wit

Arkansas, Texas, Louisiana, (except the Parishes of St. Bernard, Plaquemine, Jefferson, St. Johns, St. Charles, St. James, Ascension, Assumption, Terrebonne, Lafourche, St. Mary, St. Martin, and Orleans, including the City of New-Orleans) Mississippi, Alabama, Florida, Georgia, South-Carolina, North-Carolina, and Virginia, (except the forty-eight counties designated as West Virginia and also the counties of Berkeley, Accomac, Northampton, Elizabeth City, York, Princess-Ann, and Norfolk, including the cities of Norfolk & Portsmouth; and which excepted parts are for the present left precisely as if this proclamation were not issued.

And by virtue of the power and for the purpose aforesaid I do order and declare that all persons held as slaves within said designated States, and parts of States are and henceforward shall be free; and that the Executive government of the United States, including the military and naval authorities thereof, will recognize and maintain the freedom of said persons.

And I hereby enjoin upon the people so declared to be free to abstain from all violence, unless in necessary self-defense; and I recommend to them that in all cases when allowed, they labor faithfully for reasonable wages.

And I further declare and make known, that such persons of suitable condition, will be received into the armed service of the United States to garrison forts, positions, stations and other places, and to man vessels of all sorts in said service.

And upon this act sincerely believed to be an act of justice, warranted by the Constitution upon military necessity, I invoke the considerate judgment of mankind, and the gracious favor of Almighty God.

In witness whereof, I have hereunto set my hand and caused the seal of the United States to be affixed.

Done at the city of Washington, this first day of January, in the year of our Lord one thousand eight hundred and sixty three, and of the Independence of the United States of America the eighty-seventh.

By the President: Abraham Lincoln

William H. Seward,
Secretary of State

Frederick Douglass "Men of Color, To Arms" (1863)

In the March 1863 issue of his paper *Douglass' Monthly*, Frederick Douglass issued a call to arms for colored men. He argued that the times demanded not discussion but action, and that the Civil War had become as much the black man's war as the white man's. Using his powerful rhetorical skills, Douglass urged free blacks to enlist in the Union Army and fight for the liberation of their enslaved brothers and sisters, invoking the names of such illustrious antislavery martyrs as Denmark Vesey, Nat Turner, and John Brown. After issuing the call, Douglass left his home in Rochester to tour the North, recruiting volunteers and sending 100 of them, including his sons Charles and Lewis, to the famous 54th Massachusetts commanded by Robert Gould Shaw.

When the first rebel cannon shattered the walls of Sumter and drove away its starving garrison, I predicted that the war then and there inaugurated would not be fought out entirely by white men. Every month's experience during these weary years has confirmed that opinion. A war undertaken and brazenly carried on for the perpetual enslavement of colored men, calls logically and loudly for colored men to help suppress it. Only a moderate share of sagacity was needed to see that the arm of the slave was the best defense against the arm of the slaveholder. Hence with every reverse to the national arms, with every exulting shout of victory raised by the slaveholding rebels, I have implored the imperiled nation to unchain against her foes, her powerful black hand.

Source: Herbert Aptheker (ed.), *A Documentary History of the Negro People of the United States* (New York: Citadel, 1964), pp. 477–8

Slowly and reluctantly that appeal is beginning to be heeded. Stop not now to complain that it was not heeded sooner. That it should not, may or it may not have been best. This is not the time to discuss that question. Leave it to the future. When the war is over, the country is saved, peace is established, and the black man's rights are secured, as they will be, history with an impartial hand will dispose of that and sundry other questions. Action! Action! not criticism, is the plain duty of this hour. Words are now useful only as they stimulate to blows. The office of speech now is only to point out when, where, and how to strike to the best advantage.

There is no time to delay. The tide is at its flood that leads on to fortune. From East to West, from North to South, the sky is written all over, "Now or Never." "Liberty won by white men would lose half its luster." "Who would be free themselves must strike the blow." "Better even die free, than to live slaves." This is the sentiment of every brave colored man amongst us.

There are weak and cowardly men in all nations. We have them amongst us. They tell you this is the "white man's war"; that you will be no "better off after than before the war"; that the getting of you into the army is to "sacrifice you on the first opportunity." Believe them not; cowards themselves, they do not wish to have their cowardice shamed by your brave example. Leave them to their timidity, or to whatever motive may hold them back.

I have not thought lightly of the words I am now addressing you. The counsel I give comes of close observation of the great struggle now in progress, and of the deep conviction that this is your hour and mine. In good earnest then, and after the best deliberation, I now for the first time during this war feel at liberty to call and counsel you to arms.

By every consideration which binds you to your enslaved fellow countrymen, and the peace and welfare of your country; by every aspiration which you cherish for the freedom and equality of yourselves and your children; by all the ties of blood and identity which make us one with the brave black men now fighting our battles in Louisiana and in South Carolina, I urge you to fly to arms, and smite with the government and your liberty in death the power that would bury the same hopeless grave.

I wish I could tell you that the State of New York calls you to this high honor. For the moment her constituted authorities are silent on the subject. They will speak by and by, and doubtless on the right side; but we are not compelled to wait for her. We can get at the throat of treason and slavery through the State of Massachusetts. She was first in the War of Independence; first to break the chains of her slaves; first to make the black man equal before the law; first to admit colored children to her common schools, and she was first to answer with her blood the alarm cry of the nation, when its capital was menaced by rebels. You know her patriotic governor, and you know Charles Summer. I need not add more.

Massachusetts now welcomes you to arms as soldiers. She has but a small colored population from which to recruit. She has full leave of the general government to send one regiment to the war, and she has undertaken to do it. Go quickly and help fill up the first colored regiment from the North. I am authorized to assure you that you will receive the same wages, the same rations, the same equipments, the same protection, the same treatment and the same bounty, secured to the white soldiers. You will be led by able and skillful officers, men who will take especial pride in your efficiency and success. They will be quick to accord to you all the honor you shall merit by your valor, and see that your rights and feelings are respected by other soldiers. I have assured myself on these points, and can speak with authority.

More than twenty years of unswerving devotion to our common cause may give me some humble claim to be trusted at this momentous crisis. I will not argue. To do so implies hesitation and doubt, and you do not hesitate. You do not doubt. The day dawns; the morning star is bright upon the horizon! The iron gate of our prison stands half open. One gallant rush from the North will fling it wide open, while four millions of our brothers and sisters shall march out into liberty. The chance is now given you to end in a day the bondage of centuries, and to rise in one bound from social degradation to the plane of common equality with all other varieties of men.

Remember Denmark Vesey of Charleston; remember Nathaniel Turner of Southampton; remember Shields Green and Copeland, who followed noble John Brown, and fell as glorious martyrs for the cause of the slave. Remember that in a contest with oppression, the Almighty has no attribute which can take sides with oppressors.

The case is before you. This is our golden opportunity. Let us accept it, and forever wipe out the dark reproaches unsparingly hurled against us by our enemies. Let us win for ourselves the gratitude of our country, and the best blessings of our posterity through all time. The nucleus of this first regiment is now in camp at Readville, a short distance from Boston. I will undertake to forward to Boston all persons adjudged fit to be mustered into the regiment, who shall apply to me at any time within the next two weeks.

Statement of a "Colored Man" (September 1863)

A document which sheds light on how African Americans felt about the Union's policy during the Civil War is a statement written and signed by an anonymous "Colored Man" in New Orleans in September 1863. By that time, Lincoln's Emancipation Proclamation had been in effect for several months; yet, half of Louisiana was occupied by the Union, and was therefore exempt from its provisions. The contradictions of the federal policy were clearly expressed in the document reproduced below. Angry and frustrated, the anonymous "Colored Man" went so far as to call the Union's white officers "Slave holders [*sic*] at heart" since "the[y] are not fighting to free the Negroes," but just to save the Union. Blacks, however, cared "nothing about the union," which had enslaved them; what they cared about was their right to fight for their freedom "under Colored officers."

It is retten that a man can not Serve two master But it Seems that the Collored population has got two a rebel master and a union master the both want our Services one wants us to make Cotton and Sugar And the Sell it and keep the money the union masters wants us to fight the battles under white officers and the injoy both money and the union black Soldiers And white officers will not play togeathe much longer the Constitution is if any man rebells against those united States his property Shall be confescated and Slaves declared and henceforth Set free forever when theire is a insurection or rebellion against these united States the Constitution gives the president of the united States full power to arm as many soldiers of African decent as he deems neseesisary to Surpress the Rebellion and officers Should be black or white According to their abillitys the Collored man Should guard Stations Garison forts and mand vessels according to his Compasitys

A well regulated militia being necessary to the cecurity of a free State the right of the people to keep and Bear arms Shall not be infringed

Source: Ira Berlin et al. (eds.), *Free at Last: A Documentary History of Slavery, Freedom, and the Civil War* (New York: New Press, 1992), pp. 453–7

we are to Support the Constitution but no religious test Shall ever be required as a qualification to Any office or public trust under the united States the excitement of the wars is mostly keep up from the Churches the Say god is fighting the battle but it is the people But the will find that god fought our battle once the way to have peace is to distroy the enemy As long as theire is a Slave their will be rebles Against the Government of the united States So we must look out our white officers may be union men but Slave holders at heart the Are allways on hand when theire is money but Look out for them in the battle feild liberty is what we want and nothing Shorter

our Southern friend tells that the are fighting for negros and will have them our union friends Says the are not fighting to free the negroes we are fighting for the union and free navigation of the Mississippi river very well let the white fight for what the want and we negroes fight for what we want there are three things to fight for and two races of people divided into three Classes one wants negro Slaves the other the union the other Liberty So liberty must take the day nothing Shorter we are the Blackest and the bravest race the president Says there is a wide Difference Between the black Race and the white race But we Say that white corn and yellow will mix by the taussels but the black and white Race must mix by the roots as the are so well mixed and has no tausels – freedom and liberty is the word with the Collered people . . .

Now let us see whether the Colored population will be turn back in to Slavery and the union lost or not on the 4″ of last July it was Said to the colored population that the were all free and on the 4″ of August locked up in Cotton presses like Horses or hogs By reble watchmen and Saying to us Gen banks Says you are All free why do you not go to him and get passes And one half of the recruiting officers is rebles taken the oath to get a living and would Sink the Government into ashes the Scrptures says the enemy must Suffer death before we can Have peace the fall of porthudson and vicksburg is nothing the rebles must fall or the union must fall Sure the Southern men Says the are not fighting for money the are fighting for negros the northern men Say the did not com South to free the negroes but to Save the union very well for that much what is the colored men fighting for if the makes us free we are happy to hear it And when we are free men and a people we will fight for our rights and liberty we care nothing about the union we heave been in it Slaves over two hundred And fifty years we have made the contry and So far Saved the union and if we heave to fight for our rights let us fight under Colored officers for we are the men that will kill the Enemies of the Government.

The Destruction of Slavery in the Confederate Territories

Ira Berlin, Barbara J. Fields, Steven F. Miller, Joseph P. Reidy, and Leslie Rowland

In *Slaves No More*, the editors of the award-winning *Freedom: A Documentary History of Emancipation* explore different aspects of the African American experience in the Civil War, focusing on the active role of slaves in bringing about their own emancipation. Slave emancipation provided the basis for the development of the first forms of free labor and for the making of the black military experience in the Union Army. In this except, Ira Berlin and his colleagues explain how the actions of fugitive slaves and the consequences of military events transformed a war for the preservation of the Union into a war for the destruction of slavery. Already before Lincoln's Emancipation Proclamation, thousands of fugitive slaves had found refuge in Union camps and were laboring for the army. The pressure caused by this situation and the potential benefits of the enlistment of black soldiers in a campaign against their former masters were decisive factors in Lincoln's final decision to issue the proclamation, which took effect on January 1, 1863.

As the groundswell of antislavery sentiment in the North began to register in the halls of Congress, the military offensives of early 1862 dramatized the need for a more forthright commitment to emancipation. Shortly after the new year, the Northern armies advanced on several fronts. Moving deep into enemy territory, they encountered larger and larger numbers of slaves, some of whom had been in Confederate employ. In such circumstances, most field officers quickly applied the provisions of the First Confiscation Act and put black men (and some black women) to work on the Union side of the line of battle. As they did, federal forces became increasingly dependent on black military laborers.

The army's growing appetite for laborers deepened its complicity in the slaves' struggle for freedom. Fugitive slaves encouraged this

Ira Berlin, Barbara J. Fields, Steven F. Miller, Joseph P. Reidy, and Leslie Rowland, *Slaves No More: Three Essays on Emancipation and the Civil War* (New York and Cambridge: Cambridge University Press, 1992), pp. 31–52.

complicity by volunteering important military intelligence and by applying their skill and muscle in the Union cause. Standard usages of war authorized protection in exchange for such assistance, and few officers were so lacking in gratitude as to withhold it. But in so doing, they acted against the explicit instructions of their superiors, who had ordered the exclusion and expulsion of fugitive slaves from army lines. Conflicts multiplied within the ranks, sometimes ending in the resignation, court-martial, and even dismissal of officers determined to shield fugitives from recapture. Nevertheless, as the Union army advanced, the utility of black labor – if not the morality of protecting runaway slaves – wore upon the policy of exclusion. Whatever its advantages in the border states, it became increasingly inadequate as the Union army occupied portions of the Confederacy. Federal commanders had believed exclusion to be a panacea for their problems with slavery. It proved to be no solution at all.

General-in-Chief McClellan, whose determination to preserve the war from abolitionist taint had been established in the first months of fighting, directed the Union offensives in the east. Early in 1862, he ordered a joint naval and army expedition to establish a third Union beachhead on the Atlantic coast by invading tidewater North Carolina. In accordance with instructions from McClellan, General Ambrose E. Burnside promised to respect slavery as his soldiers smashed Confederate coastal defenses and occupied strategic positions. But slaveholders in tidewater North Carolina, some of whom had already lost slaves to the Union outpost at Fortress Monroe, did not wait to test Burnside's guarantees; they fled before the Northern advance. Federal officers recognized that those who remained did so only from lack of choice. Meanwhile, slaves – moving east as their owners migrated west – flooded into Union lines. As in tidewater Virginia, small farms and extensive slave hiring had familiarized slaves with the geography of the region and given them considerable knowledge of Confederate movements. They volunteered this information and their own labor to Burnside's short-handed command. Their presence in large numbers promised to make a mockery of any attempt at exclusion, and Burnside did not even try. Instead, he employed the fugitives... paying them for their labor and elevating them to the status of contrabands.

General McClellan, by contrast, strove to preserve his reputation as the slaveholders' friend. In March 1862, he was relieved as general-in-chief to take personal command of the massive Army of the Potomac for a campaign in tidewater Virginia. Through the spring and into the summer, McClellan inched cautiously up the peninsula formed by the York and James rivers, waging several costly battles before succumbing to the paralyzing conviction that a superior Southern army threatened to overwhelm him. Confederate forces in fact never equaled the number of Union soldiers, but McClellan's prophecy proved correct, in that the rebel army under General Robert E. Lee rallied to halt the Northern advance. Meanwhile, the turmoil created by the tramping armies allowed large numbers of slaves to escape, including many who had been brought into the area to construct Confederate defenses. . . .

The war followed a different course in the western theater. In the east, both Burnside and McClellan operated within narrow geographical bounds. In the west, the Union offensive stretched from the Ohio River deep into the Mississippi Valley. Slavery also differed markedly in the valley. Cotton was the great staple crop and plantations were large, with slaveholdings sometimes extending into the hundreds on the rich bottom lands. Slaves generally worked in gangs and often lived their entire lives within the confines of a single estate. Yet, if large units and the absence of extensive hiring deprived most slaves of knowledge of the region's geography, the community that developed within the slave quarters and the network of communication that radiated outward from each plantation allowed them to mobilize quickly to take advantage of opportunities presented by the war. However, not all slaves in the Mississippi Valley resided on plantations. Some dwelled on small farms in the interstices between the great river estates. In the region's up-country districts, small holdings predominated and slavery exhibited many of the features prevalent in tidewater Virginia and North Carolina. Throughout the Mississippi Valley, slaves quickly became aware of the federal military presence and pushed their way toward Union lines. Wherever Union soldiers entered the Confederacy, the policy of exclusion fell into disrepair.

West of the Mississippi River, military events transformed federal forces into an army of emancipation. In February 1862, General Samuel R. Curtis and his Army of the Southwest advanced upon the Confederate troops who had wintered in southwest Missouri. When they retreated into Arkansas, Curtis followed, winning an important victory at Pea Ridge in early March. . . . All along his route, Curtis encountered obstacles constructed by impressed slaves – many of whom escaped in the tumult that accompanied the arrival of Union soldiers. By the time he reached Helena, a considerable number of fugitive slaves were following in his train. A three-term Iowa congressman with solid antislavery credentials, Curtis refused to permit these slaves to be recaptured by their owners and redeployed against his army. Instead, he issued certificates of freedom on the basis of the First Confiscation Act, making the Union-controlled portion of Arkansas a haven for fugitive slaves.

East of the Mississippi River, the transformation of federal policy proceeded at a much slower pace. In February 1862, Union troops from General Halleck's Department of the Missouri . . . entered Tennessee. General Ulysses S. Grant advanced up the Cumberland and Tennessee rivers to capture Fort Henry and Fort Donelson, shattering the Confederate line of defense that protected Tennessee and the states farther south. Meanwhile, General John Pope traced the Mississippi, opening the way for federal occupation of Memphis in June. In late February, as his subordinates launched the offensive into the Confederacy, Halleck preached anew the doctrine of noninterference with slavery. "Let us show to our fellow-citizens . . . that we come merely to crush out rebellion . . . [and] that they shall enjoy . . . the same protection of life and property as in former days." Admonishing his troops that "[i]t does not belong to the military to decide upon the relation of master and slave," Halleck ordered that no slaves be admitted into Union lines. As though to leave no doubt about his firmness on the subject, he required that the order be read to every regiment and commanded all officers to enforce it strictly.[1]

Most of Halleck's subordinates executed his exclusion policy scrupulously, a comparatively easy task while they were on the move in areas with few slaves. But as Union forces overran Confederate positions, they inevitably captured slave laborers subject to the provisions of the First Confiscation Act and put them to work for the Union. The captives thereafter labored with the same tools, often in the same ditch, but now as free men protected by federal arms.

Simultaneously with the movement of Northern forces into west Tennessee, General Don Carlos Buell's Army of the Ohio advanced into middle Tennessee, occupying Nashville as its new base of operations. Many middle Tennessee slaveholders professed loyalty to the Union, a circumstance that gave Buell added reason to stand by his order to exclude slaves from army lines and, when exclusion failed, to return them to their owners. Conservative Buell remained convinced that respect for slavery on the part of the Union army would disabuse Confederates of mistaken notions about the antislavery intentions of the North, wean them from secession, and foster Southern unionism. Nevertheless, slaves fled to Buell's lines and sought admission. Sympathetic officers and men obliged. . . .

More fully than any other general in the western theater, Buell was determined to protect slave property. But changes in federal policy undercut his commitment to the rights of slaveholders. Much to Buell's dismay, the new article of war in particular gave antislavery officers and soldiers greater latitude to act upon their principles.

The policy of exclusion frayed as Northern armies took control of larger expanses of Confederate territory. It came completely undone when they reached the plantation South. There, slaves, women and children as well as men, entered Union lines in such numbers that it was nearly impossible to keep them out. Whatever the fugitive-slave policies undertaken – from rendition to unauthorized declarations of freedom – exclusion did not merit so much as a trial. Instead, Union commanders openly debated the question of universal emancipation.

The debate flared first in southern Louisiana, where General John W. Phelps squared off against the ubiquitous General Butler, under whose command federal forces captured New Orleans in April 1862. Phelps, a Vermont free-soiler who represented the growing commitment to emancipation within the Union army, believed the federal government should abolish slavery as the French had destroyed the *ancien régime*. When his troops occupied Ship Island, Mississippi, in December 1861, Phelps prepared to launch a war against slavery. But before he could act, he became a post commander within Butler's Department of the Gulf.

Unlike Phelps, Butler was no abolitionist. Finding that a good many southern Louisiana slaveholders professed loyalty to the Union, Butler took them at their word and instructed his troops to assist in maintaining plantation discipline and to return runaway slaves to loyal owners. His orders appeared to violate the additional article of war recently adopted by Congress, but federal authorities neither reprimanded him nor instructed him to do otherwise. The general who had earlier stolen a march by transforming the slaves of disloyal owners into contrabands, now reversed the process for those who fled from loyal owners. Unionism in Louisiana would be built with the support of whites, not blacks; slaveholders, not slaves....

Many slave owners, particularly those of Whig pedigree, found Butler's program attractive. Yet Union policy – some of it Butler's own doing – had proceeded too far toward emancipation to reassure all slaveholders in southern Louisiana. Upon federal invasion, many fled the region. Fugitive masters attempted to take their slaves with them to the interior, but – as in the South Carolina Sea Islands – plantation hands resisted the passage.

Again, black people drew upon their experience as slaves in struggling for freedom. Slavery in southern Louisiana – with its large waterfront estates; its dependence upon skilled workers, especially in sugar processing; and its connections with the great metropolis of New Orleans – provided slaves with the means to resist their masters. Familiar with the dense network of forests and swamps that surrounded almost every plantation, slaves took to the woods to wait out their owners' evacuation. Many of them subsequently headed for New Orleans or the Union camps on its outskirts. Some occupied abandoned estates in the midst of functioning slave plantations. Sometimes under the direction of an old driver, sometimes as groups of independent households, they began to sow subsistence crops while weeds choked the fields of sugar cane and cotton. These settlements of runaways soon attracted other fugitives, and they also affected slaves who remained at home, many of whom now refused to work under the old terms. Confronting their masters directly, they demanded an end to gang labor, the removal of overseers, and the payment of wages. Despite Butler's efforts to sustain unionist masters, the slave regime in southern Louisiana had been shaken beyond repair. Black people made it known that they would never again accept the old order.

Stationed above New Orleans at Camp Parapet, General Phelps aided their cause. He broadcast his willingness to shelter fugitives, and before long, slaves from miles around packed their few belongings and headed for his camp. When they appeared in rags, beaten and bloody, the enraged general ordered retributive raids, liberating other slaves and dramatically demonstrating the diminished authority of the planter class.

Although not opposed to freeing the slaves of outright rebels, Butler demanded that his subordinates distinguish the slaves of the loyal from those of the disloyal. Phelps knew no such distinction. The two generals warred openly, and each appealed to higher authority in Washington. Butler expected a restatement of the prevailing policy of honoring the claims of loyal owners; Phelps sought a new commitment to universal emancipation. . . .

While Butler and Phelps dueled, General David Hunter, fresh from the Kansas border wars, took command of the South Carolina Sea Islands determined to become the great emancipator. He immediately set to work making Port Royal the base for a grand assault against the Confederacy. In April 1862, he sought War Department permission to enlist black men into the Union army, in part to reinforce his short-handed command and in part to strike a blow at slavery. When the department ignored his request, Hunter began recruiting anyway – often dragooning men at work on the islands' plantations into military service. In May, he proclaimed martial law throughout South Carolina, Georgia, and Florida, even though he controlled only a few coastal outposts. Then, pronouncing slavery incompatible with martial law, he declared that the slaves in those states were free.

Although they disliked Hunter's recruitment methods, black people at Port Royal welcomed his audacious initiatives on behalf of freedom. President Lincoln was considerably less impressed, and he promptly reversed them. In acting against slavery, Hunter had moved far beyond the First Confiscation Act. . . . Northern opposition to slavery had increased during the intervening months, but Hunter's proclamation still challenged the Lincoln administration. The Secretary of War [Stanton] and the President reined the general. Stanton refused to sanction or provision Hunter's black regiment, which, as a result, eventually had to be disbanded. Ten days after Hunter abolished slavery in the Department of the South, Lincoln nullified Hunter's proclamation, reasserting his own authority over the disposition of slavery and restating his commitment to gradual, compensated emancipation.

Although he felt compelled to repudiate Hunter's bold stroke, Lincoln understood that the war was fast eroding his own policy of noninterference with slavery.... In a meeting with border-state congressmen in mid-July, Lincoln himself pointedly called attention to the changing circumstances. Warning them that time was running out for slavery, he predicted its inevitable dissolution in their own states "by mere friction and abrasion – by the mere incidents of the war."... Once more, he urged that the border states adopt a gradualist plan of compensated emancipation.[2] Events were bypassing border-state slaveholders, but Lincoln would not remain behind.

A few days after the border-state meeting, as though to confirm Lincoln's warning, Congress expanded the legal basis for the extinction of slavery. The Second Confiscation Act, approved on July 17, declared slaves owned by disloyal masters "forever free of their servitude" and ordered that they be "not again held as slaves." It thus went far beyond the First Confiscation Act, whose provisions had touched only those slaves employed in Confederate service.... The Second Confiscation Act forbade persons in federal service to decide upon the validity of a claim to a slave "under any pretence whatever" or to "surrender up" any slave to a claimant. In effect, the new law deemed free all fugitive slaves who came into army lines professing that their owners were disloyal, as well as those slaves who fell under army control as Union troops occupied enemy territory. Furthermore, it held out a promise of protection from recapture and reenslavement.... Congress contemplated another role for the freed slaves. The Second Confiscation Act authorized the President to employ "persons of African descent" in any capacity to suppress the rebellion. The Militia Act, which became law on the same day, provided for their employment in "any military or naval service for which they may be found competent" and granted freedom to slave men so employed, as well as to their families, if they, too, were owned by disloyal masters. Together, the Second Confiscation Act and the Militia Act made manifest the North's determination both to punish rebel slaveholders and to employ black men and women in the Union war effort....

The momentous events of July 1862 did not stop with the confiscation and military employment of slaves. On July 22, Lincoln informed the cabinet of his intention to issue a proclamation of general emancipation in the seceded states. Although he solicited comments from his advisers, he made clear his determination to act before the new year, regardless of opposition. At the cabinet's recommendation, however, Lincoln agreed to withhold his pronouncement until the occasion of a Union victory at arms, so that emancipation could be presented as an act of strength rather than weakness. The summer dragged on without offering such an opportunity, and in September matters took an even more ominous turn. The Confederates invaded both Maryland and Kentucky, panicking the Northern population, forcing federal troops into defensive retreat, and marking a low point for the Union.

The battle of Antietam, though hardly the hoped-for triumph, halted the Confederate offensive in Maryland and at last provided the occasion for Lincoln's announcement. On September 22, 1862, he issued the preliminary Emancipation Proclamation, serving notice that on January 1 he would declare "then, thenceforward, and forever free" all the slaves in those states still in rebellion. Lincoln pledged that the United States government would protect their freedom and, moreover, would do nothing to repress any actions taken by the slaves themselves to secure their own liberty....

The new departures had immediate repercussions in the field. Abolitionist officers, who believed that slaveholders were enemies of the Union, whatever their purported loyalty, welcomed the new legislation and presidential pronouncements, and applied them with enthusiasm. Other commanders, less principled than pragmatic, were unconcerned about the fate of slavery but desperate for laborers; they, too, welcomed the change. General William T. Sherman, whose reluctance to meddle with slavery had become notorious, simply accepted fugitive slaves into his ranks, employed those who could work, and left the others to shift for themselves....

By the late summer of 1862, black men in large numbers – as well as some black women – were already laboring for the Union army and navy. Some had been accepted under the First Confiscation Act, others in direct violation of the policy of exclusion. Now their numbers increased rapidly as federal commanders discovered what Confederate officers had known all along: Slaves and free-black people were the most readily available – sometimes the only – source of military labor....

Military labor offered thousands of black men an opportunity to escape slavery and gain the protection of the Union army. Still, they found much to criticize in their new position. Their work frequently took them away from family and friends, and the military and civilian overseers who supervised them could be as abusive as any master – sometimes more so. Despite the specification of pay and rations in the Militia Act, the government often had difficulty meeting its payroll. Black laborers routinely received their wages late, and sometimes not at all. . . . The burden of work for the Yankee army led some black men to flee military labor as they had fled slavery. When they did, Union officers frequently resorted to impressment, much as had Confederate labor agents. Still, whatever its liabilities, military labor provided fugitive slaves with obvious advantages. Even those who deserted federal labor gangs seldom returned to their erstwhile owners.

The Union army's willingness, indeed its need, to employ able-bodied black men did little to assist the black women, children, and old or infirm men who also made their way into Union lines in increasing numbers. Some women found employment as laundresses, cooks, seamstresses, and hospital attendants, but the demand for such workers paled in comparison with the calls for men to construct fortifications, move supplies, and chop wood. Old people and children had even fewer opportunities to gain a livelihood. . . .

Union commanders found a variety of ways to deal with the fugitive slaves, all of them makeshift. Some left them to fend for themselves. A few sent them North. Some placed them under the care of civilian superintendents assigned to the occupied South by Northern churches and benevolent societies. But as the number of black military laborers swelled, the army itself was forced to accept at least some responsibility for the refugees within its lines. Indeed, the black men who labored for the army often made it clear that they would not work unless their families were provided with food and shelter. During the fall of 1862, federal commanders began to organize contraband camps, placing sympathetic officers – generally regimental chaplains or other men of humanitarian bent – in charge.

Former slaves who labored for the Union army or took refuge in the contraband camps did not remain satisfied with their own escape from slavery. Almost as soon as they reached the safety of federal lines, they began plotting to return home and liberate families and friends. Some traveled hundreds of miles into the Confederate interior, threading their way through enemy lines, eluding Confederate pickets, avoiding former masters, and outrunning the slave catchers hired to track them down. Not all succeeded, but when they did, their courage helped hundreds escape bondage and informed still others of the possibility of freedom. Occasionally, these brave men and women received assistance from sympathetic Union soldiers and commanders, who accompanied former slaves back to the old estates or provided material assistance to those intent upon returning to free others. The bargain seemed mutually beneficial – the Union army gained additional laborers, and the former slaves secured the liberty of their loved ones.

The growing importance of black labor increased support for emancipation in the North. Abolitionists publicized the role of black laborers, arguing that their service to the Union made them worthy of freedom and citizenship. Other Northerners, indifferent or even hostile to the extension of civil rights to black people, also saw value in the exchange of labor for freedom. Expropriation of the slaveholders' property seemed condign punishment for treason. And they noted that by doing the army's dirty work, black laborers freed white soldiers for the real business of war. . . .

. . . [A]s public opinion turned against slavery, the proponents of black enlistment met with increasing success. In the summer and fall of 1862, the first black soldiers entered Union ranks in the Sea Islands of South Carolina, in southern Louisiana, and in Kansas.

As its advocates had hoped, the enlistment of black soldiers provided a powerful instrument in the war against slavery. Even before they had seen active service, news of the black men in blue uniforms had an electrifying effect on those still in bondage, encouraging many to strike out for the Yankee lines. When the first black regiments took the field, their subversive force increased manyfold. Black soldiers, the vast majority of them former slaves, coveted the liberator's role. Moving from plantation to plantation – up the tidal rivers of the South Atlantic coast and through the bayous and swamps of southern Louisiana – they urged slaves to abandon their owners and aided them in doing so. . . .

The possibility of military service opened the door to freedom for some slaves only to close it for others. As the enlistment of black men and the general increase of federal military activity provoked slaveholders to tighten plantation discipline, escape became more difficult and punishment more severe. Some masters called upon Confederate authorities to execute recaptured fugitive slaves as traitors in time of war, and at least one Confederate commander instituted court-martial proceedings against runaways. Other slaveholders, choosing the risks of removal over the hazards of remaining within reach of federal raids, refugeed their slaves deep into the Confederate interior.

Thus, even with the aid of federal arms, freedom advanced slowly and not always directly. Individual slaveholders could aggravate the difficulties of escape to the Yankees, and Southern armies could recapture black people who had already reached Union lines. Confederate military offensives provided harsh reminders that the Northern commitment to emancipation amounted to little without military success. Indeed, any Union retreat or rebel attack could reverse the process of liberation and throw men and women who had tasted freedom back into bondage. . . .

On New Year's Day, 1863, President Lincoln gave [emancipation] the full weight of federal authority. The Emancipation Proclamation fulfilled his pledge to free all slaves in the states still in rebellion. Differences between the preliminary proclamation of September and the final pronouncement of January suggest the distance Lincoln and other Northerners had traveled in those few months. Gone were references to compensation for loyal slaveholders and colonization of former slaves. In their place stood the determination to incorporate black men into the federal army and navy. As expected, the proclamation applied only to the seceded states, leaving slavery in the loyal border states untouched, and it exempted Tennessee and the Union-occupied parts of Louisiana and Virginia. Nonetheless, its simple, straightforward declaration – "that all persons held as slaves" within the rebellious states "are, and henceforward shall be, free" – had enormous force.[3]

As Lincoln understood, the message of freedom required no embellishment. However deficient in majesty or grandeur, the President's words echoed across the land. Abolitionists, black and white, marked the occasion with solemn thanksgiving that the nation had recognized its moral responsibility, that the war against slavery had at last been joined, and that human bondage was on the road to extinction. But none could match the slaves' elation. With unrestrained – indeed, unrestrainable – joy, slaves celebrated the Day of Jubilee. Throughout the South – even in areas exempt from the proclamation – black people welcomed the dawn of a new era.

In announcing plans to accept black men into the army and navy, the Emancipation Proclamation specified their assignment "to garrison forts, positions, stations and other places, and to man vessels" – evidently proposing no active combat role and, in fact, advancing little beyond the already established employment of black men in a variety of quasi-military positions. Nonetheless, black people and their abolitionist allies – who viewed military service as a lever for racial equality, as well as a weapon against slavery – seized upon the President's words and urged large-scale enlistment. Despite continued opposition from the advocates of a white man's war, the grim reality of mounting casualties convinced many Northerners of the wisdom of flexing the sable arm. Moreover, once the Emancipation Proclamation had made the destruction of slavery a Union war aim, increasing numbers of white Northerners thought it only fitting that black men share the burden of defeating the Confederacy.

Proponents of black enlistment adapted their cause to the new circumstances. They had few scruples about clothing their principled convictions in the rhetoric of military necessity, and such arguments found sympathetic listeners in Washington, where administration officials and legislators had awakened to the implications of protracted warfare and increasing manpower needs.... [T]he War Department took the first steps toward systematic recruitment of black soldiers. In January, Secretary of War Stanton yielded to the importunities of John A. Andrew, antislavery governor of Massachusetts and long-time advocate of the sable arm, authorizing him to raise a black regiment. Other governors received similar permission, and recruiters – many of them black – fanned out across the free states, politicizing and inspiring black communities as never before. Eventually, nearly three-quarters of the military-age black men in those states enlisted in federal military service. The War Department also expanded recruitment of black men in Union-occupied areas of the Confederacy, sending recruiting officers of high rank to tidewater North Carolina and southern Louisiana....

As black soldiers joined white soldiers in expanding freedom's domain, the Union army became an army of liberation. Although the Emancipation Proclamation implied an auxiliary role, black soldiers would not permit themselves to be reduced to military menials. They longed to confront their former masters on the field of battle, and they soon had their chance. The earliest black regiments acquitted themselves with honor at the battles of Port Hudson, Milliken's Bend, and Fort Wagner in the spring and summer of 1863, and black soldiers thereafter marched against the Confederacy on many fronts....The subversive effect of black soldiers on slavery, first demonstrated on the South Atlantic coast and in southern Louisiana, increased with the number of black men in federal ranks. By war's end, nearly 179,000 – the overwhelming majority slaves – had entered the Union army, and another 10,000 had served in the navy.

Military service provided black men with legal freedom and more. In undeniable ways, it countered the degrading effects of Southern slavery and Northern discrimination. Soldiering gave black men, free as well as slave, a broader knowledge of the world, an acquaintance with the workings of the law, access to some rudimentary formal education, and a chance to demonstrate their commitment to freedom for themselves and their people. Battlefield confrontations with the slaveholding enemy exhilarated black soldiers by proving in the most elemental manner the essential equality of men. In their own eyes, in the eyes of the black community, and, however reluctantly, in the eyes of the nation, black men gained new standing by donning the Union blue.

Notes

1 US War Department, *The War of the Rebellion: A Compilation of the Official Records of the Union and Confederate Armies*, 128 vols. (Washington, DC, 1880–1901), ser. I, vol. 8, pp. 563–5.
2 Lincoln, *The Collected Works of Abraham Lincoln*, ed. Roy P. Basler (New Brunswick, NJ, 1953–5), vol. 5, pp. 317–19.
3 US, *Statutes at Large, Treaties, and Proclamations of the United States of America*, 17 vols. (Boston, 1850–73), vol. 12, pp. 1268–9.

Index
